# Historicising Ancient Slavery

**Edinburgh Studies in Ancient Slavery**
**Series editor: Ulrike Roth, University of Edinburgh**

*Original research in ancient slavery studies*

The study of slavery is an essential element of the study of the ancient world. This series publishes the latest research on ancient slavery, including Greek, Roman and Near Eastern slavery, as well as Jewish and early Christian slavery, from c. 1000 BC to AD 500.

Written by experts in the field, from the rising star to the well-established scholar, the books offer cutting-edge research on key themes in ancient slavery studies, which will enhance as well as challenge current understanding of ancient slavery. The series presents new insights from a range of disciplines, including history, archaeology and philology.

**Advisory board**

Dr Bassir Amiri

Professor Jean-Jacques Aubert

Dr Lisa Fentress

Professor Jennifer A. Glancy

Professor Deborah Kamen

Professor Noel E. Lenski

Dr David Lewis

Professor Henrik Mouritsen

Professor Walter Scheidel

Dr Jane Webster

Dr Cornelia Wunsch

Professor Rachel Zelnick-Abramovitz

Books available

Kostas Vlassopoulos, *Historicising Ancient Slavery*

Forthcoming books

David Lewis, Mirko Canevaro and Douglas Cairns (eds), *Slavery and Honour in the Ancient Greek World*

Visit the series webpage: edinburghuniversitypress.com/series-edinburgh-studies-in-ancient-slavery

# HISTORICISING ANCIENT SLAVERY

KOSTAS VLASSOPOULOS

EDINBURGH
University Press

Edinburgh University Press is one of the leading university presses in the UK. We publish academic books and journals in our selected subject areas across the humanities and social sciences, combining cutting-edge scholarship with high editorial and production values to produce academic works of lasting importance. For more information visit our website: edinburghuniversitypress.com

Edinburgh University Press Ltd
The Tun – Holyrood Road, 12(2f) Jackson's Entry, Edinburgh EH8 8PJ

First published in hardback by Edinburgh University Press 2021

Typeset in 10 / 12 Bembo by
IDSUK (DataConnection) Ltd


A CIP record for this book is available from the British Library

ISBN 978 1 4744 8721 4 (hardback)
ISBN 978 1 4744 8722 1 (paperback)
ISBN 978 1 4744 8723 8 (webready PDF)
ISBN 978 1 4744 8724 5 (epub)


The right of Kostas Vlassopoulos to be identified as the author of this work has been asserted in accordance with the Copyright, Designs and Patents Act 1988, and the Copyright and Related Rights Regulations 2003 (SI No. 2498).

# CONTENTS

To my Brazilian friends and colleagues, in gratitude and solidarity

# SERIES EDITOR'S PREFACE

Edinburgh Studies in Ancient Slavery provides a forum for the latest research on all aspects of slavery and related forms of unfreedom around the Mediterranean basin and in its hinterland in antiquity. The exploration of slavery has been critical to research on this ancient world from the beginning of concentrated study in the nineteenth century. This is in many ways unsurprising given that there exists plenty of evidence for slavery and other forms of unfree labour and enforced subordination in antiquity, from the British Isles in the northwest, to the Persian Gulf in the southeast, from the Sumerian to the Visigothic kingdoms. Slavery in the ancient Mediterranean and beyond has manifested itself in myriad ways. The surviving evidence stretches the full panorama of our sources, material and textual, documenting cogently the pervasive nature of slavery in ancient society, across uncountable contexts and disparate settings. The diversity of the source material forcefully underpins the need for multi- and inter-disciplinary approaches, including collaborative and comparative efforts; the intricate nature of the evidence calls moreover for a preparedness to combine traditional with innovative methods, empiricist work with theoretical perspectives. Notwithstanding these evidential, contextual and methodological challenges that the study of slavery brings with it, in the light of the influence that the history of the region has had on the evolution and development of numerous modern societies and the world at large, the study of ancient Mediterranean slavery is imperative for a full understanding of the contemporary world.

The present series is not the first to give ancient slavery centre stage. The study of especially classical slavery has been an academic battle-ground at prominent modern historical crossroads, framed by its exploration under the abolitionist banner in the nineteenth century at one end – combatting the apologist uses to which the study of the classical past had been put by pro-slavery advocates, and its mobilisation on both sides of the Iron Curtain during the Cold War in the twentieth century at the other. Research agendas on ancient slavery have thus at times been powerfully influenced by modern, socio-political concerns. But even when the large political stage was not a key driver, work on ancient slavery has more often than not been inspired by, and reflective of, contemporary developments. Pioneering work on enslaved women, for example, was carried out in the 1970s, when the feminist movement was at its first peak in Western society; a decade or so later, an interest in the labour roles of enslaved individuals, and the ways in which they mobilised the world of work in creating their own identities, changed the modern appreciation of enslaved life at a time when labour force participation in Europe and the US – the hubs of research on ancient Greek and Roman slavery – was broader than ever before. It is fair to say that each generation of scholars brings its own preoccupations to the drawing-board of slavery studies, thereby ensuring the regular adjustment of our analytical gaze, and enabling the steady discovery of new facets of an institution that is not only as old as our historical records, but that has profoundly shaped social relations at the critical intersections of age, class, gender and race for generations to come. The rapid changes and momentous transformations that characterise contemporary society, often directly related to the many deeply troublesome legacies of slavery across human history, beget an opportune moment, and indeed constitute an urgent call, for a fresh, concentrated effort to reflect on the world we live in through the lens of an institution that was not less peculiar in antiquity than it is, sadly, still today, drawing on as wide a set of questions, approaches and perspectives as possible, thus also to reflect on and challenge the scholarly implication in the maintenance of the noted legacies.

Ulrike Roth

# Acknowledgements

This book has had a very long gestation. Its origins go back to 2005, when I moved to the Department of Classics at the University of Nottingham, where I also joined the Institute for the Study of Slavery. From its inception in 1998 by the late Thomas Wiedemann, ISOS has included colleagues from various disciplines and periods and has strongly fostered the comparative study of slavery, not only between ancient and US slavery, as is usually the case, but also with other slave systems across space and time. It was this stimulating intellectual community that made me to turn what was merely one of my interests into a major research preoccupation over the next fifteen years. Steve Hodkinson, then co-director of ISOS, played an instrumental role in bringing me to Nottingham and helping me make the first tentative steps in my academic career. Steve has been a great source of academic, intellectual and moral support, and our ongoing collaboration on the study of slavery has been immensely fruitful in shaping the framework presented in this volume. While at Nottingham, in 2012, I received the Philip Leverhulme Prize for my contribution to the field of Classics; this prize provided me with two years of research leave, during which I was able to do the groundwork for this volume. I am obviously immensely grateful to the Leverhulme Trust for the opportunity, as well as to my former colleagues at the Department of Classics for creating a great work environment during my decade at Nottingham. I would also like to thank my current colleagues at the Department of History and Archaeology in the University of Crete, where I moved in 2015, for the research leave that facilitated this project, as well as the help and support they have provided over the years.

Given the many new commitments that emerged after my move to Crete in 2015, I had to temporarily abandon the plan to turn the research conducted during the Leverhulme Prize leave into a book. I spent the next couple of years giving papers and publishing articles on various aspects of ancient slavery, which helped clarify the overall framework I had already devised. At the same time, the present book gradually became part of a slavery quintet, alongside: the *Oxford Handbook of Greek and Roman Slaveries*, co-edited with Steve Hodkinson and Marc Kleijwegt, whose chapters have started appearing online since 2016; the *Blackwell Sourcebook of Ancient Slaveries*, co-authored with Eftychia Bathrellou, which is approaching publication; a collection of translated stories about the lives of ancient slaves titled *Η ζωή μου όλη: καθημερινές ιστορίες δούλων από την αρχαιότητα* ('*My Whole Life': Stories from the Everyday Life of Ancient Slaves*), also co-authored with E. Bathrellou, which was published in 2020; and a narrative history of ancient slavery in the very long term, provisionally titled *Ancient Slavery and World History: Slaving in Eurasia and Africa, 2000 BCE–1000 CE*, which has been my pipe dream for quite some time now. Although they were never planned as a quintet, work on each of these books has been essential for the others, and cross-pollination has been very fruitful. Nevertheless, at times it felt that working on five different related works meant that none of them would ever be completed; now that four out of five works have been published or are reaching completion, I am starting to feel that the fifth one might not be a pipe dream after all. I would like to take this opportunity to thank Steve, Marc and Eftychia for their collaboration, ideas and support in these long journeys!

Ulrike Roth invited me back in 2018 to contribute a volume to the new series on ancient slavery that she is directing for Edinburgh University Press; this offered me a wonderful opportunity to finally put everything together. That would be reason enough to thank her; but I am even more thankful for her hard editorial work, which has forced me to rethink various black holes in my knowledge and argumentation. I hope that the final result has fulfilled most of her expectations. I am equally grateful to the two readers for the Press, who provided sympathetic but careful readings, saving me from many mistakes and offering stimulating advice, as well as to Carol MacDonald, Karen Francis and the other staff at EUP for their excellent work on the publication of the manuscript. I would also like to thank Brent Shaw and David Lewis for their valuable comments on the manuscript, as well as Mirko Canevaro, Paul Cartledge, Dimitris Kyrtatas, Noel Lenski, Robin Osborne, Jason Porter and Claire Taylor for some great conversations about slavery over the years. Needless to say, none of the above bears any responsibility for the arguments of the present work.

This book would have been impossible to write without the benefit of various chapters and articles I have written over the last fifteen years. I would like to thank the following editors and publishers for permission to re-use previously published material: Cambridge University Press, Robin Osborne, Michael Scott and Daniel Jew for permission to re-use material from Vlassopoulos 2016b in Chapter 2; Brill, the *Journal of Global Slavery*, Damian Pargas and Jeffrey Fynn-Paul for permission to re-use material from Vlassopoulos 2016a in Chapters 4, 6 and 8; Cambridge University Press and the *Journal of Hellenic Studies* for permission to re-use material from Vlassopoulos 2007a in Chapter 5; De Gruyter, Dimos Spatharas and George Kazantzidis for permission to re-use material form Vlassopoulos 2018d in Chapter 7; and finally, Ausonius, Madalina Dana and Ivana Savalli-Lestrade for permission to re-use material from Vlassopoulos 2018a in Chapter 8.

I have had the luxury of presenting various aspects of this book to audiences across the globe. In 2016 I gave the Argyropoulos Lecture in Hellenic Culture at the University of California in Santa Barbara, which allowed me to present an overview of the current project; I would like to thank Helen Morales for the invitation and the wonderful hospitality. I would also like to thank the audiences at Leicester, Nottingham, Royal Holloway, Reading, Rethymno, Manchester, Naples, Mainz, Dublin, Cambridge,

Leeds, Oxford, Rio de Janeiro, Bello Horizonte, Sao Paulo, Edinburgh, Athens, Paris, Birmingham, Newcastle, Clermont-Ferrand, New Haven, Barcelona, Washington, DC and Bonn for their responses and advice.

I find it nevertheless necessary to single out a particular audience and group of colleagues. In 2013 I spent a month teaching and giving presentations on the history of slavery at various Brazilian universities: the Universidade Federal do Rio de Janeiro, the Universidade Federal de Ouro Preto, the Universidade Federal de Minas Gerais and the Universidade de São Paulo. Brazilian colleagues and students were the original guinea pigs for the arguments of this book, and they were undoubtedly the most engaged audience I have ever had in my life. It is also perhaps unsurprising that I fell in love with the country and the people – a love renewed in my subsequent visit in 2018. For these reasons and many more, it has been very painful to observe from afar the dark turn of events in Brazil over the last few years, in particular as I am writing these sentences. As a tiny gesture of gratitude and solidarity, this book is dedicated to my Brazilian friends and colleagues: prime of place goes to Marta Mega de Andrade, who devised the plan to bring me to Rio de Janeiro and was a terrific and generous host; the gens Fabia of Ouro Preto, Fábio Duarte Joly and Fábio Faversani; Júnia Ferreira Furtado and José Antonio Dabdab Trabulsi in Bello Horizonte; and, finally, Carlos Machado, Julio Cesar Magalhães de Oliveira and Norberto Guarinello for hosting me in São Paulo.

The final word goes of course to friends and family, who have stood by me in all sorts of ways, in particular over the joyful but also difficult last few years: Apostolos Delis, Thomas Kalesios, Gelina Harlaftis, Dimitris Chrysis, Aleka Lianeri, Giorgos Augoustis, Maro Triantafyllou, Kostas Daulias, Elsa Kallonaki, Manolis Drymakis, Sophia Georgokosta, Dunja Milenkovic and Nikos Kanellopoulos; last, but not least, to Anastasia, without whose deep love, unconditional support, metaphysical ideas and divine food none of this would be the same.

# ABBREVIATIONS

| | |
|---|---|
| *AASOR* | *Annual of the American School of Oriental Research.* |
| *Actes 1971* | *Actes du colloque 1971 sur l'esclavage*, Paris, 1973. |
| *Actes 1972* | *Actes du colloque 1972 sur l'esclavage*, Paris, 1974. |
| *Actes 1973* | *Actes du colloque 1973 sur l'esclavage*, Paris, 1976. |
| *An.Ep.* | *L'Année épigraphique.* |
| CEG | P. A. Hansen, *Carmina epigraphica graeca saeculorum VIII–V a. Chr, I–II*, Berlin, 1983–9. |
| *Chambry* | E. Chambry, *Fables: Esope*, Paris, 1967. |
| CIL | *Corpus Inscriptionum Latinarum, I–XVII*, Berlin, 1862–. |
| *FD* III | N. Valmin, *Fouilles de Delphes, III. Épigraphie. Fascicule 6: Inscriptions du théâtre*, Paris, 1939. |
| *HSS* V | E. Chiera, *Excavations at Nuzi Volume 1: Texts of Varied Contents*, Harvard Semitic Studies V, Cambridge, MA, 1929. |
| *I.Bouthrôtos* | P. Cabanes and F. Drini, *Corpus des inscriptions grecques d'Illyrie méridionale et d'Épire 2.2: Inscriptions de Bouthrôtos*, Athens, 2007. |
| *I.Byzantion* | A. Łajtar, *Die Inschriften von Byzantion*, Bonn, 2000. |
| *I.Iznik* | S. Şahin, *Katalog der antiken Inschriften des Museums von Iznik (Nikaia), I–II*, Bonn, 1979–82. |
| *I.Kios* | T. Corsten, *Die Inschriften von Kios*, Bonn, 1985. |
| IC | M. Guarducci, *Inscriptiones Creticae, I–IV*, Rome, 1935–50. |
| ID | *Inscriptions de Délos, I–VII*, Paris, 1926–72. |
| *IG* I³ | D. Lewis and L. Jeffery, *Inscriptiones Graecae I: Inscriptiones Atticae Euclidis anno anteriores*, 3rd edition, Berlin, 1981–94. |
| *IG* II² | J. Kirchner, *Inscriptiones Graecae II et III: Inscriptiones Atticae Euclidis anno posteriores*, 2nd edition, Berlin, 1913–40. |
| *IG* IX(2) | O. Kern, *Inscriptiones Graecae, IX,2: Inscriptiones Thessaliae*, Berlin, 1908. |
| *IG* XII(9) | E. Ziebarth, *Inscriptiones Graecae XII,9: Inscriptiones Euboeae insulae*, Berlin, 1915. |
| *K-A* | R. Kassel and C. Austin, *Poetae Comici Graeci, I–VIII*, Berlin, 1983–2001. |

O-R            R. Osborne and P. J. Rhodes, *Greek Historical Inscriptions: 478–404 BC*, Oxford, 2017.

P. Oxy.        *The Oxyrhynchus Papyri, I–LXXXIII*, London, 1898–.

P. Turner      P. J. Parsons et al. (eds), *Papyri Greek and Egyptian Edited by Various Hands in Honour of Eric Gardner Turner on the Occasion of his Seventieth Birthday*, London, 1981.

Perry          B. E. Perry, *Aesopica: A Series of Texts Relating to Aesop or Ascribed to him or Closely Connected with the Literary Tradition that Bears his Name*, Urbana, IL, 1952.

SB V           *Sammelbuch griechischer Urkunden aus Ägypten, V*, Heidelberg and Wiesbaden, 1934–55.

SEG            *Supplementum Epigraphicum Graecum.*

SGDI           H. Collitz et al., *Sammlung der griechischen Dialekt-Inschriften, II. Epirus, Akarnanien, Aetolien*, Göttingen, 1885–99.

TAM V(1)       P. Herrmann, *Tituli Asiae Minoris, V. Tituli Lydiae, linguis Graeca et Latina conscripti. I: Regio septentrionalis, ad orientem vergens*, Vienna, 1981.

# 1

# INTRODUCTION

SLAVERY IS A DEFINING FEATURE of the ancient world.[1] Slaves constituted a signifi-cant proportion of the population of many ancient societies.[2] Slaves could be found everywhere: as personal servants, cooks, child minders, cleaners, entertainers and aman-uenses in ancient households; as farm hands, shepherds, overseers and estate managers in the fields; as unskilled workers, trained artisans, specialists and supervisors in workshops, factories and mines; as sailors, captains, fishermen, sellers, merchants, agents, bankers, book-keepers (and commodities) in marketplaces, shops, ships and ports; as actors, danc-ers, singers, sex workers, doctors, teachers, grammarians and authors in the service sec-tor; and, perhaps most extraordinarily, as policemen in classical Athens or as members of the lower, middle and upper echelons of the bureaucracy of the early imperial state in Rome.[3] Their hard work gave their masters the opportunity to enjoy a life of leisure without the drudgery of household chores, to live in relative financial comfort, to enjoy various pleasures of the senses, to delegate their simple or complex tasks and even to enjoy stupendous wealth at scales not seen again until the Industrial Revolution.

One would expect on this basis that slavery would constitute one of the major pre-occupations of ancient historians; this expectation would not be disappointed. In line with wider trends in the historical discipline that have seen social and economic his-tory become burgeoning fields ever since the 1960s, slavery became and has remained a favourite topic of research. The 600 pages of the bibliography compiled by Heinz Bellen and Heinz Heinen list more than 10,000 books and articles that relate to vari-ous aspects of ancient slavery; since this bibliography was published back in 2003, one would have to add many hundreds of books and articles that have been published in the almost two decades that have ensued.[4]

Notwithstanding this enormous output of research since the 1960s, the study of ancient slavery has been based on four fundamental and widely shared elements. The first is an essentialist approach to slavery that tries to define its trans-historical nature; the second is a top-down perspective, which considers slavery as a relationship uni-laterally defined by the masters; the third is a typological distinction between societies with slaves and slave societies; and the fourth is a deeply static account of the history of ancient slavery, in which in the millennium between the archaic period and late antiquity hardly anything changed.[5]

---

[1] duBois 2003.

[2] Scheidel 2005b.

[3] Schumacher 2001a: 91–238.

[4] Bellen and Heinen 2003. For publications since 2003, see the updated version available online at <http://sklaven.adwmainz.de/index.php?id=1584> (last accessed 22 October 2020).

[5] See how these elements are represented in the recent syntheses of Andreau and Descat 2006; Herrmann-Otto 2009; Bradley and Cartledge 2011; Hunt 2018a.

Let us briefly describe these four fundamental elements. Most ancient historians firmly believe that slavery has a trans-historical essence, even though they might disagree on how exactly to define its nature. Many historians espouse the traditional definition of slavery as a property relationship;[6] some are more inclined to conceive slavery as a form of social death, following Orlando Patterson's famous cross-cultural definition of slaves as 'natally alienated and generally dishonored persons';[7] and others are happy to combine the two definitions.[8] This essentialist approach to slavery leads directly to the adoption of a top-down perspective. Slavery is seen from the perspective of the masters, the agents who unilaterally formulated slavery and treated slaves as items of property or as socially dead; slaves are seen only as passive objects of exploitation and domination who played no role in shaping slavery as a historical relationship. Slaves could either acquiesce to slavery or revolt in order to escape slavery and acquire their freedom; but they are not seen as historical agents who played an important, if asymmetric, role in the historical configuration of slavery.[9]

The distinction between slave societies and societies with slaves was introduced by Moses Finley in the late 1960s and has been further developed over the years by various other scholars.[10] In slave societies slavery played a fundamental economic role in terms of how the elite derived its surplus; consequently, slavery also shaped deeply the social, political and cultural aspects of those societies. In societies with slaves, slavery played a marginal economic role and accordingly had a limited social, cultural and political impact. While societies with slaves were ubiquitous, slave societies have been very rare. There were apparently only five genuine slave societies in world history: classical Greece and Rome in antiquity and the New World societies of the US South, Brazil and the Caribbean. Accordingly, what distinguishes Greek and Roman slaveries and gives them their particular prominence is that they have been classified as members of a very selective club.

The consequence of the first three elements is a deeply static narrative of the history of ancient slavery. Like salt and sugar in various foodstuffs, slavery can be found in various configurations across time and space, but, like them, it always maintains its essence. If slavery is a legal relationship of property, it follows that it remained essentially the same for the whole of antiquity, since slavery was always a property relationship. If slavery is the total power of the master over the slave, then it is only if we can show that the masters progressively exercised less of this total power that we can see any historical change of slavery in antiquity. Modern scholars have generally made a good case of showing that there is very little compelling evidence for any gradual improvement in the treatment of slaves.[11] Consequently, they have concluded that slavery experienced no significant historical changes in the course of antiquity.[12]

---

[6] Andreau and Descat 2006: 18–19.

[7] Patterson 1982: 13; Bradley 1994: 10–16.

[8] Finley 1968; Fisher 1993: 5–6; Garnsey 1996: 1; for the incommensurability between the two approaches, see Lewis 2017b.

[9] See Bradley 1984.

[10] Finley 1968, 1980; for the emergence and development of the concept, see Lenski 2018b.

[11] Finley 1980: 93–122; Klees 1998; cf. Knoch 2017.

[12] See, characteristically, the account in Bradley and Cartledge 2011; for a criticism of this static approach, see Vlassopoulos 2012.

Accordingly, the problem of historical change becomes a problem of historical transition from one essentialist ideal type into another. During the archaic period Greek communities moved from being societies with slaves into slave societies; in the course of the millennium that followed, slavery is seen as essentially unchanged, until ancient communities returned to being societies with slaves in the course of late antiquity. Finley's account in his highly influential book *Ancient Slavery and Modern Ideology* is typical: historical change took place only at the beginning, with the emergence of slave societies in Greece and Rome, and at the very end in late antiquity. In the millennium that intervened, slavery hardly changed. Because it was an unchanging constant, slavery as such played no role in these historical transitions. It was rather changes within the community of freemen that constituted the motor of change: the gain of citizenship by the lower classes and the creation of a clear dividing line between free and slave in the archaic period, and the progressive blurring of the line during the early imperial period.[13]

Let us now examine some major problems created by these four fundamental elements of the dominant approach to ancient slavery. The first problem is that the essentialist and typological approaches make it difficult to account for diversity and difference. The example of slave marriage illustrates the problems it creates for both the slavery as property and the slavery as social death approaches. If slaves are property and socially dead, then we should expect that, even if they managed to create fragile marriages and families, these would not be legally recognised and would have no legal consequences. If we now turn to classical Athens, it would appear that this approach is vindicated: marriages between slaves were not legally recognised and had no legal consequences; mixed marriages between slave and free were also not recognised; masters could not marry their manumitted slaves and could not recognise their slave offspring as legitimate, even if they wanted to.[14] But if we turn to other slaveholding societies, very different patterns start to emerge. In Rome marriages between slaves, or between free and slave, were not legally recognised; but masters could marry their manumitted slaves.[15] In fifth-century BCE Gortyn in Crete, mixed marriages between slave and free were legally recognised and marriages between slaves had legal consequences.[16] In various societies in the ancient Near East masters could marry their slaves and recognise their children as legitimate heirs, while slaves could marry other free people and even adopt free people as heirs.[17] In Islamicate societies both free and slave people had the right to marry and both mixed marriages between slave and free and marriages between slaves were legally recognised; in fact, when a female slave married a slave belonging to another master, the master of the wife had to recognise the rights of her slave husband over his wife.[18] Why were slaves able to have legally recognised marriages in certain societies and not in others? How are we to explain this enormous diversity without despairing, or making token references to complexity? The dominant framework of

---

[13] Finley 1980: 67–92, 123–49.
[14] Klees 1998: 155–75; Vérilhac and Vial 1998, 42–82; Lape 2002.
[15] Wacke 2001; Willvonseder 2010; Simonis 2017.
[16] Lewis 2013; Vlassopoulos 2018a.
[17] Westbrook 1998.
[18] Ali 2010.

approaching slavery has no conceptual space for incorporating and explaining diversity, and the concept of social death as some kind of trans-historical essence of slavery is clearly problematic.

The same critique can be applied to the conceptual pair of slave societies and societies with slaves. For the distinction fails to explain both the major differences among slave societies and the existence of fault lines that on the one hand put together certain slave societies and societies with slaves, and on the other oppose them to other slave societies. Armies of slaves existed in the slave societies of the Oyo Empire in Africa and the Ottoman society with slaves, but would have been unthinkable in the slave societies of Greece and Rome;[19] wealthy slaves and powerful slave bureaucrats existed in the slave society of Rome, but were unthinkable in the US South slave society; the incorporation of freed persons into the community was relatively easy in Rome and Brazil, while freed persons were permanent outsiders in Greece and the US South.[20] How can we explain similarities between members of different typological categories and differences within the same category? The dominant conceptual approach leaves us ill prepared for dealing with such problems.[21]

This leads us to another major problem with the distinction between slave societies and societies with slaves. This distinction was based on the assumption that the economic importance of slavery determined its social, cultural and political significance and on the premise that slave societies were rare in world history. But a growing body of work over the last few decades has seriously challenged both these assumptions. Studies of global slavery have documented the existence of large-scale slave societies in various parts of Africa,[22] among Native Americans[23] and in Southeast Asia.[24] What appeared as a very selective club no longer seems that way; this challenges all the easy assumptions that resulted from the fact that the five 'genuine' slave societies posited by the original theory were all Western societies.

Its twin concept is also in trouble. The concept of societies with slaves had no internal coherence: it was a hotchpotch of very different societies whose sole common feature was that they had limited numbers of slaves. The immense growth of studies on societies with slaves keeps facing the same query: how should we assess the impact of slavery in societies where it did not have a dominant economic role? The deep impact of slavery in conceptions of marriage in Jewish and Islamic societies with slaves is a characteristic example of this phenomenon.[25] In fact, even in societies where slavery had long become extinct, like early modern England, it played a major role in life and thinking.[26] There is no automatic or predetermined way in which the economic significance of slavery relates to its impact on culture, politics or society. We need an alternative framework to explore how the economic, political, social and cultural

---

[19] Brown and Morgan 2006.
[20] Gudmestad 2018; Joly and Bivar Marquese 2020.
[21] Vlassopoulos 2016a; Lenski and Cameron 2018.
[22] Stilwell 2014.
[23] Donald 1997.
[24] Reid 1983; Condominas 1998.
[25] Flesher 1988; Ali 2010.
[26] Guasco 2014.

uses of slavery fit together in different societies, and the diverse ways in which slavery affects the economic, social, political and cultural processes of each society.

The third major problem concerns the unilateral and top-down perspective, which makes it impossible to account for the contradictions created by slave agency. In many ancient societies slaves created their own families, kinship networks and communities;[27] they developed independent economic activities, working and living on their own, and used these activities in order to acquire property and ultimately gain their freedom.[28] Our definitions of slavery have not yet managed to incorporate slave agency and the wider range of relationships that shape slavery. If the essence of slavery is the unilateral domination of the masters, how can slave agency enter the definition? If the essence of slavery is natal alienation, how should we understand slave community? The unilateral approach focuses exclusively on the relationship between masters and slaves; but the historical configuration of slavery also involved relationships between slave-owners and other freemen, between slaves and other freemen and between the slaves themselves; but there is no way of incorporating these various relationships into a definition that has no conceptual space for them.[29] We therefore need a historical approach to slavery that will enable us to study the historical agency of slaves, the diversity and contradictions which are inherent in slavery and the multiplicity of relationships which affected slavery as a historical phenomenon.

A fourth major problem concerns the overwhelmingly static account of the history of ancient slavery. If slavery has a trans-historical essence, then it can have no real history; for, as Nietzsche famously argued, nothing that has history can have a definition.[30] The current static account of ancient slavery is inherently implausible. Historians who study New World slavery have shown that during the three centuries of its existence slavery was in constant flux; how is it ever possible that slavery in antiquity remained constant during the millennium of its existence?[31] Given the radical changes that took place in the social, political, economic and cultural fields during the millennium of ancient history, how is it possible that slavery, this fundamental aspect of the ancient world, remained unchanged?

In this respect, it is worth making a final observation. Once upon a time, slavery played a key role as a causal factor in explaining various crucial phenomena and major developments of the ancient world. Slavery could account for the low level of technological development and economic growth in the ancient world.[32] It explained the emergence of ancient democracy, as the labour of slaves gave citizens the free time they needed to engage with politics.[33] It caused the Roman Revolution, as the

---

[27] For slave communities in the ancient world, see Harper 2011: 273–9; McKeown 2012, 2019; Bathrellou 2014; Hunt 2015; Vlassopoulos 2015a, 2018d.

[28] For the slaves' economy in the New World, see Berlin and Morgan 1991, 1993; for the ancient world, see Roth 2005, 2016a; Porter 2019a: 202–47.

[29] Vlassopoulos 2011a, 2011b.

[30] Nietzsche 1997 [1887]: 53.

[31] For historical narratives exploring change in New World slaveries, see Berlin 1998; Newman 2013; Burnard 2015; Helg 2016; Gudmestad 2018.

[32] Finley 1965b.

[33] Jameson 1977; Wood 1988: 5–41.

labour of slaves substituted the free peasants and created a major economic, social and political crisis.[34] For many historians, the profitability crisis of slave agriculture and the increase in the price of slaves due to the end of Roman imperial expansion led to the fall of the Roman Empire.[35] For those who considered Christianity a religion of slaves and other subaltern people, slavery played a major role in explaining the Christianisation of the Roman Empire.[36]

All of these causal explanations were quite problematic, and have rightly been abandoned.[37] But in their place, many current interpretations of these same phenomena have completely abandoned slavery as a causal factor. Other interpretations of these phenomena consider slavery as a static entity on which other factors had an effect; it is these other factors which are the independent variables that had an impact on slavery, instead of slavery affecting them in any way. In the current climate, in which ancient historians compete with each other over who will make the most extravagant claims about the level of economic growth in antiquity, slavery plays no role in explaining that growth.[38] The discovery that there were in fact significant technological innovations in antiquity means that slavery is no longer considered an important causal factor in explaining ancient technological change.[39] Accounts of the Roman Revolution no longer attribute to slavery a key causal role in the economic and political changes associated with the last century of the Roman Republic.[40] Analyses that have adopted the framework of slave societies / societies with slaves have also abandoned slavery as a causal factor. In this framework, slave societies emerged out of struggles between the free population and were transformed because of new relationships between the state and its free subjects; slavery merely provided a form of labour substitution once the lower-class citizens stopped being available for exploitation. Slavery no longer explains or causes these changes; it is merely their outcome.[41] Finally, in accounts of the major transformations of late antiquity, it is the contraction of the market and the power of the Roman state that is used to explain the end of Roman slavery;[42] it is even possible to read an account of the fall of the Roman Empire written by a slavery specialist which attributes no role to it whatsoever![43]

It is equally remarkable to notice the absence of slaves from narrative accounts of ancient history. To give an example we shall examine in detail in Chapter 8, slaves were everywhere in the Peloponnesian War: their labour was essential for serving their masters' needs, building the Erechtheion, constructing the Argive long walls and

---

[34] Toynbee 1965; Hopkins 1978: 1–98.

[35] Ciccotti 1899; Štaerman and Trofimova 1975.

[36] Allard 1876.

[37] For criticisms of these explanations, see, for example, Kyrtatas 1987; McKeown 2007a.

[38] See, for example, Ober 2015: 160; for criticisms, see López Barja de Quiroga 2010: 323; Vlassopoulos 2016d; Porter 2019b.

[39] Greene 2000; Wilson 2002; cf. Rihll 2008.

[40] For accounts that minimise or eschew the impact of slavery in favour of other factors or interpretations, see Jongman 2003; de Ligt 2004; Rosenstein 2004; Launaro 2011; Kay 2014.

[41] Finley 1980; for criticism, see Vlassopoulos 2016b: 91–4.

[42] Harper 2011: 497–509.

[43] Harper 2017b.

manning the Corcyraean, Chian and Athenian fleets. The war was a mass process of liberation and enslavement: many thousands of free people became slaves in its course, and many thousands of slaves gained their freedom. The agency of slaves was crucial for the outcome of the war. Many helots chose flight from Sparta, while others fought for Sparta; thousands of slaves fled from Athens, while many others fought for Athens; had all these various groups of slaves acted differently, the duration and the outcome of the war would have changed radically. And yet, no history of slavery pays any attention to the Peloponnesian War, and no history of the Peloponnesian War considers slaves an important historical agent in the outcome of that war.[44]

We thus face a rather bizarre situation: slavery is widely considered to be one of the most important phenomena of the ancient world, but plays little causal role in explaining many major developments in the course of antiquity. Slaves constituted a substantial proportion of the population of many ancient communities and played a significant role in many economic, social, political and cultural developments; but they are largely invisible in our narrative histories of the ancient world. The four elements that have shaped the current paradigm of studying ancient slavery have cumulatively created this paradox.

This book aims to offer an alternative framework for the study of ancient slavery, which avoids the problems we have noted while offering important new advantages. This framework is based on a processual and historicist perspective. Instead of seeking the trans-historical essence of slavery, I argue that slavery is a historically changing conglomerate of three different conceptual systems: slavery as property; slave status; and the various modalities of slavery. While these three systems have existed in all slaveholding societies, the precise ways in which they form historical conglomerates have varied greatly across space and time: the content of each conceptual system could differ significantly among different societies, and they could place the emphasis on one of these systems rather than the others. By putting aside essentialist approaches to slavery, this new framework can incorporate both diversity and historical change.

Instead of the static approach to slavery and the static distinction between slave societies and societies with slaves, the new framework adopts a processual approach. I heed the late Joseph Miller's call to shift our focus from slavery as an ahistorical institution to **slaving** as a historically dynamic agglomeration of processes that involved various agents alongside slaves and masters.[45] Such a perspective shifts our attention to the entanglement between two different factors: the diverse slaving strategies pursued by various masters and the complementarities and contradictions that they created, and the various contexts (the household, the political community, the wider world and large-scale economic operations) within which slaving took place. Strategies and contexts were held together by three distinct dialectical relationships: between masters and slaves, between free and slave and within the slave communities that slaves constructed and participated in. This novel framework enables us to re-integrate the study of slaves and slavery within the wider dynamic processes of ancient social, economic, political

---

[44] See Hunt 1998: 53–143; Vlassopoulos 2017.
[45] Miller 2012; see also Stilwell 2014.

and cultural history; it will also allow us to study the temporal and spatial diversity of ancient slavery and slaves.[46]

This new framework eschews the exclusive focus on the master–slave relationship that has characterised the traditional paradigm, and opens the way for the incorporation of slave agency within our framework for studying slavery. The entanglement between strategies, contexts and dialectical relationships enables us to approach the identity of slaves from processual and non-essentialist perspectives. Instead of approaching slave identity in monolithic terms, I suggest conceptualising slaves as enslaved persons with multiple identities. Finally, this new framework makes it possible to study the historical agency of enslaved persons and the ways in which it shaped the historical trajectories of ancient societies.

One of the major propositions of this book is that slavery was not unilaterally defined by the masters, but involved a constant tug of war. Masters might instrumentalise slavery to cover every aspect of slaves' lives, or they might only employ it for certain aspects and purposes. Slaves could try to define aspects of their lives by means of other tools, given that there were other ways of conceptualising slavery that slaves and masters could employ in certain contexts and for certain purposes. Slaves did not merely react to a relationship which was set by others; they also tried to change the rules of the game by creating a world of their own, next to, below and even against the world of their masters. They constantly tried to turn slavery into something different from what it often claimed to be. Their hopes to create families, to enhance their economic condition, to create community, to achieve recognition in the eyes of other people, even to become independent, continuously challenged and modified slavery as a relationship in any given society.[47] Slaves were historical agents, because they constantly strove to make themselves other things apart from being solely slaves, and to redefine the relationship of slavery in their own terms and for their own benefit. Of course, given the enormous asymmetry of power, slaves never achieved their aims completely or permanently; but the battles they won, or did not lose, were historically important. This focus on slave agency is in line with a growing trend towards engaging seriously with history from below in antiquity: towards excavating and reconstructing subaltern groups in antiquity as active subjects of their own histories and as historical agents in the making of ancient societies.[48]

This new framework would have been impossible without deep engagement with the comparative history of slavery.[49] I have tried to take account of work not only on the various Greek and Roman slaveholding societies, but also on the various forms of slavery in the ancient Near East[50] and Egypt,[51] late antiquity and the Middle Ages,[52] Islamicate

[46] Vlassopoulos 2016a.

[47] Vlassopoulos 2011a.

[48] Courrier and Magalhães de Oliveira forthcoming is absolutely fundamental; see also Dossey 2010; Grey 2011; Forsdyke 2012; Magalhães de Oliveira 2012, 2020; Taylor and Vlassopoulos 2015a; Grig 2017; Vlassopoulos 2018c.

[49] For works with comparative or global perspectives, see Watson 1980a; Patterson 1982; Turley 2000; Dal Lago and Katsari 2008a; Miller 2012; Zeuske 2013; Grenouilleau 2014; Lenski and Cameron 2018.

[50] Dandamaev 1984; Hezser 2005; Galil 2007; Head 2010; Culbertson 2011; Seri 2013; Dromard 2017; Lewis 2018.

[51] Bakir 1952; Loprieno 1997, 2012; Redford 2004; Hofmann 2005.

[52] Nehlsen 1972; Karras 1988; Bonnassie 1991; Melluso 2000; Pelteret 2001; Hammer 2002; Rotman 2009; Harper 2011; Lenski 2011a, 2011b, 2014; Carrier 2012; Sutt 2015; Rio 2017.

societies,[53] early modern Europe,[54] Native American societies,[55] the colonial societies of the New World,[56] Africa,[57] the Indian Ocean[58] and China.[59] The study of ancient slavery has been largely myopic in comparative terms; in the rare cases when ancient historians have engaged seriously with comparative evidence, they have largely focused on slavery in the US South.[60] Despite the value of such comparative studies, the US South is in many ways a very peculiar case, which can lead to very misleading impressions about the global history of slavery. I hope that the use of the comparative approach in this work will convince the readers of the need to expand our imaginaries in a systematic manner.[61]

I shall finish this introduction by providing an overview of the book's contents. Chapter 2 explores the historiography of the study of ancient slavery, which has been shaped by three major debates: the modernist debate concerns the extent to which ancient economies were based on slavery, in contrast to modern capitalist societies being based on free labour; the humanitarian debate tries to square the horrid realities of ancient slavery with our admiration for the political, intellectual and cultural achievements of ancient societies; while the class struggle debate assesses whether slaves constituted a class, and how the struggle between masters and slaves has affected the history of ancient societies. It was Finley who, in the course of the 1960s and 1970s, constructed the current dominant approach to ancient slavery by reformulating the three debates in novel ways: the fundamental distinction between slave societies and societies with slaves was a new way for understanding the economic impact of slavery in ancient societies; the class struggle debate took a new turn, as Finley argued that slaves did not constitute a single class, and distinguished genuine chattel slaves from serf-like groups, like the Spartan helots, who had totally different characteristics; finally, in the humanitarian debate Finley spearheaded an approach that stressed the unilateral power of the masters and its domineering and exploitative effects, and criticised attempts to describe a gradual amelioration of ancient slavery due to factors like Stoicism or Christianity. The new orthodoxy projected an overwhelmingly static history of ancient slavery in the millennium between the archaic period and late antiquity.

[53] Crone 1980; Pipes 1981; Hunwick and Powell 2002; Lovejoy 2004; Ali 2010; Loiseau 2016; Freamon 2019.

[54] Hellie 1982; Kolchin 1987; Blumenthal 2009; Guasco 2014; Hanß and Schiel 2014; Phillips 2014; Witzenrath 2015.

[55] Donald 1997; Viau 1997; Santos Granero 2009; Snyder 2010; Brooks 2011; Rushforth 2012; Cameron 2016.

[56] Kolchin 1993; Berlin 1998; Blackburn 1998; Eltis 2000; Nishida 2003; Sweet 2003; Morgan 2004; Kiddy 2005a; Bergad 2007; Gallay 2009; Read 2012; Johnson 2013; Newman 2013; Burnard 2015; Helg 2016.

[57] Miers and Kopytoff 1977; Meillassoux 1991; Lovejoy 2012; Stilwell 2004, 2014.

[58] Watson 1980a; Reid 1983, 2018; Condominas 1998; Warren 2007; Mann 2012; Hopper 2015.

[59] Watson 1980c; Hansson 1996; Crossley 2011; Sommer 2015; Ransmeier 2017.

[60] For comparisons between ancient slavery and the New World, in particular the US South, see, for example, Cartledge 1985; Bradley 1987: 1–17; Scheidel 1996b, 2002; Dal Lago and Katsari 2008c. See also the rare case of a comparison with the US North in Rosivach 1993.

[61] For the comparative approach espoused here, see Vlassopoulos 2014; for recent studies of ancient slavery that make excellent use of wider comparative evidence, see Kleijwegt 2006b; Ismard 2017a, 2017b; Lenski 2018a; Joly and de Bivar Marquese 2020.

But while this new approach to ancient slavery was taking place in the 1960s and 1970s, the study of global slavery was moving in radically new directions. The Civil Rights movement forced historians to face the dilemma of slave agency: were slaves solely damaged victims of domination and exploitation, or could they also be seen as active historical agents? To answer this conundrum, historians of US slavery created the concept of the slave community. While originally it was the study of US slavery that took the lion's share of modern historical work, the gradual shift of attention to Native American, Latin American and African slaveries brought to light forms of slavery that exhibited major differences from the familiar slavery of the US South. This awareness of important diversities across space and time had two major repercussions. On the one hand, it made historians realise that the diverse slaving systems were not separate entities, but entangled parts of wider processes; the concept of the Atlantic world which interlinked the European, Native American, colonial American and African societies through processes of empire building, commercial exchange, human mobility and cultural interaction was crucial for studying the interconnected early modern slaveries. On the other hand, the global study of slavery has led historians to challenge assumptions and approaches based on the myopic focus on Greek, Roman and American slaveries and to attempt to write the global history of slavery, instead of a sociology that examines slavery as a static worldwide phenomenon. After highlighting the implications of these developments for the study of ancient slavery, the chapter concludes by tracing developments in the study of ancient slavery over the last three decades and the ways they provide the foundations for a new conceptual framework.

Chapter 3 commences the process of building this framework by examining the concept of slavery. The first part of the chapter uses early medieval slavery as an illuminating test-case: the complexity and diversity of early medieval slavery makes it possible to challenge some implicit assumptions that have long dominated the study of ancient slavery; it also allows us to test the conceptual coherence of various key concepts in the study of slavery. The second part of the chapter builds on these insights to propose a new conceptualisation of slavery as an agglomerate of three conceptual systems: slavery as property, slave status and the various modalities of slavery. By breaking up the unitary understanding of slavery as a single essence, it explores the varying content of each conceptual system and the diverse ways in which they fitted in together across space and time.

Chapter 4 employs an instrumental approach to examine the various reasons why masters employed slavery and the contexts in which they did so. The concept of slaving strategies highlights the fact that slavery could be used for very diverse and often contradictory purposes and explores the entanglements between them. The chapter analyses slaving strategies for labour, revenue, prestige, gratification, expertise, trust and authority. It also examines how certain slaving strategies can occasionally solidify into slaving lifestyles: the lifestyles of the gentleman, the planter and the lord. The second part of the chapter explores the various contexts of slaving: the household, the political community, the wider world and large-scale economic operations. Each context had its own balance of forces and pushed slaving in different directions which could sometimes be deeply contradictory, and because these various contexts had their own historical trajectories which were independent of slavery, the history of slaving is inscribed within wider historical processes that need to be studied on their own. The final part of the chapter explores the links between slaving strategies and contexts by focusing on the various processes of slave-making: the natural reproduction of the slave population, which was shaped by both the slaving strategies of the masters and the formation of slave communities; the enslavement of members of the free population of political communities as a result of debt, conviction, self-sale or infant abandonment; the practices of violent slave-making in the wider world and the creation of slaving and no-slaving zones as a result of state-building, ideology and religion; and, finally, the slave trade and the ways it linked all the above factors.

Chapter 5 moves from slavery and the slaving strategies of the masters to the study of slaves. It utilises the explosion of interest in identities across the disciplines of history, anthropology, sociology and psychology in order to construct a new framework for approaching the complex phenomenon of slave identity. The first part of the chapter distinguishes between categorical and relational modes of slave identification and examines their implications; it further explores the distinction between primary-secondary and direct–indirect relationships on the one hand, and between definitional and prototypical categories on the other. The second part of the chapter examines three key aspects of slave identities: the categorisation of people as slaves; the various self-understandings of the slaves; and the forms of slave groupness. This conceptual framework highlights the complex and contradictory phenomenon of slave identities; while slave categorisation undoubtedly had major consequences for the lives of slaves, at the same time slaves could see themselves as free people in captivity, or build identities and groups on the basis of other factors: gender, kinship, ethnicity, religion and profession. Ultimately, the major struggle that slaves engaged in concerned the gap between the nominal slave identity imposed on slaves and its real impact in shaping slave lives. The concept of 'enslaved persons' allows us to capture the complex and contradictory character of slave identities.

Chapter 6 builds on the insights of the previous chapters by bringing together the slaving strategies and contexts examined in Chapter 4 and the identities of enslaved persons examined in Chapter 5. These two sides of the coin were inherently linked by three dialectical relationships: between masters and slaves; between free persons and slaves; and within the slave communities. The master–slave dialectic formed a spectrum with two extremes: on the one hand, it could lead to the cruel tyranny of masters exercised over slaves without any control; on the other hand, rich and powerful masters could offer their slaves significantly better opportunities than those existing for most of the free population. The free–slave dialectic depended on the intervention of the political community in the theoretically unmediated relationship between masters and slaves in order to achieve two things: to formulate slave status and the distinction between free people and slaves and to shape the master–slave relationship according to the wider interests of the community as a whole. This dialectic also formed a spectrum: on the one hand, political communities could limit what masters could do to their slaves and enhance the condition of enslaved persons; on the other, the political community might limit the opportunities that masters offered to their slaves and subordinate all slaves to the poorest and least powerful member of the free community. The third dialectic comprises the full range of relationships within the communities that enslaved persons constructed and participated in. These communities were based on kinship and family, ethnicity, religion, neighbourhood, profession or belonging to the same master. While some of these communities consisted exclusively of slaves and freed persons, in many other communities slaves participated alongside various groups of free people and citizens.

Chapter 7 attempts to apply in practice the conceptual framework presented in Chapters 3 to 6. It focuses on how enslaved persons conceived and experienced slavery and their own identities. The first section of the chapter explores the diverse modalities of slavery that co-existed in ancient societies and examines how slaves employed these modalities for various purposes. Slavery could be conceived as an instrumental relationship in which slaves existed for the purpose of serving the needs and wishes of their masters; it could also be seen as an asymmetric negotiation of power between masters and slaves: a relationship not unilaterally defined from above, but the outcome of struggle, negotiation, compromise and failure. From this point of view, slave expectations would focus on limiting the power of masters and putting forward their own agenda of aims to the extent of the possible. Slavery could also be envisaged as an asymmetric relationship of benefaction and reward; masters could opt to see slave labour as loyal service and choose to reward deserving slaves with trust, honour and material benefits; slaves could see their service as the foundation for claims to just rewards. Finally, slavery could be seen as an extreme form of bad luck; this offered slaves a way of enduring their condition, while hoping that these adverse circumstances could be reversed.

The existence of different modalities of slavery allowed masters and slaves to negotiate their respective positions and enabled slaves to conceive slavery and their relationship to their masters in their own ways. Slaves tried to modify slavery from a unilateral and instrumental form of power exercised by their masters into something more negotiable, even if in asymmetric ways. But equally significant was the fact that slaves also tried to limit the effect of slavery on their lives by ensuring that significant parts of their lives would run on principles other than slavery (gender, kinship, profession, ethnicity, religion, friendship). The second part of the chapter uses the various hopes of enslaved persons both about life in slavery and life beyond slavery in order to explore the identities and communities that enslaved persons constructed and adopted.

Chapter 8 focuses on slaving in space and time: it constructs a framework for examining the diversity of slaveholding societies, on the one hand, and the processes and forces of historical change, on the other. The first section challenges the traditional approach to Greek slavery, which assumes that systems like helotage were not 'proper' slavery, and that all Greek chattel slaveries were identical to that of Athens. The peculiarities of each slaving system resulted from the impact of wider economic, political, social and cultural processes on local slaving practices; the concept of epichoric slaving systems allows us to incorporate diversity and change into the study of local slaving practices. The second section dismantles the traditional distinction between societies with slaves and slave societies alongside the historical narratives that have been constructed on their basis. Not only are there major empirical problems with these two concepts, but they prove to be bland instruments for explaining the major differences among slave societies and the differential impact of slaving on economic, social, political and cultural processes. The concept of the intensification of the advantages for masters and disadvantages for slaves that slaving offered provides a better way of comprehending the major differences between slaveholding societies than Finley's conceptual pair.

The third section focuses on the forms and forces of change in the history of slaving. I explore four major forms of change: rise and fall; cyclical processes of intensification and abatement; conjunctures; and long-term change. These forms of change were put into motion by three major forces. The first force consisted of the wider processes that shaped the four major slaving contexts that were examined in Chapter 4. The second force faced in the opposite direction: it consisted of the impact of slaving in shaping these wider processes in particular ways. The third force, that of slave agency, is the subject of the last section. It explores how the various identities of enslaved persons shaped how they exercised their agency, examines how enslaved persons can be restored as active agents in narratives of political change and invites us to restore the agency of enslaved persons as a major factor in processes of intellectual and cultural transformation.

Finally, the book concludes with a short epilogue that summarises the major findings and considers some important avenues of future research. The study of ancient slavery will need to eschew its exclusive focus on Greek and Roman slaveries and adopt a wider framework, which will explore the entanglement between slaving and the economic, social, political and cultural processes that linked together the Mediterranean, the Black Sea, temperate Europe, the Near East and North Africa. Ancient historians need their own equivalent of the framework of the Atlantic world that is currently shaping the study of early modern slavery.

# 2

# HISTORIOGRAPHIES

THIS CHAPTER WILL CHART the development of the study of ancient slavery, with a primary focus on the last fifty years, in which the field took its current shape. It is remarkable that the study of ancient slavery is still fundamentally shaped by the conceptual framework constructed by Finley in the course of the 1960s and 1970s. There is probably no other field in ancient history which is still defined by a framework created fifty years ago, and in which the work of a single scholar is still so influential. A mere comparison of two recently published collective volumes of great scope is illuminating: *The Cambridge Economic History of the Greco-Roman World* is definitely post-Finley,[1] while the *Cambridge World History of Slavery* is equally definitely Finleyan in approach.[2] The same conclusion would apply to all works of synthesis that have appeared over the last thirty years: they all maintain the same framework.[3]

As I will try to show, the reason for this is that we still remained trapped within a number of debates that took shape in the course of the nineteenth century. It is only if one explicitly challenges the assumptions of these debates that it will be possible to construct an alternative framework. The global study of slavery has made immense advances in this respect, as we shall see later in this chapter. But because the study of ancient slavery is still dominated by the traditional debates, historians of ancient slavery have so far largely failed to take notice and take advantage of these developments for their own purposes.[4]

We currently lack a comprehensive historiography of the study of ancient slavery.[5] A number of works have explored the origins of the study of ancient slavery during the eighteenth century,[6] while the nineteenth and the early twentieth centuries are still largely shrouded in mystery, despite some valiant efforts;[7] in the last few years, there has been a growing historiographical focus on the contribution of Finley and the intellectual background of his work,[8] as well as other twentieth-century contributions.[9] But there is still no account of the development of the field as a whole; in the absence of such a comprehensive account, many ancient historians take at face value Finley's

---

[1] Scheidel et al. 2007.

[2] Bradley and Cartledge 2011.

[3] Fisher 1993; Bradley 1994; Schumacher 2001a; Andreau and Descat 2006; Joshel 2010; Hunt 2018a.

[4] For this problem, see Vlassopoulos 2014, 2016b.

[5] For an incisive exploration of some key issues, see McKeown 2007a.

[6] Deissler 2000; Harvey 2007; Grieshaber 2012; Montoya 2015.

[7] But see Vogt 1974: 170–210; Riccardi 1997; Deissler 2001; Nippel 2005.

[8] For general works on Finley, see Nafissi 2005; Harris 2013a; Jew, Osborne and Scott 2016; Palmeira 2018. On Finley and slavery, see Shaw 1998; Perry 2014; Vlassopoulos 2016b; Lenski 2018b; Bodel 2019.

[9] For the Mainz research project, see below p. 34; for the contribution of Westermann, see Joly 2019.

account of the historiography of slavery in the first chapter of *Ancient Slavery and Modern Ideology*.[10] Unfortunately, as Arnaldo Momigliano commented long ago, this is a highly misleading account.[11]

This chapter cannot even attempt to fill this important void, and it therefore has two important limitations. The first one is that its aim is rather unashamedly teleological. It will explore why the study of ancient slavery has developed in the way that it has, in order to show the limits of the current dominant paradigm; it will briefly trace the development of the study of global slavery, in order to highlight a number of important new approaches that can prove highly beneficial for the study of ancient slavery; and it will highlight recent developments in the study of ancient slavery over the last three decades, in order to reveal how the dominant paradigm has been gradually challenged and explore the foundations on which we can build an alternative framework. The second limitation concerns its coverage. Ancient slavery is a global field of study; while the historiographical review below will take account of developments in Germanophone, Francophone, Italophone, Lusophone and Hispanophone scholarship, its main focus is the historiography of the Anglophone literature which, in many important ways, has shaped the development of the field overall.[12]

## The Formation of the Dominant Paradigm in the Study of Ancient Slavery

The three debates that have shaped the modern study of ancient slavery can be called, for lack of better terms, the modernist, the humanitarian and the class struggle debates.[13] The first debate has its origins in the Enlightenment. It is a debate which is associated with famous names like those of Adam Smith and David Hume[14] and others whose names are nowadays only known to a few specialists.[15] At the centre of this debate was the new kind of society that contemporaries saw as emerging in Western Europe. This society was not based on the established hierarchies of the *ancien régime*, but on international commerce and free labour; it was totally different from ancient societies, which were based on warfare, agriculture and slavery. The distinction between a modern world based on free labour and an ancient world based on slavery is thus the legacy of an Enlightenment debate which aimed to vindicate modern society.[16]

---

[10] Finley 1980: 11–66.

[11] Momigliano 1987: 4.

[12] I am unfortunately unable to engage with untranslated Russophone scholarship for linguistic reasons. For translated Russophone studies of ancient slavery, see Štaerman 1969; Blavatskaja, Golubcova and Pavlovskaja 1972; Štaerman and Trofimova 1975; Dandamaev 1984; Štaerman et al. 1987; Marinovič et al. 1992; Kazakévich 2008. For the development of Soviet scholarship on slavery, see Raskolnikoff 1990: 1–12; Heinen 2010b.

[13] I have slightly modified the terminology employed in Vlassopoulos 2016b in the hope that this new terminology will avoid any confusions that might have been created by my earlier choice of terms. The substance of the argument remains the same.

[14] For ancient slavery and the Scottish Enlightenment, see Cairns 2006, 2012; Harvey 2007; Grieshaber 2012.

[15] For one such case, see Deissler 2000.

[16] Guerci 1979; Cambiano 1984; Schneider 1988.

These modernist debates continued during the nineteenth century and reached their climax towards the century's end, when the publication of Karl Bücher's *Die Entstehung der Volkswirtschaft* in 1893 created a spate of publications and a very audible debate.[17] On the one hand were those who argued that ancient societies were based on slavery. These scholars, who included Marxists as well as thinkers of various other persuasions, argued that the whole period of antiquity was characterised by dependence on the slave mode of production; that the emergence and decline of ancient societies was due to slavery; and that the social, political and cultural phenomena of the ancient world were deeply shaped by slavery. To give two examples, among many, the economic and technological stagnation of the ancient world was due to the impediment of slavery, and the decline of the Roman Empire was the result of the falling profitability of slavery, or of the collapse of the slave supply.[18] On the other hand were scholars of equally varied persuasions, the most famous among which was Eduard Meyer, who argued that slavery was only one among the various labour forms of ancient societies; that the importance of slavery had varied between different ancient societies and different periods; that the economic history of antiquity was not a linear stage in the evolution of societies from primitivism to capitalism, since ancient societies exhibited many similarities with modern capitalist societies; and that slavery was not the dominant economic factor which explained the economic, social and political development of antiquity.[19]

The humanitarian debate was the result of the potential clash between the universal condemnation of slavery as a result of abolitionism and the equally widespread admiration of classical civilisations, in which slavery was a ubiquitous feature. Once it was widely accepted that slavery was something wrong, the question emerged of how to square admiration of the Classics with condemnation of slavery.[20] For some scholars, the achievements of classical culture mitigated the evil of slavery; as Joseph Vogt famously argued, 'slavery and its attendant loss of humanity were part of the sacrifice which had to be paid for this achievement'.[21] Certain scholars posited that there was a progressive enlightenment in antiquity which led to the humanisation of slavery,[22] while others argued that ancient slavery was a far more humane relationship than the racial slavery of modern times,[23] or focused on exploring the human aspects of ancient slavery and its inherent contradictions;[24] their opponents denied the validity of these claims and stressed the continuity of slavery in its most cruel and oppressive forms throughout the whole course of antiquity.[25]

---

[17] See the texts collected in Finley 1979b; for these debates, see Nippel 2005; Nafissi 2005: 57–123.

[18] Weber 1896; Ciccotti 1899; see Kiechle 1969.

[19] Meyer 1898.

[20] See Vogt 1974: 170–210; Stahlmann 1992; duBois 2003.

[21] Vogt 1974: 25.

[22] See, for example, the discussion of the amelioration thesis in Wallon 1988 [1848]: 784–867; Westermann 1955: 102–20, 149–59.

[23] For the debate on the comparative humanity of ancient and modern slavery, with particular reference to helotage, see Hodkinson and Hall 2011.

[24] Richter 1958; Raffeiner 1977; Synodinou 1977; Kudlien 1991; Gamauf 2001; Waldstein 2001.

[25] For Seneca and slavery, cf. Richter 1958; Bradley 2008.

Finally, the class struggle debate was framed in the terms proposed by Karl Marx and Friedrich Engels in the famous first lines of their *Communist Manifesto* of 1848:

> The history of all hitherto existing societies is the history of class struggles. Freeman and slave, patrician and plebeian, lord and serf, guild-master and journeyman, in a word, oppressor and oppressed, stood in constant opposition to one another, carried on an uninterrupted, now hidden, now open fight, a fight that each time ended either in a revolutionary reconstitution of society at large, or in the common ruin of the contending classes.[26]

These powerful words have ultimately raised important questions: what are the best conceptual tools to analyse the various groups of slaves and their masters? Were slaves a class or not? What role did slave resistance play in the history of ancient societies? How did the slaves influence the historical development of the ancient world? When modern scholars debate these questions they are continuing a debate with the *Communist Manifesto* and its authors.[27]

The significance of these debates in the study of ancient slavery is well reflected in a collection of previously published articles edited by Finley in 1960 under the title *Slavery in Classical Antiquity: Views and Controversies*.[28] The modernist debate on the role of slaves in production is represented by the articles of Jones[29] and Westermann,[30] which minimised the importance of slavery in agriculture and stressed its significance in manufacture; the humanitarian debate is presented in articles by Vlastos on slavery in Plato's *Republic*,[31] Schlaifer's discussion of Greek theories of slavery[32] and Vogt's chapter on humanity in ancient slavery;[33] finally, the class struggle debate on the nature of slaves and the role of slavery in the historical development of antiquity is represented by Bloch's famous article on the end of ancient slavery[34] and Westermann's discussion of the variability of the statuses among ancient slaves.[35]

The study of ancient slavery followed wider trends across the historical discipline, in which the study of social and economic history increased exponentially from the 1960s onwards. The number of publications has simply exploded since the 1960s, and the level of interest has remained steady.[36] But this explosion of research has been accompanied by the emergence and consolidation of a new paradigm that is still guiding how scholars approach the topic. This new paradigm was created by Finley, one of the most important ancient historians of the twentieth century. Finley's work was

---

[26] Marx and Engels 2002 [1848]: 219.
[27] Ste. Croix 1981; Garlan 1988: 201–8.
[28] Finley 1960a.
[29] Jones 1956.
[30] Westermann 1941.
[31] Vlastos 1941.
[32] Schlaifer 1936.
[33] Vogt 1958.
[34] Bloch 1947.
[35] Westermann 1943.
[36] See the extensive bibliography in Bellen and Heinen 2003.

fundamentally shaped by the three debates we have presented above; but his contribution reshaped these debates in new ways.

Finley's first article of 1959 ('Was Greek civilisation based on slave labour?') was a direct intervention in the modernist debate, and it is best to start our discussion from that debate.[37] Instead of answering the question that he posed in the title of his article, Finley proposed changing the nature of the question. By refusing to answer whether slavery was the basic economic element of ancient societies, or whether slavery had caused technological or economic stagnation, Finley was tacitly conceding the main points that scholars like Meyer had long been arguing. Nevertheless, he was adamant that slavery had played a very important economic role in antiquity, and most of his article was devoted to documenting this position. But this important economic role should be grasped in very different terms. Finley's new research agenda on this issue became clearer in his 1968 contribution to the *International Encyclopaedia of the Social Sciences*:

> Slavery attained its greatest functional significance, and usually the greatest numerical strength, in societies in which other, less total varieties of bondage, had either disappeared or had never existed. The distinction is particularly sharp as between *genuine* slave societies – classical Greece (except Sparta) and Rome, the American South and the Caribbean – on the one hand, and *slave-owning* societies as found in the Ancient Near East (including Egypt), India or China, on the other hand.[38]

Finley proposed a distinction between two different categories of societies where slavery was present. Slavery had been present since time immemorial in countless societies, which should be characterised as slave-owning societies (or societies with slaves, as the term became widely known). But in the course of world history there has also emerged a small number of 'slave societies', in which slavery was not merely one relationship among many, but 'attained its greatest functional and numerical significance'. Finley provided a very concise explanation of what he meant by that:

> Slaves were fundamental to the ancient economy in what I have been calling, for lack of a more precise label, the 'classical period', Greek and Roman. They were fundamental both in their employment (where they worked) and in the social structure (the reliance placed on them and their labour by the highest strata, the ruling classes).[39]

Slave societies differed from societies with slaves because in the former slaves were employed in production, and in particular in agriculture and the crafts, rather than merely as servants and concubines, and because slavery provided the main source of income for the ruling classes. Slave societies emerged when slavery substituted other forms of dependent labour, such as debt-slavery or serfdom, as the main means of surplus extraction for the ruling elite.

---

[37] Finley 1959.
[38] Finley 1968: 308.
[39] Finley 1973: 79.

Finley's concept of the slave society solved a number of significant problems that had been pointed out by his predecessors. The distinction between slave societies and societies with slaves allowed Finley to take into account the objection that slavery did not play the same role in all ancient societies; it also allowed him to avoid describing the whole of antiquity as dominated by the slave mode of production. While societies with slaves were ubiquitous in Greco-Roman antiquity, it was only the classical periods of Greece and Rome that saw the emergence of slave societies. Furthermore, the concept of slave society allowed Finley to counter the objection that the majority of producers in ancient societies were not slaves, but freemen. What mattered were not numbers as such, or the population as a whole, but only the use of labour in the large landholdings of the elite, which could not be cultivated solely through the labour of the owner and his family: great landowners covered their labour needs through the use of slave labour. According to this new formulation, in classical Greece and Rome the elite did not primarily exploit the free independent producers, since they had become unavailable for exploitation as dependent labour through political means, while wage labour played a minimal role; instead, the elite primarily exploited slaves.

Finally, the concept of slave society allowed Finley to provide a periodisation of the development of ancient history. Archaic Greece and Rome were societies with slaves, where the main means of labour extraction were other forms of dependent labour like debt-bondage. But in a series of political revolutions, which Finley analysed through his interpretation of Solonian Athens, the lower classes abolished debt-bondage and gained citizenship; consequently, free people were no longer available for exploitation by the elite.[40] Accordingly, the elites turned to slavery, thus creating the first slave societies in world history. During the Roman Empire the growing deterioration in the position of the free lower classes through legislation and taxation made them again available for exploitation by the elite, and this led to the gradual demise of ancient slave societies and the return to societies with slaves in late antiquity and the early Middle Ages.[41]

Finley's conception of slave society seems capable of taking into account all objections while retaining slavery's centrality in the economic history of antiquity. But from the point of view of the modernist debate, Finley's conception conceded the most important issue at hand. In Finley's conception slavery has no explanatory role as an economic factor: it is merely a solution to the problem of labour and revenue extraction for the elite. Finley's image of the 'ancient economy' was based on two factors: the rentier mentality of the ruling elite and the consumer role of ancient cities.[42] Both factors pre- and post-dated the emergence and decline of slave societies; their structural dominance in the 'ancient economy' was thus independent of slavery. Both factors also applied to areas where slavery never became the main means of labour extraction: Roman Asia Minor and Gaul had both elites with rentier mentalities and consumer cities, although they did not use slaves as the main means of labour and surplus extraction. Accordingly, slavery was merely an answer to a labour problem and

---

[40] Finley 1964, 1965a.
[41] Finley 1965a = 1981: 162–6; 1980: 123–49.
[42] Finley 1973.

had no role as an independent economic factor in ancient history; furthermore, slavery played no role in either the emergence or the decline of the ancient world. The emergence of slave societies was the by-product of struggles among the free, and the decline of slave societies was equally the result of a changing configuration between the state and the elites, on the one hand, and the free lower classes on the other. It is telling that only Marxists could see clearly that Finley had abandoned slavery as an economic explanation in ancient history.[43]

The absence of slavery as an economic explanation in Finley's approach contrasts rather sharply with his assessment of its social, political and cultural significance:

> There is no problem or practice in any branch of Greek life which was not affected, in some fashion, by the fact that many people in that society . . . were (or had been or might be) slaves.[44]

In order to understand this contradiction, we need to explore the role of slavery in the two other debates, to which we can now turn. Finley's contribution to the modernist debate entailed abandoning the problematic identification of antiquity as a whole with the slave mode of production in favour of a distinction between slave societies and societies with slaves. In the same way, his intervention in the class struggle debate consisted in abandoning the unitary conception of slaves in favour of a novel approach. In various articles in the 1960s Finley explored a variety of groups of ancient slaves in order to show that the traditional Marxist approach that conceived all of them as a single class was misguided.[45] There were very significant differences between Athenian chattel slaves, Spartan helots, Cretan *woikeis*,[46] manumitted slaves in *paramone*[47] and debt-bondsmen,[48] and these differences had very important historical consequences: chattel slaves did not revolt and chattel slavery was never abolished, while debt-bondage was abolished in archaic Athens and Rome, and helots revolted and even managed to abolish helotage.[49] Furthermore, even among chattel slaves there were very significant differences: there was little in common between the slave miners in Laureion, on the one hand, and the slave banker Pasion or the imperial slaves in the Roman Empire, on the other.[50] Finley proposed abandoning the Marxist concept of class as well as the rigid classification between freemen, slaves and serfs.[51] The various groups of free and dependent people should be located within a spectrum of statuses that ranged from absolute freedom to absolute slavery.[52] Locating slaves and other dependent groups within the spectrum of statuses was the aim of a new research agenda:

[43]  Ste. Croix 1981: 462–3.
[44]  Finley 1959 = 1981: 113.
[45]  Finley 1960b, 1964, 1965a.
[46]  Finley 1960b = 1981: 135–9.
[47]  Finley 1960b = 1981: 139–46.
[48]  Finley 1965a.
[49]  Finley 1964 = 1981: 118–19.
[50]  Finley 1964 = 1981: 119–27.
[51]  Finley 1980: 70–7.
[52]  Finley 1960b = 1981: 146–9.

My argument is that status in ancient Greece can be analysed effectively only by borrowing an approach which has been developed in contemporary jurisprudence particularly in the analysis of property. This involves first breaking up the traditional notion of rights into a number of concepts, including claims, privileges, immunities, powers, and their opposites. Second it involves envisaging status (or freedom) as a bundle of privileges, powers and so on, and therefore the definition of any particular status, or of any individual's status, in terms of the possession and location of the individual's elements on the bundle.[53]

Finley proposed a range of privileges and powers that could be explored in order to locate different groups within the spectrum of statuses and explain their different position and history: claims to property; power over human labour and movement; power to punish; judicial privileges and liabilities; privileges in the area of family; privileges of social mobility; and sacral, political and military privileges.[54]

Finley's proposal was undoubtedly a step in the right direction. Given the enormous diversity among dependent groups in general and among chattel slaves in particular, historical research would need to discover concepts and research agendas that would enable scholars to make distinctions and explain them. But at this point we encounter a significant problem in Finley's work. This research agenda on the spectrum of statuses was completely abandoned by Finley in the rest of his publications after 1965. This is a tacit decision which was never explained, and we need to look for an explanation. One element of this explanation is that the way Finley chose to pose the problem made it inherently difficult to pursue his research agenda. Given the limitations of the evidence, it was very difficult to explore the differences between Spartan helots and Gortynian *woikeis* as regards privileges of social mobility, or the differences among Greek chattel slaves as regards claims to property. Even more problematic, though, was that Finley's spectrum of statuses was descriptive and not explanatory.[55] The spectrum of statuses does not possess any internal dynamic that can explain how different positions are created, enhanced or diminished. This was the great advantage posed by the Marxist concept of class, which Finley himself was forced to use when he needed to move from description to historical explanation.[56] As a result, Finley ended up arguing that Spartan helots and Cretan *woikeis* could not be considered as genuine slaves; they were rather 'between slavery and freedom', and should be considered more akin to serfs than slaves.[57] The spectrum of statuses was substituted by typological classification and all its essentialist assumptions.

But probably more important was the contradiction between Finley's research agenda on the spectrum of statuses and his periodisation of the development of ancient slavery. In what can only be described as a schizophrenic article, Finley moves from

[53] Finley 1960b = 1981: 148.
[54] Finley 1964 = 1981: 131.
[55] Ste. Croix 1981: 91–6.
[56] Finley 1983: 1–11; see Harris 2013b.
[57] An argument originally made by Lotze 1959.

explaining why a simple distinction between slave and free is insufficient for the complex societies of Athens, Sparta and Rome, into the following argument:

> In classical Athens and Rome, on the other hand, the traditional dividing line, the traditional distinction according to whether a man is or is not the property of another, remains a convenient rule of thumb for most purposes. For them the metaphor of continuum breaks down . . . I might close with a highly schematic model of the history of ancient society. It moved from a society in which status ran along a continuum towards one in which statuses were bunched at two ends, the slave and the free – a movement which was most nearly completed in the societies which most attract our attention for obvious reasons. And then, under the Roman Empire, the movement was reversed; ancient society gradually returned to a continuum of statuses and was transformed into what we call the medieval world.[58]

Finley had presented the spectrum of statuses as an approach of universal applicability, given the range of rights and privileges and the diverse ways in which they were distributed among various groups. He was now arguing, however, that the spectrum of statuses only applied to the Near East and to the societies with slaves which existed in archaic Greece and Rome and re-emerged from late antiquity onwards; for classical Greece and Rome, the simple and single distinction between slave and free constituted a convenient rule of thumb. The corollary of this amazing statement is that the research strategy delineated by Finley in the very same article is inapplicable to classical Greece and Rome.

Is it possible to explain this contradiction? It stems, I think, from Finley's need to account for something he accepted as a unique discovery of Greek civilisation in contradistinction with the ancient Near East; that is, the emergence of freedom and democracy. Already in his 1959 article Finley had presented the paradoxical claim that 'one aspect of Greek history is the advance, hand in hand, of freedom *and* slavery'.[59] In order for freedom and democracy to emerge, it was essential to create a clear dividing line between freeman and citizen on the one hand and slave and outsider on the other. This clear dividing line brings us to the third major debate on ancient slavery.

Finley's intervention in this debate makes a very late appearance in the form of a vitriolic attack in his book *Ancient Slavery and Modern Ideology* on Joseph Vogt[60] and his stand within the humanitarian debate on ancient slavery.[61] Finley's argument, expressed in great detail in the third chapter entitled 'Slavery and humanity',[62] can be shown to be latent in his work on slavery from his earliest publication in 1959. Already then Finley wanted to counter the tendency among ancient historians to mitigate the stigma of ancient slavery through a variety of strategies: by claiming that ancient slavery was not racial and thus more humane than modern slavery; by discovering humanity in a variety

---

[58] Finley 1964 = 1981: 132.
[59] Finley 1959 = 1981: 115.
[60] Finley's attack was focused on Vogt 1974.
[61] Finley 1980; first announced in Finley 1979a; see Deissler 2010.
[62] Finley 1980: 93–122.

of situations and relationships in ancient slavery, such as the relationship between nannies and their free masters, or in the image of the faithful slave; and finally, by claiming that there was a progressive amelioration of ancient slavery due to the influence of Stoic or Christian ideas, or through imperial legislation. In order to counter these approaches, Finley provided a definition of slavery that stressed three components in particular: the slaves' property status, the totality of the power over them, and their kinlessness.[63] This top-down definition of slavery was supplemented by a stress on the unilateral character of the relationship between masters and slaves:

> The failure of any individual slave owner to exercise all his rights over his slave-property was always a unilateral act on his part, never binding, always revocable.[64]

It cannot be doubted that, compared to the arguments of the 'humanitarian' scholars, Finley's approach, which stressed the structural role of exploitation and brutality, the unilaterality of the masters' power and the lack of any progressive amelioration of ancient slavery, was clearly more convincing. The problem was rather that this was not the only way to frame the problem and that approaching slavery in this top-down and unilateral way created as many problems as it solved.

To start with, there are significant contradictions between Finley's definition of slavery and arguments that he presented in other debates. Finley's definition stressed the kinlessness and outsider status of ancient slaves; it is thus interesting to note how in his discussion of the decline of ancient slavery Finley argued against theories which explained it through problems in the slave trade by emphasising the important role of slave reproduction in maintaining Roman slavery.[65] But surely if slave reproduction played an important role, then the definition of slaves as quintessentially kinless outsiders requires modification at the very least. This is a good example of how Finley could argue two contradictory propositions, because they served different purposes in different contexts, probably without even realising the existence of the contradiction. It is equally telling that Finley was adamant against the attempt by anthropologists of slavery to use ethnographic data in order to re-examine the role of property and unilaterality in defining slavery.[66] Given Finley's earlier disavowal of a simplistic sociology which only distinguished between free labour, slavery and serfdom and his espousal of a 'spectrum of statuses' approach, his categorical negation of any attempt to expand the definition of slavery is surely further evidence of latent contradictions.

A final point concerns Finley's understanding of the millennium of slave societies between the late archaic period and the changes of late antiquity. Finley had abandoned a static depiction of the whole of antiquity dominated by the slave mode of production in favour of a more dynamic account which included the rise and fall of slave societies. One might have expected that he would have attempted to identify and

---

[63] Finley 1980: 77; for the interconnections between Finley's definition and the similar approach of Patterson, see Bodel 2019.
[64] Finley 1980: 74.
[65] Finley 1980: 128–30.
[66] Finley 1980: 69–70.

analyse changes and developments within the millennium of ancient slave societies, but no such account is to be found in any of Finley's works. The structure of *Ancient Slavery and Modern Ideology* is characteristic in this respect: a chapter on the emergence of slave societies is followed by a chapter devoted to the structural issue of slavery and humanity, finding little change in the course of antiquity, and finally a chapter devoted to the decline of ancient slavery. This gives the obvious impression that between emergence and decline nothing significant ever changed, and this is an impression which still permeates modern scholarship on ancient slavery.[67]

The explanation seems to be the result of the constraints of the humanitarian debate. In order to counter the 'humanitarians', Finley had to adopt a static definition of slavery that emphasised its top-down and unilateral features. Given that slave agency as a factor of change was discounted by both sides, any indication of change could only have come from the initiative of the masters, and had to be discounted if the 'humanitarian' agenda were to be rejected. Finley's selection of the static account of slavery and humanity as the subject of his middle chapter, instead of the development of ancient slave societies, was thus not an accidental choice, but a decision forced on him by the terms of the humanitarian debate.

Finley's work reframed the modernist debate by devising the key distinction between societies with slaves and slave societies; he shaped the class struggle debate by arguing that slaves did not constitute a single class and positing a fundamental distinction between chattel slaves and other unfree groups, like Spartan helots and Cretan *woikeis*; his intervention in the humanitarian debate entrenched the view that slavery was a relationship of exploitation and domination unilaterally defined by the masters. The combined outcome of these contributions was to emphasise the uniqueness of slavery in classical Greece and Rome and its inherent connection to the emergence of the concept of freedom in ancient societies. This paradigm reserved no conceptual space for the historical impact of slave agency. Slave societies emerged out of conflicts between the free and changed out of new relationships among the state and its citizens; slave agency played no role. Slavery concerned the unilateral power of the masters, and this fact hardly changed in the course of antiquity: the slaves were merely victims of exploitation and domination. Overall, the narrative of ancient slavery that emerged from this new paradigm was distinctively static: between the emergence of slave societies in the archaic period and their collapse in the course of late antiquity nothing really changed. The main parameters of the paradigm created by Finley are still dominant in the field, but, as we shall see in the last section of this chapter, a number of developments over the last three decades have started to create openings for a new framework. First, however, we need to turn to the study of global slavery to look at developments outside ancient history and consider their implications.

## The Global Study of Slavery

Traditionally, and until very recently, the global study of slavery has been dominated by the study of the US South; the gradual contribution of other areas and periods

---

[67] This is the impression given by Bradley and Cartledge 2011; see Vlassopoulos 2012.

would have a transformative effect, as we shall see later. The study of US slavery had its own humanitarian, modernist and class struggle debates. As regards the humanitarian debate, until the 1950s the dominant approach was one based on racism, in which slavery figured as a means of civilising the barbarian Africans. The patriarchal institution of slavery was generally considered to have treated slaves well and have succeeded in Christianising them. This debate was completely transformed in the course of the 1950s. Kenneth Stampp's highly influential book *The Peculiar Institution* argued forcefully that American slavery was an inhumane relationship of domination and exploitation.[68] This has settled the debate for good, as no scholars have since attempted to search for a progressive amelioration of slavery for humanitarian purposes in the same way that some ancient historians have sought to explain the impact of Stoicism or Christianity on ancient slavery.

But an even stronger challenge within the humanitarian debate was offered by Stanley Elkins in the late 1950s and early 1960s. Elkins argued that slavery was a total institution which wrought serious damage on its victims by dehumanising and infantilising them and destroying their ability to resist. He famously compared slavery with the Nazi concentration camps, which, in his view, were merely an extreme version of slavery.[69] Elkins' book was supposed to be a devastating critique of slavery and its dehumanising effects; but it appeared to present enslaved African Americans and their descendants as mere damaged victims. In the context of the civil rights movement that emerged in the 1950s and the attempt to defend black culture and identity from racism, this was a highly unpalatable image for many.[70]

The combination of the civil rights movement and the emergence of social history and history from below as major new approaches and fields of study led to a radical transformation of the humanitarian and class struggle debates. A number of major studies that appeared in the early 1970s attempted to create a history from below that would restore agency to the slaves and explore the autonomy of slave culture and the groups and relationships that slaves maintained among them. John Blassingame coined the concept of the slave community as a novel contribution to the class struggle debate.[71] The concept enabled scholars to study how working conditions, family and religion constituted a slave community that allowed masters to exercise their authority while also providing slaves with the means to contest that authority, changing its terms and running various aspects of their lives on principles other than slavery; in other words, the means to build a world both beyond and below slavery. It was a superb counterargument to the image of slaves as completely dominated, damaged and infantilised that Elkins had posited; at the same time it created a historical foundation for the African American identity and culture that was erupting in the public sphere and demanding respect and recognition.

But the masterpiece that transformed the study of US slavery undoubtedly came with the publication in 1974 of Eugene Genovese's *Roll Jordan, Roll: The World the*

---

[68] Stampp 1956.
[69] Elkins 1959.
[70] King 2001.
[71] Blassingame 1972.

*Slaves Made.*[72] The very title is of course telling: it was no longer only about what the slaves suffered, but also the world they made. In order to restore slave agency, Genovese challenged the unilateral and top-down approach that had dominated the field until then. He offered a new conceptualisation of slavery as an asymmetric negotiation of power: the power relationship between masters and slaves was not a predetermined given, but a historically changing negotiation in which both sides participated, even if in clearly asymmetric ways. The history of American slavery was the outcome of that asymmetric negotiation in space and time.

Genovese's book is of course most famous for developing the concept of paternalism to account for the history of slavery in the antebellum South. The political and ideological pressures of the American Republic forced Southern masters in the antebellum period to present themselves as benevolent patriarchs who offered uncivilised Black people the benefits of assured living and Christianity in exchange for their labour. As Genovese showed, paternalism exemplified Gramsci's concept of hegemony. On the one hand, it set the terms through which both masters and slaves conceptualised their relationship; on the other hand, the slaves interpreted paternalism in a significantly different way from their masters: the benefits of paternalism exemplified not the generosity of the masters but the rights that slaves were entitled to as a result of their faithful service.

Furthermore, Genovese argued that the history of slavery could not be reduced to the relationship between masters and slaves. A number of other factors and agents intervened and fundamentally shaped slavery; the community of the free, the state institutions, the Church organisations and the republican political framework were all factors that had a significant impact. These factors pushed in different directions. State intervention in the theoretically unmediated relationship between masters and slaves had deeply contradictory results. On the one hand, it superimposed the interests of the free community over the master–slave relationship; masters were prohibited from teaching letters to their slaves or manumitting them, because these were considered as dangerous issues for the community as a whole. Other measures intended to subordinate the most connected and accomplished slaves to the lowest free White person. The result was the attempt to create a hereditary slave caste. But at the same time the state intervened in order to limit what masters could inflict on their slaves, by stipulating conditions of living or punishment. The two contradictory tendencies played a significant role in the explosive process that led to the Civil War. One of the best parts of Genovese's account was the significance it gave to the courts and the discourse of the law for the history of slavery in the South.

Genovese's conception of slavery as an asymmetric negotiation of power enabled scholars to abandon a static approach to slavery as essentially the same phenomenon across space and time and a view of slaves as passive victims of domination and exploitation. It was now possible to study slavery as a historically changing relationship in which slave agency mattered, even if in asymmetric ways. Scholars have explored various forms of slave community and sociality, with impressive results.[73] Equally

---

[72] Genovese 1974.
[73] Morgan 1998; Penningroth 2003; Walker 2004; Kiddy 2005a; Kaye 2007.

important has been the discovery of 'the slaves' economy': the economic activities and labour processes in which slaves participated on their own as largely autonomous agents and outside the direct supervision and control of their masters, from the provision grounds in which slaves cultivated agricultural products to provide their subsistence or supplement their diet, to the participation of slaves in markets as artisans, hired labourers and traders.[74]

The most important outcome of this approach is undoubtedly Ira Berlin's *Many Thousands Gone*.[75] It was the first narrative history of US slavery that attempted to show how it varied and changed as a result of the changing wishes and decisions of masters and political communities, as well as the historical role of the slaves and their successes and failures. It was the first narrative account of slavery in which slaves appeared as active historical agents, instead of being presented as just passive victims. But Genovese's conception of slavery as an asymmetric negotiation faced a key problem: how did slavery as a particular form of asymmetric negotiation differ from other forms of asymmetric negotiation, like serfdom, wage labour or patronage? How did this relational conception of slavery relate to the traditional unilateral conception of slavery as property? What was the *differentia specifica* of slavery? Followers of the Genovesian approach offered few answers to such questions; rather, different scholars followed different conceptions of slavery for different purposes without attempting to resolve the contradictions and silences.[76]

Major developments also emerged in response to the modernist debate. The American Civil War was long considered the ultimate illustration of this debate, as it pitted the capitalist states of the North, which were based on industry and free labour, with the states of the South, based on agriculture and slavery; the victory of the North and the abolition of slavery symbolised the superiority of capitalism over the pre-capitalist system of the South. But if the South was not capitalist, how could we explain the fact that planters were geared towards profit-making and were strongly linked to the capitalist world market, or that Southern political leaders like George Washington and Thomas Jefferson were both slaveowners and supporters of the Enlightenment and republicanism? One solution, favoured by Genovese, was to stress the paternalist, aristocratic and pre-capitalist culture of Southern planters and consider Southern plantations which produced for world markets as freaks of fortune that could not last long.[77] But other scholars, like Fogel and Engerman in their famous book *Time on the Cross*, insisted on the capitalist character of plantation agriculture and its profitability and productivity.[78] How could this contradiction be resolved?

The problem with both approaches was their treatment of slavery as an independent factor. Southern slavery did not exist in the ether, but was inscribed within a number of different processes. Crop production for the market produced one kind of slavery; the republican/liberal political culture produced another form of slavery;

---

[74] Mintz 1974; Berlin and Morgan 1991; Pargas 2006; Read 2012.

[75] Berlin 1998; see also Berlin 1980.

[76] For some stimulating answers, see Glassman 1991; C. Morris 1998; Johnson 2003; Glancy 2013.

[77] Genovese 1961, 1969.

[78] Fogel and Engerman 1974.

religion, family and new attitudes towards the self produced a third form of slavery; and all these various forms of slavery influenced, interacted with and contradicted each other. This is the reason that it is possible to describe certain aspects of Southern slavery as capitalist and others as paternalist. Slavery was not the coherent and independent variable which shaped everything else, but a complex conglomerate that was shaped by diverse and often contradictory processes.[79] What was now required was a new framework that would allow historians to study the interconnections between these various processes. We shall shortly see what this new framework amounted to.

Another source of new approaches came from the increasing importance of the study of slavery beyond the US South. These studies challenged the traditional unitary definition of slavery from other angles and created new frameworks of study. One main engine of change came from a particular permutation of the humanitarian debate. Historians like Gilberto Freire, Frank Tannenbaum and Elkins argued that slavery and race relations were milder in Brazil and the Spanish colonial societies compared to the US, because of the impact of Roman law, the Catholic Church and the ubiquity of miscegenation, which circumscribed the dehumanising impact of unfettered capitalism, as was the case in the US.[80]

The attempt to isolate specific factors that could account for the important differences between US and Latin American slaveries ultimately proved to be a dead end. To give one example, there were indeed real and important differences between those colonial legal systems which were based on Roman law, which accorded slaves more opportunities, and systems based on English common law, which were much more restrictive.[81] But careful study has shown that what really mattered was not the legal tradition per se, but how it was applied. Wherever colonial societies were allowed by their metropolitan overlords to choose their own laws, legal systems and their practical application were largely determined by the interests of the masters and were therefore deeply restrictive for slaves. Wherever metropolitan states, which took into account other interests apart from those of colonial masters, adopted a more proactive role in setting laws and enforcing them, the law and its application was more favourable to slaves, irrespective of whether it was based on Roman or common law.[82] Slave agency played an equally important role in how slave law was formulated and how it operated in practice.[83]

But while the initial answers were misleading, the really important contribution of this debate was to stress the existence of major differences in the economic, political, social and cultural role of slavery across the different New World societies. Slaves in Brazil and the Latin American colonies created hybrid cultures and new religions, like santería, voodoo and candomblé, while in the US there was hardly anything comparable.[84] Did African slaves manage to maintain their heritage in Latin America, while

---

[79] Oakes 1990: 40–79; Kolchin 1993: 169–84; Smith 1998; Johnson 2013.

[80] Freire 1945; Tannenbaum 1946; Elkins 1959; see also Degler 1971.

[81] For the impact of Roman slave law on early modern slavery, see Watson 1992; Harrington 1994; Cairns 2006, 2012.

[82] Watson 1989; de la Fuente 2004.

[83] Rugemer 2018; de la Fuente and Gross 2020.

[84] Raboteau 1999.

they failed to or were constrained from doing so in the US? Once scholars realised the limits of mono-causal explanations for such phenomena, it became necessary to find a new conceptual framework for dealing with them. This new approach combined the developments in the humanitarian debate with developments in the modernist and class struggle debates.

This new framework was that of Atlantic history.[85] In the course of the early modern period, empire building and market expansion created an Atlantic world-system that linked together the metropolitan societies of Atlantic Europe (England, France, Spain and Portugal), the native and colonial societies of the Americas and African societies. Imperial expansion and the creation of colonial societies worked in tandem with the production of commodities for global markets, although the two processes could produce contradictory results.[86] Human mobility was crucial for the creation and maintenance of the Atlantic world; this included imperial officials, colonists, sailors, traders, indentured servants and, of course, slaves. At the same time, empires and markets had an enormous impact in various ways on both Native American and African societies and transformed them in novel ways.

The keywords for understanding these processes are diasporas and ethnogenesis. Voluntary and forced human mobility created diasporas that crossed the Atlantic world and its various societies and cultures; but at the same time war, enslavement and economic and cultural change continuously created new ethnic, religious and cultural communities across the Atlantic world.[87] It is within this new Atlantic framework that the study of New World slavery has been pursued over the last twenty years, and similar frameworks are gradually constructed for the Indian Ocean and the Islamic oecumene that linked Africa, the Mediterranean and Asia.[88] It is of course quite remarkable that no comparable new framework has yet appeared in the study of ancient slavery, which is still restricted to thinking in terms of 'Greek' and 'Roman' slavery and eschews thinking in terms of wider systems of interactions, as we shall see in Chapter 8.

The global study of slavery has made some other important contributions as well. It was the study of African slaveries from the 1970s onwards that started to challenge the traditional understanding of slavery based on ancient and New World slave societies. Many African societies recognised a system of rights in people; households and clans possessed rights in their free members and could potentially sell them.[89] But this form of property in human beings was quite different from human property as slavery. Furthermore, while ancient and New World slaveries constituted 'closed systems', in which slaves were perennially excluded from the kinship and citizenship systems of free people, many African societies operated as 'open systems', in which slaves were

---

[85]  Benjamin 2009; Thornton 2012.

[86]  Mintz 1986; Blackburn 1997; Eltis 2000; Schwartz 2004; Tomich 2004.

[87]  Gomez 1998; Lovejoy 2000; Lovejoy and Trotman 2003; Sweet 2003; Curto and Lovejoy 2004; Curto and Soulodre-LaFrance 2005; Hall 2005; Sidbury and Cañizares-Esguerra 2011; Ferreira 2012; Brown 2020.

[88]  Hunwick and Powell 2002; Campbell 2004; Lovejoy 2004; Mann 2012; Freamon 2019.

[89]  See the discussion in Thornton 1998: 72–88.

gradually incorporated into families and clans.[90] In order to account for these peculiarities, a ground-breaking work on African slavery proposed setting aside the property definition of slavery and adopting the concept of 'institutionalised marginality'.[91]

This approach was further developed with the publication of Patterson's magisterial global sociology of slavery, *Slavery and Social Death*.[92] Patterson argued that human
property was an inadequate definition of slavery, as there were many other forms of
human property that could not be classified as slavery. He instead proposed that the
cross-cultural essence of slavery consisted of 'social death'. What distinguished slaves
was that they were not recognised members of the community and they did not possess honour. As we shall see in Chapters 3, 5 and 7, Patterson's ahistorical quest for the
cross-cultural essence of slavery led him into a methodological cul-de-sac. Furthermore, while approaches like that of Genovese were trying to find ways for conceptualising slave agency, Patterson's top-down and unilateral approach to slavery denied
any agency to slaves.[93] Given the dominance of the humanitarian debate on the study
of ancient slavery, which forces anyone who refuses the ameliorative narratives into
adopting unilateral approaches, it is of course not accidental that Patterson's approach
has been particularly popular with many ancient historians.[94]

Nevertheless, Patterson's book was the first serious attempt to expand the study
of slavery beyond the traditional focus on antiquity and the New World colonial
societies. By exploring tens of slave-owning societies across time and space, Patterson
was able to show that the idea that there had been only five genuine slave societies in
world history (Greece, Rome, US South, Brazil and the Caribbean), as Finley and his
followers had believed, was patently false. Patterson located many other major slave
societies, like those of the Pacific Northwest, the Sudan, Senegambia, Zanzibar and
Korea.[95] As a result, the easy assumptions about the economic significance of slavery
and its political, social and cultural effects could now be seriously challenged.[96]

The result of all the above developments is the emergence over the last decade of
global accounts of slavery, which for the first time are written by historians rather than
sociologists and anthropologists.[97] While social scientists like Nieboer[98] and Patterson were
searching for the trans-historical essence of slavery, the new historical approaches attempt
to incorporate the study of slavery into global historical processes that occur in space and
time.[99] The most important contribution of these works is Miller's plea to abandon the
static and a-chronic study of slavery as an institution in favour of studying the processes of
slaving.[100] This processual approach invites us to explore the variety of related processes

---

[90]  Watson 1980b.
[91]  Miers and Kopytoff 1977.
[92]  Patterson 1982.
[93]  Miller 2008; Brown 2009.
[94]  See the various chapters in Bodel and Scheidel 2017.
[95]  Patterson 1982: 353–64.
[96]  See the discussion in Lenski and Cameron 2018.
[97]  For the implications of this, see Vlassopoulos 2016a.
[98]  Nieboer 1900.
[99]  An early example was Turley 2000. More recent works include Eltis and Engerman 2011; Miller 2012;
      Zeuske 2013, Grenouilleau 2014.
[100]  Miller 2008, 2012.

that constituted slaving, the agency of the various actors that were involved in the process (masters, slaves, states, citizens) and geographical diversity and temporal change.

## Recent Developments in the Study of Ancient Slavery

This concluding section will review developments in the study of ancient slavery over the last forty years.[101] As I have argued in the beginning of this chapter, the study of ancient slavery is still conducted within the premises of the three debates that we have explored. And while certain aspects of Finley's approach have come under challenge, his redefinition of the terms of the three debates is still the dominant approach in the field. But as Thomas Kuhn argued in his theory of scientific revolutions, normal science gradually ends up facing a range of issues and problems which no longer fit in with its major assumptions and models.[102] While it is normally easy to isolate and ignore such issues and their implications, at some point it becomes no longer possible to ignore the problems; at this point, alternative models and frameworks might appear. The study of ancient slavery has reached such a stage. A lot of valuable work has reached areas and issues that the traditional framework cannot deal with or can do so only in approximate ways; many parts of the dominant edifice have been seriously challenged or undermined, and many scholars have started to appreciate the need for exploring alternative approaches and have attempted to construct novel frameworks.

The following review does not attempt to present a historiography of the field as a whole. On the one hand, important work has taken place in traditional fields of research; there have been major synthetic studies on manumission and freed persons in Greek and Roman societies, which have put this crucial aspect on a new footing.[103] On the other hand, new fields have gained prominence, like the archaeology and material culture of slavery; over the last twenty years, various scholars have explored the material traces of slaves in the archaeological record, the material culture of slaves and the representation of slaves in ancient visual culture.[104] Equally significant is the large increase in the number of studies of slavery in the societies of the ancient Near East; the sophistication of this new wave of works has raised important questions which have the potential to challenge many assumptions that are implicitly accepted by scholars who study Greek and Roman slaveries.[105] These are undoubtedly important developments,

---

[101] See also the overview of Bradley 2015.

[102] Kuhn 1962.

[103] For Greek manumission and freedmen, see Darmezin 1999; Gibson 1999; Zelnick-Abramovitz 2005; Zanovello 2016; Vlassopoulos 2019. For Roman manumission and freedmen, see López Barja de Quiroga 1998, 2007; Roth 2010b, 2011; Mouritsen 2011a; Barschdorf 2012; Perry 2013; Vermote 2016a; Husby 2017; MacLean 2018. See also the synthetic accounts of Weiler 2003; Kleijwegt 2006a.

[104] Himmelmann 1971, Zanker 1975 and Kolendo 1979 were early precursors; for recent studies, see I. Morris 1998, 2011; Schumacher 2001a; Thompson 2003; Morris and Papadopoulos 2005; Webster 2005; Petersen 2006; von Behren 2009; Binsfeld 2010; George 2010, 2013a; Borbonus 2014; Joshel and Petersen 2014; Trimble 2016; Osborne 2017; Morris 2018; Binsfeld and Ghetta 2019.

[105] See Dandamaev 1984; Flesher 1988; Westbrook 1995, 1998; van Koppen 2004; Hezser 2005; Galil 2007; Head 2010; Culbertson 2011; Kriger 2011; Seri 2013; Steinkeller 2013; Wunsch 2013; Baker 2017; Ponchia 2017; Reid 2017; Rositani 2018.

and they are an essential part of the historiography of ancient slavery; but my focus here will largely rest on how recent developments are gradually challenging the three major debates that have shaped the field so far, and on certain important studies that have started to construct new frameworks of analysis.

Starting from the class struggle debate, prime of place goes of course to the most ambitious attempt to apply a Marxist approach to the study of antiquity: G. E. M. de Ste. Croix's magisterial *The Class Struggle in the Ancient Greek World*.[106] De Ste. Croix attempted to show that the conceptual tools of Marxist theory, like that of class, could be profitably employed to analyse and explain the course of ancient history. In his view, class was the consequence of the exploitation of one group of human beings by another; accordingly, slaves could be defined as a class solely on the basis of their exploitation and irrespective of whether they ever acted collectively as a class to defend their interests. This led de Ste. Croix in two predictable directions. On the one hand, he tended to dismiss slave agency as a factor that affected historical change. In a book of over 600 pages, there is practically no discussion even of the great slave revolts of the Roman republican period. On the other hand, de Ste. Croix argued that it is the level of exploitation that can explain the major historical changes in the course of antiquity. It was the decreased profitability of the slave mode of production and the decreased available surplus that led to the collapse of the Roman Empire in the West in late antiquity. This is undoubtedly an interesting line to pursue, but it quickly faces the problem that the evidence which is brought to substantiate the hypothesis of crisis cannot support the claim and can be challenged on various grounds.[107] De Ste. Croix's particular version of class theory meant that slaves were largely considered as passive victims of exploitation and domination. In fact, a title that would better express his approach would be *The Ruling Classes of Antiquity and How They Oppressed the Lower Classes*. As a result, his work has largely stood as a dead end for the study of ancient slavery.[108]

Other scholars influenced by Marxism reached rather different conclusions. Pierre Vidal-Naquet and Jean-Pierre Vernant argued that slaves could not be considered a class, as they comprised groups with very different characteristics, and did not possess a collective consciousness.[109] But such methodological discussions were largely abandoned from the 1980s onwards; instead, scholars were content to study even slave revolts, the most extreme form in which slaves exercised their role as historical agents, without feeling the need to explore the ontology of the collective agency of slaves.[110] More recent work has even started to doubt whether events like the two Sicilian revolts and the Spartacus uprising should be seen as slave revolts; by emphasising the significance of the local contexts in which these revolts took place, the various slave

---

[106] Ste. Croix 1981.

[107] Cf. Štaerman and Trofimova 1975 and the criticism of such approaches and their assumptions in McKeown 2007a: 52–76.

[108] For a comprehensive critique of de Ste. Croix's approach from a sympathetic point of view, see Shaw 1984; cf. Vlassopoulos 2018c.

[109] Vidal-Naquet 1986a, 1986b; Vernant 1990: 11–27.

[110] Capozza 1966; Cartledge 1985; Bradley 1989; Shaw 2001; Mavrojannis 2007; Urbainczyk 2008; Forsdyke 2012.

and free groups that took part in them and the different aims and audiences of each revolt, they have raised important new questions about how to conceptualise collective slave agency.[111]

More serious challenges have emerged as regards the conceptualisation of slave status and the concept of a spectrum of statuses. Finley had argued that the emergence of slave societies in Greece and Rome in the course of the archaic period led to the substitution of the spectrum of statuses by a single distinction between slave and free. But Deborah Kamen's recent study of status in classical Athens has shown that there was in fact a spectrum of statuses, which distinguished between slaves, privileged slaves, manumitted slaves in *paramone* and freed persons who became metics.[112] Even more consequential was the challenge to the traditional distinction between chattel slaves and groups like Spartan helots or Cretan *woikeis*. While helots and *woikeis* were traditionally understood as serfs or state slaves, a series of studies, which will be examined in more detail in Chapter 8, have conclusively shown that helots and *woikeis* were the private property of their masters.[113] The peculiar characteristics of helots and *woikeis* were not the result of the fact that they had a different status from that of chattel slaves; they rather resulted from the peculiar historical trajectories of Sparta and Crete, which utilised slavery in particular ways to suit their particular needs.[114]

A significant consequence of this new approach to helots is the exploration of the processes of identity formation and ethnogenesis through which helots, *perioikoi* and exiles came to see themselves as members of a single Messenian ethnicity; the successful liberation of Messenia from the Spartans in 369 BCE was strongly linked with these processes of ethnogenesis.[115] This development has opened the window for the exploration of slave agency and the construction of slave identities. In a recent edited volume, Claire Taylor and I have called for a systematic study of the communities and networks in which slaves participated in Greek communities.[116] Peter Hunt's exploration of the construction of ethnic identities by slaves in Athens is so far the best existing study of this process.[117] The study of a very important form of slave community, that of slave families, has become particularly popular in the last few years.[118] To move to another source of slave identity, Sandra Joshel's study of how Roman slaves and freed persons presented their identities on their tombstones has stressed the importance of work in how slaves perceived themselves and wanted to be seen by others.[119] It thus raises the issue of the wider range of identities that slaves employed and their historical consequences.

---

[111] Donaldson 2012; Morton 2012, 2013, 2014. See also the comments of Daubner 2006: 176–87 on the participation of slaves in the revolt of Aristonikos.

[112] Kamen 2013. For the spectrum of work statuses of Roman slaves, see Tran 2013b.

[113] For Crete, see Link 1994, 2001; Lewis 2013, 2018: 147–65. For Sparta, see Ducat 1990, 2015; Hodkinson 2000; Luraghi 2002a, 2002b; Lewis 2018: 125–46.

[114] Hodkinson 2008; Luraghi 2009.

[115] Luraghi and Alcock 2003.

[116] Taylor and Vlassopoulos 2015b.

[117] Hunt 2015; Hunt 1998 explores slave participation in warfare.

[118] Herrmann-Otto 1994; Golden 2011; Edmondson 2011; Mouritsen 2011b; Schmitz 2012; Bathrellou 2014.

[119] Joshel 1992.

As regards the humanitarian debate, the idea that slavery is a relationship unilaterally defined by the masters, and that this relationship remained fundamentally the same for the whole course of antiquity, is still dominant in the field.[120] This approach has become dominant even in the study of ancient literature or Christianity, where the alternative ameliorative tradition used to reign supreme.[121] Keith Bradley's work is probably the most characteristic and successful application of the approach in the field of Roman slavery, whether studying how masters exercised social control over the slaves or how ancient discourses on slavery employed animal metaphors in order to conceptualise slaves.[122] Equally important are the contributions of the scholars associated with the *Groupe International de Recherche sur l'Esclavage depuis l'Antiquité* (*GIREA*).[123] Their studies have explored the relationship between masters and slaves and the employment of slavery metaphors across a range of ancient texts and authors, like Cicero, Martial and Pliny the Younger.[124] But there have also been attempts to challenge the unilateral approach. The works of the *Forschungen zur antiken Sklaverei*, a series published by the Mainz research programme on ancient slavery that was founded by Vogt in 1951, provide a telling comparison.[125] While studies published in this series can illustrate the unilateral approach espoused by *GIREA*,[126] others have argued that the relationship between masters and slaves cannot be reduced solely to exploitation and domination.[127] While not advocating a return to the ameliorative approach to slavery, a number of recent studies have started to explore the diversity of models of slavery in ancient texts and discourses and the ways in which these models can be employed in order to explore various problems and situations.[128] These studies are important steps for any effort to move beyond the ameliorative and unilateral approaches and the terms set by the humanitarian debate.

Coming to the modernist debate, there have been various studies of the link between slavery and the economic structures of ancient societies. Attention has generally focused on one historical moment: the role of the slave mode of production in late republican Italy. Keith Hopkins' study of the link between Roman imperial expansion, the crisis of the Roman peasantry and the expansion of slave employment in agriculture is still influential.[129] A particularly stimulating contribution emerged in

---

[120]  See duBois 2003; Wrenhaven 2012.

[121]  For slavery and ancient literature, see McCarthy 2000; Serghidou 2010; Sabnis 2011; Stewart 2012; Akrigg and Tordoff 2013; Owens 2019. For slavery and Christian thought, see Klein 1988, 2000; Martin 1990; Glancy 2002a; de Wet 2015.

[122]  Bradley 1984, 1994, 2000; for a critique of Bradley's approach, see McKeown 2007a: 77–96; Glancy 2013.

[123]  For the approaches of authors associated with *GIREA*, see McKeown 2007a: 41–51.

[124]  Mactoux 1980; Garrido-Hory 1981; Pérez 1984; Gonzalès 2003.

[125]  On the Mainz project, see Wiedemann 2000; Maximova 2001; Heinen 2005; McKeown 2007a: 30–41; Deissler 2010; Herrmann-Otto 2010.

[126]  Bellen 1971; Klees 1975, 1998; Herrmann-Otto 1994.

[127]  Kudlien 1991.

[128]  Thalmann 1996; Fitzgerald 2000; McCarthy 2000; Joly 2003; Leigh 2004; Tamiolaki 2010; Richlin 2017; de Wet 2018.

[129]  Hopkins 1978: 1–98.

the 1970s and 1980s from Italian Marxist historians and archaeologists that sought to link the expansion of the slave mode of production in late republican Italy with the development of commercial agriculture.[130] This has created a fruitful tradition of utilising the archaeological evidence in order to explore the role of slavery in ancient economic production.[131] More recent work has modified important aspects of Hopkins' model by stressing the variability of regional patterns of agricultural exploitation in Roman Italy, the significance of urban slavery and the consequences of financial and monetary expansion in republican Italy.[132]

More generally, the study of the economic impact of slavery in various sectors has been explored in substantially more detail for the Roman[133] than for the Greek world;[134] it is telling that while there are many book-length studies for various economic aspects of Roman slavery, there are primarily only articles devoted to the economics of Greek slavery. It is important in this respect to note current developments in ancient economic history. The new orthodoxy that has emerged over the last twenty years has broken with Finley's approach, which perceived a static and unitary ancient economy in which nothing changed for over a thousand years.[135] The new orthodoxy stresses economic growth and the significance of the development of markets; but at the same time, and for various reasons, it has largely excised slavery as an important factor in explaining the efflorescence of ancient economies.[136] This minimisation of the economic impact of slavery will undoubtedly have effects on the continuing significance of the modernist debate.

The study of slave prices, trade, markets and demography has emerged as a burgeoning field with important implications.[137] A number of scholars have presented alternative models of how the Roman slave population was replenished; Walter Scheidel has argued that the Roman slave population in the early imperial period was overwhelmingly maintained through natural reproduction, while other scholars have emphasised the significance of alternative sources, like captives, the slave trade and the enslavement of abandoned infants.[138] The issue has important implications for how Roman slavery operated, as well as the trajectory of historical change. Scheidel has also employed the corpus of surviving slave prices in order to argue that slaves were much cheaper in classical Athens, compared to imperial Rome and many other slaveholding societies.[139] This work has inspired a number of studies that have tried to account for

---

[130]  Giardina and Schiavone 1981; Carandini and Ricci 1985; Carandini 1988.

[131]  Marzano 2007, 2013; Fentress and Maiuro 2011; Marzano and Métraux 2018.

[132]  Jongman 2003; Launaro 2011; Kay 2014.

[133]  For slaves in agriculture, see Roth 2007; for slaves as managers and business agents, see Aubert 1994; Carlsen 1995. For slaves in trade, see Kirschenbaum 1987; for slaves in industry, see Prachner 1980.

[134]  Wood 1988; Rosivach 1993; Osborne 1995; Ameling 1998; Rihll 2010; Cohen 2018; Porter 2019a.

[135]  Finley 1973.

[136]  Scheidel, Morris and Saller 2007; Ober 2015; Bresson 2016. For a critique of this approach, see Vlassopoulos 2016d, 2018c; Porter 2019b.

[137]  For slave traders and slave markets, see Coarelli 1982, 2005; Duchêne 1986; Donderer and Spiliopoulou-Donderer 1993; Bodel 2005; Fentress 2005; Trümper 2009; Chioffi 2010.

[138]  Scheidel 1997, 1999, 2005b; Harris 1980a, 1999; Bradley 1987, 2004.

[139]  Scheidel 2005a; but his interpretation is challenged by Crawford 2010.

the various factors that could have produced these price differentials and which could explain the reasons why masters decided to rely on slaves instead of alternative sources of labour.[140]

But the most important challenge in this context concerns the conceptual distinction between slave societies and societies with slaves, and the traditional narrative that has been built on this basis. Finley's interpretation of the reforms of Solon as the transformation of the Athenian society with slaves into the first slave society has been seriously challenged: not only is his interpretation logically incoherent, but it cannot stand as a general model for what happened in the rest of the Greek world.[141] As Edward Harris has shown, slavery is the main source of elite income in Homer and Hesiod, and accordingly the idea that it first became so after Solon cannot stand.[142] More generally, over the last few years the twin concepts of slave societies and societies with slaves have become the subject of focused debate. While certain scholars maintain the continuing utility of the distinction, others have pointed out serious problems and have suggested alternative approaches.[143] We shall further explore this issue in Chapter 8.

I will finish this brief overview by mentioning three important recent books whose contributions are particularly crucial for redirecting the field. The first work is Niall McKeown's *The Invention of Ancient Slavery?*[144] This is the only existing study that tries to systematically explore and challenge the underlying assumptions behind the various current approaches in the study of ancient slavery. McKeown offers a historiography of the development of the field and the nature of the ancient evidence, which can be interpreted in radically different ways. By revealing the hidden assumptions of modern approaches and narratives, he invites us to think carefully about our concepts; by pointing out the grain of truth that can be found in various contradictory approaches, he invites us to search for frameworks that can accommodate diversity, complexity and contradiction.[145]

The second major contribution is Kyle Harper's *Slavery in the Late Roman World*.[146] Harper emphasises the diversity of relationships, strategies, agents and interests that affected slavery and pulled it in so many different directions at the same time. The result is an analysis that explores both the complementarities and reinforcing tendencies, as well as the conflicts, contradictions and ambiguities; late Roman slavery was not a static entity, but a historical process. Harper explores the impact on fourth-century CE slavery of three important factors. The first factor was the nexus of economic processes created by slave supply and demand, institutionalised practices and the dynamics of estate management. Roman slavery was an agglomeration of two rather distinct forms of slave use: the large-scale use of slaves by elite households for

---

[140]  Ruffing and Drexhage 2008; Harper 2010a; Lewis 2011, 2015, 2019.

[141]  Rihll 1996; Vlassopoulos 2016b.

[142]  Harris 2012.

[143]  For recent endorsements of the concept, see Hunt 2018b; Harper and Scheidel 2018. For criticisms, see Vlassopoulos 2016a, 2016b; Lenski 2018a, 2018b; Lewis 2018: 93–104.

[144]  McKeown 2007a.

[145]  See also his more recent reflections in McKeown 2010.

[146]  Harper 2011.

commercialised agriculture and luxurious living, organised in complex hierarchies of urban households and rural estates, and the small-scale employment of slaves for a variety of purposes by a wide and prosperous middling section of Roman society. The second factor concerns the nexus of domination that linked slavery with mastery and honour and the constitutive role of slavery in the formation of Roman households, in Roman reproductive patterns and the sexual economy and in the construction of identities based on honour and status. The third factor is the entanglement between the economic and social aspects of slavery on the one hand, and Christianity and the Roman state on the other. While most studies of slavery tend to perceive it as a relationship of domination and exploitation unilaterally defined by the masters, Harper correctly moves to a perception of slavery as an asymmetric negotiation of power on which masters, slaves and other groups and interests have had an effect.

Harper's image of late Roman slavery recognises its complexity and diversity: the distinction between different kinds of slave-owners and the realisation that Roman slavery was an agglomeration of very different patterns of slaveholding; the breakdown of the abstract and static 'slave society' into the dynamic nexus between supply and demand, institutions and estate management; the impact of the political community, Christian ideology and the Church on the theoretically unmediated relationship between masters and slaves; the constitutive role of slavery in the formations of households and the sexual economy of the Roman world; the role of slave agency, or how slaves, within the complex framework established by the aims and means of domination, tried to pursue their own aims within slave families and slave communities.[147]

My final example is David Lewis' recent book, *Greek Slave Systems in their Eastern Mediterranean Setting*.[148] While many studies have tried to explore aspects of slavery that cannot be reduced to the concept of property, Lewis develops a sophisticated framework for approaching slavery as a form of property, which we will examine further in Chapter 3. For the first time slavery as property is not an abstraction, but a set of interacting factors that can be explored across space and time. By using this framework, Lewis shows that we need to abandon the traditional distinction between chattel slavery, represented by classical Athens, and systems like helotage that were traditionally understood as a form of serfdom. Instead of the unitary understanding of Greek slavery, Lewis argues that slavery as property was affected by various local economic, social, political and cultural forces in order to produce diverse epichoric slave systems. At the same time, Lewis presents a comparative examination of Greek slave systems alongside the slave systems of the ancient Near East. While previous scholarship assumed that slavery in the Near East was marginal, Lewis shows that slaves constituted a major part of elite portfolios in many of these societies. This has revolutionary implications for the comparative study of Mediterranean and Near Eastern history in antiquity, as it challenges the traditional distinction between slave societies and societies with slaves. Finally, Lewis presents a model for explaining the role and significance of slavery in different ancient societies, which includes the factors that

---

[147] For a detailed assessment, see Vlassopoulos 2015b.
[148] Lewis 2018.

determine the choice of labour force, as well as the impact of political and economic geography. It is remarkable that an approach to slavery based on a cross-cultural and ahistorical definition of property does not lead to a homogenising and static account, but on the contrary opens the way for a perspective that highlights geographical diversity and chronological change.[149]

This chapter has explored the major debates that shaped the study of ancient slavery and the emergence of the still-dominant paradigm with the work of Finley in the 1960s and 1970s. We then moved to developments in the study of global slavery and their implications for the study of ancient slavery, returning lastly to recent developments in ancient history which set the stage for the development of a new framework for the study of ancient slavery. It is time to proceed.

---

[149] For a detailed assessment, see Vlassopoulos 2018–19.

# 3

# WHAT IS SLAVERY?

WHAT IS SLAVERY? How can we define this complex phenomenon? How can we come up with a definition which is cross-culturally valid while also taking into account the important differences that are attested across space and time? This chapter will proceed in a roundabout way. We will commence with an overview of slavery in the early Middle Ages; this is a topic which is quite unfamiliar to the three main audiences of this book: scholars who study slavery, specialists in ancient slavery and ancient historians. It is of course unsurprising that early medieval slavery is unfamiliar to ancient historians and to specialists on ancient slavery. But early medieval slavery is also overwhelmingly ignored by slavery scholars; not only are the sources difficult to comprehend, but early medieval slavery offends most of the assumptions they make about slavery. Why, then, use early medieval slavery as a point of entry?

There are two important reasons for undertaking this comparative exercise. On the one hand, the complexity and contradictoriness of the phenomena of early medieval slavery provide excellent food for thought for the study of global slavery, as well as of slavery in ancient societies. Early medieval slavery offers an excellent testing ground for assumptions that have been long taken for granted and should be seriously challenged. On the other hand, early medieval slavery allows us to test the conceptual coherence of the key concepts in the study of slavery. Slavery is often examined in implicit and explicit comparison with serfdom; the concept of serfdom plays an important role in defining slavery by contradistinction, and it solves important conceptual problems by incorporating servile forms and groups (such as helotage) which challenge the traditional conceptions of slavery. As I will try to show, early medieval slavery is particularly illuminating, not only in shattering some deeply held but unexamined assumptions about slavery, but also in providing important clues for the way forward.[1]

Building on these clues, the second part of this chapter will offer a new approach to slavery as an agglomeration of three distinct but interrelated conceptual systems: of slavery as property, of slavery as a form of status and of slavery as a cluster of related conceptualisations (modalities). While the three conceptual systems existed in all slaveholding societies, different societies could emphasise one system on top of the others, or combine the three systems in radically different ways. By looking at slavery as a historically changing conglomerate of interlinked conceptual systems, we can approach slavery as a global phenomenon while also accounting for the important divergences and differences across space and time.

---

[1] Rio 2017 is absolutely fundamental; see also the important contributions by Davies 1996; Pelteret 2001; Hammer 2002; Carrier 2012; Sutt 2015.

## An Instructive Case: Early Medieval Slavery and 'Serfdom'

The traditional narrative of early medieval slavery was framed in terms of the transition from ancient societies dominated by slavery to medieval societies dominated by serfdom. For anyone familiar with the actual evidence, the obvious problem was that early medieval sources continued to use the Latin vocabulary of slavery (*servus, ancilla, mancipium*) until about 1000 CE. After this temporal point, sources started to adopt new vocabularies: they employed new terms to characterise groups that have traditionally been described as serfs (for example, *homo proprius, homo de corpore*), as well as new terms for slaves, the most characteristic being the adoption of the ethnic term for Slavs to describe slaves in practically all European languages after 1000 CE.[2] Early medieval law codes have very high percentages of laws relating to slaves and give the impression of continuity. On the other hand, the documentary evidence provided by contracts and administrative records presents groups which are described with the same Latin vocabulary of slavery employed by the legal texts, but whose conditions of life and work appear like those of stereotypical serfs, instead of those of stereotypical slaves.[3]

How could one explain this contradictory picture? One solution, which was first formulated by Georges Duby and which used to be particularly popular with French historians, is to posit a 'feudal mutation' or 'feudal revolution' around 1000 CE.[4] An ancient model based on slavery prevailed up to that time, until the feudal mutation drastically changed the character of medieval societies by overturning the fundamental distinction between free and slave. By enhancing the status of slaves and reducing the status of free peasants, the new status of dependent peasants, or serfs, was created. The changes in the vocabulary are thus direct reflections of fundamental changes in social reality.[5]

Other historians have strongly disputed this narrative.[6] Conditions like those of high medieval serfdom can be observed long before 1000 CE, and consequently there is no need to posit a feudal mutation around 1000 CE. These scholars argue that the people described with the Latin vocabulary of slavery in early medieval sources were actually serfs, rather than stereotypical slaves. Therefore, the early medieval sources retained the Roman vocabulary of slavery, which no longer reflected social reality; in the same way, slavery in the law codes can also be interpreted as a relic of the past. What happened after 1000 CE, according to this alternative view, was merely the abandonment of an archaic vocabulary and legal system in favour of a new vocabulary that better reflected the social reality of serfdom that had emerged in the course of the early medieval period.[7]

The conundrum faced by medieval historians is that a significant number of people classified as slaves in early medieval Europe perfectly fit the stereotypical image of slaves familiar from Greek and Roman societies. But the same slave terminology is also

---

[2] Verlinden 1942.
[3] These issues are well presented in Sutt 2015.
[4] Duby 1971.
[5] Bonnassie 1991; Bois 1992.
[6] See, for example, Verhulst 1991.
[7] Barthélemy 2009.

employed to describe other people and conditions that appear to fit the stereotypical image of serfs. The view that all medieval people classified as slaves were slaves in the stereotypical image of slavery is untenable, but equally untenable is the view that all these same people were stereotypical serfs. How can we explain this apparently schizophrenic situation?

As Alice Rio has suggested in a recent book, constructing a radically new narrative requires adopting an instrumentalist approach.[8] Early medieval slavery was neither a simple continuation of Roman slavery until the supposed feudal mutation of 1000 CE, nor slavery in name only, and effectively an early form of high medieval serfdom. Early medieval slavery was the diverse and divergent outcome of a series of practices that employed slavery as a tool for a variety of purposes in a variety of contexts. What is peculiar about early medieval slavery is an explosion in experimentation: slavery was employed as a tool for new purposes and in new contexts. Some of these experiments were highly local, and many of them served highly specific purposes; consequently, they had a limited time span and did not survive past the early medieval explosion of experimentation. As a result of this highly instrumental and experimental use of slavery, the various aspects of slavery and slave status tended to move in different directions and take divergent trajectories. Accordingly, early medieval slavery cannot be studied in the holistic manner which is standard for Greek or Roman slaveries. Different contexts and aspects of slavery need to be studied on their own terms, because certain conditions or processes affected them in specific ways, which cannot be extrapolated to other contexts and aspects.

The best illustration of this diversity concerns early medieval ways in and out of slavery. As regards exiting slavery, early medieval manumission and freed people tell a very fascinating story. There is much here that fits what we know about manumission and freed persons in many other societies, which I will skip over. But the experimental character of early medieval slavery is best seen in the novel purposes for which manumission was employed and the new forms of the status of freed persons that emerged during this period. In many cases the status of the freed person was no longer a temporary situation that affected only the manumitted slaves, but became a hereditary condition that affected also their descendants. This happened because acts of manumission could be employed to recalibrate not only relationships between masters and slaves, but also between different groups of masters. Bequests of lands to churches were often accompanied by the manumission of the slaves who cultivated them, thus turning them into hereditary freed persons who owed gratitude to their manumittor and services to the church.[9]

But equally telling are the processes of entering slavery. On the one hand, many slaves were the result of slave raiding and slave trading. These slaves were the involuntary products of processes of warfare and trade and had no say in the processes that turned them into slaves or in their conditions under slavery. As a result, the conditions of slaves created by raiding and trading resembled most closely those of stereotypical slaves.[10] On the other hand, we also come across people who became slaves through

---

[8] Rio 2017: 10–14.
[9] Rio 2017: 75–131.
[10] Rio 2017: 19–41.

self-sale, debt or penal enslavement.[11] In many periods of their history Greek and
Roman societies posited in principle that freedom and slavery were absolute statuses,
that freedom could not be voluntarily shed or exchanged and that free members of
the community could not be legally enslaved for debt, as we shall see in more detail
in Chapter 6. In contrast, early medieval societies turned status into a negotiable commodity. People could negotiate their status and use it as a commodity that could be
exchanged for other things; as a result, they could exchange their status and turn
themselves into slaves in return for security and sustenance, to pay debts or as a punishment for crimes.

This fact has various implications. The commoditisation and relativisation of status
meant that people could negotiate the terms of their slavery; consequently, many of
the outcomes of such negotiations do not look like the stereotypical images of slaves
historians usually have in mind. People could negotiate serving as slaves for certain
days of the week, determine the conditions under which they would serve as slaves, or
stipulate the condition of their future children. The quality of this kind of negotiated
slavery could diverge significantly. While those who had few chips to bargain with
ended up in conditions that differed little if at all from those of stereotypical slaves, in
other cases people who sold themselves to a monastery could get security and sustenance for the last years of their lives and become something closer to a monk, rather
than a stereotypical slave. Slavery was employed as a tool in order to negotiate various
forms of dependence or service.[12]

The multiple terms for slavery and their multivalent meanings in the early medieval world were not archaic relics of the past without any contemporary relevance; on
the contrary, they expressed and reflected processes of negotiation between masters
and their dependants about various issues and conditions.[13] Classifying estate tenants
as slaves was a method employed by the landlords in order to enhance their negotiat-
ing position. It gave landlords the theoretical right of unilaterally imposing unlimited
dues and services and could thus be used to force tenants to accept higher levels of
extraction. Being classified under other terms strengthened the hand of the dependent
tenants, since it meant that landlords could not unilaterally impose their wishes. In
practice, some kind of negotiation was involved in all relationships between landlords
and tenants, irrespective of the classification of the latter. But the classification mattered, as it strengthened the hand of one side or the other in the constant negotiation
and renegotiation of these relationships.[14]

Where do early medieval law codes fit into this framework of negotiation and
experimentation? As we have seen above, the legal codes show that slavery remained
important in early medieval societies.[15] But Rio has argued on the basis of the practical
operation of law, as seen in legal documents like contracts, sale deeds and court records,
that early medieval law codes should be placed in the same framework of negotiation

[11] Rio 2017: 42–74.
[12] See also Rio 2011, 2015a.
[13] Rio 2015b, 2017: 209–11.
[14] Rio 2017: 175–211; Carrier 2012.
[15] For early medieval law codes and slavery, see Nehlsen 1972, 2001.

and experimentation. Law codes established the maximum claims that could be sought by the opposing sides. Early medieval law codes provided masters with a powerful bargaining tool in relation to their dependants, but what usually happened in practice was not the strict application of what the law entailed, but a negotiated settlement in which law, status, relationships, networks of support and socio-economic conditions were all bargaining chips that mattered to a lesser or greater extent depending on context and circumstances.[16]

This is why the contexts of slaving are so significant for understanding early medieval slavery. While the urban slaves living and working on their own as artisans, traders and labourers, who were a constitutive element of Greek and Roman slaveries, disappeared with the economic contraction that affected most of Western Europe in the early Middle Ages, slavery within households and on estates remained major contexts of slavery. Slavery in early medieval households most closely approximated the forms of slavery which are familiar to historians, since most such slaves worked under the direct control and supervision of their masters.[17] Slavery on estates was more complex and variegated. An estate could comprise the landlord's manor, demesne lands and tenancies. The manor was operated by slaves working under direct control and supervision, fitting the stereotypical image of slaves; demesne lands were directly cultivated by the landlords, employing either slaves who worked under their direct control or dependent tenants that devoted part of their time in cultivating the demesne lands. But most estate lands were divided into tenancies, which were given to cultivators who were classified under various terms, from the most servile to the relatively free and independent. These tenants tended to live in family units, worked the land on their own and owed their landlords fixed or fluctuating rents and services.[18]

The servile and dependent tenants more closely approximate the stereotypical image of the serfs; but it would be a major misinterpretation to assume that people working in the manor or in the demesne were slaves, while people working as tenants were serfs. It is not true that tenants were legally classified as serfs, a status that entailed certain rights, while manor dependants were legally classified as slaves, a status that meant they had no rights and could be employed as their masters saw fit. During the early Middle Ages there was no *legal* distinction between slaves and serfs. The same language of slavery was employed to classify and negotiate all working and living conditions. The major differences in the conditions of the servile groups were not the result of distinct legal statuses, but the outcome of the interplay between the various strategies of the masters and the dialectical relationships between masters and slaves, between freemen and slaves and between the members of the communities in which slaves took part (a framework which will be analysed in Chapter 6). An individual could start as a directly controlled worker serving in the manor, while later in life he could be given a tenancy to cultivate on his own. While many of the servile tenants lived in family units, landlords seemed to have significant control over marriage and residence, as seen in the cases where servile bachelors lived together with slave families and cultivated the same tenancy.

---

[16] Rio 2006, 2017: 230–6.
[17] Rio 2017: 135–74.
[18] Rio 2017: 175–211.

If the traditional narrative of the transition from slavery to serfdom is untenable, is there another narrative that we can put in its place? Rio makes an important step forward in this direction, which will need to be further amplified.[19] Medieval serfdom as a distinct *legal* status emerged after 1100 CE, as a result of a series of interrelated developments. As we saw above, early medieval Europe was characterised by widespread experimentation in the instrumental uses of slavery, but after 1000 CE the range of purposes that slavery served diminished significantly and also took radically divergent paths. A major factor in these developments was the emergence of no-slaving zones on the basis of religion, an issue we will explore further in Chapter 4. No-slaving zones were areas whose inhabitants were not subject to enslavement as a result of warfare or other practices.[20] For most of human history before 1000 CE it was considered legitimate to enslave enemies, even if they belonged to the same ethnic, cultural or religious group. The monotheistic religions that emerged in the first millennium CE had various compunctions about the enslavement of co-religionists, but in the course of the first millennium these compunctions were never solidified into law and practice.[21] For reasons that are still unclear, after 1000 CE Catholic and Orthodox Christians started to abandon the timeless principle that the defeated in war could be enslaved.[22] It was still fine to kill and maim co-religionist enemies, but no longer acceptable to enslave them. In the Mediterranean, where Orthodox, Catholic and Muslim communities continued to clash, slavery remained a significant practice and enslavement became the fate for religious outsiders who were defeated, captured or traded. The Christianisation of the Slavs and Scandinavians after 1000 CE turned central and northern Europe into the homogeneous religious zone of Latin Christendom. Consequently, warfare gradually stopped being a source of new slaves in central and northern Europe.[23]

As a result of these developments, after 1100 CE there emerged a major divergence between the Mediterranean, on the one hand, and central and northern Europe, on the other.[24] In many parts of the Mediterranean slavery was largely restricted to household service by religious outsiders; other forms of labour, like agricultural work, were now performed by dependants who were religious insiders and were classified as serfs.[25] The early medieval situation, where people classified as slaves performed all forms of labour, although their conditions could diverge very significantly, was now transformed into a major disjuncture between household service performed by foreign slaves and agricultural labour overwhelmingly performed by native serfs. In central and northern Europe slavery was gradually restricted to regulating issues of agricultural tenancy and was legally defined after 1100 CE as a form of serfdom in which serfs were

---

[19] Rio 2017: 215–45.

[20] Fynn-Paul 2009; Fynn-Paul and Pargas 2018.

[21] See the comments of Glancy 2018.

[22] Strickland 1992; Rotman 2009: 25–81; Gillingham 2012, 2015; for the case of Islam, see Freamon 2019.

[23] For these processes, see Bartlett 1993.

[24] Fynn-Paul 2009.

[25] There were exceptions to this Mediterranean rule, like the use of rural slaves in late medieval Valencia: see Blumenthal 2009: 95–101.

charged dues for marriage and inheritance rights.[26] The creation of the new legal status of serfdom and the lack of a disjuncture between household service and agricultural tenancy, alongside the religious unification of central and northern Europe, meant that slavery was effectively extinguished from this area after 1100 CE. Instead of the traditional narrative in which slavery was substituted by serfdom, we encounter a new narrative in which the early medieval period constitutes a distinct phase of its own. Early medieval slavery appears as an explosion of experimentation and new uses, some of which survived in the Mediterranean after 1100 CE, while others were gradually transformed into serfdom through a specialisation in the instrumental uses to which slavery was put.[27]

What are the wider implications of this survey of early medieval slavery? The first implication concerns the traditional distinction between slavery and serfdom. In theory, most historians would readily concede that slavery is first and foremost a legal relationship: the term slave is supposed to refer exclusively to the fact that one human being is the property of another. At the same time, the traditional concept of serfdom describes a socio-economic condition of dependent peasants who are native inhabitants of the land, possess certain rights over the land they cultivate and are obliged to surrender fixed or variable dues to their overlords. It is quite remarkable that so much in modern scholarly work has depended on what is clearly a lopsided comparison between a legal and a socio-economic concept.[28]

In practice, of course, the comparison appears more balanced, because historians have implicitly operated on the basis of a stereotypical image of slavery, in which slaves are foreigners, are exchanged as commodities, have no rights recognised by the law and work under the direct supervision and control of their masters. This stereotypical image plays an important role in scholarship, as it provides socio-economic padding to the abstract legal definition of slavery and gives plausibility to the distinction between slavery and serfdom. It allows scholars to contrast the native origins of the stereotypical serfs, whose reproduction is maintained by their families, with the foreign origins of the stereotypical slaves, whose reproduction requires the slave trade. Furthermore, while stereotypical serfs control their own labour process, as they live and work on their own, feed themselves and merely surrender part of their produce to their lords, stereotypical slaves have no control over their labour process and are fed by their masters. Finally, while the concept of serfdom is primarily describing a socio-economic condition, it also includes an important underlying legal concept. This is the idea that, in contrast to slaves, who had no rights recognised by law, serfs possessed certain legal rights, however circumscribed, concerning property and family.

The stereotypical image of slavery is of course deeply flawed methodologically: most historians never construct an explicit link between the abstract legal definition of slavery and the socio-economic stereotype with which they practically operate. As

---

[26] For the variety of forms of servitude in the late Middle Ages, see Freedman 1999; Freedman and Bourin 2005; Hanß and Schiel 2014.

[27] Rio 2017: 246–9.

[28] Bak 1980.

a result, wherever historians have come across servile groups which deviate from this stereotypical image, like helots or early medieval servile groups, they have tended to explain away their peculiar features by ascribing them to the general category of serfs.[29]

The early medieval evidence illustrates the problem with the traditional distinction between serfdom and slavery. There was enormous diversity among the people classified as slaves: many approximated the stereotypical image of serfdom, some qualified for the stereotypical image of slaves, while others could be plausibly classified either way, depending on the context or the phase of their lives. The differences did not result from different legal statuses or from belonging to different socio-economic groups, but from the interplay of context and the diverse strategies of masters and slaves. People who were legally slaves lived in conditions of stereotypical serfdom as a consequence of the interplay between the needs of the masters, the wishes of the slaves and the negotiations that ensued.

The implication is that we need to abandon for good the stereotypical image of slavery. The slave stereotype is not the natural outcome of the legal foundation of slavery as property; it is merely one of the possible outcomes of how slavery can be used. If it is a recurrent outcome, we need to study the processes that create this recurrence, instead of taking it for granted; and we also need to account for all the other historical scenarios in which slavery is employed in ways that look radically different from the stereotypical image of slavery, like the examples from early medieval Europe we examined above.

The second implication is an extension of the first. It requires us to abandon the essentialist approach on which so much in the study of slavery depends. The diverse, contradictory and fragmented forms of early medieval slavery allow us to see in a clearer light that the essentialist concepts that we usually take for granted are merely the contingent outcomes of various entangled processes. We have seen above that the condition of slavery for those who entered it through warfare or trade could be radically different from the condition of those who entered it through self-enslavement, debt or punishment. We have seen that slavery on agricultural estates might operate in radically different ways from slavery in urban households, to the extent that the divergence might ultimately result in completely different legal classifications.

We have often taken for granted a model of slavery and freedom as total and non-negotiable statuses. We tend to think that slavery and freedom did not indicate only whether somebody was property or not, but also covered the full range of an individual's life; furthermore, neither could be negotiated, as slaves could not have any legally recognised rights, and free persons could not voluntarily shed their freedom. But early medieval evidence shows that these assumptions are unwarranted; both free and slave people in early medieval societies could negotiate their status as one bargaining chip among many others. This of course does not imply that there are no societies where status is total and non-negotiable, as we traditionally assume for Greco-Roman societies. But once we no longer take the articulation of status for granted, we need to explore the precise processes through which status is articulated in each society, as well

---

[29] Cartledge 1988; Ste. Croix 1988; Hunt 2017a.

as explaining why different societies operate with different forms of status; this issue is further explored in Chapter 6.

The third implication concerns how to achieve this conceptualisation and exploration of diversity. Rio proposed an instrumental approach in order to explore the diverse and contradictory facets of early medieval slavery. This required thinking of slavery as a tool that could be employed for a variety of purposes. It implies that we need to explore the range of purposes systematically and examine how slavery was used to achieve each of them. Rio's study brings out clearly that societies have very different repertoires of aims for which they employ slavery. If the early medieval period appears remarkable for the particularly wide range of uses for slavery and the high rate of experimentation with different uses, we need to ask ourselves how other periods and societies compare with this, and the reasons for this diversity in slave repertoires. The early medieval evidence also shows that slavery as a tool is not employed in the same way to achieve all purposes; different purposes require different uses of the tool, or even modification of the tool to better fulfil the required task. But this can lead to a situation in which modified tools for different tasks might become so different and specialised that they no longer belong together in the same toolbox. This is in fact what happened by the high Middle Ages in the Mediterranean; urban slavery fulfilled a variety of purposes which were performed by foreign religious outsiders, while agricultural slavery was largely restricted to the single purpose of agricultural tenancy, leading to its separate classification as serfdom and its fulfilment by native religious insiders.

As long as historians adopted essentialist approaches to slavery, the diversity was explained away and the connecting link between the different elements was simply taken for granted. While we need to explore systematically and account for the diversity of slave conditions and uses, we also need to think carefully about what holds the various conditions and uses together.[30] The instrumental approach is essential for accounting for diversity and change, but it is insufficient for explaining connectivity and continuity. We need to find a methodological framework that allows us to accomplish both tasks together.

## The Conceptual Systems of Slavery

The methodological framework offered here proposes that slavery is a historical category which is inscribed in three distinct, but interrelated, conceptual systems.[31] Before proceeding further, it is necessary to clarify what categories are and how they operate.[32] Categories were traditionally understood in **definitional** terms; a category was defined by certain criteria, and members of a particular category were those individuals who

---

[30]  See the comments of Rio 2017: 230–42.

[31]  For slavery and conceptual systems, see Rio 2017: 73–4.

[32]  The description below does not imply that all categories should be classified as definitional, prototypical or radial. There are of course other forms of categories; I have simply chosen those forms which illuminate best the specific conceptual systems I want to explore. For categories and cognitive theory in general, see Lakoff 1987; Aitchison 2012: 39–72; Strauss and Quinn 1997.

met all those criteria. Definitional categories were particularly apt to be codified, and were usually exclusive; an individual either did or did not meet the criteria and was categorised accordingly. In the last few decades, though, cognitive scientists have discovered that a large number of categories are not definitional.[33] Human beings do not categorise birds on the basis of a definitional category of what a bird is. On the contrary, they usually rely on **prototypical** categories; that is, things that are either ideal types or best examples of a particular category. Human beings tend to take a particular bird (for example, a robin) as a prototype of what a bird is, and categorise other animals based on the extent to which they resemble the prototypical robin. One common feature of prototypical categories is that they are often graded, instead of being exclusive; while the category 'senator' is exclusive (you either meet the criteria or not), the categories 'rich person' or 'tall woman' can be graded, as the extent to which an individual is categorised as such is relative to other people.[34] Finally, certain categories can be described as **radial**; these categories constitute clusters which comprise a central sub-category and a range of other associated sub-categories. The latter cannot be derived from the central sub-category by general rules, but are only associated through conventions recognised by those who use the category. To give an example, the category 'mother' has a central sub-category (the birth model: giving birth to a child) and a cluster of associated sub-categories: the genetic model (supplying half the child's genes as birth mother); the nurturance model (nurturing a child); the marital model (being wife of the father); the genealogical model (being the closest female ancestor).[35] As we shall see, definitional, prototypical and radial categories are important concepts for understanding how slavery is inscribed in various conceptual systems.[36]

The **first conceptual system** of slavery is based on the definitional category of slavery as a form of property. This conceptual system is relational but unilateral: it establishes a relationship between two human beings, but in a way which solely focuses on the unilateral rights of the master over the slave. It is the existence of this conceptual system that makes it possible to talk of slavery on a global and cross-cultural scale. Lewis has recently offered a detailed definition of slavery as property; his scheme is based on a famous article by the legal historian Tony Honoré, which presented a cross-cultural definition of ownership.[37] This conceptualisation of property consists of a list of rights and other related characteristics: **the right to possess** – that is, the right of exclusive possession; **the right to use**, which allowed the owner to use the property in any way he saw fit, excluding illegal uses; **the right to manage**, allowing the owner to decide how and by whom the property might be used; **the right to the income** arising from the use of the property; **the right to capital** – that is, the right to alienate the property; **the right to security**, which guarantees the exclusive right of owners and their protection; **transmissibility and the absence of term**, which ensures that the previously mentioned rights are transmissible to posterity and

---

[33] Lakoff 1987: 12–57.
[34] Lakoff 1987: 21–2.
[35] Lakoff 1987: 74–6.
[36] For the significance of cognitive theory for understanding slavery, see Philips 2003–4; Lewis 2018: 66.
[37] Honoré 1961; Lewis 2018: 33–9.

not time-limited; **the prohibition of harmful use**, which sets legal limits on the enjoyment of the various rights to property; and, finally, **liability to execution**, which regulated the circumstances in which third parties could divest property from their owners.[38]

This is undoubtedly a particularly useful definition of slavery with cross-cultural application; we shall see in Chapter 8 how it allows us to re-conceptualise the various local systems of Greek slavery. But it is important to clarify some important issues with this definitional category. Many societies worldwide recognise the right of fathers to pawn or sell their children in order to deal with famine or debt; sales contracts for children from thirteenth-century BCE Emar in Syria[39] and seventh-century BCE Nippur in Babylonia[40] provide dramatic evidence for this practice in desperate conditions in the ancient Near East. Apparently this was also the case with early Roman law, which allowed a father to sell his son up to three times, a process that was later used in order to emancipate a son from his father's legal authority once the selling of children was no longer recognised as legally valid.[41] Furthermore, many African societies employed the concept of rights in people, in which corporate groups like lineages had a range of different rights over various people, including their own members; these corporate groups had the right to sell their own members, if they deemed it necessary. This is totally different from penal slavery, in which a member of the community is sold into slavery as punishment for a crime; in the case of many African communities, the rights in people that lineages held over their own members allowed them to sell members who were at no fault of their own.[42] In such cases, it is obvious that fathers or lineages have the right to alienate their sons or lineage members and sell them as slaves (the right to capital); but it is also fairly obvious that sons and lineage members are not the same thing as slaves, and that was patently clear to the members of those societies as well.[43]

Furthermore, many societies recognise sale as a means of acquiring rights over people. Chinese societies in particular recognised sale as a means through which one family acquired children from another family, who could be used as sons, wives or concubines, depending on the circumstances; they also recognised sale as a means through which families acquired servants, who were sold by their families or by the persons themselves. Such people acquired through sale may or may not be sold to third parties (the right to capital) and may have various rights recognised by law. But at the same time the individuals and families who acquired such people had various rights over them (for example, the right to use, the right to manage, the right to income, the right to security).[44] In ancient Egypt during Saite and Persian times the conceptual system of slavery as property could be employed in order to formulate annual service contracts.[45]

---

[38] Lewis 2018: 25–55.

[39] Zaccagnini 1995.

[40] Oppenheim 1955.

[41] *Twelve Tables* 4.2; Gaius, *Institutes* 1.132; cf. the interpretation of López Barja de Quiroga 2006.

[42] Miers and Kopytoff 1977; Watson 1980b.

[43] For the difference between sons and slaves in the Roman context, see Saller 1994: 71–153.

[44] Watson 1980c; Sommer 2015; Ransmeier 2017.

[45] Menu 1977.

Finally, there are cases where slavery emerged as a consequence of contracts between buyers and those who sold themselves. Such cases can be found in various societies globally. As we have seen above, Rio has examined this phenomenon in early medieval Europe, where people who sold themselves as slaves could negotiate the terms of their slavery, creating limits, for example, on the owners' rights to use and manage.[46] The phenomenon is also attested in early modern Russia, where individuals could sell themselves for the duration of their master's life, but had the right to become free after the master's death; therefore, they limited transmissibility and the absence of term.[47]

The examples we have seen above differ in various ways: in the case of fathers selling their children it is the right to capital which is the most prominent manifestation of the phenomenon; in the case of the purchase of children, brides or servants, it is precisely the right to capital which is often restricted; in the case of medieval self-sales there are restrictions to the right to use and manage, while the Russian self-sales limit the right to transmissibility and the absence of term. As with all definitions which are based on a list, at some point it becomes necessary to decide if all listed features are essential parts of the definition, and how many of them need to be present before the phenomenon under consideration morphs into something rather different. Future work will be quite crucial for exploring these issues.[48]

How exactly should we therefore conceptualise the distinction between property rights over slaves and property rights over people who are not slaves, even if they are potentially saleable and enslaveable? It is to deal with problems like this that Patterson offered his alternative definition of slavery as a form of social death, as we saw in Chapter 2. It sounds plausible that natal alienation and dishonour served to differentiate sons and lineage members from slaves. We do not have to follow the essentialist logic of Patterson's conception of slavery as social death in order to recognise the important point he has raised.[49] While property is a constitutive aspect of slavery, it is insufficient to distinguish slavery from other forms of property in human beings. This is the reason that other conceptual systems of slavery are necessary.

But there is an additional reason why slavery needs to be inscribed in other conceptual systems. The definitional conceptual system of slavery as property only tells us that someone is the property of another human being; it does not tell us anything specific about the conditions and lives of slaves. If only the conceptual system of property existed, it would often be impossible to think of slaves as members of a general group of people, as the extent to which being property determined slave lives and conditions could vary significantly from one master to another and from one slave to another. Many societies, like those in the ancient Near East or early medieval Europe, as we have seen above, left the polar opposite of slavery as a relatively abstract concept and were not particularly prescriptive concerning the practices and identities from which

---

[46] Rio 2006, 2017: 42–70.

[47] Hellie 1982: 49–64; see also the contributions in Witzenrath 2015.

[48] For the ways in which Roman jurists distinguished between different rights on slaves, see Thomas 1999; for slave labour and Greek law, see Ismard 2019: 75–114.

[49] An alternative re-conceptualisation of Patterson's concept of social death is offered in Chapter 5.

slaves were excluded. But other societies, like classical Athens or the antebellum US South, took many more steps in creating clear polarities between insiders (free citizens) and outsiders (slaves). This issue is further explored in Chapter 6.

A final point concerns the conceptual distinction between property and commodity: the term 'chattel slavery' expresses the fact that slaves were not only human property, but human commodities that were bought and sold.[50] It is true that the potentiality of being sold is inherent in slavery, but there might be limits and restrictions on the commoditisation of slaves (the right to capital). In Islamicate societies, a woman who had given birth to a child recognised by her master as her own could not be sold;[51] in Sparta, helots could not be sold outside the territory of Sparta;[52] in Roman law, a master could insert a clause in his will that a female slave could not be prostituted, and this clause was legally valid, even if the slave was sold to or inherited by third parties;[53] slaves on late Roman imperial estates could not be sold apart from their families.[54] But even in the absence of legal restrictions, for various reasons many slaves could spend their whole lives without ever being bought and sold. Like all commodities, slaves have exchange value that could potentially be materialised in various transactions; but commodities also have use value, which could only be realised when slaves entered into a variety of functions and positions. Accordingly, slaves developed roles and identities as artisans, servants, parents, relatives and members of ethnic groups and cults, as we shall see in Chapter 5. Furthermore, and in contrast with other commodities, slaves had volitions, wishes and interests of their own and could act in ways that projected those wishes and interests rather than being the instruments of their masters' wishes.

The implication of the above points is that while slaves were always potential commodities, our best way to conceptualise this aspect of slavery is to employ Igor Kopytoff's approach to commodity as a process:

> Slavery begins with capture or sale, when the individual is stripped of his previous social identity and becomes a non-person, indeed an object and an actual or potential commodity. But the process continues. The slave is acquired by a person or group and is reinserted into the host group, within which he is re-socialized and re-humanized by being given a new social identity. The commodity-slave becomes in effect re-individualized by acquiring new statuses (by no means always lowly ones) and a unique configuration of personal relationships. In brief, the process has moved the slave away from the simple status of exchangeable commodity and toward that of a singular individual occupying a particular social and personal niche. But the slave usually remains a potential commodity: he or she continues to have a potential exchange value that may be realized by resale. In many societies, this was

---

[50] Rinehart 2016.
[51] Ali 2010: 167–8.
[52] Ducat 1990: 21–2; Lewis 2018: 128–9.
[53] McGinn 1990; Perry 2013: 29–37; see also Paradiso 1999 on the legal treatment of the rape of Greek female slaves.
[54] *Theodosian Code* 2.25.1; *Codex of Justinian* 3.38.11.

also true of the 'free,' who were subject to sale under certain defined circumstances. To the extent that in such societies all persons possessed an exchange value and were commoditizable, commoditization in them was clearly not culturally confined to the world of things. What we see in the career of a slave is a process of initial withdrawal from a given original social setting, his or her commoditization, followed by increased singularization (or de-commoditization) in the new setting, with the possibility of later re-commoditization. As in most processes, the successive phases merge one into another. Effectively, the slave was unambiguously a commodity only during the relatively short period between capture or first sale and the acquisition of the new social identity; and the slave becomes less of a commodity and more of a singular individual in the process of gradual incorporation into the host society.[55]

The possible and actual commoditisation of slaves co-exists with opposite processes in which slaves are de-commoditised and inserted into relations that emphasise their singularity instead of their abstract fungibility. Accordingly, we need an instrumental approach to slavery as property. Slavery as property was a tool that masters could use for a variety of purposes; this range of purposes could be extensive or limited and could vary across space and time. At the heart of the history of slavery is a major tug of war: will slavery cover the full range of slaves' lives, and to what extent? Or will other relationships, roles and functions, the various singularities of the slaves, cover many aspects of their lives? Would it be their common status as exchangeable commodities or their singular role as artisans, achievers, mothers or devotees of Artemis that would determine various aspects of their lives? We shall further explore this issue in Chapters 5, 6 and 7.

The **second conceptual system** is based on slavery as a prototypical category. Most slaveholding societies construct prototypical images of slaves. Unsurprisingly, these prototypical images exhibit features which appear with cross-cultural regularity (manual and degrading labour; ugly features; slavish, effeminate and unbecoming behaviour, clothes and haircut; lack of independence and autonomy; the inability to live as one wishes; the practice of ignoble professions; the lack of certain moral characteristics identified with being free), as well as features that appear only in certain societies or periods (profession, colour, race, ethnicity, religion).[56] Prototypical images of slavery employ polarity to establish the features that slaves lacked, the rights denied to them, the practices forbidden, restricted or imposed on them. As Alain Testart has argued, slavery in this sense works through exclusion from whatever identity, feature or practice was valued by the slaveholding community and allowed to its members.[57] In many societies the central aspect from which slaves were excluded was kinship; in others, like Greek and Roman societies, it was freedom and citizenship. The actual content of this central aspect from which slaves were excluded matters a lot: it is one of the major issues that affect the global diversity of slavery in space and time.[58]

---

[55] Kopytoff 1986: 65.
[56] See Rosivach 1999; George 2002; Wrenhaven 2012.
[57] Testart 1998.
[58] Watson 1980b.

This second conceptual system tends to operate in absolute rather than relational terms, usually through exclusive polarities (free or slave). The definitional conceptual system of slavery as property is often institutionalised as a legally codified relationship; the same can also potentially happen to prototypical conceptual systems. Certain aspects of the prototypical system can be legally codified (the exclusion from legally recognised kinship, the denial of civic rights), while other prototypical aspects (barbarian origin, slavish behaviour) are commonly observed regularities. Prototypical aspects which might be legally codified in certain societies might be merely commonly observed regularities in others. To give one example, Near Eastern law codes prohibit people from shaving the peculiar hair lock of slaves without the express permission of the master; it is plausible that this slave hair lock was legally codified in the Near East, while the slave haircut was merely a common stereotype in the Greek world.[59] It is this second conceptual system that makes it possible to speak of slaves as occupying a distinct legal and social status.

Slavery belongs to the category of 'promiscuous institutions', to use Michael Mann's term; promiscuous institutions draw in and structure elements from many areas of social life.[60] This is the reason that slavery also constitutes **a radial conceptual system**. Its central sub-category of property is linked to a series of other associated sub-categories to form a cluster of related **modalities** of slavery.[61] An individual who was the property of another human being was also under his power; accordingly, slavery as domination was one of the sub-categories associated with the central sub-category of property.[62] Slavery could be seen as an asymmetric negotiation of power between masters and slaves: a relationship not unilaterally defined from above, but the outcome of struggle, compromise and failure.[63] As a result, slavery is often used to define relations of domination and hierarchy. Many societies employ slavery as a means of conceiving or defining various hierarchical relationships in politics, economics, society or culture.[64] This was a particular feature of ancient Near Eastern and early medieval societies (an issue further explored in Chapters 6 and 8); it was also present in Greek and Roman societies, but tended to have exclusively negative characteristics. On the other hand, the opposite direction is also commonly attested: in many societies various hierarchical relationships, like patronage or lordship, provide the conceptual system within which slavery is largely embedded.[65] Particularly remarkable is the case of ancient Egypt, where slavery was not legally codified in its definitional or prototypical forms, but was shaped by the wider modalities of hierarchy, service and domination.[66] Whether hierarchical conceptual systems will provide the language through which slavery operated or slavery will provide the means of conceptualising hierarchy and domination is one of the most important issues in the global history of slavery.[67]

[59] Potts 2011; see also Wunsch and Magdalene 2012 on slave clothing in the Near East.
[60] Mann 1986: 28; Rio 2017: 11–12.
[61] Brock 2007; Vlassopoulos 2018d.
[62] For slavery as domination, see Kyrtatas 2002; Vlassopoulos 2011a.
[63] Genovese 1974; Glassman 1991; Berlin 1998.
[64] For the role of the radial category of slavery in Christian thought, see: Martin 2000; Glancy 2002a; de Wet 2018.
[65] Reid 1983.
[66] Loprieno 1997, 2012; Hofmann 2005.
[67] Rio 2008; Ali 2010; Reid 2018.

But there were other associated modalities of slavery apart from property and domination. Slavery could be seen as an instrumental relationship in which slaves existed for the purpose of serving the needs and wishes of their masters, or it could be approached as an extreme form of bad luck.[68] Slavery could be envisaged as an asymmetric relationship of benefaction and reward; masters could opt to see slave labour as loyal service and choose to reward deserving slaves with trust, honour and material benefits; slaves could see their service as the foundation for claims to justified rewards.[69]

These various modalities of slavery could of course be mutually reinforcing; but they tended to be used for different purposes and they were also potentially contradictory. Slavery as property or as an instrumental relationship were deeply unilateral in character, as they exclusively stressed the point of view of the master. On the other hand, slavery as the negotiation of power and slavery as a relationship of benefaction and reward were relational. While the first two modalities posed no limits on the wishes and interests of masters vis-à-vis slaves, the latter two offered models that were particularly useful for slave interests and wishes. Slavery as bad luck could explain the slave condition without essentialising slaves and offer hope about change in the future. These various modalities are analysed in detail in Chapter 7. What is important in this context is to stress the potential contradictions between different co-existing modalities of slavery. One example concerns the contradictory co-existence of different modalities of slavery in Rome. The condition of slavery was considered as inherently shameful, as slaves were required to behave in ways unbecoming to free persons as a result of their slave condition, thus attracting the *macula servitutis* (stain of slavery).[70] On the other hand, slavery was considered an extreme form of bad luck, which could happen to anybody, and from which it was perfectly legitimate to hope to escape.[71] Furthermore, the modality of benefaction and reward was employed to justify why manumitted slaves deserved their freedom for services rendered. A society that considered the condition of slavery as shameful could treat manumitted slaves in radically different ways, due to the co-existence of different modalities of conceptualising slavery.[72]

The three conceptual systems we have delineated above allow us to avoid essentialist approaches to slavery and their disavowal of co-existing diversity and change in space and time; but at the same time, the entanglement between the three conceptual systems allows us to grasp the unity of slavery as a historical phenomenon alongside diversity and change. The definitional conceptual system of slavery as property is a necessary but insufficient condition for the global phenomenon of slavery. Slavery as

---

[68] For slavery as bad luck, see Williams 1993: 116–24.

[69] Zelnick-Abramovitz 2005: 6–7.

[70] Mouritsen 2011a: 10–35; see my review in Vlassopoulos 2015–16.

[71] Kleijwegt 2006c; Bodel 2017.

[72] The existence of ways of conceptualising Roman freedmen and freedwomen which did not depend on the stain of slavery modality is well brought out in: Perry 2013; Vermote 2016a, 2016b. For the contradiction, see Giannella 2014: 153–212.

property was a tool that masters employed for a variety of purposes. In order to systematically explore these diverse repertoires of employment, I propose the concept of
**slaving strategies**. The slaving strategies employed by the masters had different aims
and produced divergent groups of slaves. Slaving strategies aiming at labour created
slaves who worked in labour processes controlled and directed by the masters; slaving
strategies aiming at revenue created slaves who lived and worked on their own and
surrendered to their masters a portion of their earnings; slaving strategies that used
slaves in bureaucratic and military positions created slaves with authority and power.
Slaving strategies are explored in detail in Chapter 4.

It is at this point that the instrumental approach to slavery is most useful: slavery is
a tool that enabled masters to do certain things. But the extent to which this tool was
employed for a wide range of purposes, or for a rather limited number, is something
that historically varies significantly. The tool of slavery might be employed to its full
extent, or only certain elements of it might be utilised; it might be used to cover the
full range of slave life, or used for a limited number of aspects, while other aspects
were run on other principles. The conceptual system of slavery as property offers an
ideal type, but the extent to which all elements of this conceptual system are applicable, or limited or absent, will vary in a number of historical conditions and processes.
This is the subject of Chapter 5, which explores how slave categories operated as a
form of imposed identity alongside alternative categories employed by the slaves.

It is particularly significant that the definitional conceptual system includes a number of features that limit the portmanteau of property rights, like the prohibition of
harmful use and liability for execution. This creates a conceptual opening for recognising that the historical configuration of slavery as property is not unilaterally defined
by the property interests of the masters, but also by a variety of other agents and factors. In the majority of cases, it was the political community that affected how slavery
operated as a form of property. Apart from the political community, there were other
agents involved in the historical configuration of slavery as property and as a form of
status; as the cases of self-sale that we mentioned above show, people who sold themselves into slavery could significantly affect how slavery operated as property; from
late antiquity onwards, religious institutions also started to play a significant role. The
implication of these comments is that we need a new framework to study how these
factors affected slavery; this is analysed in detail in Chapter 6. Slavery was constituted
by the interplay between three **dialectical relationships**: the relationship between
masters and slaves; the relationship between free people and slaves; and the relationships between the members of the various communities in which slaves participated
(communities and networks of kinship, work, residence, ethnicity, cult). Each dialectical relationship pulled in different directions, which could be partly complementing
and partly contradicting each other.[73]

Let us recapitulate. I have argued in this chapter that slavery can no longer be seen as a
unitary entity with an ahistorical essence. I have argued instead that it should be conceptualised as a historical conglomerate of various elements: the different conceptual

---

[73] Vlassopoulos 2016a.

systems, slaving strategies and dialectical relationships. This processual answer is not
unique to the historical study of slavery, or even to the discipline of history in general. Instead, in order to better conceptualise what is proposed here, it is illuminating
to make a brief detour to the historical discipline of biology, which has also experienced a transition from essentialist to processual ways of thinking.[74] Modern historians
have inherited from nineteenth-century social science and its pre-Darwinian biological
foundations an essentialist conceptual apparatus of entities and species; this was based
on species conceived as fixed typological entities whose essence can be defined and
classified. Many modern biologists conceive species not as essences, but as *populations* of
genetically variable individuals whose unity rests solely on their ability to interbreed.[75]
Biological populations can tolerate a significant amount of genetic variability, but when
strong isolation mechanisms emerge, even relatively small genetic differences can lead
to the loss of the ability to interbreed between original members of a single population
and the creation of new species which can no longer mutually interbreed. Once new
species are formed, these new populations follow trajectories of their own which can
gradually diverge widely from other species which originally belonged to the same
population.

   While in essentialist approaches typological definition is explanatory, population
thinking uses historical processes as the mode of explanation. The medievalist Fredric
Cheyette has pointed out the conclusions that historians can draw from this:

> I suggest that instead of looking for structures or species with all their implied fixity
> we look at particular ways of doing things: social habits, practices, processes, each
> of which may have a multiplicity of meanings and a multiplicity of effects, and
> each of which may follow its own time-line, have its own particular history. We
> might think of these processes and practices as forming a 'population' of behav-
> iours, functionally connected, perhaps, but never stable, always variable in time
> and place.[76]

   Discarding typological essentialism in favour of population thinking enables the
global study of a historically diverse phenomenon like slavery; it requires switching
from conceiving slavery as an ahistorical essence to viewing it as a population of practices with the ability to interbreed. In the case of slavery, interbreeding equals com-
patibility, mutual intelligibility, fungibility: this is what enables a captive in a Native
American society to become a plantation slave in Virginia. Various practices might
start as part of the slaving population and subsequently develop isolation mechanisms
that make interbreeding impossible and transform them into new populations. Debt-
bondage could become a great source of slaves; but societies like Athens or Israel could
create mechanisms isolating native debt-bondsmen from slaves.[77] We have also seen
above how by the high Middle Ages native Christian serfs had developed isolation

---

[74] Sober 1980.
[75] Mayr 2006.
[76] Cheyette 2003.
[77] Lewis 2017c, 2018: 204–11.

mechanisms as regards foreign urban slaves; the single slave population of individuals and practices in the early Middle Ages had split into different populations with their own features and trajectories.

It is the definitional system of slavery as property that fundamentally maintains the 'interbreeding' of diverse slaving practices across time and space; the bundle of ownership rights remains relatively stable, even if particular rights in each bundle might be shaped or transformed in particular ways, as we saw above. While the definitional system is *relatively* stable, the other two conceptual systems of slavery tend to exhibit significantly more variation across space and time. But it would be a major mistake to consider them as optional extras; they were crucial aspects of how the tool of slavery was employed in actual historical circumstances. If we can use another biological metaphor, the definitional system of property can be seen as the skeleton of the organism, while the other two systems can be compared to the soft tissue.

As a consequence of all the above, there is no a priori way of defining populations: only their study in place and time can elucidate their variable and changing history. Population thinking allows us to move beyond essentialism and incorporate diversity and change within our framework. Its focus on interbreeding means that the proper study of slavery cannot be restricted to the study of 'slavery in society x', or slavery as an ahistorical essence: it needs to focus on the kinds of entanglements which are the stuff of global history.

# 4

# SLAVING STRATEGIES AND CONTEXTS

HAVING EXAMINED THE THREE conceptual systems of slavery in the previous chapter, we can now move on to focus on the instrumental uses of slavery as property. What were the various purposes for which masters utilised slavery, and how did these aims differ across space and time? We will start our exploration by examining the diverse slaving strategies that masters employed in the various ancient societies. This examination will reveal the widespread diversity, as well as the major contradictions and conflicts that could emerge as a result. We shall also see how these various slaving strategies could solidify into distinctive slaving lifestyles. We shall then move on to examine four major contexts of slaving: the household, the political community, the wider world and large-scale economic operations. These different contexts had characteristics and followed trajectories of their own; as a result, the study of slaving needs to seriously take into account wider processes and trends which had a formative effect on its history. Finally, we shall explore the entanglement between slaving strategies and contexts in one major process which was of fundamental importance in the history of slaving: that of slave-making.

## Slaving Strategies

As we have seen in previous chapters, many historians of slavery subscribe to a traditional sociological repertoire which projected an ideal type of slaves working under the direct control of their masters, and an ideal type of serfs as producers living and working on their own and surrendering part of their produce to their lord.[1] But ancient texts had a more complex understanding of slave work than that assumed by traditional sociology. Some interesting examples appear in the writings of Roman jurists. Let us start with Ulpian's discussion of farm equipment (*instrumentum fundi*):

> It is asked whether a slave, who was in a position like that of a tenant on the land (*colonus in agro*), is included in a legacy of the *instrumentum*. Both Labeo and Pegasus rightly denied this, because he had not been fulfilling the function of *instrumentum* on the farm.[2]

Ulpian clearly imagines slaves in the role of agricultural tenants and distinguishes them from slaves who were farm hands and thus counted as part of the farm equipment;

---

[1] For this traditional sociology in the study of ancient slavery, see Cartledge 1988, 2011; Ste. Croix 1988; Hunt 2017a.

[2] *Digest* 33.7.12.3.

Alfenus Varus, another jurist, discussed the case of a master who had rented an estate to his slave to cultivate it, but provided the oxen for the cultivation.[3] It is quite obvious from such examples that the traditional sociology is rather simplistic.[4] Another passage of Alfenus Varus explicates the law on the harbour tax of Sicily, which entailed that people were not obliged to pay harbour dues for any slaves which they were taking home for their own use:

> But what 'for his own use' is involves great uncertainty; and it is better to suppose that the phrase only covers what has been acquired in order to support life. And so on this basis the question arises over the slaves which of them were required for the man's own use, whether they were stewards, men in charge of blocks of flats, bailiffs, doorkeepers, weavers, rural labourers who were owned in order to cultivate the fields from which the head of the household derived revenue – which of these the man had bought in order to have them himself and use them for something, and whether he had not bought any of them in order to sell them. And it appeared that a head of a household had for his own use only those who were charged with looking after his own body and his care and were intended for these purposes; and that in this category masseurs, bedroom attendants, cooks, personal servants, and others who were required for this sort of purposes were included.[5]

The passage documents a distinction between the personal use of slaves, which referred to the personal service of the master and his bodily needs, and other uses of slaves, from managerial posts to artisans and cultivators. Another distinction created by Roman jurists, as Yann Thomas has shown, differentiated between the ownership of slaves and the usufruct deriving from them. The usufruct was further divided between the use of slaves under the direct authority of the master or other beneficiaries and the monetary revenue deriving from leasing a slave to a third party.[6] My final example is a story narrated by the second-century CE Christian apologist Tertullian about the family of the urban prefect Fuscianus:

> A young boy of noble birth had wandered away from his front door while his attendants were not watching. Enticed by some passersby, he slipped away from his home. He had a Greek tutor who had reared him from the outset and instructed him in the ways of pederasty. When the young boy came of age, he is brought back to Rome to enter the slave market. His father, unaware of who he is, buys him and uses him for sex. Then, after the boy had relations with the mistress of the family, the master sent him to the fields bound in chains. Both the tutor and the nurse had already been in the fields for some time undergoing punishment. The entire earlier course of events comes back to them and they recount the story of their departure. The tutor and nurse tell how their charge had died as a child,

---

[3] *Digest* 15.3.16.
[4] For slave tenants, see Giliberti 1981; Veyne 1981; Aubert 2009.
[5] *Digest* 50.16.203.
[6] Thomas 1999.

and the young man tells how his boyhood had been cut short. From this point, the stories converge. The young man had been born in Rome of a noble home. Perhaps he dropped some further hints. And so it happened by the will of God that such a dreadful curse has fallen upon this age. All three of them are shaken in spirit on this day. The passage of time that matches his age. There is something familiar about his glance and his profile. Some characteristic marks on his body catch their attention. His owners, now clearly his parents, launch a long overdue inquiry. The slave dealer is interrogated – unfortunately they were able to find him. Once the crime is fully disclosed, the parents seek relief by hanging themselves. The prefect assigns their worldly goods to their son, a wretched survivor, not as an inheritance but as restitution for sexual defilement and incest.[7]

The story illustrates the co-existence and entanglement of various slaving strategies: the use of slaves as personal servants and tutors; the use of slave labour on Roman estates; the employment of slaves for sexual gratification; the circulation of slaves between the urban and the rural possessions of their masters. Finally, there are the issues we shall examine in later sections of this chapter, like the significance of violence in slave-making and the role of the slave trade in recycling human beings.

The above references necessitate exploring the full range of slave uses and distinguishing between the various forms of slaving strategies. One set of strategies focused on the extraction of **labour** and achieved its aims through labour processes that were under the direct control of the masters. Within this first set, we can distinguish two subsets: the use of slave labour for *maintenance*, by employing slaves for the drudgery required for the everyday maintenance of households (cooks, cleaners, personal attendants and nannies),[8] and the employment of slave labour for the production of *wealth* on rural estates, in workshops and mines.[9]

Slaves employed in labour strategies would work under the supervision of their masters or their overseers, provide services or create products that their masters retained for their own use or sold in the market, and receive rations for sustenance; in other words, they were fully dependent on and under the control of their masters for most aspects of their lives. While the difference between the two labour subsets is clear enough, it is worth pointing out that occasionally the distinction between them could become blurred, in particular among masters with few slaves. This is particularly evident in one of Jesus' parables from the New Testament:

> Which of you, owning a slave working the land or tending the flocks, will say to his slave when he returns from the countryside: 'Go in and recline for dinner immediately', instead of 'Prepare me some dinner, get ready and wait on me,

[7] Tertullian, *To the nations* 1.16.13–19; see Harper 2013: 100–2.

[8] For a general account, see Schumacher 2001a: 195–210; see also Treggiari 1973, 1975a; Joshel 1986; D'Arms 1991; Schulze 1998; Harper 2011: 103–11.

[9] For a general account, see Schumacher 2001a: 91–162; see also Lauffer 1956; Giardina and Schiavone 1981; Carandini 1988; Ameling 1998; Roth 2007; Rihll 2010; Harper 2011: 144–98; Lewis 2018: 172–88; Porter 2019a: 171–89.

until I eat and drink; afterwards you too may eat and drink'? This man won't be thankful to his slave for doing what he was told, will he?[10]

For petty masters like the one portrayed in the parable, their one or two slaves would perform labour for the production of wealth as well as labour for maintenance. Furthermore, small farmers, artisans or traders could buy one or two slaves to supplement their labour needs, but such employment of slaves, if successful enough, could end up absolving masters from the need to work, and could thus allow them to enter the lower reaches of the leisure class.[11]

Accordingly, slaving for labour could produce leisure either by absolving masters from the need to work to produce wealth, or by absolving them from the need to do maintenance work for the household. Given the gendered division of labour in ancient societies,[12] it is obvious that the first form of labour would primarily apply to masters, while the second form would be primarily significant for mistresses, or the wives and female dependants of male masters. It is worth pondering what choices petty masters made in this respect: did they prioritise buying one or two slaves to enhance their wealth production or absolve them from work, or did they buy slaves in order to absolve their female dependants from the everyday chores of household maintenance? And how did women who were involved on their own in crafts, services and trade make such choices?[13] What economic, social and cultural criteria informed those choices? And if male slaves could double up as both wealth producers and maintenance providers, as shown in the Jesus parable above, is it likely that the same would apply to female slaves as well? If not, what implications does this have for the gender choices of masters?[14]

Historians have usually focused on slave labour for wealth production, claiming that this is the crucial parameter that distinguishes slave societies from societies with slaves, as we saw in Chapter 2. But this is based on a serious misunderstanding of the significance of maintenance in pre-industrial societies. Without modern technological advances that provide fresh water, electricity for lighting and cooking, washing appliances for clothes and dishes and disposable nappies, an enormous quantity of labour was required to perform essential everyday activities like cutting wood, drawing water, making bread, cooking and washing.[15] Furthermore, while pre-industrial societies might radically differ in the quantity of wealth they produced, they all required roughly the same amount of everyday maintenance work. It is thus highly misleading to underestimate the significance of slaving for maintenance in ancient societies.

Slaving for labour had a major impact on the constitution of ancient households; it enabled the free members of the household to access ways of living that would

[10] Gospel of Luke 17.7–10.
[11] Tran 2013a; Hawkins 2016; Groen-Vallinga 2017: 87–153.
[12] Dixon 2004; Harris 2014.
[13] For female participation in urban production and trade, see Treggiari 1979; Kampen 1981; Brock 1994; Groen-Vallinga 2013; Holleran 2013; Larsson Lovén 2016.
[14] But see Roth 2004, 2007: 53–87, for discussion of the various uses of female slave labour.
[15] Vlassopoulos 2016c: 669–74. For the variety and importance of maintenance work in early nineteenth-century Brazil and USA, see respectively Silva Dias 1995; Rockman 2009.

have been unavailable otherwise, thus creating a major distinction between those who aspired to a leisured mode of life and those who could not. This is well reflected in a fragment from Athenian comedy that imagines life in a primitive stage of society:

> In those days nobody had a slave, a Manes or a Sekis,
> but the women had to toil by themselves over all the housework.
> And what is more, they would grind the corn at early dawn,
> so that the village rang with the touch of the hand mills.[16]

The absence of slaves in such a primitive society had serious repercussions for the lives of women, who had to undertake such maintenance tasks. As various anthropologists have stressed, human beings do not engage with material life only in order to produce particular products, but also in order to produce particular kinds of people and modes of living.[17] Slaving was crucial for producing this particular leisurely mode of living. To give another example, in many ancient societies gender norms entailed that respectable women could not enter unaccompanied public spaces, which were considered as typically male.[18] Possessing a slave enabled respectable women to be accompanied out of home and visit places that would otherwise have been impossible or problematic.[19]

Another set of slaving strategies aimed at **revenue** extraction rather than labour; in this set masters withdrew from the labour process and used slaves like other possessions and investments which brought revenue (real property, loans and stock market shares). We can again distinguish between two subsets. In the first subset masters *hired* their slaves to other people, who either could not afford to buy their own slaves or had short-term or temporary labour needs that made hiring preferable.[20] In the second subset, masters allowed their slaves to *work on their own* as cultivators, artisans or traders, on condition that they surrendered part of their earnings.[21] The particular Roman version of the second subset was facilitated by the legal tool of the *peculium*: the male head of household (*pater familias*) could set aside various resources and entrust somebody under his authority to use them.[22] The formally constituted *peculium* involved the keeping of separate accounts by the slaves; in a looser sense, the term could also describe petty resources informally entrusted or acquired by slaves, like a couple of coins or a few chickens.[23] The *peculium* functioned as the de facto property of the slave, even though

---

[16] Pherekrates in *K-A*, fragment 10.
[17] Graeber 2006; Wengrow and Graeber 2018.
[18] Cohen 1989.
[19] Harper 2011: 340–3.
[20] Perotti 1976; Thomas 1999; Fisher 2008; Kazakévich 2008; Kamen 2011; Du Plessis 2012.
[21] Bieżuńska-Małowist 1965; Perotti 1974; Kazakévich 2008.
[22] For the significance of the *peculium*, see Buckland 1908: 187–206; Kirschenbaum 1987: 31–88; Wacke 2006; Gamauf 2009; Roth 2010b. For a comparative perspective on the *peculium*, see Patterson 1982: 182–6; for the 'peculium' in ancient Mesopotamia, see Head 2010; for ancient Greece, see Kamen 2016.
[23] For the *peculium* of agricultural slaves, see Roth 2005. For the distinction between the formal *peculium* of the legal sources and the informal use of the term to describe petty resources de facto used by slaves, see Aubert 2013.

it could be unilaterally revoked by the master; while giving slaves the capital to engage in various economic activities on their own, it also usually limited the liability of the master to third parties to the amount of the *peculium*. Slaves could use their *peculia* to produce revenue for their masters, but, as we shall see below, they could use them for other purposes, like enhancing their diet or supporting their families.

Both subsets of revenue strategies aimed at minimising the cost of supervision and engagement required by masters, while also providing them with a steady source of trouble-free income.[24] But if both subsets had the same results for masters, they could have quite different implications for slaves. In the first subset slaves were employed in labour processes outside their control, although in this case control was ceded to a person other than their master. This situation could be dangerous for slaves: their value as capital was an important reason why their masters would care about their well-being and avoid extremes of physical punishment and malnourishment. The capital value of slaves often inclined masters to think about their investment in a long-term perspective, but people who hired slaves had no such incentives and could attempt to exploit slaves without thinking about the long-term consequences.[25] Legal actions for property damages could limit what unscrupulous hirers might do to hired slaves, but the danger was clearly present, as shown by the case of Lesis that we will examine in Chapter 7.[26]

Slaves who worked on their own and gave part of their earnings to their masters experienced radically different conditions; they were in many ways indistinguishable from free independent producers. Talented and skilled slaves could profit enormously from the opportunities provided by this subset of slaving strategies. They could live relatively autonomously, and without the constant supervision and control of their masters; they could gradually amass capital that could be used to buy their freedom, and create work opportunities that could provide them after manumission with a steady living, or even with prosperity and wealth.[27] But these opportunities were always conditional: masters could force slaves who worked independently to return to labour processes directly controlled by them, even if this threat would often be unenforceable because it was economically counterproductive.

Furthermore, this subset involved deep levels of slave self-exploitation. Slaves who worked in labour processes controlled by their masters or people who hired them were generally guaranteed their maintenance. They would constantly attempt to shirk labour as far as they could get away with it, or as long as they could live with the consequences; over the long term, they would try to force their masters to abandon extra demands that would create discontent or could jeopardise the whole labour process. The ultimate aim was to make masters acquiesce to a certain level of labour demands whose performance could be guaranteed.[28] Slaves who worked on their own could

---

[24] On supervision costs of slaves, see Fenoaltea 1984 and the modifications of the theory suggested in Scheidel 2008.

[25] For these issues in New World societies, see Martin 2004.

[26] For slave hiring and slave damage, see Du Plessis 2012, 2013a.

[27] Garnsey 1981; Verboven 2012.

[28] Bradley 1984: 20–45; Klees 1998: 101–27; on the negotiations involved, see also Bradley 1979 on holidays for slaves.

not afford the luxury of guaranteed maintenance or of trying to minimise their labour effort. On the contrary, they had to increase their labour effort to the maximum possible, in order to pay their masters, guarantee their maintenance and create savings.[29] As with so many aspects of slavery, this slaving strategy involved co-existing and countervailing tendencies: it offered masters income without obligations and it increased significantly the level of slave effort; at the same time, slaves had an important incentive to work harder, as they could enjoy at least a part of the outcome of their work, an opportunity generally denied to slaves involved in the slaving strategies for labour.[30]

Slaving strategies for revenue had major consequences for the life of slaves and the history of slaving. Slaves involved in revenue strategies required a significant amount of autonomy in order to perform as profitably as possible for their masters. The result was the creation of slaves who could not easily be distinguished from free working people. This development had the potential to seriously undermine the prototypical conceptual system of slavery we have examined in Chapter 3.[31] Slaves could exploit the fact that they were often indistinguishable from free working people in order to avoid detection as slaves and to live their everyday lives as if they were free persons.[32] It is not accidental that slaves with 'white collar' jobs tended to have names that made them indistinguishable from citizens and free people; slaves could perform such tasks more successfully if they were indistinguishable, and slaves who were indistinguishable were more likely to adopt such names.[33]

Slaves who worked in labour processes controlled by their masters could often take advantage of the conditions created by slaves who worked on their own. They could take advantage of such conditions on an everyday basis, by avoiding easy detection as slaves and its consequences.[34] Fugitive slaves could attempt to hide in urban communities with significant populations of slaves who lived and worked on their own.[35] And slaves who lived and worked on their own were often at the forefront of slave militancy and revolt: slave shepherds were instrumental in the Sicilian revolt of the 130s BCE, as their autonomous living and working conditions offered them excellent opportunities to organise their resistance.[36]

We can now move to a third slaving strategy which has been effectively universal: the employment of slaves as means of **prestige creation**.[37] The sacrifice of captives and slaves on the graves of their masters is probably the most characteristic example of slavery as prestige creation; this was attested in early Mesopotamia and Egypt, as well as in societies like the Scythians in the Black Sea.[38] It was largely

---

[29] Gamauf 2009: 334–6.

[30] Egerton 2006; Roth 2010b.

[31] But see the comments of Canevaro 2018: 121–2.

[32] This is one cause of the conflicts and confusion about slave status documented in Söllner 2000; Evans-Grubbs 2013.

[33] For slave names in classical Athens, see Vlassopoulos 2010, 2015a.

[34] Vlassopoulos 2007a; Forsdyke 2019.

[35] On slave flight, see Bellen 1971; for this phenomenon in the New World, see Wade 1964; Dantas 2008.

[36] Diodorus 34/5.2.1–3, 2.27–31.

[37] Patterson 1982: 82–5.

[38] See the global account of Testart 2004.

unknown in Greek and Roman societies, though the use of gladiators in the funeral rituals of republican Italy exhibited many elements of slave sacrifice for prestige creation.[39] By and large, though, prestige creation in ancient societies focused less on conspicuous destruction and more on conspicuous display. Theophrastus' portrait of the man of petty ambition from classical Athens describes how 'if invited to dinner, he contrives to recline by the host himself; he takes his son to Delphi for a haircut; he takes care that his attendant is Ethiopian'.[40] Having an exotic slave from Ethiopia added to the prestige of petty Athenian masters, but they could not compete with the huge retinues of late Roman aristocrats:

> Some, hastening, without fear of danger, through the broad promenades of the city and over upturned paving stones, drive their horses like public horses, with their heels stamped, as the saying goes, dragging behind them trains of household members like bands of plunderers, leaving at home not even Sannio, as the comic poet says. In imitation of these men, many Roman wives, with covered heads and in covered litters, run through all quarters of the city. And as experienced leaders place at the front units dense and strong, then the light-armed troops, after them the javelin-throwers, and in the back the reserve forces, to assist the battle if chance demands it, so do the overseers of the urban households, distinguished by the staffs attached to their right hands, divide their people carefully and diligently: as if a signal was given to a soldier in the camp, near the front of the carriage the entire body of the weavers marches; they are joined by the blackened kitchen staff, and then by all the other slaves, indiscriminately, accompanied by plebeian neighbours who can spare the time.[41]

And if prestige creation in other societies required the slaughter of slaves for internment in their master's tomb, Roman masters emphasised their large retinues in alternative and more symmetrical forms of funerary commemoration, as the following Aesopic fable attests:

> A fox and a monkey were walking together, quarrelling over their noble lineage. Each was going over many arguments, when they arrived at some graves. The monkey looked at the graves and sighed. When the fox asked him why, the monkey showed her the graves and said: 'Shouldn't I cry when I see the stelae of the slaves and freedmen of my ancestors?' The fox said: 'Tell as many lies as you want. For none of these will raise from his grave in order to refute you.'[42]

The use of slaves for prestige creation was thus related to how different ancient societies allowed their members to use various media and opportunities in order to enhance their prestige.[43] Such a wider study, and the various roles of slaving within it, is an important desideratum of future work.[44]

---

[39] Wiedemann 2002: 102–24; Kyle 1998: 76–127.
[40] Theophrastus, *Characters* 21.4–5.
[41] Ammianus Marcellinus, *History* 14.6.16–17.
[42] *Perry* 14 = *Chambry* 39; see Laubry 2017.
[43] For honour in Roman society, see Lendon 2001, 2011.
[44] For a start, see López Barja de Quiroga 2020.

Another important slave strategy concerns **gratification**. By this I mean how slaving can be used to provide sensory pleasure in all its various forms.[45] Gratification slaving involved musicians, singers, dancers, actors, mimes, chariot-drivers, gladiators, barbers, masseurs, hairdressers and cooks, or the *delicia* children that amused their owners.[46] While some of these forms were covered within households, others were organised as service markets, in which slaves operated either as labourers in processes controlled by their masters or as independent workers who gave their masters a portion of their earnings. Many forms of gratification, like dancing and singing, were strongly connected to the most significant form: sex.

The sexual economy of ancient societies was organised on the basis of distinct gender roles. Respectable women could have legitimate access to sex exclusively through marriage; furthermore, given the high child mortality of ancient populations, early marriage for girls was a practical necessity merely for maintaining population levels, let alone for population increase. On the other hand, men could legitimately have access to sex outside marriage, as long as they refrained from having sex with respectable women who were under the authority of their fathers, husbands or guardians. But women without honour were fully usable, and slaves constituted the overwhelming majority of women without honour.[47] Furthermore, while girls were commonly married as soon as they reached puberty, men in many ancient societies normally deferred marriage until their late twenties or thirties, when they would have received their inheritance and could support their families. As a result, men faced a window of opportunity between puberty in the late teens and marriage in the early thirties in which sexual access took place outside wedlock and was provided by women without honour.[48]

We have so far focused on female slaves as means of sexual gratification, but the sexual norms of ancient societies meant that male slaves were also a major source of sexual gratification.[49] An important modality of ancient sexuality was based on gendered polarity: men were conceived as penetrators, irrespective of whether they penetrated men or women, while women were seen as penetrated.[50] While male desire for male beauty and the penetration of other males was considered normal and unexceptional, this model of polarity problematised the role of penetrated males. Greek societies generally maintained a creative ambiguity in this respect: some accepted the penetration of free boys, while others institutionalised homoerotic relationships between free male adults.[51] The Romans considered the penetration of male Roman citizens morally and legally reprehensible and viewed slaves as ideal for the role.[52]

---

[45] For a general survey, see Schumacher 2001a: 219–38.

[46] Horsmann 1998; Dalby 2000; Schäfer 2001; Laes 2003; Duncan 2006: 124–87; Goldman 2015; Toner 2015.

[47] Harper 2017a.

[48] For the ancient sexual economy and slavery, the best account is Harper 2013: 19–79.

[49] For the sexual use of eunuch slaves, see Stevenson 1995; Ringrose 2003.

[50] For the penetration model, see Davidson 2001; Kamen and Levin-Richardson 2015.

[51] Davidson 2007.

[52] Williams 2010.

The use of slaves for sexual gratification took a variety of forms.[53] The simplest was the casual sexual exploitation of male and female slaves by their male masters; the right of mistresses to avail themselves of the sexual services of their slaves was curtailed by the gendered prescriptions of sexual access for women.[54] More complex was the institution of concubinage, in which masters developed long-term sexual relationships with their female slaves.[55] Ancient societies dealt with long-term sexual relationships involving slaves in different ways. Near Eastern societies, like the Babylonians and Jews, accorded slave concubines special rights, and masters could recognise children born from such unions as legitimate.[56] Roman societies allowed non-aristocratic masters to marry their manumitted slaves.[57] Certain Greek societies, like Gortyn, recognised marriage between slave and free people, while others, like Athens, prohibited masters from marrying their manumitted slaves or from recognising their slave progeny as legitimate.[58]

In the course of antiquity one form of the sexual exploitation of slaves became organised on a large scale: prostitution.[59] The high levels of urbanisation reached in the ancient world created the necessary population density for the emergence of brothels; spurred by the widespread availability of slaves and the gender prescriptions of ancient sexual economies, prostitution increased exponentially. As Harper has aptly argued, prostitution was the poor man's piece of slaving: while masters could have sexual access to their own slaves, for poor people without slaves prostitution offered a particularly cheap form of access to sexual services.[60] The link between slave prostitution, gender norms and the sexual economy of ancient societies is well illustrated in a passage from the Athenian comedian Philemon:

> You, Solon, made an invention for all people. They say it was you who first saw this – the only thing designed for the people, by Zeus, and life-saving too . . . Seeing the city full of young men, their nature compulsive and erring against what was not theirs, you bought women and stationed them at places to be set up and common to all. They stand naked. Don't get deceived. Look at everything. You happen not to feel very well . . . The door is open. One obol; jump inside. There is no affectation whatsoever, nor prattle, nor snap retorts. But immediately: the woman you want, the way you want. You exit. Tell her to go to hell – she's nothing to you.[61]

A final set of strategies is the most paradoxical, for it employs slaves for **expertise, trust and authority**. Slaves could possess forms of specialised expertise that

---

[53] Fischer 2010; Cohen 2013.

[54] Evans-Grubbs 1993; Parker 2007; Todd 2013.

[55] For Athenian concubinage, see Mossé 1991; for Roman concubinage, see McGinn 1991.

[56] Westbrook 1998.

[57] Wacke 2001. The Roman term *concubinae* encompassed relations beyond that between masters and slaves; see Sandon and Scalco 2020.

[58] Vlassopoulos 2018a.

[59] Fleming 1999; McGinn 2010; Glazebrook and Henry 2011; Cohen 2015; Levin-Richardson 2019.

[60] Harper 2013: 49.

[61] Philemon in *K-A*, fragment 3.

were important for slaveholding societies.[62] This was particularly important in cases where slaves originated from societies that were more complex and technologically advanced than the societies in which they ended up as slaves. In this way, they were a crucial medium of cultural and technological transfer across societies, as we shall see in Chapter 8; whether one thinks of the expertise of the enslaved doctors, technicians and authors from the Hellenistic eastern Mediterranean, who transformed republican Rome from a cultural backwater into an imperial centre,[63] or the enslaved Romans, who in their turn offered their invaluable expertise to German and Hunnic barbarian kingdoms in late antiquity,[64] slave experts played a crucial role in various periods of ancient history. But slaving for expertise was also important for processes of knowledge transmission within ancient societies. In the absence of institutionalised systems of intergenerational training and knowledge transmission like those of the medieval guilds, buying slaves and training them was a particularly efficient way of creating, maintaining and controlling a specialised workforce. While free trainees could move or become antagonists, trainers of slave experts could control them in a much more guaranteed way.[65]

Slaves were commonly employed as agents and managers. One particular reason for this apparently paradoxical choice again concerned control. Most ancient legal systems posed serious limits on the delegation of authority from one free person to another, in particular as regards distant commercial transactions. In many pre-industrial societies it was kinship and ethnic networks that provided sufficient trust for exercising such delegated functions.[66] Slaving offered another alternative; by having full control over those with delegated authority it was possible to control in the most flexible way how it would be exercised.[67] Furthermore, delegated agency allowed masters to avoid direct engagement with commercial activities and the everyday supervision of their economic portfolios. For the Roman senatorial aristocracy the employment of freed and slave agents was an ideal way of maintaining their exclusive engagement with highly valued pursuits, while also making great profits without direct involvement.[68]

Finally, there is slaving for the exercise of power and authority. This is undoubtedly the most paradoxical form of slaving: slaves were used as soldiers, bureaucrats and even rulers.[69] The use of slave soldiers was particularly common in Islamicate societies, as well as in many African societies:[70] the most famous examples are the Mamluks, who constituted the main military force of medieval and early modern Egypt.[71] Islamicate

---

[62] For a general survey, see Schumacher 2001a: 210–18; see also Christes 1979; Kudlien 1986; Deissler 2007; Blake 2013; Lenski 2019.

[63] Treggiari 1969: 110–42; Rawson 1985; Moatti 2015: 47–50.

[64] Lenski 2008, 2011b, 2014.

[65] Scheidel 2008; Hawkins 2016: 130–91; Porter 2019b.

[66] Terpstra 2019: 33–82.

[67] Aubert 1994; Carlsen 1995, 2013; Andreau 2004; Schumacher 2010; Tran 2013b.

[68] Mouritsen 2011a: 206–47; Verboven 2012.

[69] For the public slaves of Greek and Roman cities, see Jacob 1979; Eder 1980; Weiß 2004; Hunter 2006; Lenski 2006; Ismard 2017a. For imperial slaves and freedmen, see Chantraine 1967; Weaver 1972; Boulvert 1974. For the use of eunuchs in positions of authority, see Hopkins 1978: 172–96; Guyot 1980.

[70] Crone 1980; Pipes 1981; Miura and Philips 2000; Gordon 2001.

[71] Loiseau 2016.

and African societies also commonly used royal slaves as bureaucrats and administrators who effectively ran the state apparatus.[72] It is important to note that in many slave-holding societies such forms of slaving were unthinkable: the US South is an obvious example. In such cases, the prototypical conceptual system of slavery and its institution-alisation was so preponderant that the employment of slaves in positions that challenged the prototypes became impossible. The status dissonance of slaves employed in such positions would have been intolerable for such societies.[73] Accordingly, such forms of slaving enable us to explore important parameters of the history of ancient societies.[74] It is remarkable that Greek and Roman societies never accepted *in principle* the employment of slaves in armies;[75] the role of the warrior and soldier was considered as quintessentially linked with free status.[76] On the other hand, classical Athens employed hundreds of Scythian archers as policemen: why was it possible to conceive of the use of violence by slave policemen, but not by slave soldiers?[77]

More generally, Paulin Ismard has made the major argument that the public slaves of Greek poleis offer us a powerful window into the nature of Greek states. Anthropologists have explored how non-state societies develop a range of practices in order to avoid the development of the state as an independent power apparatus.[78] While the function of every complex community required certain kinds of knowledge, democracies like Athens conceived of politics as the exchange of information among equal citizens and refused to accord to experts a separate prominent position in their political institutions. The decision to turn over the administration of public affairs to public slaves had a double effect: on the one hand it made administration invisible in Greek conceptions of politics, and on the other, by entrusting administration to slaves, it guarded against the emergence of a state apparatus with its own interests and agendas. Judges, policemen and first-class civil servants are entrenched interest groups in modern societies, but the fact that their ancient equivalents were public slaves placed serious limits on their ability to act independently.[79] This is obviously an important topic in which future research can yield rich results.[80]

Let us now reach some conclusions. I have presented above an abstract typology of slaving strategies. For some societies and for certain periods it is possible to find all of the above strategies co-existing; for other societies and periods, only certain strategies might be present, while others might be completely missing. This is undoubtedly significant: we need to ask ourselves why certain societies developed the full range of slaving strategies and others, only a certain set. But even in those societies where the

---

[72] For royal slaves in African societies, see Stilwell 2000, 2004.

[73] For status dissonance, see Davies 2017.

[74] For a comparative exploration of slave soldiers, see Brown and Morgan 2006.

[75] Practice could be a rather different issue: see the evidence collected in Welwei 1974–88. The apologetic tone in which Suetonius discusses the military employment of manumitted slaves by Augustus is telling: *Life of Augustus* 25.

[76] For the link between freedom and military service in ancient Greek ideologies, see Hunt 1998.

[77] For the slave archers of Athens, see Tuci 2004; Bäbler 2005; Couvenhes 2012.

[78] Clastres 1987.

[79] Ismard 2017a; see also Yakobson 2011.

[80] See my comments in Vlassopoulos 2015–16: 156–60.

full range of slaving strategies is attested, it is highly unlikely that all of them appeared simultaneously. A history of ancient slaving should examine the particular trajectories through which specific slaving strategies entered and exited the slaving repertory of each ancient society.

This is important because the various slaving strategies could be co-existing and mutually reinforcing, but they could also be in contradiction with each other. Slaving for labour and slaving for gratification might be easily compatible, but that might not apply to slaving for revenue, expertise and authority. Slaving for revenue or for expertise and authority tended to create autonomous, resourceful and powerful slaves. It is of course possible that the existence of such slaves might have little effect on slaves employed for labour or gratification; after all, it was always possible for different slaves to spend their whole lives within one particular slaving strategy and consequently to be little affected by the conditions of slaves employed in other slaving strategies. Apollodoros once pointed out to the ex-slave Phormion that he was lucky because he had been bought by a banker who taught him the job and eventually gave him control of the bank; had he been bought by a cook or an artisan, his life as a slave would have been completely different.[81] Apollodoros' swipe would imply that slaves in Athens had few chances of moving from a slaving strategy that offered few opportunities to another one with more openings. But it was also possible for slaves to move between different slaving strategies; Palaemon, who started life as a home-born slave in Roman Italy, was originally trained as a weaver, but learned letters through accompanying his master's son to school and subsequently became a teacher and a grammarian.[82] The wider the range of slaving strategies, the more niches were available for slaves and the more opportunities existed to enhance their condition; in this respect, the role of gender in determining which slaves had such opportunities becomes particularly significant.[83]

It is also important to examine how different slaving strategies could be entangled. Above we have treated slaving strategies for labour and slaving strategies for revenue as if they were completely separate sets of strategies. While this was largely true for many slaves, we should also recognise that there was scope for the employment of practices that were typical of slaving strategies for revenue within slaving strategies for labour. Scholars who study New World slavery have been long familiar with the importance of such phenomena.[84] Jamaican plantations operated labour processes directly controlled by the masters in order to produce their major agricultural staples like sugar. At the same time, as regards the feeding of slaves, they often resorted to the 'slaves' economy', which took various forms. In some cases masters provided slaves with a part of their sustenance and offered slaves the opportunity to cultivate garden plots or tend flocks of animals in order to supplement the sustenance provided by the masters. In other cases masters eschewed completely the obligation to provide their slaves with

---

[81] Demosthenes, *Against Stephanos I* 71.
[82] Suetonius, *On grammarians* 23.
[83] On the impact of gender on slave life in antiquity, see Treggiari 1976; Tucker 1982; Roth 2004, 2007, 2016: 442; Perry 2013; Kamen 2014; Glazebrook 2014, 2017.
[84] Berlin and Morgan 1991, 1993.

food; slaves were given plots of land and days free from working for the masters, in order to produce their own full sustenance. It was often the case that slaves produced significant amounts of food that they were then allowed to sell in the market and kept the earnings. As a result, plantation slaves in Jamaica worked in directly controlled labour processes in order to produce agricultural staples for their masters, and in labour processes controlled by themselves in order to produce their sustenance.[85]

Ancient historians have so far generally ignored the existence of such complex phenomena in antiquity. But as Ulrike Roth has argued in a number of publications, such phenomena were clearly present on Roman agricultural estates.[86] Combining evidence from the agricultural writers, the jurists and the archaeological record, she has convincingly shown that some Roman agricultural slaves possessed their own flocks, whose products could be used to supplement the food rations provided by the masters; in certain cases it is also possible that slaves were given garden plots, or even plots of land from which they could derive their full sustenance. We also need to take into account two further factors stressed by Roth: supervision and slave families. Wherever there were resident masters or masters who worked alongside their slaves, it is reasonable to expect that slaves would work in labour processes directly controlled by their masters: slaves would largely tend to follow orders and receive rations for their sustenance. In the case of absentee masters, it was often the case that slaves would still have no control over their labour process, which would now be controlled by the overseers appointed by the masters, who were usually slaves.[87] The appointment of overseers would make sense for relatively large exploitations, but given the commonly encountered patterns of dispersed landholdings in many ancient societies, many farms of absentee landlords would only employ a few slaves. In such circumstances we should expect slaves who worked with minimal supervision and who largely resembled peasant cultivators. This is the situation portrayed in Longus' novel *Daphnis and Chloe*. The novel probably dates to the Roman imperial period, but is set in the countryside of the polis of Mytilene in Lesbos during the classical period. Daphnis and his slave parents cultivate the estate of their absentee master. Supervision takes place through the occasional visits of slaves from the urban base of the master; it is telling that the adolescent Daphnis has never set eyes on his master.[88]

This brings us to the significance of slave families – for the traditional image of Roman estates populated almost exclusively by male slaves working in chain gangs is deeply misleading.[89] A recently published inscription from fourth-century CE Thera records 152 slaves on the estates of a single owner, most of whom lived in family units.[90] It would of course be wrong to assume that this example should be extrapolated across the various areas of the early and late Roman Empire; but we should now seriously consider the implications of a model in which significant numbers of rural

---

[85] Mintz 1974; Barickman 1994; Pargas 2006.
[86] Roth 2005, 2007, 2016a.
[87] For free bailiffs, see Scheidel 1990; see also the discussion in Carlsen 2013: 87–108.
[88] Longus, *Daphnis and Chloe* 4.1–9.
[89] Roth 2007, 2011.
[90] *SEG* LV, 915; see Harper 2008.

slaves on small farms and large estates lived in family units. This would have serious implications for the organisation of labour activities in estates, as well as for the experience of slavery in the rural world.[91]

These findings have major implications for the wider metanarrative of ancient slaving. Traditionally, ancient and medieval historians posited a transition period in late antiquity and the early Middle Ages in which slaves stopped working in chain gangs, as they presumably did on republican and early imperial latifundia, and became *servi casati*, hutted slaves who cultivated the land on their own and surrendered part of their produce to their master, thus gradually turning into serfs. As we saw above, slaves living in families, possessing their own agricultural *peculia* and working the land with minimal supervision were clearly present during the early imperial period. Although it would still be possible to argue for a major historical transformation in terms of the scale and ubiquity of such phenomena in the early Middle Ages, it should be obvious that their significance for the whole of classical antiquity needs to be examined anew. As we shall also see in Chapter 8, we should avoid the mistake of identifying as serfs slaves who cultivated the land on their own. The existence and scale of such phenomena will depend on cycles of intensification and abatement, as well as on the distinct and interacting processes that created the divergent epichoric systems of ancient slaving.

We should also take into account that the successful implementation of slaving strategies created winners and losers: the use of slaving for prestige enabled certain masters to increase their prestige in comparison with other masters or free people who did not possess any slaves. Lesser masters and free people without slaves might be able to circumscribe slaving for prestige in order to limit its adverse effects on their own prestige. The creation of autonomous, resourceful and powerful slaves by slaving for revenue or authority might create serious conflicts with poor free people, who could find themselves in worse conditions than those slaves. Hence the significance of the dialectical relationship between free and slave and the intervention of the political community in the relationship between masters and slaves and the slaving strategies employed by masters, as we shall explore in detail in Chapter 6.[92]

Furthermore, the prominence of certain strategies might forestall the emergence of other strategies or limit their employment. The supply of slaves was not usually unlimited; using slaves for one particular strategy could often mean that they were not available for employment in other strategies. Slave prices might also have serious implications for which slaving strategies were feasible or prioritised.[93] It is logical to assume that the higher the level of slave prices, the more limited the range of slaving strategies would be, and vice versa. But we should avoid easy assumptions about which particular slaving practices would be prioritised by high or low slave prices. In societies where prestige and gratification were particularly important as slaving strategies, high slave prices might prioritise their employment for these social ends. Among the hunter-gatherers of the Pacific Northwest, who had relatively limited

---

[91]  Roth 2016: 442–7.
[92]  For these issues, see the comments of Miller 2008.
[93]  Scheidel 2005a, 2008.

economic complexity and inequality, slavery was crucial primarily because it enabled a distinction between the mass of commoners and the leisured elite; slaving for leisure was therefore crucial and predominant in such societies.[94] This is a major reason why slaving in many societies was primarily geared towards the acquisition of women, who could best fulfil the roles of gratification and the provision of leisure.[95] In other societies, where slaves were expensive, like in ancient Mesopotamia, they could be employed primarily in positions of expertise and authority.[96]

People might employ slaves as one option among many in order to fulfil certain aims: one could cultivate the land with one's slaves, hire workers or lease it to share-croppers.[97] But sometimes such slaving strategies solidified into distinctive **lifestyles**: not merely one strategy among many, but a particular way of living. In such cases the employment of slaves was not one option among many, but a necessary element of this way of living. Furthermore, while slaving strategies might be available to a significant part of the population in various societies, slaving lifestyles were usually available to the privileged few. Finally, while certain slaving strategies produced equivalent life-styles, this by no means applied to all strategies, as we shall see.

The slaving strategy for leisure could produce the lifestyle of a leisure class of gen-tlemen who delegated drudgery to slaves in order to engage solely with honourable and pleasure-bringing activities.[98] The slaving strategy for wealth could produce the lifestyle of the planter: the master of an operation which was both an extended patri-archal household and a means of generating fabulous wealth.[99] The slaving strategy for expertise, trust and authority could produce the lifestyle of the lord, who used slaves (soldiers, attendants, agents) in order to exercise power over the rest of his commu-nity.[100] It is significant that the slaving strategies for revenue and gratification do not seem to produce equivalent lifestyles; but we should not make the mistake of assum-ing that if a slaving strategy did not produce an equivalent lifestyle, its importance was limited. We rather need to think carefully about the processes that solidified certain slaving strategies into slaving lifestyles.

The lifestyles of the leisured man, the planter and the lord could be joined together, as in certain African societies, or kept apart.[101] There is no doubt that the lifestyle of the leisured gentleman is widely attested in many ancient societies; in fact, what seems peculiar about Greek and Roman societies is the extent to which this lifestyle became an achievable aspiration for wider sections of society, beyond the tiny elites of wealth and power. In fact, in societies like Sparta this lifestyle was extended to the whole citi-zen population, which became leisured gentlemen, while all labour was undertaken by the helots.[102] It could be potentially argued that the lifestyle of the planter can also

---

[94] Donald 1997.
[95] For the link between gender and slave prices, see Harper 2010a.
[96] Dandamaev 1984; Head 2010; Richardson 2019.
[97] See, for example, Menander, *The difficult man*, 327–32; Vlassopoulos 2016c.
[98] For the lifestyle of the leisured gentleman, see Veblen 2007 [1899]; Daloz 2009.
[99] For the lifestyle of the planter, see Oakes 1982; Bowman 1993; Dal Lago 2005; Burnard 2015.
[100] For the lifestyle of the lord, see Meillassoux 1991: 141–200.
[101] Stilwell 2014: 89–175.
[102] Lewis 2018: 125–46.

be attested with the emergence of villa systems across the late republican and early imperial Mediterranean, although whether this is actually true would require further study: is there really an ancient equivalent to the early modern planter?[103] Finally, certain aspects of the lifestyle of the lord can also be attested in the Near Eastern and Roman worlds, though not to the full extent that they are attested in African societies, for example.[104]

We need more focused work on how slaving lifestyles emerged in ancient societies and whether some of them were occasionally or regularly combined, or remained separate.[105] But the concept of the slaving lifestyle enables us to distinguish between issues which are usually confused in general discussions of ancient slavery. Ancient historians tend to focus on the slaving strategy for producing wealth as the distinguishing characteristic of ancient 'slave societies'; but did this slaving strategy produce its own lifestyle, as in the case of the planters of New World slavery? And should we not distinguish between the slaving strategy for wealth and the significance of the slaving lifestyle of the leisured gentleman, which was produced by the slaving strategy for maintenance? It is telling that whenever ancient authors think of primitive or utopian societies where slavery was absent, it was primarily the absence of slaving for leisure that captivated their imagination, rather than other slaving strategies.[106]

## Slaving Contexts

Our next step is to distinguish a number of discrete contexts of slaving: the household, the political community, the wider world and large-scale economic operations.[107] The first three occur in all slaveholding societies; the last is only present in certain societies. None of these contexts relates solely to slavery; each context also engages a large numbers of factors that can be completely unrelated to slavery. While the slaving strategies and the dialectical relationships of slavery we will examine in Chapter 6 are factors which are peculiar to slavery, the contexts of slaving present us with major factors that are relatively independent and follow trajectories of their own. The paradox is that the history of slavery involves both factors peculiar to slavery and factors that shape slavery while following their own paths.

The first context is that of the **household**. For human history before the last two centuries, the household, by closely linking production and reproduction, has provided the context of most human activities. Most slaves have been part of households;[108] accordingly, the divergent shape and aims of households within a single society, or between different societies or periods, has a significant impact on

---

[103] See the Mediterranean-wide overview of villas in Marzano and Métraux 2018.

[104] MacMullen 1990: 190–7; Lenski 2009; Baker 2017; López Barja de Quiroga 2020.

[105] The best current comparative analysis of slaving in ancient societies is Lewis 2018.

[106] Athenaeus, *Deipnosophists* 6.263b–d, 267e–f; cf. Aristophanes, *Wealth* 510–26; for the cultural and political significance of slaving for leisure, see Osborne 1995.

[107] I have modified the terminology employed in Vlassopoulos 2016a in order to make it less ambiguous; the substance of the argument remains the same.

[108] Flory 1978; Saller 1994; Moggi and Cordiano 1997; Culbertson 2011.

slaves and slavery.[109] One important axis is the extent to which household heads had free rein to pursue their aims, or were limited by countervailing tendencies and factors. Were household heads allowed to marry, recognise as heirs and bequeath their property to whomever they wanted, or were there rules that imposed, prohibited or prioritised particular courses of action?[110]

In societies which allowed household heads to do as they saw fit – the ancient Near East, for example – they could marry their slaves, recognise their slave offspring as legitimate children and bequeath their property to enslaved spouses or to the offspring of those relations.[111] In the society represented by Homer, the head of the household could decide whether to recognise his slave offspring and whether to treat them the same as the rest of his children.[112] It was social relations between people that determined who got married to whom, rather than general legal rules that restricted marriage and legitimate offspring to the free. Marriage between free people was not the sole way of acquiring legitimate children; there was greater scope for sexual and familial relationships between masters and slaves, as the offspring of such relationships could become full members of the community. In societies where political communities imposed a high rate of prescription, like classical Athens, slaves were excluded as potential marriage partners, and the offspring of such relationships would remain slaves or would not be recognised as legitimate heirs.[113]

This leads us to the form of marriage and the aims and purposes it served in different societies. Many ancient societies either fully recognised polygyny or enabled males to take a second wife under certain conditions, such as the first wife being sterile.[114] Greek and Roman households were fundamentally shaped by their peculiar obligatory monogamy, a rare phenomenon in global history.[115] We can distinguish in this respect between two different aspects: marriage as a form of procuring legitimate heirs, and marriage as a means of creating alliances between families and kinship groups.[116] In certain societies, like classical Athens, marriage constituted the main system through which the head of the household could procure legitimate heirs; children born out of wedlock could not be legally recognised as legitimate, irrespective of the wishes of the head of household. In other cases, like, for instance, Islamicate societies, the procurement of legitimate heirs did not require marriage to free women. Free males could marry free or slave women; masters could not marry their own slaves unless they manumitted them, but they could marry slaves belonging to other people. Masters could also procure legitimate children from their own female slaves. Once a slave concubine (*umm walad*)

[109] For comparative perspectives on households, see Thompson, Thirsk and Goody 1976; Wall, Hareven and Ehmer 2001. For households and families in antiquity, see Rawson 2011; Laurence and Strömberg 2012; Huebner 2013.

[110] Goody 1969; Thomas 1984.

[111] For the household model in Near Eastern societies, see Schloen 2001; Marti 2014.

[112] Homer, *Odyssey* 14.199–213.

[113] For the distinction between open and closed slave systems in regard to marriage and kinship, see Watson 1980b.

[114] For polygyny in ancient societies, see Friedl 2000; Testart and Brunaux 2004.

[115] Scheidel 2009, 2011.

[116] Roubineau 2015: 55–62.

gave birth to a child recognised by her master as his own, she could no longer be sold and automatically gained her freedom upon the master's death.[117] To generalise, certain societies recognised only marriage with free people as a means of procuring legitimate heirs; others recognised mixed marriages between free and slave; finally, many societies did not require marriage as a means of procuring legitimate heirs, and some of them even put a premium on the acquisition of female slaves in order to procure more children. Such differences had obvious consequences for the formation and reproduction of ancient households and the role of slaves; future work will need to examine such differences systematically, as well as provide historical explanations for such phenomena.

Finally, we need to pay attention to the set of traditions and assumptions that shaped the forms of productive and reproductive labour within the household. Gender assumptions often determined what kind of labour slaves performed, but gender often affected slaves differently from free people.[118] Where gender assumptions dictated that agricultural work was performed by the female members of the household, male slaves found themselves working in the fields alongside women, while in New World societies, where agriculture was a male task, female slaves often worked on plantations alongside men.[119] The nexus between gender norms, forms of childcare and forms of female labour that were compatible with them shaped how female slaves were employed in ancient households.[120] Slaving strategies pursued within households have already being explored above, and are also explored in Chapter 6.

The second slaving context is that of the **political community**: it concerns the multiple ways in which the forms, aims and processes of communities shaped slaving within them. The form of the community affected whether any of their members could be enslaved. Many communities accepted that enslavement could be a justified result of moral failure by their members or imposed as punishment for egregious crimes and when people failed to pay fines or debts.[121] In other communities internal enslavement was possible because householders were allowed to deal with household members as they saw fit: child exposure and the sale of family members were legitimate practices.[122] But some communities decided that communal solidarity necessitated the abolition or limitation of debt-bondage and debt-slavery (Biblical Israel, Solonian Athens, republican Rome);[123] some came to perceive a general state of freedom as pertaining to everybody who was a non-slave, and attached certain entitlements as inherent to this state, which free people could not lose or shed. This is an issue that we will examine in detail in Chapter 6.

---

[117]  Ali 2010.
[118]  On gender norms and female labour, see Dixon 2004; Harris 2014.
[119]  For the New World, see Morgan 2004. For antiquity, see Roubineau 2015: 62–9; Glazebrook 2017.
[120]  Roth 2007.
[121]  Westbrook 1995; Rio 2015a.
[122]  Oppenheim 1955; Zaccagnini 1995; Hellie 1982; Rio 2011.
[123]  For Israel and the Levant, see Chirichigno 1993; Westbrook and Jasnow 2001; Lemaire 2015. For Athens, see Harris 2002a; Lewis 2017c. For Rome, see Kleijwegt 2013; Lerouxel 2015; Bernard 2016; Pottage 2020.

The social imaginaries of political communities had a major impact on slaving; this concerned how the radial conceptual system of slavery and the various modalities of slavery (Chapters 3 and 7) operated in each society. In communities that made kinship their major organising principle, it served both to exclude slaves as natally alienated outsiders and also to provide a means of gradually incorporating them within the community.[124] Other communities included slavery within wider systems of classification: in China slaves were included in the wider category of debased people, which included convicts and people performing defiling services,[125] while in Thailand slaves were included (alongside beggars and the destitute) in the *sakdina* system of merit that classified the whole population.[126] In medieval Europe a classification based on the status distinction free–slave was accompanied by a tripartite classification on the basis of social functions (priests, warriors, peasants). The co-existence of the two systems could be used in order to tar as servile all those performing agricultural labour; on the other hand, the theoretical reciprocity of the tripartite system could be successfully employed in order to challenge the servility of the peasants.[127]

Other communities turned asymmetric relationships of reciprocity like clientship into the focus of their social imaginary, providing a model which assimilated the relationship between master and slave to that of patron and client.[128] In many Southeast Asian communities the legal status of slaves was rarely delimited: slaves were largely conceived as one group among the various dependants of a powerful lord; what mattered was the power of the lord and the form of the relationship, rather than the legal status as such.[129] A comprehensive study of how political communities in antiquity shaped and employed the various modalities of slavery is an urgent desideratum of future work. In this respect, it is worth highlighting the peculiar case of ancient Egypt, where slavery was not legally codified in its definitional or prototypical forms but was shaped by the wider modalities of hierarchy, service and domination.[130]

Equally significant are the means through which communities establish order. We can trace a spectrum ranging from the settling of disputes through appeal to oral norms and mediation all the way to the establishment of a formal and distinct judicial apparatus enforcing a code of written laws.[131] In communities based on norms, slave status might be informal and imprecise in terms of everyday life: for second-generation slaves who were born into the community, had an important master or had amassed some wealth and network links these factors might be more important in terms of settling disputes than their slave status. Communities with formal systems tended to create clear-cut distinctions of status and their formalised institutions tended to exclude slaves. But at the same time formal systems could also create new institutionalised opportunities for slaves, like the Roman institution of the *peculium*,

---

[124] Miers and Kopytoff 1977.
[125] Hansson 1996: 29–54; Crossley 2011: 188–91.
[126] Turton 1980; Nunbhakdi 1998.
[127] Freedman 1999; Arnoux 2012.
[128] Glassman 1991; for patronage and slavery in Rome, see López Barja de Quiroga 2020.
[129] Reid 1983.
[130] Loprieno 1997, 2012; Hofmann 2005.
[131] Pirie 2013: 26–51.

which allowed slaves to engage in legally enforced contracts and obligations, or the legally enforced slave rights of *coartación* and *papel* in Latin America, which we shall examine in Chapter 6.[132] Formalised legal systems might also provide institutional avenues for redressing slave grievances: a significant number of late Roman laws consisted of reactions by the Roman authorities to formal appeals by free and enslaved people to address issues of status and other concerns.[133]

The third context is that of the **wider world**; by this I refer to the systems of political, military, economic and cultural interactions that reached beyond the borders of individual communities and linked them together in various ways.[134] The majority of slaves in global history have been produced through warfare, raiding and international trade. This means that slavery was directly inscribed in the changing history of the forms of warfare, predation, exchange and state- and empire-building that linked together communities into wider systems of international relations. We shall explore these issues in detail in the last section of this chapter. For the time being, a key concept for understanding the impact of the wider world on slaving is that of slaving zones and no-slaving zones (defined above, p. 44).[135] Slaving zones were the geographical zones from which a particular community drew its slaves; no-slaving zones were geographical zones whose inhabitants were not enslaveable from the point of view of a particular community. We can further distinguish between perfect no-slaving zones, within which no free person could be enslaved, and imperfect no-slaving zones, in which enslaveability was limited in varying degrees.

As we have seen above, many political communities allowed their members to become enslaved for debts or as a penalty; the slaving zones of such communities included their own members. But many other communities took measures to ensure that their own members were not enslaveable, and their own slaving zones were exclusively oriented towards the exterior. In externally oriented slaving zones it becomes crucial to know whether there were particular criteria about which persons are enslaveable, or anybody was fair game. If there were no specific criteria, then it was possible that the slaving zones of different communities would be overlapping. In the Greek interstate world of the archaic, classical and Hellenistic periods, everyone was potentially enslaveable. A characteristic example is the travails in the fourth century BCE of the Athenian Nikostratos, who went to recover three slaves who had escaped from his farm, was captured and sold in the neighbouring island of Aegina as a slave but was redeemed by his relatives and returned back to Athens and freedom.[136] A master and enslaver could relatively easily become enslaved in his turn.

But gradually, political and ideological processes started to create extensive no-slaving zones. Political consolidation and the expansion of empires was a main force

---

[132]  See de la Fuente 2007; Geary and Vlassopoulos 2009; de la Fuente and Gross 2020.

[133]  For status disputes and the Roman legal system, see Evans-Grubbs 2000, 2013; Söllner 2000; Connolly 2004–5; 2010.

[134]  Vlassopoulos 2007b: 143–202.

[135]  Fynn-Paul 2009; Fynn-Paul and Pargas 2018.

[136]  Ps.-Demosthenes, *Against Nikostratos* 6–8; Sosin 2017; see also Parmenter 2020 for similar processes in the Black Sea.

for the emergence of no-slaving zones. The unification of southern Mesopotamia into the Babylonian state in the course of the second millennium BCE meant that only people outside this area were enslaveable in Babylonia.[137] Other forms of political consolidation, like the Achaemenid Empire, do not seem to have enforced a no-slaving zone for their inhabitants. We find plenty of Anatolian and Syrian subjects of the Achaemenid Empire as slaves in Greece or Egypt, and they are highly unlikely to have been captured by Greek or Egyptian armies; consequently, we have to assume that these people became slaves as a result of various slave-making processes that took place within the Achaemenid Empire, like warfare, banditry or self-sale.[138] On the other hand, we come across cases like the Ptolemaic Empire, which took measures to prohibit the enslavement of its Syrian subjects; but it is telling that those measures aimed at limiting the enslavement of subjects by private citizens, while accepting as legitimate the enslavement of subjects by public authorities for reasons like debt to the state.[139] In other words, the Ptolemaic Empire is an example of an imperfect no-slaving zone, within which enslavement was limited in certain respects but by no means completely eliminated.

The expansion of the Roman Empire across the Mediterranean, the Black Sea and temperate Europe from the republican period onwards created the largest no-slaving zone in world history until then. Consequently, it offers a good example of discussing the various elements of imperial no-slaving zones. The Roman Empire was of course an imperfect no-slaving zone.[140] Although Roman citizens were normally not enslaveable within the empire, there still existed certain exceptions: lower-class people convicted of serious crimes became penal slaves, while free women who married slaves against the will of their masters could become slaves.[141] Until 212 CE the Roman Empire also included a large number of communities whose members were not Roman citizens; these communities had their own rules regarding enslavement, and in some of them the enslavement of their members was legitimate.[142]

But an important way in which the Roman Empire constituted a major no-slaving zone resulted from the outcome of wider processes rather than legal prescription. The Roman Empire could be compatible with widespread violence and enslavement of its subjects, as was the case, for example, during the period of the Roman Revolution between the 130s and the 30s BCE; but, as Tim Cornell has shown, this was accompanied by a gradual process in which many areas which were originally war zones ultimately became provinces with no military presence or only low-level military activities.[143] People in the peripheral areas of the empire could of course be part of the slaving zones of barbarian communities outside the empire, and some of them were

---

[137] Van Koppen 2004.
[138] Lewis 2011, 2015.
[139] *SB* V, 8008, 33–61; see Bieżuńska-Małowist 1974: 10–39; Scholl 1990: 16–27.
[140] See the discussion in Glancy 2018.
[141] For penal slavery, see Millar 1984; McClintock 2010. For women enslaved according to the SC Claudianum, see Harper 2010b. For forms of enslavement in the Roman Empire, see Wieling 1999: 1–30.
[142] Harris 1994, 1999; cf. Silver 2011.
[143] Cornell 1993.

indeed enslaved.[144] But inhabitants of the core areas of the empire became part of a no-slaving zone during the early imperial period as a result of the *pax Romana*. This was undoubtedly an imperfect no-slaving zone; even during the early imperial period, revolts or civil wars could lead to the enslavement of the defeated, as was the case with the Jewish rebels in the first and second centuries CE.[145] But it would be wrong not to recognise the significant impact that the Roman Empire had in creating in practice an imperfect no-slaving zone in many areas around the Mediterranean in the early imperial period. Finally, it is important to stress that imperial no-slaving zones could diminish or collapse: this is what happened to an important extent in late antiquity,[146] as the emergence of barbarian kingdoms within the former imperial territories made large segments of the population again part of various overlapping slaving zones.[147]

Ideology played an equally important role in regard to no-slaving zones. Already from the classical period there is an attested predilection against enslaving fellow Greeks.[148] This predilection never became international law, and the cases in which Greek states enslaved the inhabitants of other Greek communities are undoubtedly numerous.[149] The ideology mattered, though, for a variety of reasons. On the one hand, it facilitated the creation of ransoming mechanisms through private initiative or bilateral treaties that limited the enslavement of fellow Greeks or the trade in Greek captives.[150] On the other hand, the enslavement of the inhabitants of Greek communities was considered an extraordinary measure, justified only in particular circumstances.[151] It is not accidental that captivity and the enslavement of the defeated opponents is effectively absent from Greek iconography, while it constitutes such a major aspect in the iconography of imperial states like those of Assyria and Rome.[152] Given that Greek warfare overwhelmingly consisted of wars among Greek communities, captivity and the enslavement of enemies was not seen as a legitimate means of celebrating military success. In any case, the ways in which ethnic and cultural identities affected the creation of no-slaving zones in antiquity will require further study.

Undoubtedly, though, of even larger significance was the emergence and expansion of monotheistic religions in the course of the first millennium CE. Monotheistic religions created new kinds of ideological and ultimately political communities in which slaves were in theory equal members with the free.[153] This was potentially a revolutionary change, but for centuries after its emergence, Christianity was content with the enslavement of Christians by their fellow co-religionists.[154] On the other

---

[144] Lenski 2008.

[145] Josephus, *The Jewish War* 6.414–20; Bradley 2004.

[146] The collapse of the no-slaving zone of a Roman province in late antiquity is described in Augustine, *New Letters* 10; see Lepelley 1981; Rouge 1983; Szidat 1985; Harper 2011: 92–5.

[147] Lenski 2014; for early modern African examples of the collapse of no-slaving zones, Thornton 2018.

[148] Garlan 1987; Klees 1998: 19–60.

[149] See the material collected in Volkmann 1961; Pritchett 1991: 203–312; see also Gaca 2010.

[150] Ducrey 1968, 1999; Bielman 1994; Rigsby 1997; Gabrielsen 2003.

[151] See, for example, the apologetic account of Polybius in regard to the enslavement of Mantineia by the Achaean League in 223 BCE: *History* 2.58.8–13: Texier 1979; Nicholson 2018.

[152] de Souza 2011.

[153] But see Glancy 1998 on the obstacles slaves faced for participating in Christian communities.

[154] See Harper 2016.

hand, Islamicate societies were adamant from the very beginning about the creation of no-slaving zones for all Muslims and the members of other religious groups which had submitted to Islamic authorities.[155] Finally, around 1000 CE Catholic and Orthodox Christians came to accept the principle of no-slaving zones for co-religionists, even if the question of who exactly constituted a co-religionist was debatable.[156] This was a revolutionary change in the history of global slaving: by 1200 CE Christianity and Islam had created 'perfect' no-slaving zones in wide swathes of Eurasia.[157]

It is obvious, therefore, that there was no automatic process that led from the emergence of monotheistic religions to the creation of huge religion-based no-slaving zones. The historical conjunctures that led to these developments are little studied yet. As Jennifer Glancy has suggested, one of the reasons that led Christians to question the enslavement of fellow Christians might have less to do with the principles of Christian religious ideology per se, and more with the clash with other religious groups. While Christians were content with the enslavement of co-religionists, they were increasingly unhappy about non-Christians, like the Jews, holding Christian slaves.[158] This concern could have gradually paved the way for the prohibition of the enslavement of co-religionists. Future work will have to explore the various processes that ultimately led to such momentous changes, while also taking into account the role of slave agency in these processes.[159]

The two sides of the coin were joined: the expansion of no-slaving zones in certain areas meant the expansion and intensification of slave-making zones in other areas. As we saw in Chapter 2, Americanists and Africanists have gradually moved to a consensus that it is impossible to study early modern slavery outside the framework of the creation of the Atlantic world and its imperial systems, networks of trade, and diasporas. Slavery in the US South, among Native Americans in the Great Lakes and in the kingdom of Congo were not separate species, but slaving practices that became entangled and interdependent (we might say interbred) in the process of the creation of the Atlantic world.[160] Similar approaches have now become commonplace as regards the modern Indian Ocean,[161] and more tentatively as regards the medieval Mediterranean.[162] What is now needed is a similar approach that will explore how the wider world in antiquity interlinked the slaving strategies of different ancient societies, as we shall see in Chapter 9.[163]

While households, communities and the wider world are contexts universally encountered in world history, the fourth context of **large-scale economic operations** is more restricted in time and space.[164] This context involves societies with

---

[155]  Freamon 2019.
[156]  Barker 2018.
[157]  Fynn-Paul 2009; Gillingham 2012.
[158]  Glancy 2018.
[159]  See, for example, the case of the Christian slaves of Jewish masters in the *Theodosian Code* 16.9.3.
[160]  Thornton 1998; Eltis 2000; Gallay 2009.
[161]  Campbell 2004.
[162]  Rotman 2009.
[163]  For a first step in this direction, see Lewis 2018: 274–90.
[164]  Cf. Zeuske 2013: 139–49, 298–381.

deep inequalities in wealth and power, in which the economic strategies usually pursued within households were expanded and transformed into large-scale operations employing hundreds or even thousands, like the portfolios of a Mesopotamian temple, a large estate, a factory. The New World slave plantations are characteristic examples of this context; but the urban households of elite Romans with hundreds of slaves, or the large workshops of classical Athens, are equally relevant. Many of these operations maintained the organisational form of the household, but their scale and complexity made them clearly distinguishable from ordinary households; other large-scale economic operations, like the thousands of slaves in the Athenian silver mines, were not organised as households.[165]

Modern historians have examined the link between large-scale economic operations and New World slavery with great detail and sophistication. They have explored the commodity chains in sugar, tobacco, cotton and coffee that linked together the early modern Atlantic economies;[166] the division of labour and technological organisation of plantations;[167] the triangular economy between Europe, Africa and the Americas in the early modern period;[168] the links between the various assets and forms of capital that were involved in slaving within large-scale economic operations.[169] And while there is no doubt that early modern large-scale economic operations involved diverse complex processes, there is little doubt nowadays that the concept of capitalism will be crucial for understanding them.[170]

In comparison to the study of early modern large-scale economic operations, ancient historians are currently little prepared to tackle its ancient forms. While some ancient historians are happy to use the term capitalism to study ancient large-scale economic operations,[171] there is no effort so far to engage with current historical debates about early modern capitalism or to define what is meant by the term.[172] John Clegg has recently argued that what made early modern slavery capitalist was dependence on the market for all the various production factors. Early modern planters depended on capital markets for funding the acquisition of plantations and their equipment, labour force and provisions; they also depended on international commercial markets for selling their products and making profits that would enable them to finance their debts and avoid foreclosure.[173]

It is highly doubtful that this total market dependence is particularly relevant for ancient large-scale economic operations. Markets were undoubtedly important for ancient large-scale economic operations, but total market dependence was probably quite limited. Even the great Roman landowners, who were clearly geared towards large-scale commercial production, were not totally dependent on markets for the

---

[165] Lauffer 1956; Rihll 2010.
[166] Mintz 1986; Schwartz 2004; van Norman 2013; Beckert 2015.
[167] Curtin 1998; Newman 2013; Burnard 2015.
[168] De Zwart and van Zanden 2018.
[169] Tomich 2004; Johnson 2009, 2013; Schermerhorn 2015.
[170] Beckert and Rockman 2016.
[171] Harper 2011: 60–6; Bresson 2014.
[172] But see Banaji 2016.
[173] Clegg 2015.

various factors.[174] This means that we need to create an alternative conceptual framework; this framework should avoid importing into ancient economic history implicit assumptions from how markets operate in early modern and modern economies, while also recognising the significance of markets for ancient large-scale economic operations and slaving.[175] We also need to explore further the products and their commodity chains that fuelled ancient large-scale economic operations and slaving. While psychotropic substances like coffee and tobacco and other goods like sugar were clearly constitutive of early modern slaving and large-scale economic operations,[176] the extent to which the same applies to ancient large-scale economic operations requires discussion. Ancient wine is certainly relevant in this respect, but we also need to explore the major differences between wine and early modern psychotropic substances.[177]

Finally, in order to understand ancient large-scale economic operations we need further work on divisions of labour.[178] In the case of certain products like sugar, the investments involved in building and equipping mills and the labour requirements of processing the product made large-scale operations essentially a highly cost-effective solution.[179] Does the same apply to ancient estates cultivating products like grain, wine and oil? And if not, were there really as many large-scale operations as we tend to think? What were the reasons for those large-scale operations that really existed? Was there a division of labour in the Athenian shoe-making workshop that employed ten slaves,[180] or the shield-making workshop that employed tens of slaves?[181] Or did all these slaves merely replicate multiple times the activities that would be undertaken by one or a few persons in a simple workshop? Without further work into such questions, our understanding of ancient large-scale economic operations will remain distinctly limited.[182]

## Slave-making

Slaving contexts and slaving strategies were interlinked in various ways. I will focus on one particular process in which they were entangled: that of slave-making.[183] This is an area where the experience of New World slavery has had very problematic effects on

---

[174] For export markets and the expansion of slavery in the Roman world, see the classic Giardina and Schiavone 1981.

[175] For a start, see Bang 2008; Harris, Lewis and Woolmer 2015.

[176] De Zwart and van Zanden 2018; see also Mintz 1986 on sugar and slavery.

[177] For ancient wine, see Purcell 1985; Tchernia 1986; Brun 2003; Fentress and Maiuro 2011. For wine exports and slavery in the case of late republican Gaul, see Laubenheimer 2013; Tchernia 2016: 86–92; Fentress 2019.

[178] For classical Athens, see Harris 2002b. For Rome, see Hawkins 2016; Groen-Vallinga 2017. For a wider perspective, see Persson 1988.

[179] Schwartz 1985.

[180] Aeschines, *Against Timarchos* 97.

[181] Lysias, *Against Eratosthenes* 8.

[182] Harris 1980b; Acton 2014; Porter 2019b.

[183] For a general comparative account, see Zeuske 2013: 261–97; for the representation of these processes in Greek and Roman thought, see Mélèze-Modrzejewski 1976; Wieling 1999. The best current analysis for this process in the eastern Mediterranean is Lewis 2018: 269–94.

the study of other slaveries. New World slavery was exceptional globally, because the provision of slaves to New World societies was almost exclusively through the slave trade. There are admittedly some exceptions to this rule, as regards, for example, the early attempts to enslave Native American groups through warfare and brigandage. But these were relatively minor contributions compared to the fact that New World societies acquired the vast majority of their slaves by buying them from various African communities. In most cases, slave-making was undertaken by African communities and slaving entrepreneurs, and European and American traders only bought the end product of processes they cared little about.[184] As a result, until fairly recently the slave trade was examined separately from the slave-making processes of African history, while African history was considered as essentially geared towards slave-making.[185] Over the last few decades, though, scholars have increasingly realised that African slave-making was only one particular outcome of various processes of African history which need to be examined on their own terms.[186]

In the case of ancient slave-making, though, the New World model is deeply misleading. There is no doubt that the slave trade was important, but equally important were processes of warfare, state-making, piracy and ethnic construction. This wider framework of analysis is necessary for the study of the processes of slave-making in antiquity.[187] A first process concerns the formation of slave communities we will examine in Chapter 6. Until fairly recently, the natural reproduction of slave populations was considered effectively impossible, and accordingly the familial and sexual relationships involving slaves and other people were little explored. US slavery, where slaves reproduced naturally after 1750 CE, was considered exceptional; but the study of the demography of US slavery, as well as the demography of other slave systems, has revealed that under certain conditions the natural reproduction of slave populations was perfectly feasible.[188] Furthermore, a priori reasoning has shown that natural reproduction could have played a very significant role in Roman slavery.[189] Given the large size of the slave population of the Roman Empire in the early imperial period and the low population density of the barbarian areas outside the empire, it would have been practically impossible for the Romans to renew their slaves primarily through enslaving or trading the inhabitants of the areas outside the empire, as this would have depleted these areas of any people within a short period of time. Accordingly, natural reproduction must have played a significant role in Roman slavery, the consequences of which we shall examine later.[190] To what extent this model might also apply to other slaveholding societies in antiquity is subject to debate.[191]

---

[184] Pétré-Grenouilleau 2004: 25–7; Grenouilleau 2014: 322–4.
[185] Lovejoy 2012.
[186] Thornton 1998; Heywood and Thornton 2007.
[187] For a comparative perspective, see Patterson 1982: 105–71.
[188] Bergad 2007: 96–131; Klein 2010: 162–87.
[189] Scheidel 1997.
[190] For Roman house-born slaves, see Herrmann-Otto 1994. But see also the arguments of Bruun 2013.
[191] Vlassopoulos 2010, 2015b examine how slave names can be used to study the significance of reproduction for slavery in classical Athens; but see also Schmitz 2012.

The second process involved forms of slave-making within ancient societies. Historically, the four most significant were self-sale, enslavement for debt, penal slavery and the enslavement of abandoned infants.[192] The study of these processes in Greek and Roman societies faces particular challenges. As we have seen above, certain political communities in antiquity took measures to abolish or discourage internal processes of slave-making like enslavement for debt or self-sale. Penal slavery was limited in Greek societies,[193] while the Romans conceptualised penal slavery in different ways than other forms of slavery.[194] There are good reasons, therefore, to believe that these processes of slave-making were significantly less important in antiquity compared, for example, with the early Middle Ages.[195] Nevertheless, the nature of our sources and the discourses that dominate them might be rather misleading.[196] Greek and Roman societies conceived freedom as a total and unalterable status, as we shall see in Chapter 6. Accordingly, they tended to leave outside their purview or keep silent about practices that challenged this conception of freedom. A careful study of the sources, though, can reveal that there were quite a number of people who would sell themselves or their children into slavery, while the abandonment of infants was also a major source for slaves.[197] The attempt of the Roman state to legislate on such issues in late antiquity makes the issue for the first time visible on a large scale in our sources; but we should not be misled into thinking that this is evidence of the marginality of such phenomena in earlier periods.[198]

The third process concerns the various forms of violence through which people were turned into chattels. I will start by pointing out that violence produces captives; in other words, violent slave-making must be approached within the wider phenomenon of captivity in its various forms: prisoners of war and slaves were just two among various possible outcomes of captivity.[199] We need to explore the processes through which people were made into captives, the reasons for taking captives, the processes through which people were extricated from captivity, the various fates of captives and the particular reasons why different societies turned variable proportions of captives into slaves.[200] Did captors enslave all captives, or did they kill adult males and enslave only women and children?[201] How did communities deal with the captivity of their own members, and how did they try to solve the complex social and legal problems that captivity created?[202] While there are

[192] For comparative perspectives, see Campbell, Miers and Miller 2009; Campbell and Stanziani 2013; De Vito and Lichtenstein 2015.
[193] Daverio Rocchi 1975.
[194] Millar 1984; Gustafson 1994; McClintock 2010; Groen-Vallinga and Tacoma 2015.
[195] Rio 2008, 2011, 2015a, 2017.
[196] Vlassopoulos 2016c.
[197] Harris 1980a, 1994; Ramin and Veyne 1981; Vuolanto 2003; Evans-Grubbs 2010.
[198] Harper 2011: 391–425.
[199] For prisoners of war in ancient Greece, see Ducrey 1968, 1999; Bielman 1999.
[200] Maffi 2007; Huntzinger 2014; Robert 2014.
[201] Gaca 2010.
[202] For captivity and Roman law, see Buckland 1908: 291–317; Amirante 1950; Watson 1961; Cursi 2001. For captivity and Jewish law, see Malka and Paz 2019.

particular studies about captivity in the Near East,[203] Egypt,[204] Greece,[205] Rome[206] or the early Middle Ages,[207] the subject has never been explored systematically and in a long-term perspective.[208]

Captives could be fully incorporated into the captor community, resettled as bound tenants or turned into slaves.[209] Furthermore, certain communities developed mechanisms which enabled them to ransom their captives; while there are currently studies of particular cases, like the ransom mechanisms of Greek poleis or the mechanisms developed by the Church in the early Middle Ages, we need a systematic study of ransoming mechanisms in their long-term history in antiquity.[210] And while ancient historians are familiar with the institutionalised ransoming mechanisms of Greek poleis, they tend to forget the existence of ransoming mechanisms among the barbarian communities, like the fifth-century BCE case of Thracians travelling from Thrace to the island of Lesbos and back in order to ransom some of their captured compatriots; how common were such ransoming mechanisms among non-Greek communities?[211] Ransoming mechanisms could be successful because of the existence of a veritable ransoming market; in many cases, slave-makers could fetch a higher price by ransoming their captives in 'closed markets' to their relatives, friends and compatriots than by selling them as slaves in the open market. For the pirates that captured Julius Caesar, it was obviously more profitable to ransom him than sell him as a slave, provided of course that ransoming mechanisms existed and were safe, and the attendant risks were worth it.[212]

But the most difficult question is the exact link between the processes of violence and the processes of slave-making. For a long time the study of African slave-making was based on the assumption that African warfare consisted of raids with the single purpose of capturing slaves.[213] Gradually, scholars have realised that most African warfare was conducted for the usual range of military and geopolitical purposes; these wars created slaves, but warfare was rarely conducted with the single purpose of producing slaves.[214] It should be taken for granted, therefore, that in the normal course of things

---

[203] Gelb 1973; Oded 1979; Seri 2013; Steinkeller 2013; Wunsch 2013; Garcia Ventura 2014; Ponchia 2017; Lewis 2018: 231–3, 254–7.

[204] Gundlach 1994; Redford 2004; Janzen 2013; Bußmann 2014; see also van Minnen 2000 on Graeco-Roman Egypt.

[205] Klees 1998: 19–60; Roy 2012.

[206] Bradley 2004; Leigh 2004: 57–97; Wickham 2014; Boatwright 2015.

[207] Huntzinger 2009.

[208] For a good start, see the studies in Sánchez León and López Nadal 1996; Heinen 2008.

[209] For the fate of captives in the ancient Near East and Egypt, see Galil 2007; Menu 2004b. For the fate of captives in Native American societies, see Santos-Granero 2009; Snyder 2010; Brooks 2011; Cameron 2016.

[210] For Greek ransoming, see Bielman 1994; Sosin 2017. For Roman ransoming, see Connolly 2006; for the Christian tradition of ransoming, see Osiek 1981; Klingshirn 1985.

[211] Antiphon, On the murder of Herodes 20; see also Aelian, fragment 71.

[212] Gabrielsen 2003: 392–5; cf. Lewis 2019: 93–103.

[213] Meillassoux 1991; Welwei 2008 is unfortunately based on antiquated Africanist literature that adopts this perspective.

[214] Thornton 1998: 98–125; Stilwell 2014: 29–59.

the usual forms of violence within and between political communities will often produce slaves as one of its consequences. What need to be studied in more detail are
the actual links between warfare and slave-making and their diverse forms. For anyone who has read Thucydides, slave-making on a significant scale was an important
consequence of warfare between Greek states, as we shall see in Chapter 8. And yet,
traditional images of Greek slavery assume that practically all slaves in Greek cities
like Athens were barbarian slaves acquired through the slave trade. What happened
to all those Greek captives who were enslaved?[215] Were they ultimately ransomed, or
have we missed a significant element of the slave populations of Greek cities? One
also gets the impression that the warfare between Rome and its neighbouring Italian
communities in the early and middle republican period led to slave-making on a much
more extensive scale than the equivalent forms of warfare among Greek poleis.[216] Is
this actually true, or is it just the impression given by our different kinds of sources,
and the lack of a city-centred narrative like that of Livy for ancient Greece? Hans van
Wees has argued that in the course of the classical period Greek states gradually moved
from conquest and subjugation of defeated communities and their members to heavier
reliance on incorporation of the defeated into hegemonic alliances or as members
with equal rights.[217] Whatever the case, we need to explore in more depth historical
changes in the link between warfare and slave-making.

Furthermore, the volume of violent slave-making cannot be considered constant.[218] Angelos Chaniotis has argued that the emergence of Hellenistic kingdoms
made warfare more ubiquitous and larger in scale than in previous periods.[219] During
the same time, the process of Roman expansion led to significantly increased levels
of warfare across the eastern basin of the Mediterranean and violent slave-making on
a massive scale.[220] The other period that saw warfare and violent slave-making on a
major scale is the period of the mass internal and external violent challenges to the
Roman order in late antiquity and the early Middle Ages, including the emergence
of powerful new barbarian states, the renewed conflict between Rome and Sassanian
Iran and the various dynastic conflicts.[221]

We also need to take into account some peculiar inflections which affected violent slave-making in particular ways. One factor was the emergence of empires in
Eurasian history. This meant an enormous disparity between powerful imperial centres and the areas of concentrated wealth that they controlled on the one hand, and
the relatively impoverished and weak peripheries on the other. Such empires could
embark on massive campaigns of conquest and pillage, which resulted in huge numbers of captives, many of which ended up as slaves. The Egyptian campaigns in Nubia
were often a form of mass pillage of flocks and captives,[222] while Roman campaigns

---

[215] See the answer of Garlan 1987.
[216] Volkmann 1961; Harris 1979: 54–104; Welwei 2000; Wickham 2014.
[217] van Wees 2007: 284–5.
[218] Volkmann 1961.
[219] Chaniotis 2005: 1–17.
[220] Hopkins 1978: 1–98; Shaw 2014.
[221] Hutzinger 2009; Lenski 2014.
[222] Redford 2004.

like that in Dacia were good examples of how conquest could lead to slave-making on a mass scale.

On the other hand, slave-making was also important for poor peripheries. Some communities with low population densities had systematic recourse to captivity as a means of replenishing their population and labour force.[223] Furthermore, pillage was always a major form of wealth accumulation in poor societies with few resources, limited infrastructures and few other means of investment and wealth-making; in such circumstances, low-level pillage and slave-making was a constant phenomenon.[224] The Germanic, Sarmatian, Hunnic and Saracen societies in the early empire and late antiquity are characteristic examples of the development of slave-making that was parasitic on empires and their concentrated wealth.[225]

A particular version of pillaging is what is traditionally described as piracy.[226] In many ancient societies ships were owned by wealthy individuals, who could use them to trade or pillage; these political communities enforced a state monopoly on violence only on certain occasions, while also permitting their members to practice violent accumulation on their own for most of the time. But the emergence of triremes in the late archaic Mediterranean changed the situation abruptly. Traditional warships required relatively small crews of up to fifty people and were relatively cheap to build; but triremes required crews of up to 200 people, while their construction necessitated extensive networks for the provision of the necessary materials. As a result, trireme fleets were beyond the capacities of most wealthy individuals and were constructed and owned by states. In this way there emerged a new form of state that monopolised the exercise of violence and the means to it. Ancient societies were now divided between monopolistic states with state fleets and oligopolistic states that allowed their members to use their private vessels for violent accumulation.[227] Societies like the Aetolians and the Illyrians are good examples of oligopolistic states whose members practised violent slave-making on a widespread scale, given the opportunity.[228] Once markets and empires created significant concentrations of wealth, they generated the incentive to create infrastructures for large-scale pillaging and slave-making by people in the impoverished periphery: the organisation of large war bands that could attempt campaigns of slave-making on a large scale. The Cilician pirates of the late Hellenistic period, who acquired quasi-state features, are characteristic examples of this phenomenon.[229] It is one of the greatest ironies of ancient history that empire building and slave-making on the back of barbarian peripheries could in turn create barbarian slave-makers on a mass scale.[230]

---

[223] For Native American examples, see Viau 1997; Snyder 2010; Brooks 2011.

[224] For these phenomena in early medieval Europe, see Bartlett 1993: 292–314.

[225] Lenski 2008, 2011a, 2011b, 2014, 2018a: 29–30.

[226] For piracy and slave-making, see Garlan 1987; Gabrielsen 2003; Lewis 2019.

[227] Gabrielsen 2001, 2013.

[228] For Illyrian piracy, see Dell 1967; for Cretan piracy, see Brulé 1978; for Etruscan piracy, see Giuffrida Ientile 1983; for Aetolian piracy, see Scholten 2000.

[229] Rauh 1997; see also Mavrojannis 2018, 2019.

[230] See the overall account of empires, peripheries and violence in Heather 2010.

The fourth process of slave-making involved the slave trade. This process linked the demand side of the various slaving strategies explored in the previous section with the supply side of the three processes of slave-making explored above. The study of the ancient slave trade poses some of the most difficult methodological problems in the study of ancient slavery. Until fairly recently most scholars of ancient slavery had concluded that little could be said about the ancient slave trade, given the paucity of quantifiable evidence. It was also thought that the slave trade could be conceived as a constant process that could be simply taken for granted. But things have gradually changed over the last twenty years for various reasons. On the one hand, the study of the New World slave trade has revealed that it is one of the most crucial parameters for the history of slaving. The origins, number and gender ratios of the people sold in the slave trade were crucial for how slavery operated in the slave-buying societies and what kinds of slave communities emerged in them. On the other hand, ancient historians have found innovative ways of thinking about the slave trade despite the paucity of quantifiable evidence.[231]

Before the first millennium BCE, violent slave-making and natural reproduction were the most important mechanisms for large-scale slave systems. Once a slave population had reached a certain level, its maintenance could only rely on natural reproduction as a constant source of supply. Raiding, warfare and trade could occasionally contribute large numbers, but they could not be relied on for producing large numbers of slaves on an annual basis. It was only in the few cases of predatory and expansionist states that engaged in constant campaigning, pillage and conquest that violent slave-making could supply slaves on a constant basis. Ultimately, though, expansion would reach its limits, and warfare would no longer supply slaves on a regular basis; at this stage, either natural reproduction would have to maintain the slave population or the number of slaves would dwindle abruptly or gradually.

This is an important model for understanding slavery in the ancient Near East before the first millennium BCE. Slavery was ubiquitous and slaving strategies for leisure, gratification, income or positions of authority should be considered constant. But on top of this groundwork, violent slave-making could produce large numbers of slaves for a few generations; this increased slave population could expand in new slaving niches, like the use of slaves for the production of wealth. In the course of the first millennium BCE a fundamental change took place. The connectivity processes that had started in the Levant in the course of the third millennium BCE and had expanded into the Aegean during the second millennium now reached the whole of the Mediterranean and the Black Sea.[232] These processes were multiform: they included the opportunistic exploitation of various micro-ecologies and the redistribution of their products through Mediterranean connectivity. What is traditionally described as Greek colonisation is one version of this process: favourable micro-ecologies, like that of Cyrene, were seized in order to produce great wealth by redistributing large grain harvests or specialised products like silphion.[233] Another related process was the

---

[231] Scheidel 1997; Harris 1999; Harper 2010a.

[232] See the account of Broodbank 2013.

[233] Horden and Purcell 2000: 65–77; Purcell 2005.

creation of dispersed hinterlands through colonisation or trade networks: a city like Athens could draw its food supply not solely from its own territory, but also through cleruchies like Lemnos, colonies like Amphipolis and an extensive commercial network in the Black Sea.[234] A third process was the emergence of consumer societies: the cultivation of taste and desire and the use of disposable income in order to consume a wide variety of products with special characteristics originating from various areas. The wide circulation across the Mediterranean of wine and oil products, despite their ubiquitous local production, is an excellent illustration of the emergence of consumer societies.[235]

It is within these wider processes that we need to situate the emergence in the course of the first millennium of interlinked large-scale markets across the Mediterranean and the Black Sea.[236] Interlinked and large-scale markets shaped slaving in three important ways. The first is that they enormously expanded the volume and the reliability of slave supply: instead of the occasional glut produced by a raid or a successful campaign, buyers could now be guaranteed steady supply on a large scale, as commercial networks could now reach across the Mediterranean, the Black Sea, Near East and temperate Europe and draw slave supplies from various areas. The second effect was that the entanglement of micro-ecological exploitation, dispersed hinterlands, consumerism and connectivity exponentially increased the demand for slaves. Slaves could now be employed to provide labour for the processes of large-scale production of agricultural staples like grain, wine and oil, as well as manufactured products like textiles, pottery and metal utensils. With steady supply guaranteed, there was now scope for the creation and maintenance of large-scale slave systems based on slave labour. The emergence of large-scale systems of slave-based agriculture on islands like Corcyra and Chios, which specialised in commercial crops like wine, is of course not accidental.[237]

The third effect was that greatly increased and constant demand mediated by markets modified the link between violence and slave-making in important ways. It has long been known that slaves in the Greek world were constantly drawn from certain areas like Phrygia, Thrace and the Black Sea.[238] Why were these areas exporters of slaves on such a constant basis and in such large numbers? In areas like Thrace and the Black Sea this was the outcome of state-making. The emergence of powerful states like the Odrysian kingdom of Thrace and the Royal Scythians in the Black Sea created forces that could produce large numbers of slaves as a result of their expansion. In areas like Phrygia, it is possible that we have to deal with the opposite process, in which the collapse of the Phrygian state in the course of the archaic period led to the absence of state structures and a free for all which provided a constant supply of slaves.[239] In both

---

[234]  Horden and Purcell 2000: 115–22.
[235]  Foxhall 1998, 2005.
[236]  For Mediterranean-wide markets, see Harris, Lewis and Woolmer 2015; Bresson 2016.
[237]  Rihll 1996.
[238]  For the Black Sea, see Finley 1962; Braund and Tsetskhladze 1989; Hind 1994; Gavriljuk 2003; Avram 2007; Braund 2008; Tsetskhladze 2008; Fischer 2016; Parmenter 2020. For Thrace, see Alexianu 2011. For Phrygia, see Lewis 2011, 2015.
[239]  Thonemann 2013; Lewis 2015: 317–21.

cases, the existence of nearby slave markets provided a powerful inflection of the usual forms of warfare and state-making. Around 400 BCE the Thracian prince Seuthes was able to use the mercenary army of the Ten Thousand in order to establish his authority over many Thracian communities; but the need to pay his mercenaries and the existence of slave markets in nearby Greek colonies like Perinthos meant that attacking a settlement, capturing its inhabitants and selling 1,000 persons in the local market was both profitable and easily feasible.[240]

Many historians of the ancient economy have become fond of waxing lyrical about the development of markets in antiquity and their beneficial outcomes.[241] But the development of the slave trade is an important reminder that ancient markets could create immense misery alongside increased prosperity, something that has not escaped most people in the contemporary world, even if it is not always obvious to modern academics. More specifically, we need to explore whether the specific inflection of warfare by the slave trade applies also outside areas like Thrace and Phrygia, or should be seen as a peculiar phenomenon of certain geopolitical settings.[242]

---

[240] Xenophon, *Anabasis* 7.3–4.
[241] Ober 2015, Bresson 2016; my own responses in Vlassopoulos 2016d, 2018c.
[242] Lewis 2018: 282–6.

# 5

# ENSLAVED PERSONS

HAVING EXAMINED HOW SLAVERY is constituted by three conceptual systems and how masters employ the tool of slavery to pursue various slaving strategies, it is time to move to the slaves. This requires asking a number of important questions. What is a slave? How did slaves see their condition? What aims did slaves pursue? Ultimately, it is impossible to answer any of these questions without recourse to the issue of slave identity. But at that point we come across a major paradox: despite the explosion in the study of identities across the humanities and the social sciences over the last thirty years, the study of slavery has engaged with matters of identity only to a very limited extent. This is a great pity, as identity studies can make a major contribution to the study of slavery.

Let me start the discussion with a key observation: slavery is quintessentially an imposed identity. This does not mean that it is impossible for slaves to take up this imposed identity and make it their own; this is undoubtedly a real possibility, as we shall see. But it means that, given its imposed character, we need to think very carefully about the implications of this basic fact, and we should avoid assuming that this imposed identity was the sole identity that slaves had. This chapter will use a conceptual repertoire developed by scholars exploring identity across anthropology, sociology, psychology and history in order to explore in detail the complex and contradictory aspects of slave identity. My main argument is that we need to abandon the unitary and monolithic understanding of slave identity in order to explore the multiple identities of *enslaved persons*.

## Identification Modes and Forms of Relationships

The first distinction we need to introduce to the study of slave identities is that between categorical and relational modes of identification.[1] In a **categorical** mode of identification people belong to the same category because they share the same features; all people with blond hair belong to the category of blondes, while people are categorised as pensioners because they receive a pension. A **relational** mode is not based on shared features, but on relationships between people; kinship, where persons are identified on the basis of their relationships to parents, relatives and ancestors, is perhaps the most characteristic relational mode of identification. Slaves partake in both modes of identification. On the one hand, slaves can be defined categorically (as those human beings who constitute property, or those who are socially dead, etc.);

---

[1] Calhoun 1997: 29–50.

as we shall shortly see, though, there are different kinds of categories to which slaves belong, and these different kinds of categories have very serious consequences about how slaves are conceptualised. On the other hand, slaves could be defined relationally: slaves usually belonged to particular masters,[2] and it was the relationship to their particular masters that defined them.

The fact that slaves can be defined both categorically and relationally has very significant implications for the history of slavery; while both modes of identification are in principle compatible with each other, they also have very different implications, which can potentially lead to significant divergences and disjunctures. The categorical mode focuses on the features shared by all slaves, irrespective of their particular characteristics and conditions, and reduces all slaves to their common denominators. The relational mode focuses on the particular relationship between a specific master and a specific slave; as a result, it emphasises the particular features of the master and the slave and their specific relationship. When the emphasis is placed on the relational mode, the slaves of a powerful master might be in significantly different conditions from the slaves of an ordinary master, as the features of the particular master to which slaves are related might become more consequential than the features that all slaves share *qua* slaves; the same also applies to the quality of the particular relationship between a specific master and a specific slave. We shall examine the dialectical relationship between masters and slaves in more detail in Chapter 6.

In terms of global history, there are many societies that prioritise the relational mode and focus on the particular relationship between specific masters and slaves; the early modern societies of Southeast Asia are a telling example in this respect.[3] In such cases, the categorical content of being slave (that is, the prototypical conceptual system we examined in Chapter 3) is either not institutionalised or largely inconsequential; what really matters are the particular features of masters and slaves and the quality of their relationship. As a result, slavery tends to be assimilated to other asymmetric relationships, like those of parents and children or patrons and clients; accordingly, the more preponderant the relational mode, the greater the tendency for slavery to be assimilated to other asymmetric relationships.[4] This observation underlies the significance of the categorical mode in the history of slavery; without the identification of certain features as peculiar to slaves and the employment of this categorical mode for a variety of purposes, slavery would dissolve into multiple specific relationships between particular masters and slaves.

The above comments imply that we need to more closely examine the concepts of categories and relationships. Starting with relationships, we can distinguish between direct and indirect relationships. **Direct** relationships are based on personal encounters between the people involved, like those between parents and children, teachers and pupils and coaches and athletes. **Indirect** relationships link people without personal

---

[2] Roman law recognised the category of the slave without a master (*servus sine domino*), as well as the penal slave, who did not belong to any particular master but was a slave of 'punishment' (*servus poenae*): Buckland 1908: 1–6; 277–8; 578–80; McClintock 2010.

[3] Reid 1983, 2018.

[4] For one particular example from Africa, see Glassman 1991.

encounters. Organisations like states, churches and companies of course involve direct relationships between co-workers, priests and parishioners, employees and managers; but at the same time they also involve a huge nexus of indirect relationships between the elite hierarchy of those organisations (the government and chief state bureaucrats, the Pope and bishops, the boards of directors), the various employees and members of these organisations and the people with which these organisations interact (subjects, parishioners, customers); few people have direct relationships with prime ministers or the Pope, but millions engage in indirect relationships with them.[5]

In the case of slavery, the overwhelming majority of slaves in most societies were primarily involved in direct relationships with their masters, fellow slaves and other people with whom they interacted. But it is important to point out that in certain societies some slaves came to be enmeshed in a nexus of indirect relationships. This is particularly true for Roman slaves of the early imperial period: the extensive portfolios of the Roman aristocracy, scattered across various provinces and multiple settlements, the large-scale aristocratic households with hundreds of slaves and the empire-wide bureaucracy of imperial slaves created indirect relationships which affected the lives of these slaves in significant ways. The thousands of slaves of Caecilius Isidorus[6] and Melania the Younger,[7] or the portfolio of Trimalchio, as satirised by Petronius,[8] are characteristic examples of how many slaves could live their whole lives without ever coming into direct contact with their masters; in such cases, it was a nexus of indirect relationships and structures that substituted the direct relationship between masters and slaves (see also the case of Daphnis discussed in Chapter 4).[9]

Notwithstanding the importance of these indirect relationships, we should not lose track of the fact that most slaves experienced slavery as a direct relationship with their masters. Accordingly, it is important to introduce another distinction between primary and secondary relationships.[10] **Primary** relationships involve persons as a whole, with all their features, roles and capacities; relationships between lovers, spouses, friends and family members are characteristic examples, where it is the full range of the features, roles and capacities of the people involved that affects these relationships. On the other hand, **secondary** relationships primarily link people as enactors of specific social roles: my relationship with the accountant, the postman, or the policeman is primarily determined by our specific roles and the extent to which we meet the criteria of those roles rather than by our overall features and characteristics. In practice, of course, the stronger and more significant the direct relationship between two people, the likelier it is that a secondary relationship will be affected by more features outside the respective role repertoires and will be assimilated to a primary relationship. While in theory my relationship to my academic colleagues and students is a secondary relationship based on the criteria of our respective roles, the depth of certain direct relationships

[5] Calhoun 1991, 1992.
[6] Pliny, *Natural History* 33.135; see Brunt 1975.
[7] Palladius, *Lausaic History* 61.5–6; see Harper 2011: 192–5.
[8] Petronius, *Satyricon* 52; see Veyne 1961; Andreau 2009; Verboven 2009.
[9] Harper 2011: 33–66, 100–200.
[10] Cooley 1962; Calhoun 1991, 1992.

with particular colleagues and students will mean that our interactions will become assimilated to primary relationships.

In theory, the relationship between master and slave was a secondary relationship, in which masters and slaves were linked by the specific social roles they enacted. But in practice, the fact that most relationships between slaves and masters were direct, and the depth of these relationships, meant that there was a constant tendency of slavery to become assimilated to a primary relationship. For those slaves who worked in the fields or mines and had limited contact with their masters, or whose contact was based on a limited range of issues, slavery would mean involvement in an overwhelmingly secondary relationship. Household servants, slaves who offered prestige or gratification, slaves in position of trust and authority or slaves who worked alongside their masters in their fields and workshops would likely have a relationship that extended over a wider range of issues and would more often tend to become assimilated to a primary relationship. This would mean that the relationship would not be determined solely by the respective social roles of master and slave, but by a wider range of features and factors. A telling example of this comes from a petition from early imperial Oxyrhynchos in Egypt. In the course of narrating how a third person severely injured her female slave, the slave-owner Thermoutharion describes their relationship:

> I loved and took care of my serving girl, Peina, a homebred slave, as though my own little daughter, in the hope that when she came of age I would have her to nourish me in my old age, since I am a woman who is helpless and alone.[11]

There is no doubt that the petitioner chose to present her relationship to her slave in terms of a primary relationship. It is of course telling that we are given a utilitarian explanation for this assimilation: the slave-owner was hoping that the slave would take care of her in old age. The petition also mentions that the slave was injured on her way to her singing lessons; it is likely, therefore, that the slave was trained to become an entertainer, a profession that was strongly linked to the sex industry. It is possible that the strong sentimental relationship between mistress and slave co-existed with the sexual exploitation of the slave in order to maintain her mistress; the complexity of slavery as a primary and secondary relationship is quite evident.[12]

The above observation has a number of implications. On the one hand, it is obvious that in many cases there would be significant advantages for slaves in trying to turn secondary relationships into primary ones. It would mean that their lives would be affected less by the fact that they were slaves and more by the quality of the relationship with their masters. On the other hand, we should carefully avoid any simplistic assumptions. If I have a secondary relationship with a nice person, there are good reasons why I should try to assimilate it to a primary relationship, as I will benefit from the positive features of the other person which are outside the repertoire of his/her

---

[11] *P.Oxy.* L, 3555.

[12] But similar contradictions existed in relationships between family members: see the salutary comments of Glancy 2002b.

respective role. But if the same relationship involves a nasty person, there is every reason to keep this relationship within the requirements of the secondary roles, as I will
be adversely affected by the negative features of the other person which are outside
the respective role repertoire.

Keeping the relative distance of the secondary relationship was something that
slaves often attempted for a variety of reasons. A particularly important one resulted
from the dangers of asymmetry and the misreading of context. While it was often
the case that masters allowed slaves to step outside the requirements of their secondary roles and assume attitudes and engage in acts that were appropriate in a primary
relationship, it was always possible for masters to change the setting at a moment's
notice and severely punish slaves who behaved inappropriately.[13] Slaves had to tread
carefully and judge the moment appropriately. This means that we need to explore the
roles and personas that slaves adopted in their various interactions with their masters.[14]
We shall further explore these issues in Chapter 6.

Let us now move to categories. As we have seen in Chapter 2, categories were
traditionally understood in **definitional** terms; a category was defined by certain criteria, and members of a particular category were those individuals who met all those
criteria. Definitional categories were particularly apt to be codified, and were usually
exclusive; an individual either did or did not meet the criteria and was categorised
accordingly. In the case of slavery, the most common definition of the category of
slave was that of an individual who was a piece of property. This definitional category
was normally exclusive: one was either the property of somebody else, and therefore
a slave, or was not, and therefore a free person.

But slaves were also often categorised in **prototypical** ways.[15] Most slaveholding societies construct prototypical images of slaves. Unsurprisingly these prototypical
images exhibit features which appear with cross-cultural regularity as well as features
that only appear in certain societies or periods (see the discussion above at pp. 52–3).[16]
For most modern people, whether slavery specialists, scholars who do not specialise
in slavery or lay people, the prototypical image of a slave is that of a black rural slave
in the antebellum US. We often implicitly categorise other people on the basis of the
extent to which they fit this prototypical image; as a result, the lay public and the non-
specialists (as well as quite a lot of slavery specialists) often find it difficult to categorise
as slaves people who do not easily fit the prototypical image of the black slave.

While definitional categories of slaves are usually exclusive, prototypical categories of slaves are often graded. As a result, some slaves completely fit the prototypical
image of slave, while other slaves in the same society fit the prototype only to a limited

---

[13] An issue well brought out in how literary texts employ such interactions to explore various issues: see
Fitzgerald 2000.

[14] For the personas adopted by slaves in their interactions with their masters, see Genovese 1967;
Blassingame 1972: 284–322; Wyatt-Brown 1992; King 2001.

[15] Lewis forthcoming.

[16] For physical characteristics and clothing associated with the prototypical image of slaves in ancient
societies, see Zimmermann 1980; Potts 2011; Thalmann 2011; Wrenhaven 2011, 2012; Wunsch and
Magdalene 2012. For slave names as marks of distinction, see Solin 2001; Robertson 2008.

extent, or not at all. Ps.-Xenophon complained that in fifth-century BCE Athens it was impossible to tell apart poor citizens from slaves and metics because they all dressed equally terribly;[17] Seneca reported the apocryphal story that the Roman Senate considered a proposal to force all slaves to wear the same clothes but had to abandon it for fear that the slaves would thus realise how many they were and might consequently revolt.[18] At the same time, the prototypical category of slave might also be applicable to a variable degree to individuals and groups who were not slaves. Non-slave individuals and groups might perform servile tasks, wear servile clothes, sport servile haircuts, exhibit servile features or behave slavishly. Finally, many slaves might fit the prototypical category of free persons, making it very difficult for third parties to identify them as slaves.[19] As I have explored elsewhere in regard to classical Athens, certain names made it possible to identify particular people as slaves, while other names that slaves bore made this impossible because they were widely shared by citizens as well.[20]

Most slaveholding societies construct both definitional and prototypical categories for slaves. Definitional and prototypical categories are obviously essential for the categorical mode of identification of slaves we have examined above, but they tend to perform different tasks. Definitional categories are particularly apt for legal purposes, and this is why they are often legally codified; prototypical categories, on the other hand, are particularly important for social and political purposes. The definitional category of slave is usually physically invisible; as a result, the categorisation of a particular individual as the property of another individual might be known only to a few people.[21] On the other hand, the prototypical category is usually highly visible because it is based on bodily and behavioural characteristics; as a result, it provides stereotypes that can be used to shape social interaction in particular ways.[22]

Given the fact that definitional categories are exclusive but prototypical categories tend to be graded, it is fairly obvious that there is potential for major contradiction between the two types of categories. We have already seen that many slaves might fit the prototypical category only to a limited extent or not at all, while many non-slave individuals or groups might fit the prototypical category partly or fully. Furthermore, it would be a mistake to assume that slaveholding societies employ definitional and prototypical categories in the same way and to the same extent. Societies with high levels of institutionalisation and developed legal systems will tend to use definitional categories of slaves to a much higher degree. On the other hand, societies with limited institutionalisation and relatively simple legal systems will tend to employ prototypical

---

[17] Ps.-Xenophon, *Constitution of the Athenians* 1.10; see Cataldi 2000.

[18] Seneca, *On mercy* 1.24; see George 2002.

[19] For status confusion in the Greek world, see Vlassopoulos 2007a, 2009; Forsdyke 2019; for status confusion in the Roman world, see Söllner 2000; Connolly 2004–5; Evans-Grubbs 2013.

[20] For slave names in classical Athens, see Vlassopoulos 2010, 2015b; for the names of Roman home-born slaves, see Bruun 2013; for the names of Babylonian slaves, see Hackl 2013; for slave names in Hellenistic Greece, see Lewis 2017a.

[21] Visually identifiable marks, like collars, tattoos and branding, were applied only to particular groups of insubordinate slaves as a punishment or as a means of preventing flight: see Jones 1987; Hillner 2001; Kamen 2010; Trimble 2016.

[22] Osborne 2011; see also Glancy 2002a on the corporeality of slavery.

definitions to do much more work than in other societies. A telling example concerns disputes about slave status in medieval societies; given the limited institutionalisation and use of written documents, the employment of prototypical features (like the performance of servile tasks) was crucial for deciding the categorisation of particular individuals as slaves.[23]

## Categorisation, Self-understanding and Groupness

It is time to move from identification modes to the wider issue of identity. An important first step in approaching identity stems from the provocative contribution of Rogers Brubaker and Frederick Cooper.[24] They have argued that the explosion of identity studies has created a situation in which identity is conceptualised in radically incompatible ways. Traditional understandings of identity as monolithic and stable have been undermined by newer approaches which have underlined the constructed character of identity. The constructionist approach has conceptualised identities as multiple, contradictory and changing; but if this is the case, does it still make sense to talk about *identity*? And how should we deal with the fact that, despite the constructivist insights, identities are generally experienced as monolithic and stable, rather than as changing constructions? Brubaker and Cooper argue that the concept of identity is trying to do too many things at the same time, while succeeding in none. Instead, they have proposed breaking up the unitary concept of identity into three different aspects. The advantage of their proposition is double: on the one hand, it makes it easier to distinguish between different phenomena which are often misunderstood if placed under the single label of identity; on the other hand, the three aspects that they distinguish focus on processes rather than entities or essences and in this respect enable us to study identity issues from a historical point of view.

The first aspect of identity concerns **categorisation** or classification. It is the process through which individuals and groups are given particular labels, whether they are aware of them or not. While the process of categorisation emphasises the external classification of individuals and groups, the process of **self-understanding** focuses on the internal identification of individuals and groups. These two processes are distinct but co-existing and mutually constitutive aspects of identity. People identify themselves and categorise others, and at the same time they are aware of how others identify themselves and categorise them.[25] Although the two aspects influence each other, this influence can take a variety of forms. In many cases, self-identification and categorisation might create the same outcome; to take a hypothetical example, I see myself as a Greek living in Italy, and both the Italian state and my colleagues and neighbours categorise me in the same way. Or my self-understanding might be radically different from how other people perceive me: I understand myself as a Greek citizen of

[23] Rio 2017: 194–209.

[24] Brubaker and Cooper 2000; I have slightly modified their terminology to make it easier to comprehend.

[25] Jenkins 2008: 37–48.

Albanian origins, while other people simply categorise me as an Albanian. On the other hand, I might be unaware of or misperceive how other people categorise me; I consider myself as being clever, but I am unaware or misunderstand the fact that most people around me categorise me as being stupid. Finally, it is possible that how other people categorise me might significantly change how I understand myself, or that I succeed in convincing other people to categorise me in the way I understand myself. The fact that others categorise me as an Albanian might stop me from considering myself as a Greek citizen of Albanian origins and make me self-identify as Albanian; alternatively, I might succeed in convincing people around me to categorise me as a Greek citizen of Albanian origins.

While categorisation and self-understanding are essential aspects of all forms of identity, we need to distinguish a third aspect that applies only to certain forms of identity: **groupness**. This refers to the process through which categorisation and self-understanding combine with other aspects to create groups. Groupness is a potentiality for many forms of identity, but whether an identity acquires groupness and the extent of its groupness are variable outcomes of historical processes. Categories and categorisations are necessary foundations for groupness; the members of a group must share certain features (being members of a category) in order to constitute a group; otherwise, they are merely a temporary collectivity, like a crowd or a mob. At the same time, categories are not sufficient for groupness. A category might exist only in the eye of the categoriser and might be unknown or have no meaning or significance for the people categorised as such: the category of blue-eyed people who speak French is certainly valid, but unless the people in that category are aware of that categorisation and identify themselves as such, this category would have zero groupness. Accordingly, groupness requires both categorisation and self-understanding. People who belong to the same category and identify as such share a collective identity; but for a collective identity to become groupness, a third element is required, that of a network linking together at least some of those who share a collective identity and leading to common activities.[26] Groupness is the combination of categorisation, self-understanding and networking.[27]

How does the above conceptual framework of identity relate to slavery? As an imposed identity, slavery is before anything else an act of categorisation. People were categorised as slaves, whether on the basis of definitional or prototypical categories, as we have seen above.[28] There is no doubt that because this act of categorisation was performed by individuals and organisations with authority (masters, states), with whom slaves had a highly asymmetric relationship of power, it would have a significant impact on the lives of slaves, whether they liked it and accepted it or not. But it would be highly misleading to assume that simply because slaves were categorised as

[26] For such an approach to ethnic identity, see Vlassopoulos 2015d.
[27] For collective identity and groupness, see Domingues 1995; Vandenberghe 2007a, 2007b; Jenkins 2008: 102–17.
[28] For status identification in antiquity, see Reinhold 1971; Gardner 1986; George 2002; Faraguna 2014.

such, this was also how they understood themselves. A passage from Aristotle gives a typical example of this misleading view:

> And the term piece of property is used in the same way as the term part: a thing that is a part is not only a part of another thing, but absolutely belongs to another thing, and so also does a piece of property. Hence, whereas the master is merely the slave's master and does not belong to [the slave], the slave is not merely the slave of the master, but wholly belongs to the master.[29]

In this passage Aristotle sees the identity of slaves as wholly determined by their function as slaves to their masters. While masters do not belong to their slaves – that is, they have other identities and functions distinct from their role as masters (fathers, athletes, architects, citizens, magistrates) – the slaves' identity is solely defined by their role as slaves.[30] There is no doubt that masters were in a considerably better position to self-identify with all their other roles apart from their role as masters and to ensure that these other roles and categories shaped their lives in significant ways. And given the fact that many aspects of their lives were shaped by their categorisation as slaves, it is also plausible to assume that this categorisation often became an important form of self-understanding for slaves.

But this was by no means the full story. To start with, many slaves had lived significant periods of their lives as free people before becoming slaves. Many of these people understood themselves as free people in captivity, rather than as slaves. Given that many of them managed to regain their freedom through manumission, flight, liberation, ransoming or captive exchange, this self-understanding was far from implausible.[31] The father of the Athenian Euxitheos was captured during the Peloponnesian War, sold as a slave on the island of Leukas and spent many years there, to the extent that he acquired the local accent; he finally came across an actor who ensured his return to Athens.[32] Despite the long passage of time as a slave in Leukas, it is probable that Euxitheos' father understood himself primarily as a free Athenian in captivity, even though for many purposes he would have to accept the consequences of his categorisation as a slave. Perhaps the most characteristic example of this way of self-understanding comes in Achilles Tatius' novel *Leukippe and Kleitophon*. Leukippe, the female protagonist who comes from a noble family of Byzantion, is sold as a slave to the Ephesian Thersandros. Leukippe resists Thersandros' various attempts to seduce her and make her his lover, at which point Thersandros claims his right as her master to violate her and punish her for her insubordination. Leukippe's answer is telling:

> Arm yourself then. Take up your whips against me, the torture wheel, the fire, the iron blade. Have your councillor too, Sosthenes, fight by your side. I, naked, alone, a woman, I have one weapon: my freedom. But freedom cannot be beaten

[29] Aristotle, *Politics* 1254a.9–13.
[30] Klees 1975: 188–90.
[31] For Greek inscriptions recording the 'return to liberty', see Bielman 1994.
[32] Demosthenes, *Against Euboulides* 18.

up by blows, nor cut up with iron blades, nor burnt in fire. I will never surrender it. Even if you set me on fire, you will find that fire is not as hot.[33]

It is obvious that Leukippe's claim would have been practically impotent in any non-fictional context: once she had become a slave, her former free status was not going to save her from violation or torture; the claim only makes sense in the fictional context of the erotic novel, where the reader knows that the female protagonist will by definition avoid being violated until she is happily reunited with her lover at the end of the novel.[34] And yet, it is precisely the absurdity of the claim that illustrates the significance of this mode of self-understanding for slaves. A particularly vocal final example concerns late antique texts which emphasise the pre-existing Christian identity of captured individuals for how they perceived and experienced their lives under slavery.[35]

Furthermore, and like free people, slaves adopted various other roles apart from that of slave. Slaves created families and kinship groups, and were thus lovers and spouses, parents, children and relatives;[36] slaves had various skills and performed many tasks, and had accordingly a variety of professional roles: artisans, traders, bankers, sailors, builders, entertainers, cultivators;[37] slaves had ethnic identities from their life before slavery or acquired/constructed new ethnic identities in the course of their life in bondage;[38] slaves participated in various cults and were thus worshippers and devotees of many deities.[39]

I want to focus in particular on two aspects of slave identity: gender and work. Until fairly recently, scholars often adopted an androcentric perspective on slavery or conceived it as a gender-neutral experience; this is a charge from which my own work cannot be exempted. But over the last twenty years a growing number of works has started to assert the profound implications of gender on slave experience in antiquity.[40] This attention to gender has started to redress the imbalance in the coverage of our sources; while agricultural treatises might give the impression that rural slaves were exclusively male, a careful reading of the sources can reveal the significant role of slave women on ancient estates.[41] While androcentric perspectives have conceptualised *vilicae* as merely the wives of *vilici* (overseers), recent gender-sensitive work has shown the independent role of *vilicae* in the estate economy.[42] The study of Roman freedwomen has revealed the role of gender in the process of manumission and the conflicted ways in which freedwomen negotiated their transition from chattels to respectable female citizens.[43] While

---

[33] Achilles Tatius, *Leukippe and Kleitophon* 6.22.

[34] Harper 2013: 19–22, 2017.

[35] For Malchus in fourth-century CE Syria, see Jerome, *Life of Malchus* 6; Lenski 2011a, Gray 2015. For Saint Patrick in fifth-century CE Ireland, see his *Confession* 1.16–19; Thompson 1985; McLuhan 2001.

[36] Willvonseder 2010; Mouritsen 2011b; Schmitz 2012.

[37] Joshel 1992; Daoust 2019.

[38] Hunt 2015.

[39] Bömer 1981, 1990; Hodkinson and Geary 2012; Fischer 2017.

[40] Joshel and Murnaghan 1998; Reduzzi-Merola and Storchi Marino 1999; Glazebrook 2017.

[41] See the pioneering work of Roth 2007; for female labour in agriculture, see Scheidel 1995, 1996a.

[42] Roth 2004; see also Setälä 2002.

[43] Wacke 2001; Weiler 2001; Kleijwegt 2012; Perry 2013.

family was important in the life of ancient slaves, the fact that manumission inscriptions often record women being manumitted along with their children, but almost never fathers with children, raises important questions about the differential impact of gender on the slave family.[44] Not only was gender an important aspect of slave identity, but it also created profound differences in how slaves experienced slavery and life under slavery.

Given the significance of work in the lives of slaves, this was obviously an important aspect of slave identity. We have seen in Chapter 4 how the variety of co-existing slaving strategies created a large and diverse number of work tasks and professions for ancient slaves. Work provided a means of categorising slaves: masters could appoint slaves to particular tasks, and, in particular in elite households, the division of labour among slaves could be very developed.[45] At the same time, work could provide a means of slave self-understanding, as attested by the numerous inscriptions and reliefs in which Roman slave and freed persons record their profession or work task.[46] It is of course worth pointing out that professional identity was a gendered experience: the difference between the large number of male slaves and freedmen commemorated with their professional identities and the general absence of professional identities from the epitaphs of female slaves and freedwomen is eloquent testimony of how gender affected identity and experience.[47]

To understand better the role of work in slave identity the concept of work status is particularly useful. Jean Andreau introduced the concept in ancient history in order to distinguish between the different groups involved in Roman financial activities; the concept has been further developed by Nicolas Tran.[48] Work status can be distinguished from either legal status or the wider social status associated with honour, prestige and lifestyle. Work status refers to 'the material organization of an individual's working life, the mode of his remuneration and the influence it exerted on his mentality, the possibility of uniting in work, the manner in which work was conceived relative to the rest of life, how work was chosen and could be changed, or work's relationship to the state'.[49] Given the diverse slaving strategies and the work niches they created for slaves, work mattered for slaves in very different ways and created distinct work statuses.

Tran has explored the various work statuses of slaves and freed persons in Roman ports. One work status concerned drudge slaves, like warehousemen, porters, oarsmen and boat haulers. These slaves performed manual labour and were largely unskilled or had limited professional training. They usually worked under the direct control of their masters or supervisors and received rations as remuneration, but some of them were allowed to work on their own on condition of surrendering part of their earnings to their masters. A second group involved trusted slaves in a variety of

[44]  Tucker 1982.
[45]  Treggiari 1975a.
[46]  Joshel 1992; Hasegawa 2005: 30–51; George 2006; Daoust 2019.
[47]  Treggiari 1976, 1981; Günther 1987; Malaspina 2003.
[48]  Andreau 1999: 3–4; Tran 2013a.
[49]  Tran 2013b: 663.

capacities: shipmasters, agents accompanying a ship, commercial agents or business managers. These slaves possessed various skills (navigation, literacy, accounting), were given different degrees of autonomy or initiative, were remunerated in diverse ways and often had significant opportunities to become financially comfortable.[50] Work statuses divided slaves into different groups; at the same time, slaves might share the same work status with other freeborn or manumitted workers. In this respect, it is also worth underlining the fact that some slaves were the de facto masters of other slaves (*servi vicarii*), a phenomenon which was quite common in the Roman world for the trusted slaves analysed above. It should be obvious that for slave-owning slaves and their *vicarii* it was their different work status that was more significant than their common legal status as slaves.[51]

As is evident, slaves did not understand themselves exclusively on the basis of the imposed category of slavery. But is it not true that law, which was based on the exclusionary definitional category of slavery as property, only recognised their role as slaves and refused to acknowledge as legally consequential their other roles? Patterson's famous description of slavery as social death is precisely an attempt to drive home this point.[52] Irrespective of how much slaves tried to create families and professional, ethnic or religious communities, from the point of view of the slaveholding societies in which they lived all of these roles were legally invisible and the only role that mattered was that of slave.

There are various points that need to be addressed in this respect. To start with, while slavery as social death is a recurrent tendency in slaveholding societies, the extent to which the various roles of slaves are recognised by law is historically variable. To give only one example, as noted in brief in earlier chapters, Islamic law recognised slave marriage as legally consequential. Male and female slaves could marry other slaves or free persons, and once they married, male slaves had the same rights vis-à-vis their wives that free husbands had. In fact, when a female slave married a male slave, both her master and her slave husband had rights over her and needed to find a compromise in which both rights were honoured when they came into conflict.[53] Ancient Near Eastern and Islamic laws stipulated that if a female slave had given birth to a child recognised by the master as his own, she could no longer be sold and would have to be manumitted once the master died.[54] Examples could be multiplied, but it should be fairly obvious that social death is not some kind of universal sociological law of slavery, but a phenomenon that varies across time and space; both the regularity of social death and its limits and modifications are phenomena that need to be examined historically, rather than simply taken for granted.

We can in fact improve on Patterson's concept by making two observations. The first is the need to distinguish between different arenas and orders of social life. We can distinguish between the **interaction order** of everyday life and the **institutional**

---

[50] Tran 2013b.
[51] For *vicarii*, see Baba 1990; Reduzzi-Merola 1990.
[52] Patterson 1982.
[53] Ali 2010: 65–96.
[54] See above, p. 3; Westbrook 1998; Ali 2010: 164–86; Tsai 2014; Reid 2017.

**order** of those aspects of life that take place within institutionalised organisations (the political institutions, the legal system, etc.).[55] Both the interaction and the institutional order include a variety of **arenas**: in the interaction arena we can distinguish the arenas of work, family, sociality, cult, exchange, etc.[56] Free and slave people participated in various such arenas and adopted a variety of roles, some of which were relevant for specific arenas only, while others were relevant across different arenas. Both free and slave people adopted diverse roles in the various arenas of the interaction order; in fact, the interaction order would not have functioned if the various roles adopted by the slaves were not recognised by the free and slave people who interacted with them. Ps.-Xenophon's *Constitution of the Athenians*, a source critical of Athenian democracy and society, presents a characteristic illustration of this phenomenon:

> If anyone is also surprised at the fact that here they allow their slaves to live in luxury and, some of them, magnificently, they could be shown to be doing this too with good reason. For where there is a naval power, it is necessary to be a slave to one's slaves for the money – so that we may be taking the slave's earnings – and to let them free. 'But in Lacedaemon, my slave feared you'. But if your slave fears me, there will be a risk that he even offers his money so as not to be in danger. Where there are wealthy slaves, it is no longer to my benefit that my slave should fear you. This is why we established that the slaves too have equal rights to free speech as the free, and the metics as the citizens.[57]

Although we cannot take this observation as a disinterested description of Athenian reality, its logic is quite clear.[58] The Athenian interaction order of exchange involved slave artisans and traders, who worked and lived on their own and paid their masters a fixed or variable proportion of their earnings. If one applied the prototypical category of slavery, in which slaves behaved slavishly and feared free people, the transactions would have benefited the free customers and financially damaged both the slaves and their masters. As a result, the Athenian interaction order required that people involved in exchanges would treat other people not only on the basis of the category of slavery but to a significant degree on the basis of professional categories. In the Athenian interaction order of exchange (but apparently not in that of Sparta) the alternative self-understanding of slaves on the basis of profession was in fact recognised by their exchange partners.[59]

The multiple self-understandings of slaves could therefore be recognised in various arenas of the interaction order. But, in contrast to free people, there was no automatic recognition of slave self-understandings across the different arenas. If customers recognised a slave in his professional self-understanding in the arena of exchange, it was still possible that in his interactions with his master or in the arena of cult he was merely

---

[55] Jenkins 2002: 68–76.
[56] Rabbås 2015.
[57] Ps.-Xenophon, *Constitution of the Athenians* 1.11–12.
[58] Cataldi 2000; Cohen 2000.
[59] Canevaro 2018: 120–1.

categorised as a slave. The recognition of the various self-understandings of slaves in the different arenas of the interaction order was not as easy or automatic as that of free people. It took a lot of work for slaves to have their self-understandings recognised in particular arenas and more work to have them recognised across the different arenas. Some slaves would have more or less succeeded in this work, while many others would have more or less failed.

But while at least a certain degree of success was plausible in the arenas of the interaction order, things tended to be much more difficult as regards the institutional order. As we commented above, social death is a recurring phenomenon across space and time. Even if slaves succeeded in having their alternative self-understandings recognised in various arenas of the interaction order, the institutional order would often recognise solely their categorisation as slaves.[60] This disjuncture stresses the value of distinguishing between the interaction and the institutional order. At the same time, social death in the institutional order was far from universal, as we saw above. The question of why certain institutional orders recognised certain slave self-understandings while others imposed a blanket version of social death is certainly an important one that has been little explored. What role did slave agency play in these outcomes? To what extent were they the unintended outcome of the premises employed by the legal system? How did slaves take advantage of such openings? These are questions that future research will need to address.[61]

I will finish this discussion with three comments. We have established the existence of a disjuncture between the categorisation of people as slaves and the existence of alternative self-understandings of slaves as free people in captivity and as having a variety of familial, kin, professional, ethnic and religious roles, and we have explored how this disjuncture operated in the various arenas of the interaction and the institutional order. The best way to capture this disjuncture and to explore its historical ramifications is by introducing a distinction between nominal and actual identities.[62] **Nominal** identities refer to the theoretical implications of being categorised with a particular label; **actual** identities concern the extent to which a particular categorisation is applied in reality and shapes the lives of those classified under the label. There could be a significant disjuncture between the nominal identity of slave, which in theory could exclusively affect all aspects of slaves' lives, and their actual identities, where their alternative self-understandings could affect various aspects of their lives instead of the slave categorisation or where the alternative self-understandings mitigated the effects of the nominal slave identity. The struggle to create as big a gap as possible between the nominal slave identity and the actual identities of slaves was one of the major processes that affected the global history of slavery.

My second point is that the extent to which slave self-understandings were recognised by the institutional orders depended to some extent on the categorisation

---

[60] Canevaro 2018: 121–2.

[61] Cf. Zeuske 2013: 221–60. For a comparative perspective from the Americas which stresses the role of slave agency, see de la Fuente and Gross 2020.

[62] I have tried to clarify Jenkins' terminological distinction between nominal and virtual identities: Jenkins 2008: 99–101.

models and modes of identification employed by each institutional order. Certain societies, like early modern Europe and Thailand, recognised a spectrum of statuses in their institutional order;[63] but, as recent studies have noted, Greek institutional orders operated on the basis of a single categorical distinction between free and slave.[64] When it came to groups with privileges, such as public slaves, Greek institutional orders did not create distinct status positions and a spectrum of statuses; instead, they chose to treat public slaves like free people for certain purposes, such as the conferral of public honours, and as slaves for other purposes, such as punishment.[65] It sounds plausible that institutional orders which employ spectra of statuses are more likely to recognise the alternative self-understandings of slaves, while institutional orders which employ binary and exclusive categorisations are less likely to do so. Nevertheless, the case of Islamicate societies suggests caution: Islamic law operated with a binary and exclusive categorisation between slave and free and without spectra of statuses, while at the same time recognising various slave self-understandings. Clearly, we should avoid simplifications before the issue has been explored in depth.

Consequently, we should eschew a one-dimensional approach to slave status. Some scholars have adopted Finley's proposal of incorporating legal, social, political and economic aspects of status (see above, Chapter 2) into a single spectrum of statuses. Kamen's study of status in classical Athens presented a unified spectrum which included various aspects of status; this allowed her to distinguish between chattel slaves, privileged chattel slaves and freed persons with conditional freedom.[66] But, as Lewis has argued, this unified approach can produce highly misleading results, and we should instead distinguish between institutionalised and non-institutionalised aspects of status.[67] Slavery as property was institutionalised in ancient communities, though this institutionalisation took rather different forms or had different inflections among the various Greek and other Mediterranean and Near Eastern communities, as we shall see in Chapter 8. Non-institutionalised aspects of status (wealth, comportment, education, achievement, authority) were significant as well, but formed distinct spectra, which did not necessarily align with the legal spectrum. The case of rich slaves, like the Athenian slave bankers or slaves who exercised power or influence, like public slaves or the slaves of Roman magnates, are excellent illustrations of how different spectra of status might not align, thus producing the phenomenon of status dissonance.[68]

The extent to which legal and non-legal aspects of slave status will align, thus effectively creating a single spectrum, or will diverge significantly, thus producing major issues of status dissonance, is also the result of historical conditions and processes. Few societies, if any, have managed to make the different aspects of slave status align closely, and the antebellum US South is probably one of the closest approximations. In other societies status dissonance might be very extensive, in particular where

---

[63] Turton 1980; Bush 1992.
[64] See in particular Azoulay and Ismard 2018.
[65] Ismard 2017a: 57–79; Lewis 2018: 72–92.
[66] Kamen 2013; see also my review in Vlassopoulos 2015–16.
[67] Lewis 2018: 72–92.
[68] On status dissonance, see Davies 2017.

slaves manned armies and bureaucracies and had opportunities to become very rich, as in many African and Islamic societies and, in important ways, in imperial Rome as well.[69] Most slaveholding societies were probably in between these two extremes; in these societies various forms of status dissonance produced by misalignment between different uses of slavery existed and could produce significant outcomes, but the prototypical conceptual system of slave status espoused by the political community put a ceiling on the extent of status dissonance.

My third point concerns Patterson's concept of social death. I have tried to show that while there is obvious value in the concept, it can also be deeply misleading if taken as the universal essence of slavery. I would like to heed Vincent Brown's call to reconceptualise social death not as a constant and universal condition of slavery but as a recurrent existential threat that slaves faced.[70] The institutional order, and in important ways the interaction order as well, presented slaves with the constant spectre of social death. It required a lot of effort by slaves to face this existential threat and try to limit as much as possible its effects on their lives. For many slaves the threat became their everyday reality; others mitigated the threat with more or less success and for longer or shorter periods; a lucky few managed to overcome the threat in one way or another.

Let us now move to the third aspect of identity: that of groupness. As we have commented above, while the combination of categorisation, self-understanding and networking that constitutes groupness is a potentiality for many forms of identity, the groupness of different identities varies significantly across space and time. Accordingly, whether and to what extent the slave categorisation would acquire groupness is something that needs to be explored historically, rather than taken for granted.[71]

There were strong factors that worked against slave groupness. Many masters owned one or just a few slaves, who would spend most of their time with their masters and their families, rather than with other slaves.[72] This, alongside other wider factors, would strengthen the significance of relational modes and minimise the opportunities for slave groupness. Furthermore, the major asymmetries of power, and the fact that most institutional orders did not accord slaves any rights, made slave groupness fragile and dangerous. The threat of severe punishment made most public expressions of slave groupness a very dangerous affair and provided strong incentives for slaves to act and think in individual or relational terms.[73] While relational modes existed in all slaveholding societies, in certain societies they acquired particular prominence. In such cases, both categorisation and self-understanding tended to focus on the particular relationship between specific slaves and masters and the quality of this relationship.

---

[69] For African societies, see Stilwell 2000; for the Ottoman society, see Toledano 2017.

[70] Brown 2009.

[71] See the reflections of McKeown 2019.

[72] For small-scale slaveholders in classical Athens, see Lewis 2018: 180–93; Porter 2019a: 130–68. For slaves owned by Roman craftsmen and traders, see Tran 2013a. For slaves in the labour strategies of middling and small households in the Roman world, see Groen-Vallinga 2017: 87–153. For small-scale slaveholders in late antiquity, see Harper 2011: 100–43.

[73] See the general argument of Kolchin 1983; for individual strategies of ancient slaves, see Hunt 2017b.

This would imply that the relationship between slave and master would matter more for practical purposes than the categorical identification of slave, and that slave self-understanding would give prominence to the relationship with the master and with fellow-slaves of the same master, rather than to the status of slave shared with other slaves belonging to other masters.

This is in my view one of the prominent differences between Greek and Roman slaveries. Greek slaveries placed relatively limited emphasis on the relational mode; this was partly because relational modes of identification had limited purchase in Greek societies. Lineages were relatively short, there were few corporate groups based on real kinship (unlike corporate groups based on fictive kinship, like tribes and phratries) and these corporate groups rarely functioned collectively.[74] Romans shared with other Italian societies the corporate kinship group (*gens*) and its shared gentilicial name; it is of course highly significant that Roman freed persons took the gentilicial name (*gentilicium*) of their former masters and were in this way included into the corporate kinship group.[75]

I want to illustrate this difference between Greek and Roman slaveries through some examples. The number of cases in which Greek slaves mention their masters' names in their dedications or epitaphs is extremely small;[76] many extant Greek dedications and epitaphs must belong to slaves, but the absence of mention of the slave identity or the name of the master makes identification impossible. This is the reason that unless we are given extra clues by the onomastics or some other oblique reference to slavery, it is often difficult or impossible in Greek epigraphy to attribute epitaphs or dedications to slaves.[77] On the other hand, there are innumerable epitaphs or dedications in which slaves refer to their Roman masters.[78] This is of course very common in Latin epigraphy,[79] but it is telling that most of the Greek inscriptions in which slaves mention their masters concern the slaves of Roman masters.[80] Dedications made by slaves independently from their masters are particularly telling, as they show how slaves of Roman masters conceived of their identity: an ostracon with a Latin inscription from the Cave of the Nymphs in Ithaca records the presence in 35 BCE of Epaphroditus, the slave of Novius, perfumer in the Via Sacra;[81] a bilingual, Greek and

---

[74] For kinship, lineages and corporate groups in Athens, see Humphreys 2018. From a comparative standpoint, see the significance of lineages and corporate groups in Chinese societies: Ebrey and Watson 1986; Naquin and Rawski 1987.

[75] For the Roman gens, see C. J. Smith 2006. But it is important to note that many Roman freedmen did not become Roman citizens (the so-called Junian Latins). This raises some very interesting questions about what the shared *gentilicium* meant for this category of non-citizen freedmen. For Junian Latins, see below, Chapter 6.

[76] Among the very few examples, mostly from Roman times, see *SEG* XV, 787 (Malos); *IG* XII(9), 116 (Tamynai); *I.Byzantion* 185 (Byzantion).

[77] For a Greek dedication which can only be attributed to slaves because of the onomastics of the dedicators, see *IG* II², 2940.

[78] See the cases collected in Eck and Heinrichs 1993. For the identification forms of Roman slaves and their development over time, see Oxé 1904.

[79] See the overview of slaves and freedmen in Latin epigraphy in Bruun 2014.

[80] See, for example, *SEG* XIX, 782 (Polyetta); *SEG* XLVI, 1475 (Miletos); *I.Kios* 49 (Kios); *TAM* V(1), 71 (Silandos).

[81] *An.Ep.* 1932, no. 22.

Latin, rupestral inscription from Wadi Menih in the eastern Egyptian desert records the presence in 6 CE of Lysas, slave of Publius Annius Plocamus.[82] These slaves found it essential to record as part of their own identity the name of their Roman masters.

My next example is a Latin inscription on an altar from second-century CE Chester in Britain:

> To Fortune the Home-Bringer, to Aesculapius, and to Salus the freedmen and slaves (*familia*) of Titus Pomponius Mamilianus Rufus Antistianus Funisulanus Vettonianus, son of Titus, of the Galerian voting-tribe, imperial legate, gave and dedicated this.[83]

This altar was set up by the freedmen and slaves of a Roman imperial officer; it is a collective dedication by a group of people whose connecting link is that they were current and former slaves of the same master. It is telling that the inscription employs the Latin term *familia*, which describes a group of slaves belonging to the same master; equally notable is the mention of the freedmen separately from the slave *familia*.[84] My next example is a Greek inscription from Miletos, dating to the imperial period:

> Tiberius Iulius Frugi Damianus, son of Titus Damianus, chief priest of [the province of] Asia, [member of the tribe] Cornelia; the *familia* honours its own master.[85]

In this example, the *familia* of fellow slaves honoured their own master, a priest of the imperial cult. While the inscription is in Greek, it is telling that it uses the transliterated Latin term *familia*; equally telling is the fact that these slaves belonged to an influential Roman citizen. My final example concerns the collective burial monuments (*columbaria*) of the slaves and freed persons belonging to the great aristocratic families of Rome in the early imperial period.[86] There is of course nothing equivalent from the Greek world, and this shows the significance of the relational mode for Roman slaves and freed persons.[87]

The last two examples point out the need for careful analysis. The inscriptions from Chester and Miletos and the Roman *columbaria* illustrate the intermeshing of two factors: on the one hand, we see the significance of the relational mode linking masters and slaves as a means of slave self-understanding, but on the other, we do actually see here examples of slave groupness, in the form of the *familia* of fellow slaves belonging to the same master. The relational mode did not necessarily preclude the emergence of slave groupness; but it is plausible to assume that forms of slave groupness based

---

[82] *An.Ep.* 1999, nos 1720–1.
[83] *CIL* VII, 164.
[84] Flory 1978.
[85] *SEG* XLVI, 1475.
[86] See, for example, *An.Ep.* 1996, no. 253, which records a burial monument destined for the freedmen, freedwomen and slave *familia* of Marcella, Messalla and Regillus.
[87] For Roman *columbaria*, see Buonocore 1984; Caldelli and Ricci 1999; Hasegawa 2005; Bodel 2008; Penner 2012; Galvao-Sobrinho 2012; Mouritsen 2013; Borbonus 2014. For grave plots in the Greek world, see Zelnick-Abramovitz 2017.

on the relational mode would tend to pose serious limits on the emergence of forms of groupness which were based on the common status of slavery and irrespective of belonging to different masters. In other words, the relational mode tended to promote forms of slave groupness that could not be easily extended to include slaves belonging to different masters. This factor is an important aspect in the history of ancient slavery.

Slave groupness could also emerge on the basis of the alternative slave self-understandings. Slaves could constitute or participate in groups on the basis of cult, ethnicity, profession or kinship. We shall explore such slave groups in detail in Chapter 6, so I will refrain from giving specific examples here. Slaves could thus participate in a wide range of groups, but these groups were not necessarily composed exclusively of slaves. Let us take the case of groups based on kinship and family. In societies which prohibited mixed marriages between free and slave, slave groupness on the basis of kinship would tend to create groups exclusively composed of slaves. Of course, even under such circumstances, many of these kinship groups would become mixed over time. Slaves would have relatives who had been manumitted; in cases like Rome, where many manumitted slaves became citizens, many slaves would have free and even citizen relatives, with all the historical consequences that this had.[88] And in those societies where mixed marriages between slave and free were recognised, like ancient Near Eastern societies, Islamicate societies or Gortyn in Crete, kinship groupness would by definition include both slave and free people.

Groupness based on ethnicity or religion could of course create communities composed only of slaves.[89] It is rare, nevertheless, to find cults exclusively for slaves in antiquity; on the contrary, slaves usually participated in mixed cults, some of which had devotees from the citizen community, while others had devotees from free foreigners who originated from the same regions as the slaves.[90] The same tends to apply to groupness on the basis of ethnicity: the Thracian community in Athens and the Jewish community in Rome included both free and slave members, even if the proportions might vary according to community, time and space (further discussed in Chapter 6). Finally, groupness on the basis of profession was the least likely to create groups consisting only of slaves. This was because there were hardly any professions that were restricted to free people, and very few that were restricted to slaves; as a result, professional groups tended to be mixed (further discussed in Chapter 6).[91] Furthermore, the various work statuses of ancient slaves, even within the same work environment, as we saw above (Chapter 5), could also potentially destabilise any form of slave groupness based on work.

We can now register a paradox. Notwithstanding the strong factors that worked against the emergence of slave groupness, slaves did in fact participate in a variety of groups. But slave groupness was often not based on their identities *qua* slaves, but on the various other self-understandings which co-existed with their categorisation as slaves. The slave categorisation was most prominent when slaves acted individually and in relation to their masters; it could be less prominent when slaves acted collectively and

---

[88] Mouritsen 2011b.
[89] See the examples discussed in Zoumbaki 2005.
[90] Bömer 1981, 1990; McKeown 2012; North 2012; Fischer 2017.
[91] For the professional identities of skilled workers, see Tran 2017.

within forms of groupness that had little to do with slavery per se. This is not to deny that there also existed forms of slave groupness based on the slave categorisation, like the *familiae* of Roman fellow slaves we have examined above. But if we wish to study slave groupness, we must be prepared to explore situations in which slaves constructed groups on the basis of factors that had little to do with slavery.

There is an important implication from all the above observations. Historians continue to use the term slave as a shorthand, without realising that in this way they affirm the institutional order of many slaveholding societies, which claimed that the categorisation as slave was all that mattered. But, as we have seen, slaves possessed alternative self-understandings which were not based on slavery; there was often a significant disjuncture between the nominal slave identity and the actual slave identity; and many forms of slave groupness were not based on slavery. It is for these reasons that it seems to me necessary to reconceptualise 'slaves' as **'enslaved persons'**. If the term 'slave' implies that categorisation as slave was all that mattered, the term 'enslaved person' recognises the real impact of the slave category on the lives of the enslaved, while at the same time opening for historical exploration the extent to which there was a significant gap between nominal and actual identities and the historical processes and factors that created these gaps. This is not a nominalist plea to change our vocabulary by banishing the term slave from it; I do not think this is likely to happen, and there is no point in merely exchanging one term for another, if the way we approach these terms remains the same. Thinking of slaves as enslaved persons is a first step towards changing our approach to the history of slavery.[92]

I will finish this chapter with a final comment. A particularly useful tool for conceptualising the complex and contradictory identities of enslaved persons is the theory of recognition developed by the critical theorist Axel Honneth. Honneth has argued that recognition constitutes the moral grammar of social conflicts; building on Hegelian philosophy and the conceptual interactionism of G. H. Mead, he has suggested that the struggle for recognition comprises three distinct aspects. The first aspect is love and focuses on emotions; love is the recognition of the emotional needs of human beings and an essential element of healthy psychological development. The second aspect of recognition is respect and focuses on rights, and in particular legal rights; the rights that communities accord to their members enable them to make claims to dignity and consequently develop their sense of moral autonomy. The third aspect is esteem, and focuses on recognition for the particular features, capacities and achievements of each human being.[93]

We have seen above how social death constituted an existential threat that enslaved persons continually faced; the various struggles for recognition resulted from the mighty desire of enslaved persons to defy the threat of social death. Emotional recognition as love is an essential quest of all human beings; the slave quest for love, friendship and support materialised in the formation of families, kinship groups and

---

[92] I generally agree with the criticisms offered by Rinehart 2016: 13–15, as regards other reasons for adopting the term 'enslaved persons'.

[93] Honneth 1996; see also Zurn 2015.

social networks that we shall examine in more detail in Chapter 6. Given the overwhelming focus of past research on the master–slave relationship, it is important to
note that many enslaved persons primarily sought emotional recognition from third
parties: other enslaved persons and free persons apart from their masters. But while this
refocusing is salutary and necessary, it would be a mistake to forget that many slaves
would also seek emotional recognition from their masters by trying to turn their secondary relationships based on the roles of masters and slaves into primary relationships.
This is obviously relevant for the various sexual relationships between masters and
slaves, which we examined in Chapter 4; but the phenomenon is not restricted solely
to sexual relationships, and we badly need a systematic examination of all its facets.[94]

The second aspect of the struggle for recognition is obviously the one that is least
relevant for ancient enslaved persons, but this is still particularly useful, as it highlights
the peculiarity of slaves in comparison with other subaltern groups. It is of course
extremely rare in world history before the nineteenth century for slaves to fight for
the recognition of legal rights.[95] The difference in this respect between slaves, who
were not recognised as an *estate* (a group of people with certain privileges and duties
towards other *estates* and the community as a whole),[96] and late medieval serfs, who
were recognised as an *estate* within the community and who fought to have their rights
to property and marriage legally recognised, is telling.[97]

Instead, it was the struggle for the recognition of esteem, alongside emotional recognition, that attracted the energy and initiative of enslaved persons. They could seek
recognition for their moral characteristics and their various skills and achievements, as
we shall see in Chapter 7. As with so many aspects of slaving, the quest for esteem was
a contradictory process; on the one hand, it gave enslaved persons something essential
for all human beings and allowed them to overcome the threat of social death; but on
the other hand, the slave quest for self-esteem could be employed by masters to get
enslaved persons to work better and cultivate the values accepted by the masters.[98] As
with the quest for emotional recognition, enslaved persons did not seek esteem only
from their masters. The creation of communities based on profession, religion and
ethnicity were alternative means through which enslaved persons sought and found
esteem.[99]

Honneth's theory is geared towards understanding the identities, moralities and
social conflicts of modernity; accordingly, it is not developed with a view to exploring pre-modern societies and groups like slaves.[100] Nevertheless, such an extension
and further elaboration would be undoubtedly fruitful, as the theory of recognition
captures particularly well the struggles and identities of enslaved persons.

---

[94]　See the studies in Dondin-Payre and Tran 2017.
[95]　See the framework of Genovese 1979; cf. Helg 2016.
[96]　On estates, see below, pp. 127–8.
[97]　Blickle 2003.
[98]　Joshel 1992; McKeown 2007a: 24–8; Roth 2010b.
[99]　For Roman honour communities including slaves, see Lendon 2001: 95–103.
[100]　But see Honneth 2012 for his discussion of the master–slave dialectic in Hegel.

# 6

## Dialectical Relationships

HAVING PRESENTED A GENERAL framework for studying the identities of enslaved persons in Chapter 5, we shall now move to examine in more detail three major dialectical relationships that shaped the identities of enslaved persons and defined how they exercised their agency. These are the relationships between masters and slaves; between free and slave; and between the members of the communities that slaves created or participated in. It was the concatenation of these three dialectical relationships that held together the slaving contexts and strategies that we examined in Chapter 4.

### The Master–Slave Relationship

In order to understand this relationship, we need first to examine the various kinds of slaves and masters; since we examined the various kinds of slaves in the previous chapter, we will now focus on the forms and scale of mastery and its impact on slaving. It is rather strange that there are innumerable studies of slaves, but there have been very few studies that focus on ancient masters and their diversity.[1] The best existing study concerns late Roman masters, who can be divided into four different categories: the first two groups, the illustrious households of the senatorial aristocracy and the elite households of the equestrian and local aristocracies, comprised roughly the wealthiest 1.5 per cent of Roman society, while the 'bourgeois' households of merchants, artisans and professionals in the cities and the prosperous agricultural households in the countryside constituted roughly 10 per cent of the Roman population. According to Harper's estimations, Late Roman slave-owners owned about five million slaves, close to 10 per cent of the overall population, divided equally between the illustrious and elite households on the one hand, and the bourgeois and agricultural households on the other.[2] This means that a tiny proportion of the population (the illustrious and elite slave-owners) controlled as many slaves as the rest of the free population.[3] Roman slavery was an agglomeration of two rather distinct forms of slaving by two different kinds of masters: the large-scale use of slaves by illustrious and elite households, organised in complex hierarchies of urban households and rural estates,[4] and the small-scale employment of slaves for a variety of purposes by a wide and prosperous middling section of

---

[1] For studies of diverse groups of masters in the early modern world, see Oakes 1982; Bowman 1993; McCurry 1995; Dal Lago 2005; S. D. Smith 2006.

[2] For estimations of the patterns of slave ownership in classical Athens, see Lewis 2018: 168–94; for estimations of patterns of Italian slave ownership in the imperial period, see Scheidel 2004, 2005b.

[3] Harper 2011: 33–66.

[4] Harper 2011: 144–200.

Roman society.[5] There has been an ongoing debate as to whether on top of the tiny elite of the 1.5 per cent and the prosperous sections in the next 10 per cent of the population, we should also envisage a third group of masters with relatively limited means, at least for certain ancient societies. Lewis has recently argued that slaveholding in classical Athens extended far beyond the top 10 per cent of the Athenian population, and the argument sounds eminently plausible.[6] Whether we can extend this tripartite model to other ancient societies, and what functions and consequences slaveholding had for such wider groups, will require further work. For current purposes, it is sufficient to illustrate the issue with the tragic story of a young slave who belonged to a grammarian in early imperial Pergamon:

> The slave boy in question was owned by a grammarian. Every day, the teacher used to go to the baths accompanied by another slave and would leave behind in the house the slave in question, locking him in. His job was to look after the house and prepare the meal. One day, however, he felt extremely thirsty; there was no water inside, and so he drank a great amount of old wine. From that point onwards, he was persistently unable to sleep; later his temperature rose and he died from the lack of sleep and the delirium that befell him.[7]

The tragic end of this slave boy would have never occurred, had he belonged to a bigger household than that of this relatively poor grammarian.[8]

The huge slave retinues of elite Roman households could not be governed by direct relationships between masters and slaves, and required complex organisational hierarchies. This brings us to a fourth category of masters, that of organisations. When Augustus transformed the political structure of the Roman state, like previous Roman officeholders he employed his own slave staff in order to perform the various administrative and governmental functions that were now in the remit of the emperor.[9] The *familia Caesaris*, the slaves and freedmen of the emperors, formed an extensive hierarchy that both served the emperor personally and fulfilled the functions of an imperial bureaucracy. Because the *familia Caesaris* was inherited by each imperial successor, its members served under many different emperors and often had long-term careers.[10] Alongside the imperial slaves and freedmen, there were the public slaves employed by the Roman and Greek cities.[11] Finally, temples and sanctuaries had their own slaves;[12] the large sanctuaries and temple states in the Near East could own thousands of slaves.[13] And once

---

[5] Harper 2011: 100–43.

[6] Lewis 2018: 167–94.

[7] Galen, *On the affected parts* 8.132K.

[8] On the social milieu of ancient grammarians, see Kaster 1988.

[9] For the *familia Caesaris* as a household, see Schumacher 2001b.

[10] Chantraine 1967; Weaver 1972; Boulvert 1974.

[11] Eder 1980; Weiß 2004; Lenski 2006; Ismard 2017a; Luciani 2020.

[12] For one example of temple slaves in Sicily, see Heinen and Eppers 1984.

[13] For slaves in the temple states of Asia Minor, see Hülsen 2008. For the wider category of *hierodouloi*, oblates and temple dependants, see Scholl 1985; Dromard 2017: 76–117.

the Church became a major organisation of the Roman Empire, Church slaves further increased the number of slaves of organisations.[14]

While imperial slaves had at least a nominal human master, public slaves belonged to organisations rather than to individual human masters. Given the fact that Greek and Roman cities were run by office-holding elites who often changed annually, people who gave orders to public slaves would change constantly, while public slaves maintained organisational continuity. The fact that public slaves did not have personal human masters gave them important advantages.[15] The significance of this fact is underlined by the example of consecrated slaves. In many ancient communities slaves could be consecrated to particular deities and sanctuaries; consecrated slaves no longer had a personal master, and as sacred property they maintained a status that was in many ways equivalent to that of freed persons.[16]

The dialectical relationship between masters and slaves had a contradictory nature.[17] On the one hand, when the power of masters over slaves was not circumscribed by other forces and factors, it could lead to the most tyrannical and cruel treatment of slaves.[18] The master was the equivalent of a little king who could rule his subjects as he saw fit. A characteristic illustration of this phenomenon is a story narrated by Cassius Dio about Vedius Pollio, a Roman equestrian in the early imperial period:

> Most of the things he did it would be wearisome to relate, but I may mention that he kept in reservoirs huge lampreys that had been trained to eat men, and he was accustomed to throw to them such of his slaves as he desired to put to death. Once, when he was entertaining Augustus, his cup-bearer broke a crystal goblet, and without regard for his guest, Pollio ordered the fellow to be thrown to the lampreys. Hereupon the slave fell on his knees before Augustus and supplicated him, and Augustus at first tried to persuade Pollio not to commit so monstrous a deed. Then, when Pollio paid no heed to him, the emperor said, "Bring all the rest of the drinking vessels which are of like sort or any others of value that you possess, in order that I may use them", and when they were brought, he ordered them to be broken. When Pollio saw this, he was vexed, of course; but since he was no longer angry over the one goblet, considering the great number of the others that were ruined, and, on the other hand, could not punish his servant for what Augustus also had done, he held his peace, though much against his will.[19]

A sadistic master like Vedius Pollio could feed his slaves to his lampreys; it is obvious that at the time of the narrative (the reign of Augustus) there was no law prohibiting Pollio from killing his slaves in this horrific manner, though this would come to change in the course of the early imperial period, as we shall see below. Somebody

[14] For a case-study of how one pope dealt with Church slaves, see Serfass 2006.
[15] Ismard 2017a: 57–79; see also Bruun 2008; Luciani 2019.
[16] Zanovello 2018.
[17] Dondin-Payre and Tran 2017.
[18] For the role of violence in ancient master–slave relationships, see the overviews in Hunt 2016; Lenski 2016; see also Parker 1989; Richlin 2017: 90–105.
[19] Cassius Dio, *Roman History* 54.23.

who objected to the practice could only attempt to dissuade the master (as Augustus did at the beginning) or intimidate him, if he was in the position to do so (as Augustus ultimately did). In fact, as Hopkins has pointed out, in the absence of legal restraints it was largely the cultivation of the appropriate morality and dispositions in masters that constituted the only realistic form of control; stories like these acted as forms of moral policing.[20]

Faced with such conditions, some slaves responded with violence, as in the famous case of Larcius Macedo, another cruel master and former slave, who was killed by his own enraged slaves.[21] Such explosions of slave violence against cruel masters could light the fire for slave rebellions, as was how the key narrative of the slave revolt in Sicily around 135 BCE described the cause of the slave revolt in Sicily around 135 BCE. The revolt erupted when the slaves of Damophilos and Megallis, a pair of cruel masters, could no longer bear their travails, and their rage was transformed into a rebellion once an appropriate leader was found.[22] Nevertheless, in most cases the fate of enslaved persons who reacted with violence would have been that of the slaves of Larcius Macedo: torture and execution. Collective violence, and, in fact, oppositional collective action in general, was very risky and dangerous for slaves.[23]

This is the reason that most slaves attempted to deal with their masters in alternative ways, which were not openly oppositional. This limited the risk, but also increased the rate of success; forms of action that did not directly threaten the authority of the masters were more likely to elicit their acquiescence because in this way masters would not lose face. This theatricality of master–slave interaction is well brought out by James Scott's concept of hidden transcripts in the relationship between elites and subaltern groups.[24] Slaves adopted a public transcript of deference in their interactions with masters, while also retaining a hidden transcript which was employed offstage among themselves.[25]

A common slave tactic was to limit the expectations of their masters. The instrumental modality of slavery required slaves who were living tools that existed with the sole purpose of fulfilling their masters' wishes. But at the same time, the everyday operation of slavery required a significant amount of slave initiative for the successful fulfilment of tasks.[26] This contradiction is well illustrated in a story from Aesop's *Life*. Xanthos, the philosopher master, has ordered his slave Aesop to follow his orders strictly:

'Pick up an oil-flask and towels, and let's go to the bath.' Aesop said to himself: 'Masters who are harsh in their demands for service are themselves the cause of their troubles. I will give a lesson to this philosopher, so that he might learn how

---

[20] Hopkins 1993: 8–9; on slavery and the role of exemplary stories, see Parker 1998.

[21] Pliny, *Epistles* 3.14; see Williams 2006; McKeown 2007b.

[22] Diodorus Siculus 34/5.2.1–24; Shaw 2001: 80–6.

[23] For the violent retribution of *the senatus consultum Silanianum*, see Harries and Du Plessis 2013.

[24] Scott 1985, 1990.

[25] On public and hidden transcripts of Roman freedmen, see Vermote 2016a: 439–524. For transcripts on the speech of slaves in Plautus, see Richlin 2017: 311–50.

[26] For the contradiction between instrumentality and initiative, see the comments of Giannella 2014: 99–152.

he should give orders.' So Aesop picked up the stuff mentioned above and, without putting oil in the flask, followed Xanthos to the bath. Xanthos took off his
clothes, gave them to Aesop and told him: 'Give me the oil-flask.' Aesop gave it
to him. Xanthos took the flask, found it empty when he tried to pour oil, and said:
'Aesop, where is the oil?' Aesop said: 'At home.' Xanthos said: 'What for?' Aesop
responded: 'Because you told me "pick up an oil-flask and towels"; you didn't
mention oil. And I was supposed to do nothing more than what I was told. For if I
didn't obey this instruction, I would be liable to a beating.' Then, he kept silent.[27]

It is of course unlikely that masters in those circumstances would usually accept
Aesop's point and not punish their slaves; the asymmetry in the relationship would
always allow masters to react with violence and anger, irrespective of who was right.
Dissimulation was thus a risky strategy, as the donkey Lucius found when he dissimu-
lated ignorance of the labour he was supposed to do in a bakery and got a beating
for his lack of initiative.[28] Nevertheless, enslaved persons who were willing and able
to play this tactic in the long term would ultimately force their masters to abandon
certain tasks or negotiate the best conditions for performing them.[29]

But the most successful strategy required enslaved persons to take advantage of the
fact that slavery often tended to be a primary relationship that involved people as a
whole, rather than a secondary relationship in which people interacted solely in their
roles as masters and slaves (an issue explored in Chapter 5). By employing modalities
of slavery like the negotiation of power or the reciprocal exchange of benefactions
and rewards, slaves could turn to their favour the features of primary relationships. An
excellent illustration of this comes from one of the Hellenistic mimiambs of Herodas.[30] The mimiamb depicts Bitinna, a jealous mistress who has sexual relations with
Gastron, one of her slaves, deciding to punish him cruelly when she suspects him of
cheating. Kydilla, a female fellow slave, tries to save Gastron by chastising her fellow
slave Pyrrhias for not showing sympathy with Gastron's plight, while also offering her
mistress a reason for reconsidering her decision:

**Kydilla**: Pyrrhias. You wretch! You deaf one! She's calling you. Ah! But one
will think that it is a grave-robber you pull to pieces – not your fellow-slave.
Do you see with how much force you are now dragging him to be tortured,
Pyrrhias? Ah! It is you whom Kydilla will see, with these very two eyes,
in five days, at Antidoros', to be rubbing your ankles with those Achaean
things that you recently shed.

**Bitinna**: Hey you. Come back here, keeping this man bound exactly as when
you were taking him away. Call me Kosis the tattooer and ask him to come
here, bringing needles and ink. You must turn many-coloured in one go.
Let him hang as gagged, as the . . . honourable Daos!

---

[27] *Life of Aesop* G38; Hopkins 1993: 10–21.
[28] Ps.-Lucian, *The Ass* 42.
[29] Bradley 1990.
[30] See Fountoulakis 2007.

**Kydilla**: No, mummy. Let him off now. I beg you. – As your Batyllis may live, and you may see her entering a husband's house and take her children in your arms. This one error . . .

**Bitinna**: Kydilla, don't give me grief, or I will run out of the house. Shall I let him off? This seventh-generation slave? And which woman won't justly spit on my face when she sees me? No, by the Tyrant! But since he, although a man, does not know himself, he will now find out, with this inscription on his forehead.

**Kydilla**: But it is the twentieth, and the Gerenia festival is in four days.

**Bitinna**: I'll let you off the hook now. And be grateful to this girl here, whom I cherish no less than Batyllis, as I reared her in my own arms. But when we have poured libations to the dead, you will then celebrate festival after festival bitterly.[31]

Kydilla employs a confrontational transcript towards her fellow slave Pyrrhias, for failing to show solidarity towards a fellow slave, but as regards her mistress her public transcript is completely different. Kydilla employs her primary relationship with her mistress to ask for lenient treatment for Gastron as a personal favour; at the same time, she knows how to give her mistress an excuse not to execute her original threat of punishment without losing face. The case shows clearly the consequences of the asymmetry of power and the existence of solidarity among the slaves. But at the same time, it illustrates the significance of individual action: Pyrrhias opts to follow orders instead of helping his fellow slave, while the successful defence of Gastron comes through the individual action of Kydilla, who utilises her personal relationship with Bitinna to achieve it. The smaller the units within which slaves operated, the more localised and individualised their resistance and identity would tend to be.[32]

While the preponderance of the master–slave relationship over other relationships could lead to enormous cruelty, the very same phenomenon could be of utmost importance and benefit to some slaves. The various terms for house-born slaves (*oikogenes*, *verna*) emphasised the bond between slaves and the masters' household.[33] Masters could bestow on their slaves names linked to their family onomastic tradition;[34] and they tended to place higher value and trust on house-born slaves.[35] The primary relationship between masters and slaves is also stressed by the phenomenon of *threptoi*, which is particularly prominent in certain areas, like Asia Minor. *Threptoi* could be slave or free persons, who were raised by third parties instead of their natural parents; in the case of slaves, it was often their masters and mistresses who played the role of raising *threptoi*. By employing this term, the emphasis could

---

[31] Herodas, *Mimiamb* 5.

[32] See the comparative perspective of Kolchin 1983.

[33] For Roman *vernae*, see Herrmann-Otto 1994.

[34] For the onomastics of slaves in the Greek world, see Vlassopoulos 2010, 2015a; Lewis 2017a; for the names of *vernae* and their implications, see Bruun 2013.

[35] See, for example, the priority in liberating home-born over bought slaves by the Achaean League in 146 BCE in order to meet their need for soldiers; Polybius, *History* 38.15.1–6.

be placed on the affective bonds of the primary relationship rather than on property or social death.[36] Bitinna's comment above, that she did what her slave Kydilla requested because she had raised her herself, is a good illustration of how this affective bond could occasionally function.

A powerful master could also protect his slaves against third persons. Historians of the US South have shown that while in the antebellum period black slaves were rarely lynched when they killed or assaulted whites, the lynching of black 'offenders' became very widespread after the abolition of slavery. Masters would protect their slave property against lynching, even for the purely selfish reasons of not forgoing their capital investment; there was nobody to protect black people when slavery was abolished.[37] The slaves of a powerful master could become more important and influential than many free persons or other lesser masters: the *familia Caesaris*, where a slave of the emperor might run whole provinces and give orders to freemen and nobles, is a characteristic illustration of this phenomenon.[38] A Greek inscription from an early imperial ossuary from Jericho records the burial place of Theodotos, who proudly records that he was the freedman of Queen Agrippina, the wife of emperor Claudius; while most inscriptions from this ossuary simply record the names of the deceased, the identity of Theodotos' former mistress was obviously too important to be omitted.[39]

But the phenomenon can be illustrated with other examples as well. My first example concerns an incident in the life of Cato the Younger, the famous Roman senator of the first century BCE:

It is said that, while in Syria, something ridiculous happened to Cato. When he was walking into Antioch, he saw outside, by the city gates, a large crowd of people drawn up on either side of the road. Among them, ephebes with military cloaks and boys had decorously positioned themselves in two separate groups, while some men, priests or magistrates, bore clean garments and garlands. Cato thought it most likely that the city was offering him a reception to honour him, and was getting angry at those of his men who had been sent in advance for not having prevented the event. He asked his friends to dismount and started to proceed with them on foot. When they arrived close, the man who was arranging all this and marshalling the crowd, a man already advanced in years, holding a staff in his hand and a garland, advanced and met Cato before the others and, without even greeting him, kept asking where they had left Demetrios and when he would appear. Demetrios had been a slave of Pompey. At that time, the whole world, so to speak, looked to Pompey, so court was paid to Demetrios at excess, as he had great influence with Pompey.[40]

---

[36] Ricl 2009.
[37] Johnson 1997: 427–8.
[38] Weaver 1972: 224–96; Duncan-Jones 2016: 143–52.
[39] *SEG* XXXI, 1405; see Eck 2013.
[40] Plutarch, *Life of Cato the Younger* 13.

In the eyes of the citizens of Antioch, Demetrios, the former slave of Pompey, was more significant than Cato, a scion of a noble family and a Roman senator. An early imperial inscription from Bithynia illustrates the same phenomenon:

> In the year 12, the village of the Okaenoi honoured Doryphoros, the estate manager of the excellent Claudia Eias, with a stele, statues, seating in the first row and prayers, throughout his life, together with his wife Potamias, for her virtue and her love for her husband. [The village bestowed these honours] because he has been our outstanding patron.[41]

The free villagers honour the slave manager of the estate of a Roman aristocrat, who was clearly an important landowner in the area, and maybe owned the lands cultivated by the villagers. That a slave manager could act as the patron of free villagers is a telling example of the consequences of the preponderance of the master–slave dialectic over other relationships.

## The Free–Slave Relationship

The second dialectical relationship that shaped slaving and enslaved persons was that between free and slave. This dialectical relationship took place in the context of the political community that we analysed in Chapter 4, but the relationships shaped by this context also affected all other relationships, as we shall see. The intervention of the political community in issues relating to slavery had two sides. On the one hand, it defined the distinction between free and slave, between citizen and outsider; on the other hand, the political community could decide to intervene in the theoretically unmediated relationship between masters and slaves, to superimpose other concerns on those of masters and slaves and even to subordinate the relationship between masters and slaves to those other concerns. By defining the distinction between slave and free, the political community shaped the prototypical conceptual system of slavery that we examined in Chapter 3; the intervention of the political community in the relationship between masters and slaves shaped how the definitional conceptual system of slavery as property operated in practice; and the radial conceptual system of the various modalities of slavery offered tools that the political community could employ for shaping the other two conceptual systems and their practical application.

Let us start with the distinction between slave and free. Unfortunately, this distinction is subject to some major conceptual problems and blind spots, which require some discussion before we can move on.[42] The first thing to notice is a methodological disjuncture: while slavery is primarily studied as an economic and social phenomenon, freedom is primarily conceived as a political, intellectual and cultural phenomenon.[43]

---

[41] *I.Iznik* 1201.

[42] See the comments of Alston 2011.

[43] For studies of freedom as a political and intellectual phenomenon in antiquity, see Wirszubski 1950; Dover 1988; Raaflaub 2004; Saxonhouse 2006; Arena 2012.

As a result, slavery and freedom are explored by scholars with different interests, disciplinary training and methodologies, and are rarely examined in tandem.[44] This disjuncture has important consequences. The Greeks could talk about the enslavement of Greek cities by the Athenians;[45] but because this reference to slavery concerns a political process rather than a socio-economic phenomenon, it is not considered as 'real' slavery but merely a metaphorical use; accordingly, no modern account of Greek slavery has anything to say about the use of the language of slavery in Greek interstate politics.[46] In Chapter 3 we have explored the different conceptual systems of slavery, while in Chapter 7 we will focus on the various modalities of slavery that composed the radial conceptual system; this wider framework can enable us to avoid the artificial separation that has characterised previous scholarship and allow us to examine economic, social, political, intellectual and cultural uses of slavery in tandem.

The conception of freedom as a political and cultural phenomenon has led to a deeply influential metanarrative. The concept of freedom, we are told, was nonexistent in the societies of the ancient Near East; its discovery by the ancient Greeks was supposedly one of their most momentous contributions to world history.[47] As with much else in the creation of the current orthodoxy, it was Finley who suggested that there was a paradoxical connection between slavery and the emergence of political freedom. As we saw in Chapter 2, Finley argued that Near Eastern subjects did not have political rights and their societies were characterised by a spectrum of statuses with innumerable gradations. It was the victory of Greek lower classes in acquiring citizens' rights during the archaic period that led to the creation of slave societies and the emergence of a single dividing line between slavery and freedom.

As we shall see in Chapter 8, this metanarrative is deeply misleading,[48] but what is of interest here is one of its consequences. If freedom was absent from Near Eastern societies, we can simply take for granted what we understand as freedom in ancient Greece and Rome as the only possible form of freedom;[49] if freedom was primarily a political and cultural phenomenon, then there is no reason to study in any detail its legal and social aspects, which are usually at the centre of attention when historians examine slavery. In this respect, it is telling that while there are innumerable articles and books devoted to the study of slaves, there is hardly any study devoted to free people as such. One of the reasons we do not study free people as such, is that we recognise that gender, political rights and wealth created major disjunctures between free people, which makes it more useful to focus attention instead on categories like rich and poor, citizens and metics, men and women. In Chapter 5 I have commented on the implications of this for the study of slaves: in the same way that we recognise

---

[44] Tamiolaki 2010 is a rare example of studying freedom and slavery in tandem. Patterson 1991 is an interesting study, but his methodology and assumptions are unfortunately unsound; cf. Hunt 2017a.

[45] Thucydides 1.98; see Brock 2007.

[46] Vlassopoulos 2011a; cf. Lewis 2018: 57–79, forthcoming.

[47] Raaflaub 2004; see the characteristically triumphalist account of Meier 2011.

[48] For critiques, see Rihll 1996; Vlassopoulos 2016b; Lewis 2018: 81–92.

[49] For the concept of freedom in non-Western societies, see Reid 1998, Snell 2001; von Dassow 2011, 2013, 2018.

that freedom was merely one factor among many others that affected the lives and conditions of free people, we should also recognise that slavery was merely one factor among many that affected the lives of enslaved people. Here, though, my interest lies in the opposite direction: while we have devoted a lot of attention to exploring the legal and social status of slaves, we have largely eschewed devoting the same amount of attention to the legal and social status of free people, with important consequences for the study of slavery; the relative lack of specific attention to the legal and social status of free people leaves the study of the legal and social status of slaves seriously unbalanced.[50]

We can start by abandoning once and for all the idea that the concept of freedom was unknown in the ancient Near East. If we refer to the definitional conceptual system of slavery as property, slaves were the property of their masters, while free people were not property. On the basis of this conceptual system, there is no doubt that freedom was a basic category of law in all societies of the ancient Near East. Not only was there no such thing as a spectrum of statuses in the Near East, but these societies also relied on a single fundamental distinction between free and slave.[51] Furthermore, Near Eastern societies were clearly familiar with the concept of the citizen as a member of a political community.[52]

The differences between Greek and Roman societies, on the one hand, and Near Eastern societies, on the other, concern rather the second and third conceptual systems of slavery. While the definitional system was solely concerned with whether an individual was property or not, the prototypical system concerned a range of practices and features that were considered typical of slaves or free people respectively, and of rights and claims which were considered as characteristic of free people and negated to slaves. One difference between Greco-Roman and Near Eastern societies is how they conceptualised prototypical status. Greek and Roman political communities tended to conceive freedom as a totalising, non-negotiable and unalterable status. By totalising status I refer to the tendency for this status to cover a growing proportion of aspects of life: being a free adult man meant to be treated with respect, to be autonomous, to not receive orders from other people, to be inviolable from physical punishment, torture and sexual exploitation; to be a free woman meant access to the lifestyle of sexual honour and marriage. By unalterable status, I mean the tendency to assume that freedom is ascribed at birth and cannot usually be lost in the course of an individual's life within his community, even if an individual wants to shed freedom.[53] The totalising and unalterable aspects tend to reinforce the fact that status is non-negotiable: it cannot be used as a chip that can be exchanged for other things, and it cannot be broken in pieces and negotiated in parts. The non-negotiable and unalterable aspects of the free

---

[50] Roman historians have dealt with issues concerning the legal and social status of free people to a much greater extent than Greek historians by looking at various forms of free status that did not entail citizenship, like the status of Latins, colonists and informally manumitted slaves: see Humbert 1976; Sirks 1983; Gardner 1986; Kremer 2006; Coşkun 2016. For an account of Roman citizenship that pays serious attention to the various groups that composed it, see Gardner 1993.

[51] Lewis 2018: 86–9; cf. von Dassow 2014.

[52] Von Dassow 2011, 2018; see also Vlassopoulos 2007b: 101–22.

[53] Cf. Thomas 2007.

status are also strongly linked to its totalising aspect: in societies where free status is unalterable and non-negotiable, the totalising tendency is consequently strengthened; in societies where people can willingly shed their freedom, negotiate parts of it or lose their freedom as a result of debt or punishment or as a consequence of their actions (as we have seen in our examination of early medieval slavery in Chapter 3), the totalising tendency is consequently weakened in practice.

I use the word tendency to stress the important point that this was a process that took various paths, left various exceptions and could be reversed. While free people in ancient Greece could not be flogged, it was curiously permitted to flog athletes;[54] while Greek soldiers could not be physically punished, this did not apply to Roman soldiers;[55] while Greeks considered the anal penetration of a male citizen's body acceptable under various circumstances, the Romans prohibited it under all circumstances;[56] while free Greeks could not generally be enslaved as a punishment, there were exceptions to this rule;[57] while free Romans usually could not be enslaved within their community, from the early imperial period onwards the *senatus consultum Claudianum* prescribed that free women who co-habited with slaves could become slaves.[58] Putting the issue in this way highlights the fact that there is no inherent link between being free and the totalising claims to autonomy, respect and inviolability. In the course of the history of the Roman Empire ordinary and elite Roman citizens gradually lost the right of inviolability from physical punishment and torture; this obviously did not mean that they stopped being free.[59] The tendency, followed by Greek and Roman political communities, to make free status totalising and unalterable was a contingent outcome of historical processes rather than the trans-historical quintessence of freedom.

In order to understand how political communities shaped the prototypical conceptual system of slavery, we can distinguish between two extremes. On the one hand, the political community might define very closely a range of practices and rights that were prohibited or negated to enslaved persons, or were exclusively allowed only to free people or solely to members of the political community. On the other extreme, the political community might leave quite abstract the content of being slave and the range of practices and rights prohibited or negated to enslaved persons. In the latter case, it would primarily be the relationship between masters and slaves and the relationships within slave communities that would determine the various aspects of slave lives; as a result, one might expect very widespread diversity among enslaved persons.

Let us offer some examples to illustrate these observations. A major aspect of Athenian law was that free people would pay monetary penalties for offences, while enslaved persons who committed the same offences would have to be physically punished instead.[60] Furthermore, while citizens could freely testify and could not be

---

[54] Crowther and Frass 1998.
[55] Kiesling 2006.
[56] Williams 2010.
[57] Daverio Rocchi 1975.
[58] Harper 2010b.
[59] Garnsey 1970; Aubert 2002.
[60] See, for example, the punishment regulations concerning the cult of Apollo Erithaseus: *IG* II², 1362.

tortured to extract their testimonies, slave testimony in court was only acceptable if extracted under torture.[61] But the political community did not enforce the free–slave distinction solely in relation to the legal system. Various ancient sources relate that in the early sixth century BCE the Athenian lawgiver Solon prohibited slaves from exercising in the gymnasium and participating in pederastic relationships. Athletics and pederasty were becoming major aspects of the free lifestyle, and by prohibiting slaves from participating in these activities Solon was trying to police the boundary between freemen and slaves.[62] On the other extreme, we can find various Near Eastern societies where slaves could participate in the legal system on equal terms, or even in social practices that were elsewhere prohibited to slaves, like marriage and adoption. To illustrate these observations, we can turn to two fourteenth-century BCE texts from Nuzi, in modern-day Iraqi Kurdistan. The first text is a record of a court case:

> Hanate, maidservant of Tulpun-naia, with Hiiar-elli and Sukr-apu appeared in a lawsuit before the judges on account of Halb-abusa, for Hiiar-elli and Sukr-apu had given Halb-abusa into daughtership to Hanate. Three times the judges sent deputies to them, Kari, son of Akap-senni, Hanadu, son of Kuttanni and Simi-kari, son of Nirpiaia, the three deputies of Hanate, but Hiiar-elli did not consent to come. In the lawsuit Hanate prevailed and the judges gave Halb-abusa to Hanate.[63]

In this case we encounter a female slave who made a contract with two free people to adopt their child as a daughter. Not only was a female slave allowed to procure a child from free people, but in the case of breach of contract, as was the issue here, the courts supported her claim. My second example comes from another court document:

> Thus say the judges of Karra: Kusuh-atal, slave of Kiliske, appeared before us. And a constable was assigned to Kusuh-atal. They went to his wife to take his wife. Because Kusuh-atal would take his wife, three times with vigour, Kirip-seri, son of Arrutuppa, struck Kusuh-atal. And Ar-teia, the constable, the word brought back, Kirip-seri struck Kusuh-atal three times with vigour. And I saw that he struck him.[64]

In this remarkable case a slave was promised a free girl as his wife. When the promise was not honoured, the slave was in the position to use a constable in order to enforce his legal claim. This is the clearest indication both of what it meant for a slave to have the right to marry a free person, as well as for the political community to recognise and enforce this right.

We can then summarise the above argument by suggesting that in certain communities, such as classical Athens, freedom is not only the state of not being property, but

---

[61]  Todd 1993: 167–200; Hunter 2000.
[62]  Mactoux 1988; on slaves and Greek athletics, see also Crowther 1992; Golden 2008: 40–67.
[63]  *AASOR* XVI, no. 43.
[64]  *HSS* V, no. 27.

additionally the means of access to a particular lifestyle.[65] This relates to the claims to respect and inviolability we mentioned above, but is best illustrated from the point of view of gender. As Harper has argued, in the case of Greek and Roman women freedom was not primarily a matter of rights, but above all else the means of access to the lifestyle of sexual honour, and of participation in the marketplace of marriage and wifehood, which was prohibited to female slaves.[66] This is undoubtedly correct for Greek and Roman societies, but, as we have seen in the case of Nuzi, in other societies freedom was only tenuously connected to a particular free lifestyle, as slaves had access to many practices which were elsewhere restricted to free people, like marriage and adoption.

A final difference concerning the distinction between free and slave involved the radial conceptual system of slavery. In the Near East, people used the modality of slavery as domination (Chapter 7) in order to conceptualise various other hierarchical relationships among free people; thus an inferior could address a superior as his master, and the king's subjects could be described as his slaves. These uses did not define a legal relationship of property, nor were they necessarily derogatory; they rather tended to express a measure of politeness and deference, depending on the context. On the other hand, the use of the modality of slavery as domination to refer to relationships of power and service among free people in the Greek world was almost exclusively derogatory, and was not employed to express deference or politeness.[67]

The above comments have shown the need for a radical and full-scale re-appraisal of the conceptual pair of freedom and slavery in ancient societies. The traditional dichotomies that have long dominated discussion need to be set aside. We have seen that the distinction between freedom and slavery can be set within three different conceptual systems which can have very divergent and contradictory implications; different societies have combined these three conceptual systems in various ways, or have placed their emphasis on one conceptual system instead of the others. We need to leave aside the traditional conceptualisation of slavery as a socio-economic and freedom as a political and cultural phenomenon and create instead a unified framework of analysis. A historical anthropology of status and personhood in ancient societies is urgently required, if we are ever to understand how phenomena like the totalising tendency of freedom emerge and develop.[68] And of course pointing out the correct distinctions and differences between ancient societies is necessary, but is only the first step; historically explaining these differences should be our ultimate task.

Let us now move to the issue of the intervention of the political community in the master–slave relationship. We can start from the obvious point that the support of the political community was indispensable for masters to be able to exercise their power over slaves. This is a point superbly made by Plato:

'Let us look at those individuals in our cities who are wealthy and possess many slaves. These men, Glaukon, resemble tyrants in that they rule over many; the

---

[65] See also Campa 2018.
[66] Harper 2017a.
[67] Lewis 2018: 84–6.
[68] See the interesting comments of Pottage 2020.

difference is that a tyrant rules over more.' 'Yes, this is the difference.' 'To your knowledge, are these men fearless and not afraid of the slaves?' 'Yes. What would they be afraid of?' 'Of nothing', I said. 'But do you understand why?' 'Yes. Because the city as a whole runs to the help of every individual.' 'Well put', said I. 'However, if some god carried off one man who owned at least fifty slaves or more, took him out of the city, along with his wife and children, and placed him in a deserted place, together with his other property and his slaves, at a place where no free man would run to his help, how great and what sort of fear do you think he would experience for himself, his children and his wife, lest they be killed by the slaves?' 'I'd think he'd be most fearful', he said. 'So wouldn't he be forced to start cajoling some of his slaves, and give them many promises, and manumit them, though he needn't? And wouldn't he show himself as his slaves' flatterer?' 'It'd be inevitable', he said; 'otherwise, he'd perish.' 'And what would happen', I said, 'if the god established many others around him as neighbours, people who would not condone one man being the master of another, but instead punish with the gravest punishments such a person, if they came across one?' 'I think he would find himself amidst even more evil,' he said, 'surrounded solely by enemies.'[69]

This support of the political community took a variety of forms; I will simply mention state support for catching fugitive slaves as an essential prop of maintaining masters' control.[70] But while the role of state intervention in supporting masters is relatively easy to grasp, what requires more discussion is its contradictory effects. A comparative perspective from New World slaveries is particularly illuminating in this respect. Alan Watson has brought attention to the importance of the public dimension of slave law in the New World.[71] Most ancient slave laws concern the legal formulation of private transactions that arise from the fact that slaves were property, or acted as agents in transactions; such laws are also commonly attested in early modern slave codes. But early modern codes also included provisions which concerned the public impact of relationships between masters and slaves; such provisions were relatively rare in surviving ancient laws on slavery. A good illustration is the laws that prohibited the teaching of reading and writing to slaves in the American South. In antiquity masters were left free to choose whether to educate their slaves or not,[72] but in the American South the right of masters to direct their slaves' education as they saw fit was overridden by the intervention of the political community. Slave literacy was seen as a threat to the community as a whole and had to be eliminated, even if this would limit a master's freedom and the profitability of his slaves.[73] Slave spatial mobility was also seriously curtailed as it was considered dangerous for the free community, even though such measures limited the profitability of slaves for their masters. Such provisions are

---

[69] Plato, *Republic* 578d–579b.

[70] Fuhrmann 2012: 21–43; for the capture of fugitives in Mesopotamia, see Reid 2015.

[71] Watson 1989: 66–7.

[72] For the education of slaves in antiquity, see Forbes 1955; Booth 1979; Klees 1998: 218–49.

[73] For concerns about slave literacy in antiquity, see, for example, Columella, *On rural affairs* 1.8.4; but, as far as we know, there were no equivalent ancient laws prohibiting slave literacy.

rarely attested in antiquity, and it is worth asking whether this is due to the nature of our surviving sources or whether this constitutes a major difference in how political communities intervened in the relationship between masters and slaves.[74]

We have seen that the dialectical relationship between masters and slaves could move in opposite directions: either towards the total tyranny of masters over slaves, or towards situations where the link between masters and slaves, the participation of slaves in their masters' households and the creation of resourceful and influential slaves were common phenomena. The same bifurcation can be observed in the intervention by the political community in the relationship between masters and slaves.[75] On the one hand, it could ameliorate slave conditions by curbing the total power of masters and according rights to enslaved persons; it could also offer enslaved persons the opportunity to enhance their condition vis-à-vis their masters by employing the mediating institutions of the political community. On the other hand, state intervention could destroy any protection or privilege the slaves might enjoy from their masters and subordinate all slaves, irrespective of their individual features, achievements or position, to a condition of subservience to even the lowest free person.[76]

In other words, the free–slave dialectic creates a process of constituting slaves as either a caste or an *estate* (for the concept, see above p. 112). By *estate* I understand a group of people which is defined by law and has certain privileges and duties towards other *estates* and the community as a whole: the nobility, the clergy and the third estate of *ancien régime* France are characteristic examples. By looking at slaves as an *estate* one focuses on the rights and duties that slaves lacked, but might also be granted. By caste I understand a hereditary status characterised by endogamy and social barriers sanctioned by custom, law or religion. By looking at slaves as a caste one underlines their condition as outcasts, marginalised people who cannot and should not be part of society: the condition of social death described by Patterson.

For a variety of reasons, the potential of turning enslaved persons into either an *estate* or a caste was never fully realised in the global history of slaving. There were important reasons that the process of constituting enslaved persons as an *estate* was always circumscribed: because slaves were property, their primary relationship was that with their masters, rather than with the community as a whole or with other groups; most of the acts of enslaved persons did not come under the purview of the community, but were solely under the remit of their masters. If masters were happy with slave activities, the slaves could go on unhindered; if masters were displeased, they were free to punish the slaves as they saw fit. Enslaved persons usually came under the purview of the community only when their acts affected other people apart from their masters, like when a slave defrauded or injured a third person; even in this

---

[74] See, for example, the law of Caesar stipulating that one out of three shepherds should be free; given the mobility of slave shepherds and their important role in slave uprisings, the law intended to ensure public peace: Suetonius, *Life of Julius Caesar* 42.1.

[75] For state intervention in slavery, see Geary and Vlassopoulos 2009.

[76] For slaves and the institutional orders of ancient societies, see Knoch 2017; Ismard 2019.

respect, this was often treated as an affair between the slave's master and the third party involved. The following passage from the *Digest* is telling:

> Again, an insult can be effected against someone personally or through others: personally, when a head of household or matron is directly affronted; through others, when it happens by consequence, as when the affront is to one's children or slave.[77]

An insult to a slave by a third party was conceptualised as a legal issue between the third party and the slave's master.

Slaves did not have a corporate identity: they could not speak in their own name and they did not have representatives of the group as a whole. This is precisely where slaves differed from other dependent groups in world history, such as late medieval serfs and other dependent communities. Peter Kolchin's seminal comparative study of US slaves and Russian serfs brings this out very eloquently; even though Russian serfs were very similar in many respects to US slaves, and could be bought and sold, it was their corporate existence in the form of the peasant commune and their recognition as an *estate* which constituted a significant difference from US slaves.[78]

Equally, the process of turning enslaved persons into a caste was often arrested. Slaves were employed in many different capacities, from the highest of an imperial slave to the lowest of a slave in the mines; they could have the most variable ethnic origins and could also belong to the same ethnic group as their masters. Slaves could form conjugal relations with their masters and could be adopted into their masters' family; if manumitted, they could even become citizens and their children could be fully incorporated among the free population. Masters could use their slaves in order to enhance their position vis-à-vis other members of their community; this tended to undermine the line separating the free from the slaves.[79] Accordingly, as long as masters were free to do whatever they wanted with their slaves, use them in any possible way or manumit them as they saw fit, slaves could not become full outcasts.

But although the process towards constituting enslaved persons either as an *estate* or a caste could never be fully completed, it is important to note how political communities could move in one direction or the other. The slave codes of the various New World societies moved in either direction in different ways and with different paces.[80] The slave codes of the US South, in particular in the antebellum period, tried precisely to turn slaves into a hereditary caste, but with certain rights that resembled those of an *estate*.[81] On the one hand, they effectively prohibited manumission and severely restricted the activities in which slaves could lawfully participate, while also trying in various ways to eliminate the category of free Black people; on the other hand, they placed various limits on the authority of masters by legislating on the proper treatment of slaves in terms of nutrition, hygiene, punishment and protection

---

[77]  *Digest* 47.10.1.2.
[78]  Kolchin 1987.
[79]  Meillassoux 1991: 143–235.
[80]  Oakes 1986.
[81]  Morris 1996.

of life. But since slaves were never allowed a legal persona, could not sue for their rights and had no corporate recognition, the process was inherently self-defeating.[82]

The process took a different form in the Spanish and Portuguese colonies. There the slaves ultimately gained two legal rights which they could protect in court. The one was *coartación*: this was an agreement between the master and the slave that provided for manumission on payment of a certain amount of money. Once the agreement was made, the master had no right to refuse to manumit the slave, and the slave had the right to sue in order to enforce the agreement. The other right was *papel*: the right of the slave to be sold to a different master. In both cases the slaves acquired legal rights which they were able to defend on their own by suing in the courts. Of course, even in this case the process never reached the point at which slaves became an *estate*: the process stopped significantly before this stage.[83]

This comparative analysis is a useful setting for examining the interventions of ancient political communities. They could intervene in order to limit what masters could do to their slaves, and in particular to circumscribe how slaves could be punished and to offer avenues for redress for slaves who had excessively cruel masters. As the above case of Vedius Pollio shows, during the republican period the Roman political community largely eschewed intervening in how masters punished their slaves and merely relied on moral pressure to avoid the worst excesses. But during the early imperial period the Roman state decided to intervene in a number of important ways.[84] The first intervention concerned the right of masters to punish their slaves by death:

> Thus, slaves are under the power of their masters, and this power is derived from the law of nations, for we may perceive that among nearly all nations masters have the power of life and death over their slaves, and whatever is acquired by a slave is acquired by his master. But, at present, it is not permitted to any persons living under Roman dominion to be guilty of cruelty to their slaves which is atrocious, or without a cause recognized by the law. For, according to a Constitution of the Divine Antoninus, anyone who kills his slave without a cause shall be punished as severely as one who kills the slave of another; the inordinate severity of masters is also repressed by a Constitution of the same Emperor.[85]

Another example shows how the Roman state provided an institutional arena for adjudicating slave complaints against their masters for cruel treatment, as well as accusations of illegal slave behaviour, by stipulating actions that could be heard by the city prefect of Rome:

> 1) He must hear the complaints of slaves against their masters who have fled for refuge to the Imperial statues, or have been purchased by their own money in order to be manumitted . . . (5) Where anyone accuses a slave of having

---

[82] Johnson 1997.
[83] De la Fuente 2004, 2007.
[84] Knoch 2017: 45–119.
[85] *Digest* 1.6.1–2.

committed adultery with his wife, the case must be tried before the Prefect of the City . . . (8) When it is said that the prefect must hear the complaints of slaves against their masters, we should understand that this does not mean that they can accuse their masters (for a slave is never allowed to do this, unless for specific reasons), but that they may humbly apply to him where their masters treat them with cruelty, harshness, or starve them, or may state to the Prefect of the City that they have been forced to endure indecent attacks. It was also a duty imposed upon the Prefect of the City by the Divine Severus, that he should protect slaves from being prostituted by their masters.[86]

In late antiquity the Christian Roman emperors legislated to prohibit Jewish masters from converting their Christian slaves by offering such slaves their freedom; unsurprisingly, some slaves took advantage of this window opened by state intervention and falsely accused their Jewish masters of converting them in order to secure their manumission.[87]

An event in 104 BCE shows the consequences of the intervention of the Roman state: when the Romans discovered that many free Bithynians had been sold into slavery illegally, they invited people illegally enslaved to reclaim their freedom by appealing to Roman authorities across the empire to facilitate their liberation. A large number of enslaved persons appealed to the Roman governor in Sicily, who liberated 800 slaves within a few days. Worried, elite masters convinced the governor to turn away any other slave applicants; according to some ancient sources, the dismissal lit the fire of a major revolt.[88] The story is an excellent illustration of the opportunities opened for slaves by the intervention of the political community and of the potential clash between the interests of masters and the priorities of the political community; it also reminds us of the importance of thinking of slaves as free people in captivity, as we saw in Chapter 5.

On the other hand, intervention by the political community was not always in favour of enslaved persons. The Augustan legislation concerning manumission is a characteristic example. One of these laws put clear limits on the number of slaves who could be manumitted through the testament of their masters by making the number of manumitted slaves a fixed proportion of the overall number of slaves possessed by the master.[89] The Augustan intervention also prescribed that certain categories of slaves, like those who had been shackled as a punishment, could never become formally manumitted and gain Roman citizenship as a result.[90] The purpose of this legislation was to protect the rights of the inheritors by limiting excessive post-mortem manumissions and enhance the rights of patrons on the property of their freedmen and freedwomen, as well as to pressure slaves to conform to certain kinds of behaviour in order to avoid falling under conditions that would ensure they could not be formally manumitted.[91]

---

[86] *Digest* 1.12.1–8.
[87] *Theodosian Code* 16.9.3; see Glancy 2018.
[88] Diodorus Siculus 36.3.1–6; cf. Morton 2012: 163–72.
[89] Gaius, *Institutes* 1.42–4.
[90] Gaius, *Institutes* 1.13; see Roth 2010b, 2011.
[91] Mouritsen 2011a: 33–5.

This brings us to the important issue of the role of the political community in defining whether and how enslaved persons could exit slavery and whether they could be incorporated within the political community.[92] We should distinguish between a number of important aspects. The first aspect is whether the manumission of slaves was within the exclusive purview of masters, came under the oversight of the political community or required its assent, or was taken over from masters and became the exclusive prerogative of the community.[93] In many societies manumission took place through various public rituals, like *manumissio vindicta* and *manumissio censu* in ancient Rome[94] or manumission in the assembly or the theatre in various ancient Greek communities.[95] While some of these public rituals might simply serve communication purposes, in other cases they might express the requirement of communal assent to manumissions.[96] In the case of Sparta, the community decided that the manumission of helots by their private masters was dangerous for the wider interests of the community; as a result, only the community could manumit helots, normally due to public considerations rather than the private concerns of masters and slaves.[97]

A second aspect concerned the extent to which manumitted slaves could access the institutional order. Imperial Rome was famous for allowing so-called formally manumitted slaves who had reached a certain age and/or satisfied certain requirements to become Roman citizens, while the freeborn children of such manumitted slaves became Roman citizens with full rights.[98] As we shall see in Chapter 8, while most Greek communities excluded freed persons from becoming citizens, there is evidence that this was not the case with all Greek communities. In this respect, it is also important to distinguish between a freed status that was transitional and only applied to one person, and one that was considered hereditary, thus turning manumitted slaves into a form of caste.[99] Despite the widely entrenched idea that all manumitted slaves of Roman masters became Roman citizens, it is becoming gradually accepted by scholars that perhaps only a minority of Rome's freed population also became citizens. After the early imperial reforms, a significant proportion of Roman freedmen and freedwomen became Junian Latins; these did not possess citizenship, although they could potentially acquire it, if they fulfilled certain additional conditions. As a result, Junian Latins could live as free people for the remaining of their lives, but could not transmit their property to their spouses and children; their property would accordingly be inherited by their former masters. Junian Latins lived as free people, but they died as slaves.[100]

---

[92] Kleijwegt 2006a; Husby 2017.

[93] See Daube 1946.

[94] Bellen 2001; Kleijwegt 2009; Husby 2017.

[95] Zelnick-Abramovitz 2005: 184–207; Mactoux 2008; Vlassopoulos 2019.

[96] Zelnick-Abramovitz 2009, 2013.

[97] Lewis 2018: 128–39.

[98] Mouritsen 2011a: 66–119, 248–78; Vermote 2016b.

[99] For free Black people in the US as 'slaves without masters', see Berlin 1974; for hereditary freedmen in the early Middle Ages, see Rio 2017: 75–131.

[100] Sirks 1983; Weaver 1990; López Barja de Quiroga 1998; Roth 2010b, 2011; Corcoran 2011; Koops 2014; Hirt 2018.

A third aspect concerned the prototypical conceptual system we examined above. In societies where the prototypical system was limited and enslaved persons were allowed to participate in most activities and practices of free persons, the incorporation of former slaves into the free community was relatively easy, even if they were not given formal access to the institutional order. In cases where enslaved persons could marry free people or own real estate, as we shall see in Chapter 8, the incorporation of manumitted slaves into the kinship networks of free people in one or two generations was relatively smooth.

Finally, we need to pay attention to the ways in which the political community had a significant impact on slaving and enslaved persons for reasons that had little to do with slavery per se. Relations among the members of the political community could create opportunities and openings that enslaved persons could take advantage of. Ps.-Xenophon describes a characteristic facet of this phenomenon in classical Athens, briefly mentioned earlier on:

> But again, slaves and metics enjoy extreme licence in Athens, and it is not allowed to strike them, nor will a slave make way for you. I will explain why this is the local practice. If there was a law that the slave or the metic or the freedman could be beaten by the free man, then very often one would strike Athenians, having mistaken them for slaves. For the people here do not wear better clothes than the slaves or the metics, and they are not at all better in appearance.[101]

The key to understanding the above passage is the position of the lower classes among the citizens. Athenian citizenship was exercised without any exclusion based on wealth or profession. The Athenian citizen body comprised people who were rich, comfortably well-off, struggling to make ends meet, poor, even destitute; it comprised the aristocrat and the landowner together with the wage labourer, the artisan, the shop-keeper and the merchant.[102] The upper-class reactionary could not maltreat lower-class people randomly, because those of the lower classes who were citizens had political power and would not accept maltreatment stoically. But since among lower-class people it was difficult to differentiate between citizens and foreigners, freedmen and slaves, it was prudent to abstain from aggressive behaviour in general. Thus, the unintentional effect of democratic citizenship was that slaves, freedmen and foreigners were protected by association, simply because it was difficult to distinguish them from the citizens easily.[103] Plato famously argued that the love of freedom in democratic societies gradually extended beyond the political arena and undermined all forms of authority and domination, including the relationship between parents and children, masters and slaves and even humans and animals; despite the obvious hyperbole, it is undoubtedly a process worth exploring.[104]

Another example of the same phenomenon is the Athenian law of *hubris*. The law protected from dishonourable mistreatment not only citizens and metics, but also

---

[101] Ps.-Xenophon, *Constitution of the Athenians* 1.10.

[102] For poverty and Athenian democracy, see Taylor 2017.

[103] Vlassopoulos 2007a, 2009. For means of distinguishing between different groups in Rome and their limits, see Reinhold 1971; Gardner 1986; George 2002.

[104] Plato, *Republic* 562b–563d; see Klees 1998: 355–78.

slaves. Scholars have debated whether the law assumed that slaves possessed honour, or emphasised the hubristic disposition of the aggressor, rather than the honour of the victim.[105] It seems probable that the major preoccupation of the law was to curb the hubristic behaviour of citizens by prohibiting all opportunities for exercising such behaviour, even if they concerned slaves. But while the protection of slaves was not the primary concern of the law, it is undeniable that at least on certain occasions it would have allowed slaves to avoid mistreatment and see punishment meted out to those who had mistreated them. It is also worth pointing out the various ways in which ancient communities offered asylum to their free and enslaved inhabitants, from altars and sanctuaries to the statues of Roman emperors and ultimately Christian churches. These practices were obviously of utmost importance for slaves who tried to escape from the barbarity of their masters, publicise their travails or change masters.[106]

But the most significant way in which the political community affected slaving and enslaved persons concerned moments of conflict and crisis. When faced with external crises like wars, political communities often turned to their male slaves.[107] In certain cases, communities manumitted slaves and even offered them citizenship in order to enhance their military manpower: the liberation and enfranchisement of thousands of Athenian slaves before the battle of Arginousai in 406 BCE is a telling example.[108] The same pressures applied to internal crises, conflicts and civil wars. While Greek and Roman slaves could not normally testify against their masters in court, ancient states were willing to allow exceptions when the interests of the state or the ruler were in danger. In cases of sacrilege or conspiracy, slaves were allowed to inform against their masters; the interests of the community allowed slaves to ruin their masters and win money and freedom for their act.[109] During the civil war in Corcyra, in the course of the Peloponnesian War, democrats and oligarchs offered freedom to the slaves in order to enhance their chances of prevailing in the conflict;[110] slaves also played various roles in the civil conflicts that convulsed the last century of the Roman Republic.[111] Slaves could also prove useful in the aftermath of a conflict for building a powerful base, as was the case with Sulla after the first Roman Civil War:

> To the plebs he enrolled the youngest and strongest of the slaves of the proscribed men – more than 10,000. He manumitted them, declared them Roman citizens and called them Cornelii, after himself, so that he could have at his disposal 10,000 plebeians, ready to follow his commands.[112]

---

[105] Cf. Fisher 1995; Canevaro 2018.

[106] Gamauf 1999; Derlien 2003; Ismard 2019: 191–222.

[107] For slaves and crisis situations, see Klees 1998: 409–31; for the employment of slaves in warfare, see Welwei 1974–88.

[108] For slaves and Arginousai, see Hunt 2001; Hamel 2015; see also Herz 2001 for Ephesos and its slaves during the First Mithridatic War.

[109] Schumacher 1982; Osborne 2000.

[110] Thucydides 3.73.

[111] For the role of slaves in civil conflicts at Rome, see Annequin 1973; Sartori 1973; Létroublon 1974; Flambard 1977; Bradley 1978, 2011; Thein 2013.

[112] Appian, *Civil Wars* 1.11.100; see Treggiari 1969: 162–92.

We should finally briefly mention that the political community was not the sole institution that defined the distinction between free and slave and intervened in the relationship between masters and slaves. Perhaps the most significant alternative institution in the course of antiquity resulted from the emergence of monotheistic religions like Christianity.[113] The development of the Church as a major institution in the course of the early imperial period, and its aggrandisement, co-option by but also relative independence from the Roman state created an alternative pole. The role of the Church in the history of ancient slavery was until recently perceived in the terms set by the amelioration narrative of the slavery and humanity context we have examined in Chapter 2. Many ancient historians have rightly concluded that the Church had no intention to promote the abolition of slavery; but because they have accepted the terms of the slavery and humanity debate, they have failed to understand that the Church had its own particular agenda in regard to slavery, which could affect state policy, and that as a separate institution it could provide important contexts and practices that created opportunities for slaves to enhance their condition.[114] The impact of Christian ideology on the Roman law of slavery and the endless controversies created by slave attempts to become ordained as priests and monks without the permission of their masters are excellent illustrations of these issues.[115]

## The Relationships Within Slave Communities

We have seen in our historiographical exploration in Chapter 2 how historians of New World slavery created the concept of slave community. This concept has allowed scholars to explore in depth the processes by which slaves created a world of their own and the unique importance of the slave community for slave identity and resistance.[116] It is deeply unfortunate that this concept had until very recently almost no impact on the study of ancient slavery.[117] It is therefore essential to explore some important aspects of New World slave communities, before we examine slave communities and their relationships in antiquity. I want to focus here on some extraordinary phenomena that the study of New World slavery has revealed, and ponder their implications for antiquity.

Slave communities in the New World were constructed along four main axes. The first was that of ethnicity. Most slaves in New World societies came from Africa, which constituted a kaleidoscope of innumerable local communities and certain regional linguistic and ethnic groups, as well as some larger political entities, which

---

[113] Tannenbaum 1946 and Elkins 1959 already highlighted the Catholic Church as an institution that significantly affected master–slave relationships in Latin American societies; nothing equivalent existed in Protestant New World societies, on which see Gerbner 2018.

[114] Klein 1988, 2000; Harper 2011; McKeown 2012; Vaucher 2017.

[115] Waldstein 1990; Evans-Grubbs 1995; Melluso 2000; Lenski 2011c; Harper 2016.

[116] For recent critical assessments of the concept, see Kaye 2002; Ben-Ur 2018.

[117] But see now Harper 2011: 273–9; McKeown 2012, 2019; Bathrellou 2014; Hunt 2015; Vlassopoulos 2011a, 2011b, 2015a, 2018d.

could possess wider political identities.[118] Slaves from Africa in the New World could sometimes maintain their original local, regional and larger identities and attempt to construct communities on the basis of these identities.[119] More often, though, the conditions created by the slave trade and the slaving strategies of their masters led to the emergence of new ethnic identities among slaves, freed persons and their descendants. These new ethnicities were based partly on elements from their various African backgrounds; partly on categorical modes of identification imposed by the masters and the political communities of the New World; and partly on elements and identities constructed out of the interaction between slaves and freed persons in the New World. Finally, the most radical development was that in certain New World societies the variety of African and Creole ethnicities led gradually to the emergence of a single and shared Black ethnicity for all slaves, freed persons and their descendants.[120]

Some ethnic slave communities created their own leadership and devised impressive rituals for selecting their leaders. Once a year in various places (Brazil, New England, New Orleans), when the free community elected its leaders, the slave community would organise elaborate pageants in which they elected their own leaders. These leaders were either slaves of important masters, or were distinguished for their personal characteristics, like bravery and bodily strength. They would often play the role of mediators between slaves and masters or between the slave community and the free community; for example, slaves who had absconded and feared punishment from their masters would request the intercession of their slave leaders. The slave kings of Congo and of other slave nations in Brazil and Cuba are justly famous;[121] but particularly important is that even in societies where slaves were relatively few, like New England, we also come across the election of slave governors and kings.[122]

The second axis around which slave communities were constructed was that of religion. In all New World societies there are clear signs of the development of cults and religious practices which allowed slaves to construct common bonds.[123] These cults and religious practices took diverse forms. Slaves continued adhering to cults and practices that they brought from their homelands; to give a significant example, Brazilian slaves originating from western Africa maintained the Islamic religious affiliation that was prominent in their homeland.[124] In Brazil there also emerged various religious sodalities within the Catholic Church, sometimes incorporating various groups of mixed-race people, Creoles, Africans, slaves and freed persons, sometimes restricted to slaves or specific categories of slaves. These sodalities were characterised by a syncretistic combination of African deities and practices with Catholic cult, possessed their own shrines and had their own festivals, but also participated as distinct groups in

---

[118] For the political, ethnic and cultural environments of early modern Africa, see Brooks 1993; Haour 2007; Thornton 2012: 60–99; Stilwell 2014: 60–123.
[119] Falola and Childs 2005; Hall 2005; Konadu 2010.
[120] Mintz and Price 1992; Gomez 1998; Lovejoy 2000; Lovejoy and Trotman 2003; Sweet 2003; Heywood and Thornton 2007; Sidbury and Cañizares-Esguerra 2011.
[121] De Mello 2002; Walker 2004; Kiddy 2005b; Fromont 2013.
[122] Piersen 1988: 117–40.
[123] Thornton 1998: 183–271.
[124] Reis 1993; Reis, dos Santos Gomes and Carvalho 2020.

religious practices of the society at large.[125] This is the clearest example of slave communities with their own corporate existence and participation as a recognised distinct group within activities of the society as a whole. In the US South slaves created their own version of evangelical Christianity and religious community, but without the independent corporate existence of the Brazilian sodalities.[126] In many New World societies slaves also created Creole cults and religious practices, like voodoo, santería and candomblé.[127] Cemeteries, funeral rites and the afterlife were another field in which enslaved persons created their own spaces and rituals, stressing their existence as a community.[128]

The third axis was constituted by the link between locality and labour that characterised the profoundly rural world of the plantations in various societies of the New World. Medium and large plantations that employed from a dozen up to hundreds of slaves created slave communities that coalesced around their common labour in agricultural and other related activities; this community on the basis of labour was further enhanced by the typical spatial separation between the master's mansion and the slave quarters on many plantations.[129] Finally, the fourth axis took place in urban contexts, primarily in Latin American societies, where urban slavery was more developed. A significant proportion of urban slaves lived and worked on their own, as part of slaving strategies for revenue that we examined in Chapter 4. These autonomous slaves created communities that mixed ethnicity, neighbourhood and professional activities in complex ways.[130]

This comparative exploration has raised a number of issues. As far as I can tell, ancient societies appear to have nothing equivalent to the elected leaderships of slave communities in peacetime, like the kings of Congo that we find in New World societies. This raises a number of questions. It might be the case that since ancient historians have not explored ancient slave communities until very recently, they have not yet gathered the existing evidence. It is also possible that the nature of our surviving sources makes such phenomena relatively invisible, and that we have to read the sources against the grain. One good example comes from Thucydides' description of the civil war between democrats and oligarchs in Corcyra during the Peloponnesian War:

> The next day passed in skirmishes of little importance, each party sending into the country to offer freedom to the slaves and to invite them to join them. The mass of the slaves answered the appeal of the democrats; their antagonists being reinforced by eight hundred mercenaries from the continent.[131]

How precisely did this take place? Did each party send a group to every farm and the slaves heard first the one group and then the other? Did the democrats send delegations

---

[125]  Russell-Wood 1974; Kiddy 2005a; see also Howard 1998 on Cuban *cabildos*.
[126]  Genovese 1974: 161–284; Raboteau 1999, 2004.
[127]  Bastide 1978; Reis 2001; Sweet 2003; de Carvalho Soares 2011.
[128]  Roediger 1981; Reis 2003.
[129]  Blassingame 1972; Genovese 1974; Kaye 2007.
[130]  Reis 1997, 2005.
[131]  Thucydides 3.73.

to the farms that belonged to democrats or democratic sympathisers and the oligarchs accordingly? But then how did most slaves manage to join the democrats? How did they reach a decision? Individually or collectively, and on what criteria? Perhaps the easiest assumption is that the slaves had their own form of leadership, which was able to take the decision on behalf of the mass of the slaves within a short time. Perhaps it is such examples that might allow us to excavate the existence of forms of slave leadership in antiquity. But perhaps the right answer is that the forms of slave leadership that are attested in the New World are the historical outcome of the particular entanglement of processes of the early modern Atlantic; if the ancient Mediterranean experienced different entanglements, it would be highly misleading to expect to find the same phenomena in antiquity.

The same question can also be raised in regard to slave communities based on religion. We have seen how enslaved persons in the New World transferred religions and cults from their homelands, created new Creole syncretistic cults and religions and inflected the religions of their masters in new ways. To what extent can we find similar phenomena in antiquity? According to the fundamental study of Franz Bömer, there was no such thing as slave religion in antiquity: slaves participated in cults that originated from their homelands or in the religious practices of their masters, but there were neither cults that were exclusively attended by slaves, nor slave inflections of the master cults.[132] It is again worth asking whether we have not searched hard enough, or whether we have asked the wrong questions so far.[133]

It is necessary to start our survey by reiterating here some points that were raised in Chapter 5, concerning the self-understanding and groupness of enslaved persons. As I argued there, enslaved persons did not understand themselves exclusively as slaves: they also understood themselves as free people in captivity and built identities and communities on the basis of a number of other roles they held while being slaves: as members of families and kinship groups, as members of original and new ethnicities, as members of religious and professional groups. In certain cases, times and places these roles would lead to the construction of communities that were exclusively composed of slaves; but enslaved persons in ancient societies often participated in mixed communities that also included citizens, other free people and freedmen.

The formation of slave communities was affected by a range of factors. The first factor consisted of the processes of slave-making we have examined in Chapter 4. In this respect, one crucial parameter was the balance between the proportion of slaves that derived from violence and trade, who were therefore outsiders, and the proportion of slaves that derived from natural reproduction or internal enslavement, who were insiders.[134] This ratio was heavily reliant on the sex ratio of the slave population. In situations where violence and trade played an overwhelming role in the maintenance and expansion of the slave population, the sex ratio of the imported slaves was crucial: wherever there was a heavy imbalance towards the importation of male slaves, this would make the formation of slave families and the natural reproduction of the

---

[132] Bömer 1981, 1990.
[133] Cf. Zoumbaki 2005; Hodkinson and Geary 2012; Padilla Peralta 2017.
[134] Scheidel 1997, 1999, 2005b; Harris 1999; Bradley 2004; Hunt 2018a: 31–48.

slave population significantly more difficult.[135] Wherever the natural reproduction of slaves played an important role, over the course of time it would tend to equalise the sex ratio among the slave population.[136]

But the ratio between imported and local slaves was also significant from a cultural and social point of view: as studies of New World slavery have shown, the distinction between African and Creole slaves had major consequences for the communities and practices of enslaved people.[137] The same is obviously relevant for ancient slave communities. Should we imagine populations of foreign slaves who hardly spoke the local language and were unfamiliar with local culture and practices? Or should we assume that a significant part of slave populations were cultural and linguistic insiders who could easily understand, participate in and take advantage of local practices and institutions?[138] The remarkable number of rescripts in the *Codex of Justinian* that result from slave petitions regarding their status might not be evidence of slave knowledge of Roman law, as they would probably have used legal 'brokers' to frame these petitions; nevertheless, they are clear attestations of slaves who were sufficiently familiar with the Roman legal system to attempt to use it in their own favour.[139] Can we imagine slaves who were cultural and linguistic outsiders being able to pursue such paths?[140] And if the best solution is to imagine slave populations composed of significant numbers of both insiders and outsiders, how should we envisage the interaction between these groups? A recent synthetic work on ancient slavery illustrates the need to examine such issues systematically: while the chapter on enslavement accepts that natural reproduction played the dominant role in replenishing the Roman slave population,[141] when it comes to discussing slave culture, the book only examines the culture of slave outsiders, like Greek slaves at Rome; the culture of native Roman slaves and its historical consequences are completely excised from the account.[142] We need to move past the stereotype of slaves as outsiders and examine the implications of cases in which a significant proportion of slaves did not have foreign origins.

We need, furthermore, to think about the significance of the slaving zones from which foreign slaves originated.[143] Did these areas exhibit major economic, social and cultural differences with the communities in which slaves ended up? Did these areas maintain other links with the importing communities apart from violent and commercial slave-making? Were there free people from these areas that moved back and forth to the importing communities, or who ended up living as free residents in these communities?[144] One of the major aspects of the early modern slave trade in

[135] Thornton 1983; Schmitz 2012; Mouritsen 2011b.

[136] For reproduction in New World slavery, see Bergad 2007: 96–131; Klein 2010: 162–87.

[137] Mintz and Price 1992; Barcia 2008, 2012; Mintz 2010; Price 2011.

[138] Petersen 2006; Hunt 2015: 142–50, 2018: 83–98; MacLean 2018.

[139] Connolly 2010.

[140] For a comparative perspective from the New World, see Owensby 2009; Schweninger 2009; de la Fuente and Gross 2020.

[141] Hunt 2018a: 40–7.

[142] Hunt 2018a: 92–8.

[143] Hunt 2015: 150–3.

[144] For interconnections between Africa and Brazil, see da Costa e Silva 2000; Strickrodt 2004; Ferreira 2012; Reis, dos Santos Gomes and Carvalho 2020.

Africa is that a very significant proportion of enslaved Africans were completely unfamiliar with the New World societies where they ended up and came from societies that exhibited major social, economic and cultural differences from the New World colonial societies.[145] Ancient historians need to ask themselves to what extent this also applied to antiquity.

Distances between slaving zones and importing communities in antiquity were significantly smaller and often rather negligible; as a result, most foreign slaves would have a certain level of familiarity with the communities where they ended up as slaves.[146] Furthermore, there were significant political, social, economic and cultural links between areas like Thrace, Phrygia and Scythia and the Greek communities which imported slaves from these areas on a mass scale; not only were Thracians familiar with Greek deities, but the Thracian goddess Bendis had a major cult in Athens and received the third largest sacrifice of the Athenian state. The Greeks did not come across Thracians and Scythians solely as slaves, but also as powerful kings, aristocrats, traders, mercenaries and immigrants.[147]

What were the consequences of these major differences between ancient Mediterranean and early modern Atlantic slaving? Were there in antiquity processes of ethnogenesis that created new Creole ethnicities out of the experience of slaving, as was the case in the New World? And if we can find no such examples from antiquity, how should we explain this difference?[148] Should we assume that the relative absence of Creole slave cultures in the ancient Mediterranean, in comparison with the Atlantic world, is the consequence of the high volume of intercultural contact and exchange that existed between Mediterranean communities irrespective of slaving?[149] Or is it the case that we have not sufficiently explored our literary, epigraphic, legal, papyrological and material record from antiquity for Creole slave culture and community?[150]

The early modern Atlantic involved contact between varieties of monotheistic Christianity and the significantly different religious practices of enslaved persons imported from Africa.[151] In the ancient Mediterranean the encounter between the religions and cults of the masters and those of imported slaves took place in a very different religious context, in which religious differences were relatively circumscribed and the mutual adoption of cults and ideas between different communities was relatively common; is this the reason we do not seem to have slave religions or slave-inflected cults in antiquity, or have we not asked the right questions yet?

An inscription from early first-century CE Laureion in Attica records the foundation of a cult to Men Tyrannos by Xanthos, the slave of Gaius Orvius.[152] Xanthos originated from Lycia in Asia Minor, and the cult of Men was popular in various parts of Asia Minor, although it had entered the Aegean centuries before the foundation

---

[145]  Thornton 1998.
[146]  Lewis 2011, 2015.
[147]  Vlassopoulos 2013a: 119–28.
[148]  See the comment of Hunt 2015: 132.
[149]  I. Morris 1998, 2011.
[150]  Cf. Webster 2005.
[151]  Sweet 2003; Thornton 2012.
[152]  *IG* II², 1366.

of Xanthos.[153] It is difficult to see this as a slave cult, or as a cult introduced by a foreign slave; but did the ethnicity of this slave have no impact whatsoever on the foundation and operation of this cult? This example raises important questions about slave agency and the role of slaves as cultural agents, which we shall examine in Chapter 8. Another epitaph from the mining area of Laureion, but this time from the fourth century BCE, gives some tantalising evidence about how local and foreign could be entangled in the ancient Mediterranean:

> Atotas the miner
> From the Black Sea Atotas, the great-hearted Paphlagonian,
> put to rest his body from the toils far away from his fatherland.
> Nobody vied [with me] in [my] art; I am from the stem of Pylaimenes,
> who died subdued by the hand of Achilles.[154]

Whether Atotas was a slave or a freedman at the time of his death is impossible to tell; that he must have started as a slave miner is effectively certain. We are dealing with a person who was proud of his manual skill and of his national origins. And, what is most tantalising, he was able to express his ethnic credentials in a language that could appeal to the Greek reader of this epitaph. The epigram uses Homeric expressions; Atotas is described as *megathymos Paphlagon*, which brings to mind the verse of the *Iliad*, in which Paphlagonians are described with exactly the same adjective.[155] Interestingly, though, the Homeric version of the death of Pylaimenes is different from that of Atotas, since in the *Iliad* he is killed by Menelaos.[156] Clearly, Atotas could combine a good knowledge of Greek mythology with national pride and his own version of mythical events.[157] Atotas' ethnic self-presentation in Greek terms would have been impossible without the peculiar tool of Greek mythology.[158] What was peculiar in Greek mythology was its spatial location not solely in the Aegean world, but across the Mediterranean, the Black Sea and the Near East; furthermore, the concept of the foreign hero, like the Trojans or their Paphlagonian ally Pylaimenes, allowed non-Greeks to incorporate their ethnic identities within a Mediterranean-wide canvas.[159]

The above comments show why the study of ethnic, religious and cultural communities in which enslaved persons participated will need to engage more systematically with wider debates about ethnogenesis and cultural interaction in antiquity (and vice versa, of course).[160] We are told that in early imperial Rome a significant part of the Jewish population of Rome consisted of former slaves who had been manumitted, as the Jewish philosopher Philo reports:

---

[153] Lane 1971; Bömer 1990: 195–213.
[154] *IG* II², 10051; see Bäbler 1998: 94–7; Lauffer 1956: 200–4.
[155] Homer, *Iliad* 5.577.
[156] Homer, *Iliad* 5.576.
[157] For this text, see Raffeiner 1977: 14–16, 87–8.
[158] Vlassopoulos 2011b; Hunt 2015: 136–8.
[159] Vlassopoulos 2013a: 161–70.
[160] Among the rare extant studies, see Hunt 2015.

How come then that Augustus acknowledged the great section of Rome on the other side of the Tiber, which he knew was occupied and inhabited by Jews? The majority were Romans who had been manumitted. That is, they had been taken to Italy as captives and were manumitted by those who had bought them, without being forced to falsify their ancestral customs. So he also knew that they organized prayers and held gatherings for this purpose, especially on the holy seventh day, when they publicly receive training on their ancestral philosophy. He also knew that they collected money for sacred purposes from first-fruits and sent it to Jerusalem with those who would offer the sacrifices.[161]

The Jewish ethnic, religious and cultural community of Rome included free immigrants of the Jewish diaspora, as well as enslaved Jews;[162] but can we generalise from this example about how other diaspora communities operated in the ancient Mediterranean?[163]

The second factor that affected slave community formation resulted from the nexus between the various slaving strategies and contexts (see above Chapter 4). The large number of slaves concentrated in households or the various forms of large-scale economic operations provided opportunities for the construction of various slave communities. Concentrations of slaves in households or estates with a relatively balanced sex ratio were potentially congenial for the formation of slave families and kinship networks.[164] They also led to the formation of slave communities which were based on ownership by the same master and membership of the same household. This was particularly prominent in the Roman world, as we have seen in Chapter 5.

In this respect, we need to think about the spatial arrangements that might have facilitated family life among slaves. As we mentioned above, the provision of separate cabins for slave families in New World societies like the US South was clearly significant for family life; classical archaeologists have searched for equivalent spatial arrangements for slaves in antiquity, primarily in the residential quarters of Roman villas.[165] Irrespective of the various answers, it is clear that there was usually nothing equivalent to separate slave quarters in Roman villas, and in many cases slaves shared the living space of their masters.[166] How far this relative lack of spatial autonomy might have affected the formation of slave families and kinship networks will require further study.[167]

On the other hand, in situations where many households possessed one or two slaves, this would make more difficult both the formation of families and kinship groups and the formation of slave communities based on common ownership. Nevertheless, as studies of other slaveholding societies have shown, even where households possessed

---

[161] Philo, *Embassy to Gaius* 155–7.

[162] Noy 2000: 255–67; Tacoma 2016; see also Gnoli 2005–8 on a Parthian former slave in Roman Italy.

[163] See the comments of McKeown 2019.

[164] Treggiari 1975b; Roth 2007.

[165] Carandini and Ricci 1985; George 1997; Thompson 2003: 83–9; Marzano 2007; Roth 2007; Joshel and Petersen 2014: 162–213.

[166] But see now Fentress, Goodson and Maiuro 2016: 115–79; Molina Vidal et al. 2017.

[167] Martin 1993, 2003; Mouritsen 2011b: 136; Schmitz 2012.

one or two slaves, enslaved persons could create families with slaves belonging to different households.[168] The difference in slave concentrations and the slave communities that they led to is probably one of the major differences between Greek and Roman forms of slaving. Small groups of slaves would more often face the threat of family separation that perennially hovered over the heads of slave families. The threat of sale was a powerful tool in the hands of masters in order to coerce obedience; but it also commonly resulted from the slaving strategies of masters, whether transforming their human capital into monetary capital through sale or dividing slave families for inheritance purposes.[169] In Chapter 7 I analyse a characteristic example of the threat of family separation and the collective action of enslaved persons which thwarted it. It is finally worth pointing out that we should not think of slave families exclusively in terms of marriage and biological relationships; global studies of kinship have shown the variety of materials and relationships from which communities constitute kinship, while studies of New World slavery have revealed that African slaves could create various groups of quasi-families, even in the absence of balanced sex ratios.[170]

While slave communities were facilitated by slaving strategies for wealth or maintenance that created large concentrations of slaves, an alternative path for the formation of slave communities was provided by slaving strategies for revenue, expertise or trust. These strategies generally created slaves who lived and worked on their own; such slaves had significantly higher degrees of autonomy, resources and social connections for creating their families and kinship networks. At the same time, such slaves worked among other slaves, freed persons, free foreigners and citizens; consequently, they were more likely to participate in mixed communities on the basis of profession, residence, cult and ethnicity.[171] These communities brought together people of different statuses for the purposes of work, trade, commensality, cult and travel.[172] An excellent illustration of this phenomenon is offered by a dedicatory inscription from fourth-century BCE Athens:

> The washers dedicated this to the Nymphs and all the gods after a vow: Zoagoras son of Zokypros, Zokypros son of Zoagoras, Thallos, Leuke, Sokrates son of Polykrates, Apollophanes son of Euporion, Sosistratos, Manes, Myrrhine, Sosias, Sosigenes, Midas.[173]

This is a dedication from a group of washers, which includes ten men and two women. We do not know the precise legal status of the persons involved. Four people have Greek names commonly borne by freemen accompanied by their

---

[168] Nishida 2003: 52–4; see the comments of McKeown 2019.

[169] Bradley 1984: 51–70; Mouritsen 2011b: 139–40.

[170] For the complexity of kinship, see Carsten 2000, 2004; for quasi-families, see Sweet 2013.

[171] Bathrellou 2014.

[172] For this mixed sociability, see Randall 1953; Vlassopoulos 2007a, 2011b; Rauh, Dillon and McClain 2008.

[173] *IG* II², 2934.

patronymic: Zoagoras and his son Zokypros are probably metics from Cyprus, while Sokrates and Apollophanes are obviously freemen, and possibly even citizens. Thallos, Sosistratos and Sosigenes are names borne by Athenian citizens and other free foreigners, but not securely attested for slaves otherwise. Sosias is a Greek name, common among citizens, but also very common for slaves; and the last two males have typical names of foreign slaves, both of them Phrygian: Manes and Midas.[174] The people without patronymics can thus be either slaves or freed persons, most probably a combination of both. Finally, both women have impeccable Greek names and are possibly free, or even female citizens. We have here a mixed association of free Greek men and women, and what can be a combination of freed persons and slaves; this mixed community is constructed on the basis of shared professional activities and cultic adherence to deities linked with water, and accordingly associated with the washers' profession.[175]

This group of washers appears to be rather informal; but around the same time there emerged one of the most important developments in ancient sociability: the creation of formal and institutionalised associations on the basis of profession, cult and ethnicity. These associations tended to adopt the model of the Greek polis as a blueprint for organising their internal affairs; they held assemblies and passed decrees, elected magistrates, organised festivals and celebrations, possessed collective funds and properties, created their own burial grounds and took care of the funeral rites of their members.[176] In the course of the Hellenistic and early imperial periods such forms of associations expanded into the eastern Mediterranean and the Near East, as well as into the western Mediterranean and temperate Europe, where they acquired peculiar Roman inflections.[177] The social composition of these associations ranged widely: while certain associations were relatively exclusive or primarily attracted the middling sort, many included slaves and freed persons.[178] It is remarkable that in certain associations slaves could even be elected magistrates, alongside freeborn citizens and freedmen, as in the following inscription from early imperial Cartagena in Spain:

These officials superintended: Caius Poplicius, son of Caius; Lucius Cervius, son of Lucius; Marcus Caeicius, freedman of Caius Numerius; Lucius Talepius, freedman of Aulus; Cnaeus Tongilius, freedman of Publius; Lucius Paquius Silo, freedman of Longus; Quintus, slave of Caius Veratius; Pilippus, slave of Caius Marcius [of the] Pontilii; Quintus, slave of Pupius Claudius.[179]

---

[174] For slave names in classical Athens, see Vlassopoulos 2010, 2015a.

[175] Vlassopoulos 2011b.

[176] Arnaoutoglou 2003; Harland 2003; Gabrielsen 2007; Ismard 2010; Fröhlich and Hamon 2013; Gabrielsen and Thomsen 2015; Taylor and Vlassopoulos 2015a; Vlassopoulos 2015c.

[177] Waltzing 1895; Ausbüttel 1982; van Nijf 1997; Tran 2006b; Liu 2009; Perry 2011; Dondin-Payre and Tran 2012.

[178] Tran 2006a; Verboven 2007; North 2012: 73–4; McKeown 2019.

[179] CIL II, 3433.

The magistrates include two freeborn citizens, four freedmen and three slaves. In fact, in another early imperial inscription from Minturnae in Italy, the whole board of magistrates consisted of slaves:

> These *magistri* gave the gift to the deity Spes: Antiochus, slave of Quintus Pullius; Bacchides, slave of Marcus Paccius; Seleucus, slave of Marcus and Caius Aurelius; Philinus, slave of Caius Cosconius; Philocles, slave of Numerius Furius; Philomusus, slave of Lucius Cahius; Gorgia, slave of Caius Allenius; Alexsander [sic], slave of Marcus Antius; Barnaeus, slave of Aulus Morasius; Deiphilus, slave of Titinius Curtius and Caius Publius; Afrio, slave of Caius and Marcus Statius; Sosia, slave of Marcus Badius.[180]

Future work will have to ponder in more depth the implications of the participation of enslaved persons in mixed associations and their acquisition of positions of authority within them.[181] An inscription records an association that was willing to accord funerary rites to its slave members, even when their masters refused to release the body of the slave: in such cases, an effigy of the slave body would be used.[182] It is telling, therefore, that imperial laws forbade associations from enrolling slaves among their membership without the permission of their masters.[183]

While we should not assume that the participation of enslaved persons in associations was in itself an act of resistance or something that would necessarily be displeasing to their masters, we also need to explore how participation in associations enabled slaves to enhance their condition and create social networks that could prove highly useful. A vocal example comes from an inscription from Hellenistic Delos, in which the slave Theogenes appeals to the deities Helios and the Hagne Thea to punish a woman who promised to take his money and secure his manumission but betrayed him; but Theogenes also appeals to all *therapeutai*, presumably fellow members of a cult association to the Hagne Thea, to curse the woman by the hour.[184] Even if his fellow associates could not give him practical support in his plight, their moral support was clearly desirable.[185]

But such communal links could have practical effects, as we can see from the admonitions of the bishop Ignatius of Antioch to Polycarpus, bishop of Smyrna, in the early second century CE:

> Don't behave arrogantly towards slaves, whether male or female; nor should they puff themselves up, but be slaves more zealously for the glory of God, so that God may grant them a better freedom. They shouldn't desire to get manumitted from the common fund, so that they might not be found slaves to desire.[186]

---

[180]  *CIL* I², 2689.
[181]  For slave *magistri* and *ministri*, see Schumacher 2006: 13–16; Tran 2014.
[182]  *CIL* XIV, 2112.3–5; see Bendlin 2011.
[183]  *Digest* 47.22.3.2.
[184]  *ID* 2531.
[185]  For cases of practical support, see Rädle 1970.
[186]  Ignatius, *Epistle to Polycarpus* 4.

Christian communities were mixed associations, which included free people, freed persons and slaves. It is obvious from Ignatius' advice that the slave members of the Christian community of Smyrna were trying to convince their fellow members to use the common funds in order to buy their freedom, presumably from their non-Christian masters. This is a telling example of how participation in mixed associations could provide enslaved persons with resources and connections that could have significant impact in their lives.[187] In 340 CE the Christian Synod of Gangra voted to anathematise anyone who taught slaves to despise their masters, or to withdraw from their service under the pretext of religion; participation in certain mixed Christian communities could provide enslaved persons with grounds to resist the authority of their masters, as well as a network of support.[188]

It would be misleading, though, to give a one-dimensional image of slave communities as sources of affection, solidarity and support. While they provided all these things, they were also continuously torn by conflicts and contrasting interests.[189] I will bring this discussion to a close by turning our attention to a final source that illustrates the tensions and conflicts that tore apart master households, relationships between masters and slaves and relationships within the slave community. The following story comes from the apocryphal *Acts of Andrew*, usually dated to the late second or early third century CE. The text narrates how the Apostle converted Maximilla, the wife of Aigeates, the Roman proconsul of Patras; as a devout Christian, Maximilla decided to abstain from sex with her husband, and convinced her slave Euklia, with promises of reward, to secretly take her place in the spousal bed:

> Eight months later, however, Euklia demanded from her mistress to set her free; Maximilla gave her what she asked on the same day. After a few days, she also asked for a substantial sum of money; Maximilla gave it to her immediately. Then she asked for some of her jewels; Maximilla had no objections. Put simply, although on each occasion Maximilla would give her clothes, linen, head-bands, this was not enough for her; boasting, puffed up, she revealed the affair to her fellow slaves. They were indignant at her bragging, and at the beginning they tried to silence her with their railing. But she would laugh and show them the gifts she had received from their mistress. Her fellow slaves recognized these and were at a loss as what to do . . . When they found out about the affair . . . they caught Maximilla as if she were some foreign guest . . . Some of them wanted to make the affair known and inform Aigeates; others tried to stop them, pretending they felt affection for their mistress. So they tried to silence those with them, and beat them as if they were mad men, in order to make them clear off . . . After an hour, the slaves who were fighting against their fellow slaves about her rushed into her room. They spoke to her in flattery, expecting to get something from her, as they were slaves of Aigeates. The blessed Maximilla did not refuse to give them what

---

[187] Harrill 1995: 158–92; cf. Shaner 2018: 87–109.

[188] *Concilium Gangrense* canon 3; cf. de Churruca 1982; Grieser 2001; McKeown 2012: 296–7.

[189] For cases of conflict within slave communities, see *An.Ep.* 2008, no. 792; *An.Ep.* 2010, no. 108; Tomlin 2008, 2010.

they demanded . . . Thus, she ordered that 1000 denarii be given to those feigning love for her, commanding them not to reveal the affair to anyone. They swore, more than once, to keeping silent about what they had seen. But, instigated by their father the devil, they immediately rushed to their master, with the money in hand. And they told him the whole story . . . Aigeates, indignant at Euklia for her boasts to her fellow slaves and for her words, which defamed the mistress, cut off Euklia's tongue, mutilated her and ordered that she be thrown out. After a few days without any food, Euklia was eaten up by dogs. And his other slaves, those who had told him what I mentioned (they were three), he crucified.[190]

In a situation of potential grave conflict between the mistress and her husband, it was a female slave who could be used as the solution to the problem. But while Euklia did very well out of her pact with her mistress, her wish to brag to her fellow slaves led to her terrible destruction; her fellow slaves clashed about how to handle the situation and potentially profit from it, and the result was catastrophic for many of them. The asymmetry of master–slave relations and the usual conflicts that can be found in all human relationships ensured that the formation of slave communities was always a fragile process, fraught with constant danger; many slaves often preferred individual strategies that were less risky.[191]

We have explored three different dialectical relationships and their impact on slaving and enslaved persons. As we saw, each relationship pointed in different directions and emphasised different concerns; but at the same time they influenced each other and should always be examined in their historical entanglement. We have seen that each relationship could point in contradictory directions: the master–slave relationships could create the absolute tyranny of the masters, or create slaves with resources and authority; the free–slave relationship could intervene to limit what masters could do to their slaves and to offer opportunities to enslaved persons, or subordinate all slaves irrespective of their networks and accomplishments to the lowest free person; slave communities could be sources of solidarity and support, but also sources of tension and conflict. Slave communities like slave families could be a powerful tool in the hands of masters for enforcing their control and reproducing the slave system, and simultaneously a way in which slaves could overcome social death, create lives beyond slavery, enhance their condition and resist their exploitation and domination. The entanglement between the different relationships could reinforce each other, but also create major contradictions. We have also stressed diversity, as in the case of slave communities: while some of them included exclusively slaves, in other communities slaves participated alongside various free people. Finally, the free–slave relationship and the relationships within slave communities stress the need to move beyond the exclusive focus on the link between masters and slaves which has so far dominated the study of ancient slavery, and to examine the full range of relationships and factors that affected the history of slaving.

---

[190] *Acts of Andrew* 17–22; see Glancy 2002: 21–4.
[191] Kolchin 1983; Hunt 2017b; Ben-Ur 2018.

# 7

# THE SLAVE VIEW OF SLAVERY: SLAVE HOPES AND THE REALITY OF SLAVERY[1]

HOW DID ENSLAVED PERSONS in antiquity view their condition? How did they see themselves? What hopes did they have about the future? The traditional approach to these issues in the study of ancient slavery was framed within the humanitarian debate on ancient slavery that we examined in Chapter 2. The possible answers in this debate have been preconditioned by its top-down and unilateral perspective; slavery is seen as a relationship of domination and exploitation unilaterally defined by the masters. In this perspective, slaves were merely passive objects of exploitation and domination: their agency was shaped by the fact that their status was unilaterally defined by others, and that they existed instrumentally, in order to serve the aims and purposes of others.[2] Many ancient historians have come to accept Patterson's famous definition of slavery as social death.[3] But if slavery is tantamount to social death, then it is a truly hopeless situation. The only hope a slave might entertain is to reverse the 'day of slavery', gain his freedom and, within this new condition, entertain the full range of hopes that those who are socially alive can dream of.[4] For the other side within this debate, this might as well be true, but masters could gradually become more benevolent for a variety of reasons and treat their slaves in a better way. Generally speaking, slaves could hope to find humane masters that would treat them well; in the longer term, ideologies like Stoicism or Christianity could convince masters of the shared humanity of slaves and of the need to behave appropriately.[5]

This chapter attempts to re-orient the discussion by exploring in detail the implications of the alternative approach we have explored in Chapters 3 and 5. Slavery was not a single thing, but a conglomerate of different conceptual systems; enslaved persons were not exclusively defined by their servile identity, but exhibited a variety of other roles and identities. How did enslaved persons employ the various modalities of slavery in order to understand themselves and their condition? How were these modalities employed in order to fulfil their various hopes and desires and realise their roles and identities? What limits did these modalities place on how enslaved persons thought and acted? What do modalities and identities tell us about how enslaved people exercised their agency? What challenges did slaves face in fulfilling their hopes

---

[1]  The title of this chapter is a tribute to Schwartz 1977.

[2]  For a critique of such approaches, see Vlassopoulos 2016a.

[3]  Patterson 1982: 13; see Fisher 1993: 5–6; Bradley 1994: 10–16; Cartledge 2011: 79; Harper 2017a; Hunt 2017a, 2018a: 18–19.

[4]  For a recent assessment of Patterson's approach, see Bodel and Scheidel 2017.

[5]  Richter 1958; Vogt 1974; Waldstein 2001.

and desires? In a nutshell, this chapter is an attempt to look at slavery from the slaves' point of view, while exploring all the serious methodological problems involved in exploring this difficult issue.

We should start this exploration from a general proposition. As far as we can tell, nobody in antiquity disputed the legitimacy of slavery as an institution and called for its abolition.[6] That does not deny the existence of very significant debates concerning slavery in antiquity, but we need to be clear about the nature of these debates and what was at stake. Perhaps the easiest way to frame this is by saying that ancient discourses on slavery took it as a fact of life. Think of death, another fact of life, as an analogy for how ancients talked about slavery: perhaps it is bad for those to whom it happens; perhaps we should struggle to keep it at arm's length as much as we can; perhaps some people deserve it for what they have done or who they are; perhaps it is an accident of fortune; perhaps it is beside the point, an insignificant detail when other things are more important; perhaps inflicting it on some people is a legitimate means for other people to achieve desirable things (victory, glory, power, wealth); perhaps inflicting it on (certain) people is shameful and unjust.[7] These debates were very significant; but by accepting slavery as a fact of life, it meant that no slave or group of slaves in antiquity ever conceived the abolition of slavery as such, or fought for it. This is a point that is generally conceded by most scholars and usually tends to terminate discussion;[8] but we need to move on from this proposition into examining the contradictory conglomerate of ideas and discourses about slavery and their historical impact.

## Modalities of Slavery

The reconstruction of slave agency requires the realisation that ancient societies did not have a single model through which to conceptualise slavery and shape relations between masters and slaves. In every society there existed a variety of such models, which we can call modalities of slavery, as we saw in Chapter 3; they had different implications, which were partly overlapping and partly contradicting each other, and they could be used for different purposes and in different ways. I shall start by trying to illustrate the range of such modalities that could co-exist in the work of a single author. My case-study is Artemidorus' early imperial handbook, *On the interpretation of dreams* (*Oneirokritika*). Enslaved persons are present in Artemidorus' handbook both as dreamers and as elements in the dream repertoire. But it is crucial that slaves do not appear as a single category with identifiable features; instead, the identity and the features of the slaves as a category can change significantly, depending on the point of view from which Artemidorus approaches them.[9]

---

[6] Gregory of Nyssa is the sole ancient exception; but while he disputed the legitimacy of slavery as an institution, he never called for its abolition. See Garnsey 1996: 80–5; Harper 2011: 345–6; cf. Ramelli 2016: 172–211; Vlassopoulos 2018b: 323–5.

[7] See the collection of passages illustrating these various debates in Garnsey 1996.

[8] See the characteristic reaction of Bradley 1997.

[9] For slaves and slavery in Artemidorus, see Annequin 1987, 2005, 2008; Klees 1990; Pomeroy 1991; Hahn 1992.

I will offer a few examples that illustrate this point, and tease out their implications. I shall eschew discussing the central modality of slavery as property, as the significance of this modality has already been discussed in Chapter 3.[10] My first example is a neat illustration of the instrumental view of slavery, in which slaves exist solely as means for fulfilling the wishes and needs of their masters:

> Together with their other outcomes, slaves also have a certain correlation with the bodies of their masters. Indeed someone who had imagined that he observed his slave having a fever fittingly fell ill himself; for the connection that a slave has in relation to the dream-observer, the body has in relation to the soul.[11]

In this case a slave's illness does not even refer to the future of the slave; because the slave only exists for the sake of his master, the slave's illness actually predicts something concerning the master. A rather different perspective emerges from the juxtaposition offered in the next passage:

> To observe a lion that is tame and simpering and approaches harmlessly is good and delivers assistance to a soldier from a king . . . to a citizen from the magistrate and to a slave from his master; for this animal resembles these people, due to its power and strength.[12]

In this case, the lion stands as a metaphor for relations of power: enslaved persons are juxtaposed with soldiers and citizens, as people who had the subordinate position in relations of power with masters, kings and magistrates. Slavery is conceptualised as a relationship of domination, in which two asymmetric sides negotiated power.[13]

The third example shifts from domination and power to adversity:

> And a thunderstorm and hurricane and winter storm bring about dangers and losses. But alone for slaves and poor people and those who are in a difficult position they foretell a release from their present ills; for following great storms good weather arises.[14]

Slaves were individuals who faced difficult circumstances, and this brought them together with the poor; slavery is considered as an extreme form of bad luck, which with perseverance and good fortune one could eventually overcome.[15] Our final passage moves again in another direction:

> To be struck by a thunderbolt . . . frees those slaves who are not trusted. But those who are trusted or honoured by their masters, or who possess much property, it removes from that trust and honour and property.[16]

---

[10] For slavery as property, see, for example, Artemidorus, *The interpretation of dreams* 1.78.

[11] Artemidorus, *The interpretation of dreams* 4.30.

[12] Artemidorus, *The interpretation of dreams* 2.12.

[13] For slavery as domination, see Kyrtatas 2002; Vlassopoulos 2011b.

[14] Artemidorus, *The interpretation of dreams* 2.8.

[15] For ancient views of slavery as a form of bad luck, see Williams 1993: 116–24.

[16] Artemidorus, *The interpretation of dreams* 2.9.

The thunderbolt is a symbol of radical reversals of circumstances for diverse groups of people. Having delineated various categories among free people, Artemidorus moves on to explore the differential meaning of the thunderbolt by distinguishing two categories among slaves: slaves without favour and trust, and slaves who are trusted and honoured by their masters and enjoy material benefits as a result. This focus on trust and honour as aspects that differentiate certain slaves from others points towards an alternative modality of slavery. Slaves who enjoy trust, honour and property from their masters have clearly earned them as a result of their behaviour and actions. From this point of view, slavery is not an instrumental relationship in which slaves merely exist in order to serve the needs of their masters; it is rather a reciprocal relationship of mutual benefaction and reward between masters and slaves in which both benefit from it, even if in widely asymmetric ways. Equally significant is the reference to honoured slaves: it is one example among many of why the essentialist understanding of slavery as a state of dishonour proposed by scholars like Patterson can be quite misleading.[17]

Let us now tease out the implications of the passages above. Slavery could be conceived as property or as an instrumental relationship in which slaves existed for the purpose of serving the needs and wishes of their masters; but property and instrumentality were not the only means of conceiving and employing slavery. Slavery could be seen as an asymmetric negotiation of power between masters and slaves: a relationship not unilaterally defined from above, but the outcome of struggle, compromise and failure.[18] From this point of view, slave expectations would focus on limiting the power of masters and putting forward their own agenda of aims, to the extent that this was possible.[19] Slavery could also be envisaged as an asymmetric relationship of benefaction and reward; masters could opt to see slave labour as loyal service and choose to reward deserving slaves with trust, honour and material benefits; slaves could see their service as the foundation for claims to just rewards. From this point of view, slaves would focus on eliciting the master's goodwill and the various rewards that came with it.[20] Slavery could be seen as an extreme form of bad luck, which could happen to anybody through no fault of their own, and could be potentially reversed with a change of fortune; this offered slaves a powerful means of facing adverse circumstances that might not last forever.[21]

These observations show the limits of the unilateral approach to slavery. The modality of slavery as service and reciprocal benefaction allowed slaves to conceive themselves not as instruments to satisfy the needs of their masters, but as people who had lived their lives in an exemplary manner that illustrated their virtues. A characteristic example comes from a first-century funerary inscription from the columbarium of the Statilii at Rome:

[17] For criticisms of Patterson's theory concerning slavery and dishonour, see Stilwell 2000; Lendon 2001: 95–103; Brown 2009; Rabbås 2015; Canevaro 2018.

[18] For such an approach, see Genovese 1974; Glassman 1991; Berlin 1998.

[19] For an impressive, if rare in its clarity and visibility, example from eighteenth-century Brazil, see Schwartz 1977.

[20] Zelnick-Abramovitz 2005: 6–7.

[21] See the comments of Bodel 2017: 89–93.

Iucundus, slave of Taurus, litter bearer; as long as he lived, he was a man and acted on behalf of himself and others; as long as he lived, he lived honourably; Callista and Philologus dedicated (this).[22]

The inscription eloquently records how Iucundus wished to be seen: as a slave who fulfilled the expectations of his male gender and who lived as a honourable person, irrespective of the social death of slavery. Another particularly telling source is a funerary inscription from early imperial Brixia in Italy:

Marcus Hostilius Dicaeus. 'I came to this city when I was fourteen years old. In the household in which I arrived I stayed; never did I change to another household or master except for this, my eternal home. I have lived for seventy years. No-one called me before the praetor, no one sent me to a judge. You, who stand here and read this, if this is not the best of things, tell me, what is better?'[23]

Having lived his whole life as a slave and freedman in a single household constitutes for this former slave indisputable evidence of his moral probity. The fact that he was never sold to another household recognised his value; the fact that he stayed in the same household after his manumission recognised his continued value and contribution.[24] The same spirit is expressed by one of the freedmen in the *Cena Trimalchionis* of Petronius' satirical novel:

'Then why have you been a slave?' Because I went into service to please myself, and preferred being a Roman citizen to going on paying taxes as a provincial. And now I hope I live such a life that no one can jeer at me. I am a man among men; I walk about bare-headed; I owe nobody a brass farthing; I have never been in the Courts; no one has ever said to me in public, 'Pay me what you owe me'. I have bought a few acres and collected a little capital; I have to feed twenty bellies and a dog: I ransomed my fellow slave to preserve her from indignities; I paid a thousand silver pennies for my own freedom; I was made a priest of Augustus and excused the fees; I hope to die so that I need not blush in my grave . . . I was a slave for forty years, and nobody knew whether I was a slave or free. I was a boy with long curls when I came to this place; they had not built the town-hall then. But I tried to please my master, a fine dignified gentleman whose little finger was worth more than your whole body. And there were people in the house who put out a foot to trip me up here and there. But still – God bless my master! – I struggled through. These are real victories: being born free is as easy as saying, 'Come here.'[25]

The pride of this freedman in having lived in slavery as a decent person is underlined by his argument that having made a success of his life under the conditions of slavery is a major achievement. It is particularly telling that he stresses the fact that he lived

[22] *CIL* VI, 6308.
[23] *An.Ep.* 1980, no. 503.
[24] Kleijwegt 2006c: 96–9.
[25] Petronius, *Satyricon* 57.

for forty years as a slave and nobody knew whether he was a slave or a free person, a point to which we shall return.[26]

Conceiving of slavery as a job that could be performed with success and pride obviously conceded the legitimacy of the system and the masters' power, even if it allowed some slaves to maintain their dignity. The same combination is illustrated by another characteristic example that shows the hegemony of masters over slaves as well as the way slaves interpreted the power of their masters. It comes from Galen's description of how people with different characters react to punishment:

> Behaviour of this kind can also be seen every day in slaves. Those who are caught stealing or doing something else of the kind, even when whipped, starved and disgraced by their masters, are not angry; but those who believe they are suffering or have suffered any of these things unjustly have inside them an anger that is always savage and craves vengeance on the wrongdoer.[27]

Galen argues that (many) slaves accepted the legitimacy of their masters' authority over them and the legitimacy of being punished for actions considered as theft. At the very same time, though, he describes how slaves reacted with anger to punishment that they considered unjust and undeserved. While masters considered their power to punish as absolute, slaves considered that power as circumscribed by justice, in the same way that citizens considered the power of state authorities to punish them.[28] The juxtaposition of slaves, citizens and soldiers in Artemidorus' work we examined above was not accidental: the modality of domination could be employed by slaves to conceptualise their relationship to their masters and the limits of that power.

The modality of reciprocal benefaction was employed by both masters and slaves for a variety of reasons and contexts. The extent to which this modality differed from the instrumental view of slavery is most telling when masters employ the language of honour in order to conceptualise the relationship with their slaves and express their utter disappointment that the slaves did not show proper gratitude for the honour, as seen in a third-century CE petition from Oxyrhynchos in Egypt:

> I have a slave, who formerly belonged to my father, by the name of Sarapion, and I considered that he had done no base deed whatsoever, as he was part of my inheritance and had been entrusted by me with our household. He, I do not know how, at the instigation of certain folk, disdaining the honour I afforded him and the provision of the necessities for life, purloining some items of clothing from our household with which I had provided him and even other items which he also took possession of for himself from our own property, he secretly run away.[29]

---

[26] For the language of freedmen in Petronius, see Boyce 1991; for the discourses employed in the public transcripts of freedmen, see Vermote 2016a: 439–524.

[27] Galen, *On the doctrines of Hippocrates and Plato* 5.7.66–7.

[28] See, for example, the female slave from Ptolemaic Egypt complaining of being treated unjustly in Scholl 1990: no. 73.

[29] *P. Turner* 41; see Llewelyn 1992: 55–60, 1997: 9–46.

Masters might consider benefactions to their slaves as a form of benevolent gratitude, as illustrated by this excerpt from a late-antique collection of jokes:

> A scholar visited his estate after some time and saw some sheep going to browse. Hearing them bleating, he asked for the reason. His manager answered in jest, 'They greet you.' 'For my sake give them a holiday and do not take them out to graze for three days.'[30]

The joke is obviously built on the misleading similarity between slaves and sheep: the idiotic scholar's ludicrous offer of a holiday for his sheep would have made sense as a holiday gift from a master pleased to see his grateful and obedient slaves greeting him respectfully.[31] In other cases, masters could explicitly present gifts to their slaves as a reward for their loyal service, as shown by a first-century BCE manumission inscription from Thessalian Azoros:

> Aristoteles, son of Demochares, and his wife Adea, daughter of Philotas, and their son Demochares, son of Aristoteles, citizens of Larissa, emancipated gratis Zosime, their slave, because she was well-pleasing.[32]

The slave's good behaviour constituted in her masters' eyes the reason for the gift of manumission gratis. But what to the master might appear as a magnanimous unilateral gift, to the slave might appear as a right earned for faithful service, as also expressed in one of the Aesopic tales of Phaedrus we will encounter below (p. 159). The potential of different understandings to clash comes out in a famous example of slave retaliation described by Tacitus:

> Soon afterwards one of his own slaves murdered the city-prefect, Pedanius Secundus, either because he had been refused his freedom, for which he had made a bargain, or in the jealousy of a love for a boy, in which he could not brook his master's rivalry.[33]

The promise of manumission was a unilateral act from the point of view of the master, which he was under no obligation to honour; and yet Tacitus makes it quite clear that this is not how this particular slave conceived of it. The murder was instigated by the sense of betrayal felt by the slave for the dishonouring of the agreement he had negotiated with his master. Tacitus also offers an alternative interpretation of the slave's motives, which raises issues we will discuss below (pp. 155–8).

The existence of different modalities of slavery allowed masters and slaves to negotiate their respective positions and enabled slaves to conceive slavery and their relationship to their masters in their own ways. Slaves tried to modify slavery from a unilateral and instrumental form of power exercised by their masters into something

---

[30] *Philogelos* no. 47.

[31] On slave holidays, see Bradley 1979.

[32] *IG* IX(2), 1296A.

[33] Tacitus, *Annals* 14.42; for this event, see Bellen 1982.

more negotiable, even if in asymmetric ways. But equally significant was the fact that slaves also tried to limit the effect of slavery on their lives, by ensuring that significant aspects of their lives would run on principles other than slavery (kinship, profession, ethnicity, religion, friendship). The struggle to limit the effects of slavery on slaves' lives was one of the most crucial elements in the historical trajectory of slavery in antiquity. This struggle consisted of many different factors and elements and was deeply contradictory. It obviously depended on the extent to which masters attempted to employ slavery in order to shape the full range of their slaves' lives, or preferred to use it for only limited purposes. The more masters were willing to accept the latter option, the more the slaves' attempts to limit the effects of slavery were likely to succeed. An illuminating window on how slaves tried to run their lives comes from exploring their various hopes, both within and without slavery.

## Exploring Slave Hopes under Slavery

Let us start with a relatively direct source on slave hopes and fears: that of oracles. Ancient societies had a very wide spectrum of divination practices. We have already encountered the tradition of dream interpretation in the handbook of Artemidorus; other examples include the questions and responses addressed to institutional oracles, like Delphi and Dodona, and sortition oracles, on which I shall focus.[34] Sortition oracles depend on an apparently random and therefore divinely inspired link between the enquirer's question and a list of possible answers. While dice oracles were common in many parts of the Mediterranean world, for our purposes the written collections of sortition oracles are of particular interest.

The earliest version known to us is the so-called *Sortes Astrampsychi*, a collection composed in the early imperial period but preserved in two late-antique recensions.[35] The enquirer would select his question among a list of ninety-two numbered questions; he was then invited to randomly choose a number from one to ten and add this to the number of the chosen question. Enquirers would then consult a table in which the added sum (for example, 68 + 7 = 75) would correspond with a particular decade (a collection of ten numbered answers) among a list of 103 decades. The enquirer would then consult within that decade the numbered answer that corresponded to the number from one to ten that he had randomly chosen – for example, answer 7 of decade 75 – and, lo and behold, he would find an answer that corresponded exactly to the question he had asked. In other words, for every question there was a set of ten possible answers. Among the list of ninety-two questions, there are two slave-related questions asked by masters concerning fugitive slaves (36: 'Will I find the fugitive?'; 89: 'Will the fugitive escape my detection?'), while another one might be construed as the same question asked from the point of view of the fugitive slave ('Will my flight be undetected?').[36] But there also exist three questions that were clearly asked

---

[34] For an approach to oracles in terms of dealing with risk, see Eidinow 2007; for slave hopes in the institutional oracles, see Eidinow 2012; Desbiens 2017.

[35] Browne 1983–2001.

[36] On the interpretative issues surrounding this question, see Eidinow 2012: 247, n. 14.

by the slaves themselves: number 32 asked 'Will I be freed from servitude?'; number 46 enquired 'Will I come to terms with my master?', and number 74, 'Am I going to be sold?'[37]

I shall examine slave hopes for freedom in the final section of this chapter, so I postpone examining those answers for that section. Let us start by presenting the list of answers for the question concerning relations between masters and slaves:

'You won't come to terms with your masters' (33.1)
'You won't come to terms with your masters now' (5.2, 39.6, 11.7)
'You won't come to terms with your masters just yet' (49.10)
'You won't come to terms with your masters. It's not to your advantage' (100.4)
'You will come to terms with your masters after a while' (41.5)
'With effort you will come to terms with your masters' (10.9)
'You will come to terms with your masters and benefit' (45.3)
'You will come to terms with your masters and be treated with affection' (74.8)

The answers can be divided along three axes: the first on the basis of whether the reconciliation will take place (6) or not (4); the second concerns the manner of the reconciliation, and whether it will be immediate (2), postponed (5) or achieved after some effort (1); the third concerns the outcome of the reconciliation, with two answers focusing on the particular benefits that the slave will derive out of it; the presumed negative effects of the lack of reconciliation are not specified. A good idea of what it meant for a slave to be on bad terms with his master, and how a slave hoped to improve his condition under those circumstances, comes from a fourth-century BCE lead letter from Athens:

Lesis is sending [a letter] to Xenokles and his mother [asking] that they by no means overlook that he is perishing in the foundry, but that they come to his masters and that they have something better found for him. For I have been handed over to a thoroughly wicked man; I am perishing from being whipped; I am tied up; I am treated like dirt – more and more!

There are various interpretative issues with this letter, which there is no space to treat here in detail.[38] A crucial issue is whether we should envisage the letter as being written by Lesis himself, or composed by somebody else on his behalf. Whatever the answer, it is obvious from the letter's rhetoric, as expressed through its vocabulary, alliteration and asyndeton, that it describes a situation of despair. The most plausible interpretation is that Lesis was a young slave who was placed by his masters to work in a foundry, where he was maltreated and faced terrible conditions. His hope for deliverance lay with Xenokles and his own mother, whom he was requesting

---

[37] For the link between slaves, slavery and sortition oracles, see Kudlien 1991; Eidinow 2012. See also the discussion of Kudlien's approach in McKeown 2007a: 30–41.

[38] *SEG* L, 276: for publication of this text and variant interpretations, see Jordan 2000; Harris 2004, whose interpretation I generally follow; Eidinow and Taylor 2010.

to visit his masters and persuade them to take him out of the foundry and find him another, less oppressive, placement. We can neither tell what exactly the relationship between Xenokles and Lesis was, nor what the relationship between Xenokles and Lesis' mother might have been. But whatever the case, this is a clear illustration of why we should not reduce slavery to a binary relationship between masters and slaves; Lesis hoped that employing his wider network of kinship and support would succeed in convincing his masters to improve his lot. This shows how slave hopes often revolved around the creation and maintenance of such networks and communities of kinship and support, as we shall see below.

Let us now move to the answers to the question concerning slave sale:

'You won't be sold. It won't benefit you. Stand fast' (55.5)
'You won't be sold just yet, but it won't benefit you' (30.6)
'You won't be sold to your benefit' (58.8)
'You won't be sold, but you will be set free with a bequest' (87.10)
'You will be sold, but not just yet' (60.1, 14.4)
'You will be sold and you will be sorry when you don't profit at all' (43.3)
'Where you will be purchased, you'll have regrets' (64.7)
'You will be purchased and it will go well for you with those to whom you're sold' (84.2)
'You will be sold and you will be set free' (85.9)

As with the previous question, the answers can be divided along three axes: the first is according to whether the slave will be sold (6) or not (4); the second in regard to whether the outcome will be positive (3), negative (5) or undefined (2); the third concerns the timescale, and whether the sale will be immediate (4) or postponed (3). Among the answers which state that the slave will not be sold, two predict that this will not be to the slave's benefit (30.6, 58.8), although one advises the slave to stand fast and not try to improve his luck by fleeing (55.5); equally, two answers predict that the slave will be sold and will regret his new masters and surroundings (43.3, 64.7). On the other hand, it is predicted that the slave will not be sold, but rewarded with freedom and a bequest (87.10), that he will be sold and freed (85.9) or that he will be sold, but succeed with his new masters (84.2).

Sale constituted one of the most critical moments in a slave's life. As such, it was potent with both hope and fear. Hope concerned the possibility of gaining freedom or of enhancing one's condition, as we have already examined. Fear obviously related to the unknown circumstances that awaited the slave in his new surroundings; 'better the devil you know' was often an apt summary of how slaves thought about changing masters.[39] But fear did not concern only the risk of the unknown: it also concerned the risk of dismantling existing networks and communities of kinship, emotion and support in which the slave already participated. A telling example is the incident narrated

---

[39] See, for example, Philogelos, no. 122: 'A man from Abdera was trying to sell a pan which had lost its ear-shaped handles. When asked why he had made away with the handles, he responded: "So that it might not hear that it is on sale and run away"'. See Harper 2011: 248.

in the *Life of Melania the Younger*, a late-antique scion of one of the richest senatorial families, who, along with her husband Pinianus, decided to divest themselves from their riches and follow an ascetic mode of life:

> While they were planning these things, the Devil, the enemy of truth, subjected them to an enormous test. Since he was jealous at the great zeal these young people showed for God, he prompted Severus, the brother of the blessed Pinianus, and he persuaded their slaves to say: 'we realize we haven't been sold yet, but if we are forced to be sold, rather than be put on the open market, we prefer to have your brother Severus as our master and have him buy us'. [Melania and Pinianus] were very upset by this turn of events, at seeing their slaves in the suburbs of Rome rising in rebellion.[40]

The plan of Severus, Pinianus' brother, was to acquire his brother's property on the cheap; to achieve this aim, he incited the slaves in his brother's landholdings to revolt, in order to put pressure on Pinianus to sell the whole portfolio to him at a bargain price, rather than opt for the higher price he would acquire if the properties were sold piecemeal to the highest bidders on the market. But the crucial question for our purposes is what made the slaves demand not to be sold, or, if that were not possible, to be sold to a single master who was a relative of their former owner. The answer is not explicitly provided in this particular passage, but can be plausibly supplied: it was caused by the slaves' wish to preserve the families and communities that they had managed to create and the mode of life with its customs and accommodations which they were used to.

The case of the slave family is a good example of the contradictory form of this process. The slave family was an important factor in building stability in slaveholding societies.[41] It ensured the natural reproduction of the slave force; slaves with families were less likely to flee; and the threat of family separation was a potent weapon in the hands of the masters. The issue is brought out well in one of the Aesopic fables:

> A dove who lived in a certain dovecote was boasting about the number of children she had given birth to. The crow heard her and said 'Stop your bragging! The more children you have, the greater the slavery you bring into the world!' The fable shows that the most unfortunate slaves are the ones who give birth to children in captivity.[42]

But at the same time, family and kinship were major tools for creating slave communities of emotion, support and solidarity.[43] The slave family was both a tool in the hands of masters and a means through which slaves could organise their resistance. The significance of creating family and kinship for slaves comes out well in a number

---

[40] Gerontius, *Life of Melania the Younger* 10.
[41] Bradley 1984: 47–80.
[42] *Perry* 202.
[43] For a vivid portrayal of female slaves' hopes of finding a husband, see *Life of Aesop* G29–30.

of inscriptions that provide a very different perspective from that of the Aesopic fable above. The first is an inscription of the imperial period from Lydia:

> Eutychos, slave agent of Iulia Tabille, along with his wife Epigone as a vow to Men Axiottenos on behalf of their son Neiketas, because he was saved by the god when he was ill.[44]

The vow made by this slave and his wife in order to ensure the health and safety of their son shows eloquently that they did not consider giving birth to slave children a misfortune. The complexity of slave families and the communities that could be built on their basis is clearly shown in another inscription from the same area:

> Helikonis honoured Amerimnos, her husband; Amerimnos his father; Terpousa her own son; Neikopolis the grandmother; Alexandros and Demetria and Terpousa their brother; Aigialos the foster-father; Gamos his brother in law; the relatives and the fellow-slaves honoured Amerimnos. Farewell![45]

The inscription illustrates the extended kinship network of this particular slave: his parents, grandparents and foster-parents, siblings, wife and children and in-laws, as well as other relatives and fellow slaves. It is particularly telling to see how Roman jurists took account of the significance and implications of these forms of slave community and the slave agency that was based on them.[46] The passage below concerns discussion of what forms of slave activity should be legally classified as flight:

> The same Vivianus further says that . . . if [a slave] concealed himself until his master's wrath abated, he would not be a fugitive any more than one who, having in mind that his master wished physically to chastise him, betook himself to a friend whom he induced to plead on his behalf . . . Vivianus goes on to say that if a slave leaves his master and comes back to his mother, the question whether he be a fugitive is one for consideration; if he so fled to conceal himself and not to return to his master, he is a fugitive; but he is no fugitive if he seeks that some wrongdoing of his may be better extenuated by his mother's entreaties.[47]

Vivianus considers whether slaves who absconded in order to request the intercession of friends and relatives with their masters should be considered fugitives, and argues against this view; but it is an eloquent example of how slave networks and communities should be taken into account in interpreting slave actions. We have already seen slaves employing communities of kinship and their related networks in the letter of Lesis we saw above (p. 155), or the attempts of Christian slaves to use Church funds

[44] *TAM* V(1), 442; see also Chaniotis 2009.
[45] *SEG* XL, 1044; see Martin 2003, Zoumbaki 2005.
[46] For slave agency in the work of Roman jurists, see Giannella 2014.
[47] *Digest* 21.1.17.4–5.

for their manumission (pp. 144–5).[48] Examples like these, in which slaves made use of the communities and networks they created beyond their masters, could pose a clear threat to the masters' authority, as is clearly expressed by Libanius in the following passage:

> Nor again is it right for a slave, if he demands justice for wrongs suffered, to look to just anybody, and to present himself before anyone who is not his owner and implore his aid, while ignoring his master. For he would no longer belong entirely to his master, but he would present his protector with the lion's share in any division of his loyalty and personal services. Certainly, it is right that he should secure justice, but he should secure it through his master. To do so through somebody else often means the master losing his slave altogether, since he is despised as a result of the assistance rendered by another.[49]

The above discussion has, I hope, illustrated the extent to which slave hopes under slavery often aimed to create a world of their own, with relationships defined by emotion, kinship, ethnicity and work, rather than the imposed identity of slavery. Slave hopes that focused on their relationship with their masters also show why slavery should not be treated solely as a unilateral and instrumental relationship: slave hopes express the slave attempt to shape this relationship as an asymmetric negotiation of power, or an asymmetric exchange of mutual service and benefaction.

## The Slave Hope for Freedom

Notwithstanding these slave efforts to turn slavery into something different from a mere instrumental relationship, the fulfilment of such aims was always beyond the reach of many slaves, and success was always fragile. Escaping slavery altogether, either by means of flight or through manumission, was commonly one of the defining hopes in the slave experience.[50] The issue is illustrated evocatively in a passage from Phaedrus' *Fables*:

> A slave who was running away from his cruel master happened to meet Aesop, who knew him as a neighbour. 'What's got you so excited?' asked Aesop. 'Father Aesop – a name you well deserve since you are like a father to me – I'm going to be perfectly frank, since you can be safely trusted with my troubles. There's plenty of whipping and not enough food. I'm constantly sent on errands out to the farm without any provisions for the journey. If the master dines at home, I have to wait on him all night long; if he is invited somewhere else, I have to lie outside in the gutter until dawn. I should have earned my freedom by now, but my hairs have gone grey and I'm still slaving away. If I had done anything to deserve this,

---

[48] For the significance of such networks and communities for ancient slaves, see Rädle 1970; Vlassopoulos 2011a.

[49] Libanius, *On protection systems* 21.

[50] Weiler 2003: 215–75.

I would stop complaining and suffer my fate in silence. But the fact is that I never get enough to eat and my cruel master is always after me. For these reasons, along with others that it would take too long to tell you, I've decided to go wherever my feet will lead me.' 'Well,' said Aesop, 'Listen to what I say: if you must endure such hardship without having done anything wrong, as you say, then what is going to happen to you now that you really are guilty of something?' With these words of advice, Aesop scared the slave into giving up his plans of escape.[51]

The fugitive slave eloquently presents his grievances: physical maltreatment, lack of adequate nourishment, the frustration and humiliation of serving others meekly, the lack of personal time and space. Escape from slavery would be the obvious solution to all these problems. But the hope for manumission has been frustrated so far and is likely to remain beyond reach: under the circumstances, flight seems the only way forward. It is only the fear of even worse conditions, should the attempt at flight fail, which convinces the slave to abandon his plans.[52] Particularly notable is the slave's complaint that he 'should have earned [his] freedom by now': the conceptualisation of slavery as an asymmetric relationship of mutual service and benefaction is crucial for the slave's understanding of his claim to freedom as the result of his faithful service.

The way in which this hope for freedom is represented in ancient literary texts tells us something significant about conceptions of slavery in antiquity. On the one hand, there is no doubt that one can find multiple examples of discourses that tried to naturalise slavery, by presenting slaves as inferior beings who were fit for that particular role, or deserved the fate of slavery.[53] From this point of view, the slave hope for freedom is something that could only be portrayed as monstrous, futile or perverse.[54] It is therefore remarkable that one can find numerous portrayals of the slave hope for freedom from a wholly sympathetic point of view. The following passage from Menander is a characteristic example:

**Onesimos**: There is only one thing you've not said, that you'll be freed. For if he thinks you're mother to the child, then obviously he'll buy your liberty.
**Habrotonon**: I don't know that. I'd like it.
**O**: Don't you know? But will I get some thanks for this myself, Habrotonon?
**H**: By both the goddesses, I shall consider you the cause of all my happiness.
**O**: Suppose you stop the search for her on purpose and you give it up and leave me in the lurch, what happens then?
**H**: My goodness, why should I? Do you think I long for children? Gods above, I only ask for freedom. That's the prize I want for this.
**O**: I hope you get it.
**H**: Well, do you like my plan?

---

[51] Phaedrus, *Fables* Appendix 20.

[52] For slave flight in antiquity, see Bellen 1971; for fugitives in Roman law, see Klingenberg 2005.

[53] This theme is well explored in Garnsey 1996: 35–52; Rosivach 1999; Thalmann 2011; Wrenhaven 2012: 43–89.

[54] The portrayal of the Scythian slaves in Herodotus (4.1–4) is characteristic; see Harvey 1988.

**O**: I do, extremely. If you try to cheat, I'll fight you then. I'll find a way. But for the moment let us see if this is really true.

**H**: So you agree with me?

**O**: I do.

**H**: Then quickly hand the ring to me.

**O**: Here, take it.

**H**: Dear Persuasion, be my friend, be at my side and make the words I speak succeed.

**O**: The girl's a clever creature. When she found she couldn't get her liberty through love and was just wasting all her pains this way, she takes another road. But I shall stay a slave forever, snotty, paralysed, incapable of making schemes like hers. Perhaps I shall get something from the girl, if she succeeds; that would be fair – poor fool, what empty hopes you have, if you expect to earn, from any woman, gratitude! I only hope my troubles don't increase.[55]

The audience is presented with two slaves scheming to gain their freedom with a plan that will inadvertently lead to the happy ending of the plot. The slaves express on numerous occasions their hope for freedom, which is presented as a matter of fact, and without any negative connotations. This sympathetic portrayal of the slave hope for freedom makes evident the fact that in a society like classical Athens a variety of alternative conceptualisations of slavery co-existed. If slavery is an extreme form of bad luck, then the hope for freedom is an understandable attempt to mitigate adverse circumstances. If slavery is an asymmetric relationship of mutual service, then the slave hope for freedom is a legitimate attempt to obtain a reward for faithful service.[56]

Let us now return to the answers provided in the *Sortes Astrampsychi* to the question of whether a slave will gain his freedom:

'You won't be freed just yet' (3.1)
'You won't be freed just yet: don't expect it' (68.2, 4.6)
'You won't be freed just yet, but after a time' (50.4, 21.9)
'You will be freed, but not just yet' (76.3)
'You will be freed after some time, but don't be distressed' (96.7)
'You will be freed with an appeal once you've paid money' (53.5)
'You will be freed with a good bequest' (40.8)
'You won't be freed. Be silent' (23.10)

As above, the answers can be analysed along three axes. The first axis concerns whether the manumission will take place or not; only one answer categorically denies that pos- sibility. Another three focus on the fact that the hope for freedom will not be realised immediately, without explicitly denying that it could happen in the future. Another two predict that the manumission will not take place soon, but promise manumission

---

[55] Menander, *Epitrepontes* 538–66.
[56] For the representation of slave hopes of escape from slavery in Plautus, see Richlin 2017: 417–77.

at some time in the future, while another one makes the same promise, but stated in a more positive manner. The second axis concerns the circumstances of the manumission: one answer predicts that freedom will be gained by an appeal, after paying money, while the other predicts that manumission will be accompanied by a bequest from the master. Finally, the third axis concerns responses to the emotional state of the slave hoping for freedom: one answer asks the enquirer not to be distressed because the manumission will not happen for some time, while in another the bad news that the manumission will not happen is supplemented by the telling command: 'Be silent'. Overall, the inclusion of the query on manumission in the list of questions is a telling indication of how normal the slave hope for freedom is considered.

If the slave hope for freedom is presented sympathetically, its realisation presents us with some of the most challenging questions in understanding slavery. Various ancient sources illustrate the terrible choices that slaves faced in attempting to materialise the hope of freedom. Studying these choices, and the problems they raised, is an excellent litmus test for figuring out what exactly the hope for freedom consisted of. They also illustrate the significance of gender for the lived experience of slavery; the following examples focus on choices and dilemmas that affected female slaves in particular.[57]

Our best means for exploring this issue comes through the corpus of manumission inscriptions, one of the most common forms of the Greek epigraphic record. In some areas of the Greek world, like the two inscriptions from Delphi presented below, manumission inscriptions set out in detail the conditions under which slaves have gained or will gain their freedom. Our first example comes from the first century CE:

> Euporia sold to Apollo Pythios two bodies, whose names are Epiphanea and Epaphro, for a price of six mnas . . . under these conditions: that they will remain [with Euporia] for the rest of her life, without reproach, doing everything that they have been ordered . . . and after her death, Epaphro shall give my grandson Glaukias, the son of Lyson, three babies of two years old. If she does not have the babies, she should give 200 denarii. And Epiphanea shall give my son Sostratos after five years a three-year old child, and after three years a three-year old child to my grandson Glaukias.[58]

The inscription records the conditional manumission of two female slaves, Epiphanea and Epaphro. The first condition concerns *paramone*, the obligation of the manumitted slaves to remain with their former owners and serve them for a period of time, commonly until the latter's death, as is the case here.[59] But the manumission also contains a second condition that will apply at the time of the manumittor's death: in order to gain their full freedom, the two slaves are obliged to surrender to the mistress' relatives a number of children over a span of time: three two-year-old babies in the case of

---

[57] For gender and manumission in the Greek world, see Tucker 1982; Wrenhaven 2009; Glazebrook 2014; Kamen 2014. For gender and manumission in the Roman world, see Wacke 2001; Weiler 2001; Kleijwegt 2012; Perry 2013.

[58] *FD* III, 6.38.

[59] Zelnick-Abramovitz 2005: 222–48; cf. Sosin 2015.

Epaphro, while in the case of Epiphanea the obligation is to surrender a three-year-old child after five years, and a second three-year-old child after another three years.

The obligation for female slaves to surrender one or more children in order to gain their full freedom is by no means rare in the ancient world.[60] From the master's point of view, the aim of this condition is patently obvious: it would provide free of cost the new generation of slaves that would replace those who were manumitted. But from the slave's point of view the condition illustrates the difficult choices that the hope for freedom entailed. For the fulfilment of this condition effectively meant that female slaves had to have sex in order to get pregnant and use their children as bargaining chips for gaining their own freedom. In a world of very high infant mortality, where one out of three children would die before their first birthday and half the children before the age of five, clearly attitudes towards children could not have been the same as contemporary societies with extremely low infant mortality.[61] And yet, it would be misleading to think that ancient people did not get emotionally involved with their children, or that slaves merely thought of babies as means to an end.[62] The inscriptions we saw above, and the hope for recovery and health for slave children, document the extent to which slaves cared for their children. But this still leaves our question unanswered. Slaves cared deeply about their children and their families, even under conditions of slavery, which made families fragile and the ability to protect loved ones limited. What did the hope of freedom consist of, if attaining it meant surrendering your new-born children as the new generation of slaves in exchange for your own freedom?

This kind of question becomes even more difficult to answer in the case of our next example, a first-century BCE inscription from Delphi:

> Philagros, son of Archytas, sold to Apollo Pythios a female body called Dioklea, born in the house, for a price of three mnas . . . Dioklea shall remain with Kleopatra, the mother of Philagros, obeying all orders to the extent of her ability; Kleopatra will have the power to punish her in any way she sees fit, except for selling her. And when something happens to Kleopatra, Dioklea will be free and she can go anywhere she wants . . . if Dioklea has a child in the time of *paramone*, she will have the right to choke it, if she wants; if she wants to raise it, it will be free, but if she does not want this, neither Dioklea nor anyone else will have the right to sell the child.[63]

The manumission includes the usual condition of *paramone*; but its stipulations as regards children are quite different from those in the previous example. The manumission document gave Dioklea the right either to raise any child born during the *paramone* as a free person, or to kill it. These conditions are easy to understand: effectively, the manumittors gave the former slave full rights over the child, allowing the slave the right to decide whether the child will be raised and surrendering any right to

---

[60]  Zelnick-Abramovitz 2005: 229–31.
[61]  For infant mortality in ancient societies, see the simulations in Saller 1994: 43–69.
[62]  For an overview, see Laes 2011.
[63]  *SGDI* 2171.

the slave's progeny. It is the final condition that is more difficult to interpret: if the former master was happy to surrender his rights over the child, why did he then prohibit Dioklea from selling the child? A plausible interpretation has been suggested: Philagros wanted to safeguard that Dioklea would remain with his old mother until her death. If Dioklea could sell her children, she could then use the money raised in order to buy up her time in *paramone*, a provision attested in many Delphic manumissions.[64] This is another example of how the hope for freedom could clash with a number of hopes that slaves entertained under slavery, and clearly also entertained once freed.

The frustration of the hope for freedom by the complexities of what life in freedom actually meant is the subject of a famous exhortation by a former slave, the philosopher Epictetus:

> The slave wishes to be set free immediately. Why? Do you think that he wishes to pay money to the collectors of the 5% tax? No; but because he imagines that hitherto through not having obtained this, he is hindered and unfortunate. 'If I shall be set free, immediately it is all happiness, I care for no man, I speak to all as an equal and like to them, I go where I choose, I come from any place I choose, and go where I choose'. Then he is set free; and forthwith having no place where he can eat, he looks for some man to flatter, someone with whom he shall sup: then he either works with his body and endures the most dreadful things; and if he can obtain a manger, he falls into a slavery much worse than his former slavery; or even if he becomes rich, being a man without any knowledge of what is good, he loves some little girl, and in his unhappiness laments and desires to be a slave again. He says: 'What evil did I suffer in my state of slavery? Another clothed me, another supplied me with shoes, another fed me, another looked after me in sickness; and I did only a few services for him. But now a wretched man, what things I suffer, being a slave to many instead of to one.'[65]

This exploration of hope and slavery has tried to underline three issues. The first is that slave hopes provide an excellent litmus test for thinking carefully about the historical experience of slavery and the various conceptualisations of slavery in ancient societies. The exploration of slave hope gives the lie to the essentialist and instrumentalist approaches, which have exercised such a powerful influence on the study of slavery. Hope places slave agency at the forefront of our attention, and this requires us to think carefully about the relationship between slave agency and the various practices employing slaving for a variety of aims. This leads to my second point: instead of a top-down relationship unilaterally defined by the masters, the exploration of slave hopes has revealed a co-existence of different conceptualisations of slavery. A major aspect of this phenomenon was the extent to which masters attempted to employ the tool of slavery to shape the full extent of slave life, and slaves attempted to use other tools (kinship, religion, ethnicity, work, residence) in order to shape various aspects of

[64]  Zelnick-Abramovitz 2005: 229–30.
[65]  Epictetus, *Discourses* 4.1.33–7; see Herschbell 1995.

their lives into a world that existed beyond and below slavery. As a result, a significant part of slave hopes concerned life within slavery, but a life that was affected by slavery as little as possible. Obviously, and this is my third point, the hope for freedom had an immense value for slaves. Exploring this hope has major implications, both for how slaves envisaged freedom and the difficult choices they faced in the process of realising their hope.

# 8

# SLAVING IN SPACE AND TIME

THIS CHAPTER FOCUSES ON SLAVING in space and time: its aim is to construct a framework for examining the diversity of slaveholding societies on the one hand, and the processes and forces of historical change on the other. The first section challenges the traditional approach to the various local systems of Greek and Roman slaveries and its implicit assumptions. It focuses in particular on the widespread assumption that systems like helotage were not 'proper' slavery and that all Greek chattel slaveries were identical to that of Athens. The peculiarities of each slaving system resulted from the impact of wider economic, political, social and cultural processes on local slaving practices; the concept of epichoric slaving systems allows us to incorporate diversity and change within the study of local slaving practices. The second section dismantles the traditional distinction between societies with slaves and slave societies and the historical narratives that have been constructed on their basis. Not only are there major empirical problems with these two concepts, but they prove to be particularly blunt instruments for explaining the major differences among slave societies and the differential impact of slaving on economic, social, political and cultural processes. The concept of the intensification of the advantages for masters and disadvantages for slaves that slaving offered provides a better way of comprehending the major differences between slaveholding societies than Finley's traditional distinction.

The third section focuses on the forms and forces of change in the history of slaving. I explore four major forms of change: rise and fall; cyclical processes of intensification and abatement; conjunctures; and long-term change. These forms of change were put into motion by three major forces. The first force consisted of the wider processes that shaped the four major slaving contexts that were examined in Chapter 4. The second force faced in the opposite direction: it consisted of the role of slaving in shaping these wider processes in particular ways. The third force, that of human agency, is the subject of the final section. I focus in particular on the issue of slave agency: the section explores how the various identities of enslaved persons shaped how they exercised their agency, examines how enslaved persons can be restored as active agents in narratives of political change and invites us to restore the agency of enslaved persons as a major factor in processes of intellectual and cultural transformation.

## Epichoric Systems of Slaving

The study of slavery in antiquity follows a number of implicit assumptions which are worth unpacking. Many studies employ labels like 'ancient' or 'Greco-Roman' slavery, which imply a fundamental continuity for about a millennium.[1] I will come back to this assumption in later sections of this chapter. For the time being, I want to focus on the implicit assumptions behind the other commonly used labels: 'Greek' and 'Roman' slavery. If we assume that these labels express what is usually understood as Greek and Roman history respectively, the label 'Greek slavery' should refer to forms of slavery across the Greek-speaking eastern Mediterranean, or at the very least the Greek communities in the Aegean and the Black Sea; and it should have a chronological range covering the archaic, classical and Hellenistic periods of Greek history at the very least. The label 'Roman slavery' should cover the area under the authority of the Roman state, starting from the original nucleus of the city-state of Rome, and progressively covering the whole of Italy and then the Mediterranean and temperate Europe; chronologically, it should have a range from the early republican period to late antiquity, or at least until the end of the early imperial period.

It might come as a surprise, but this is not at all how these labels actually operate in the study of ancient slavery.[2] A cursory perusal of major syntheses immediately reveals that the label 'Greek slavery' is effectively tantamount to slavery in classical Athens.[3] Why is this the case? The first reason is that, as we have already seen, the servile systems of many Greek communities are not considered as 'proper' slavery. Scholars have long been baffled about how to interpret those forms of dependent labour in ancient Greece that do not seem to fit the stereotypical image of slaves, like Spartan helots, Thessalian *penestai* and Cretan *woikeis*.[4] Until very recently, most scholars understood these groups as a form of serfdom, imagining helots as dependent peasants: they were not acquired and reproduced through the market, but were subjugated native inhabitants who formed their own families, had a strong sense of community and ethnic identity, cultivated the land of their masters and rendered them part of the harvest.[5] While there is very little that is actually known about the *penestai*,[6] the Gortyn law code provides substantial evidence concerning the Cretan *woikeis*. The provisions regarding the children and property of the *woikeis* and mixed marriages between *woikeis* and free people have been traditionally interpreted as recording rights to family and property possessed by the *woikeis*, which made them clearly different from slaves and similar to medieval serfs.[7] A popular solution to distinguishing 'proper' slaves from such groups is to employ the term 'chattel slavery' for 'proper' slavery, and some other circumlocution (communal slavery, serfdom) for other forms of servile dependence.[8]

---

[1] Herrmann-Otto 2009; Bradley and Cartledge 2011; Hunt 2018a.
[2] See the comments in Vlassopoulos 2012.
[3] Fisher 1993; Klees 1998; Andreau and Descat 2006; the chapters on Greek slavery in Bradley and Cartledge 2011; Hunt 2018a.
[4] Lotze 1959 classified these groups as 'between slavery and freedom', a view criticised below. For the servile groups of Sparta, Crete and Thessaly, see below; for the less well-known groups, like the Mariandynoi of Herakleia in the Black Sea, see Paradiso 1991, 2007; Baralis 2015.
[5] For older examples of this approach, see Ste. Croix 1981: 137–58; Garlan 1988: 85–118; Fisher 1993: 22–33. For more recent expressions of the same approach, see Cartledge 2011; Hunt 2017a.
[6] See Ducat 1994.
[7] Willetts 1955: 46–51; Lévy 1997; Gagarin 2010.
[8] For the logical inconsistencies in the term 'chattel slavery', see Lewis 2018: 9.

The other reason why 'Greek slavery' is implicitly restricted to classical Athens concerns the nature of our evidence. Classical Athens is by far the best known ancient Greek community; most sources for the archaic and classical period concern Athens, and their diversity (historiography, law-court speeches, drama, essays and dialogues on philosophy and society, inscriptions) enables historians to have an in-depth understanding of Athenian slavery.[9] As regards the archaic and classical periods, there is exiguously little evidence for slavery in other Greek communities. The situation improves from the Hellenistic period onwards, when epigraphic sources offer historians evidence on slavery in many Greek communities apart from Athens.[10] But the almost exclusively epigraphic evidence for slavery in Greek communities apart from Athens means that we have a very limited picture, usually geared towards manumission practices.[11]

At this point a third implicit assumption enters to save Greek historians from the problem of how to study slavery outside Athens. The traditional approach to slavery employed by Greek historians predisposes them to adopt static accounts. If slavery is a relationship of property unilaterally defined by the masters, then there is no reason to expect that this relationship would vary across space and time. This static approach has led to the largely implicit assumption that 'chattel slavery' operated in essentially the same ways in all Greek communities from the archaic period onwards; accordingly, the better-known Athenian slavery is considered as representative for all forms of 'chattel slavery' in the Greek world.[12] In this respect, it is worth pointing out the paradox of Egypt and the Black Sea. In the Black Sea there is a variety of literary, epigraphic and archaeological sources ranging from the archaic to the early imperial period;[13] in Egypt, the mainly papyrological evidence commences in the second millennium and reaches late antiquity.[14] It is therefore interesting to observe that the specialist literature for these areas has made some effort to take into account diachronic perspectives, which is largely absent from other regional studies; but the wider phenomena we described above have ensured that these perspectives have had no effect on the wider discipline of ancient slavery, whose approach remains static.

The triple consequence of the fact that systems like Spartan helotage are not considered 'proper' slavery, that most sources concern classical Athens and that slavery is considered as a static relationship, is the implicit restriction of the label 'Greek slavery'

---

[9] But the wealth of evidence is also accompanied with problems of vision: see Vlassopoulos 2016c.

[10] See the overviews of Hellenistic slavery in Heinen 1976, 1977.

[11] For the epigraphic evidence for ancient slavery, see Chaniotis 2018.

[12] Tellingly, the chapter on Hellenistic slavery in Bradley and Cartledge 2011 covers only the Hellenistic Near East; there was no need to discuss slavery in the Hellenistic Aegean, as nothing apparently had changed or was different from classical Athens; see Thompson 2011: 213.

[13] For slavery in the Black Sea, see Nadel 1976; Gibson 1999; Heinen 2001; von Behren 2009; Parmenter 2020.

[14] For slavery in Pharaonic Egypt, see Bakir 1952; Menu 1977; Cruz-Uribe 1982; Loprieno 1997, 2012; Hofmann 2005. For slavery in Hellenistic, Roman imperial and late antique Egypt, see Fikhman 1973; Bieżuńska-Małowist 1974, 1977; Straus 1988, 2004; Scholl 1990; Bagnall 2011; Rowlandson forthcoming. There is regrettably little effort to look at slavery in Egypt in the long term, bridging the gap between Pharaonic and Greco-Roman periods; but see Heinen 1978. The sourcebook on Egyptian slavery from Pharaonic times to late antiquity, which was being prepared by the late Jane Rowlandson, will make a significant difference when published.

to 'slavery in classical Athens'.[15] The same comments can be applied to the label of 'Roman slavery'. In some ways, it is better balanced chronologically than the Greek label, as it tends to cover both the republican and the early imperial periods.[16] But the label tends to focus on Rome and Italy, or, in the most expansive form, the Latin-speaking western Mediterranean. Most of the time there is very little attention paid to slavery in the Greek-speaking provinces of the empire; as a result, slavery in the Greek-speaking eastern Mediterranean in the Hellenistic and early imperial periods is effectively a no-man's-land, as it lies outside both the 'Greek' and the 'Roman' labels as currently applied.[17] Even in those cases where 'Roman slavery' includes evidence from the eastern Mediterranean, there is little attempt to explore whether slave systems in these areas differed from 'Roman slavery', or how eastern Mediterranean systems might have interacted with the slave system of the Roman imperial overlord.[18]

It is high time that we challenge this nexus of largely implicit assumptions. I suggest that we need to set aside the 'Greek' and 'Roman' labels as currently employed. In their position, we need a new framework of multiple epichoric (local) slaving systems, which co-existed in space and changed over time, as Lewis has shown in his fundamental recent synthesis (already discussed in Chapter 1).[19] These epichoric systems were the result of the entanglement between the factors we have examined in the previous chapters: the various conceptual systems of slavery, the contexts and strategies of slaving and the various dialectical relationships. But they were also shaped by wider economic, social, political and cultural processes, as we shall see in the third section of this chapter. Finally, these various epichoric systems did not exist in isolation; they interacted with each other and mutually shaped each other in various ways. In the remainder of this section, I will show why the traditional labels are misleading and why we need an epichoric framework; to keep things manageable, I will restrict my comments to the label of 'Greek slavery'.

We can start by showing why the traditional assumption that servile systems like helotage are not 'proper' slavery is deeply misleading; in challenging this assumption, we shall explore an alternative interpretation of the peculiarities of systems like helotage which does not depend on essentialist classification, but on the study of historical processes. Our point of embarkation will be the definitional conceptual system and the detailed definition of slavery as property which we discussed in Chapter 3. Helots and *woikeis* were undoubtedly the property of their masters and had no recognised rights that distinguished them from Athenian slaves and made them similar to late medieval serfs. Spartan and Gortynian masters held helots and *woikeis* as property and

---

[15] For general works which give some attention to Hellenistic slavery, see Garlan 1988; Herrmann-Otto 2009: 102–10.

[16] General accounts of Roman slavery tend to focus on the late Republic and in particular the early imperial period; see, for example, Bradley 1994; Joshel 2010. For studies focusing on the republican period and its own particular features, see Štaerman 1969; Bieżuńska-Małowist 1986; Dumont 1987; Bradley 2011; Shaw 2014; Husby 2017; Richlin 2017.

[17] Among the rare exceptions, see Blavatskaja, Golubcova and Pavlovskaja 1972; Briant 1973; Marinović et al. 1992; Bussi 2001. But much of this work suffers from the problems analysed below.

[18] For recent attempts to explore this issue, see Harper 2011: 367–78; Youni 2012.

[19] Lewis 2018.

exercised the various rights of ownership over them. The peculiarities of helots and *woikeis* in comparison to Athenian slaves were due to the particular social, economic, political and geopolitical conditions of Sparta and Gortyn in relation to Athens, and not because helots and *woikeis* were not real slaves. Classical Sparta and Crete had limited engagement with Mediterranean markets and accordingly could not resort to the reproduction of their slave labourers through the market; consequently, their systems depended on the natural reproduction of the slaves, and this is the reason that slave families were encouraged. The Gortynian regulations concerning the family and property of *woikeis* do not record any rights of the *woikeis*, but rather regulate the property rights of their masters to the belongings of the *woikeis* and to the children born from their sexual unions.[20]

It is undeniable that the helots of Messenia lived effectively as communities of dependent peasants, but this resulted from the peculiar conditions of Spartan history. Spartan masters were absentee landlords who lived far away, and could not oversee the helots continuously; absentee masters had to give great leeway to their slaves, and the result was that helots effectively operated as dependent cultivators. The political, social and economic balance of relations among Spartan citizens put a clear limit on the ways in which Spartan masters could exploit and employ their helots. Finally, helotage was shaped by Sparta's geopolitical situation; Sparta was surrounded by enemies who did not have a similar system of helotage and were willing to incite the helots to revolt; as a result, helots had to be managed carefully.[21] Because of its geopolitical and economic conditions, the Spartan community significantly restricted the right to capital of Spartan masters: helots could not be sold outside Spartan territory, and they could not be manumitted by their masters, but solely by the Spartan community. All the above factors had significant implications for the form and history of helotic slavery; but helots were still slaves, though with peculiar features. The differences between Spartan helots, Gortynian *woikeis* and Athenian slaves reflected the particular conditions of each community and were the result of various historical processes.[22]

This observation does not apply solely to 'strange' servile systems like those of Sparta and Gortyn; it also applies to those Greek communities who are traditionally assumed to have forms of 'chattel slavery' essentially identical to that of classical Athens. In order to document this, I will now turn to the distinction between free insiders and slave outsiders in ancient Greek communities.[23] Greek historians tend to take the exceptional case of classical Athens as representative of the Greek world as a whole. The Athenian distinction between insiders and outsiders is based on three major elements: the restriction of the right to own real estate to citizens (*enktesis*), the restriction of marriage to marriages between citizens (civic endogamy) and the restrictive definition of the citizenship right to the offspring of citizen marriages. The ownership of real estate was the exclusive privilege of Athenian citizens and those few foreigners who had explicitly been granted the same privilege. Marriage was also gradually restricted to Athenian

---

[20] Link 1994, 2001; Lewis 2013, 2018: 147–65.
[21] Ducat 1990, 2015; Hodkinson 2000; Luraghi 2002a, 2002b; Lewis 2018: 125–46.
[22] Hodkinson 2008; Luraghi 2009.
[23] Vlassopoulos 2018a.

citizens; before 451 BCE, marriage between a male Athenian citizen and a non-citizen woman was legitimate and the children born from this marriage were legitimate successors of their father. After Pericles' citizenship law, only marriage between Athenian citizens could produce legitimate children; finally, at some point in the first half of the fourth century BCE the Athenians outlawed marriages between Athenian citizens and foreigners and instituted penalties for foreigners marrying Athenian men and women. Athenian law did not allow for marriages between free and slave and did not accord any legal consequences to marriages between slaves; an Athenian father could not recognise his slave children as his own, even if he wanted to. Metics rarely gained the right to citizenship, and manumitted slaves did not become citizens; if they chose to remain at Athens, they were included within the category of metics. Finally, rules for inheritance limited to a very significant extent the ability of individuals to bequeath their property as they saw fit: in the absence of children, patrilineal and matrilineal relatives had very strong claims to a person's property.[24]

But can this model be extended to the rest of the Greek world? Let us start with Longus' novel *Daphnis and Chloe*, which we have already discussed in Chapter 4. The two protagonists are foundlings adopted by a free (Chloe) and a slave (Daphnis) family of shepherds respectively. They grow up together tending their flocks and finally end up falling in love. At that point Daphnis decides to ask for Chloe's hand in marriage from her father, who ultimately accepts the offer; but the wedding has to be postponed until Daphnis' master visits his estate, because the master's permission is necessary for Daphnis to marry.[25] It is remarkable that a marriage between a slave groom and a free bride is presented without any comment, as simply something that happens and does not require any explanation.

Alongside this fictional example from literature we can set the case of fifth-century Gortyn, as illustrated through the famous code. The regulations of the code regarding slave marriage are quite remarkable:

> If the slave goes to a free woman and marries her, their children are to be free; but if the free woman [goes to] the slave, their children are to be slaves. And if free and slave children are born from the same mother, when the mother dies, if there is property, the free children are to have it; but if there should be no free children, her relatives are to inherit it.[26]

Gortynian law clearly envisaged the possibility of mixed marriages between free and slave and accepted the legality and legal consequences of such marriages. The law set residence as the parameter that would decide the status of children born from such unions; if the couple resided at the house of the free woman, then the children became free, but if the couple resided at the slave's house, then they came under the authority of the slave's master and the children would become slaves. Equally significant, but hardly noticed, are the implications of the regulations concerning marriage between slaves at Gortyn:

[24] Harrison 1968; Todd 1993: 167–200; Vérilhac and Vial 1998: 42–82; Humphreys 2018.
[25] Longus, *Daphnis and Chloe* 3.29–31.
[26] *IC* IV, 72, VI.56–VII.10; Gagarin and Perlman 2016: 386–9.

If a divorced female slave should bear a child, she is to bring it to the master of her husband . . . in the presence of two witnesses. And if he does not accept it, the child is to be in the hands of the master of the female slave . . . If an unmarried female slave should be pregnant and give birth, the child is to be in the hands of the master of her father; but if the father is not alive, it is to be in the hands of the masters of her brothers.[27]

As we have mentioned above, the purpose of the regulations of the code in regard to slave marriages is not to establish the right of slaves to marry, but rather to determine the property rights of masters over the children of slaves.[28] The children of a divorced female slave did not belong to her own master, but rather to the master of her divorced husband; the children of an unmarried female slave would not belong to her own master, but to the master of her father, or of her brothers, if the slave father was no longer alive. But while the law did not establish a slave right to marriage or protection against separation for the slave family, at the same time it recognised that slave marriages had legal implications.

Many slaveholding societies apply the principle that it is the status of the mother that determines the status of the children (*partus ventrem sequitur*), and accordingly that the children of a female slave belong to the mother's master; this is undoubtedly a principle that makes it fairly easy to decide property rights over slave children.[29] On the other hand, the provision in the Gortyn law creates a fairly complex situation: in order to decide who has property rights over slave children, it needs to be determined whether the slave mother has been married or not, and to whom; furthermore, in case the slave was not married, it is essential to establish her kin, who might be owned by different masters, because it is the owner of the slave *kyrios* of the female slave (her father or brother) who will have property rights over the children, instead of the master of the slave mother. In other words, instead of employing the matrilineal principle for determining property over slave children, as many slaveholding societies like classical Athens did, Gortyn applies to the slave population the patrilineal principle of kinship and inheritance employed by the free population, despite the evident complications that such an application would create.[30] Slave marriage is recognised by the law not as a slave right, but as an act with legal consequences, because it alters who has property rights over the slave children.[31]

Similar issues are raised by certain manumission inscriptions from Hellenistic Bouthrotos in Epirus. While manumissions at Bouthrotos normally record individual manumittors, many record a wider group of manumittors that probably constitute some kind of family or kin group, as in the two inscriptions below:

[27] *IC* IV, 72, III.52–IV.23.
[28] Lewis 2013.
[29] For the ownership of slave children in Roman law, see Wieling 1999: 9–15; Willvonseder 2010: 2–10.
[30] Maffi 1997: 119–51.
[31] On the matrilineal principle and its different application in various slaveholding societies, see Kriger 2011.

Eurymmas, Tauriskos and Aristomachos [have manumitted] Sibylla and Antigonos.[32]

Eurymmas, Tauriskos, Aristomachos and Sibylla [have manumitted] Euboula.[33]

In the first inscription three male individuals manumit a female slave (Sibylla) and a male one (Antigonos). In the second inscription the manumitted female slave now joins the same three males to manumit another female (Euboula). Clearly, since her manumission Sibylla has joined her former masters in some kind of relationship; she is either merely joint owner of another slave or has become through marriage or adoption a member of the group comprised by the three males.[34] It is likely that at Bouthrotos it was possible for a former slave to enter in some capacity into the family group of her former owners, a situation that was legally impossible in classical Athens.[35]

I move on to a series of manumission inscriptions from central Greece in the Hellenistic period, which illustrate the link between slavery, inheritance and citizenship. The first inscription from Delphi dates to 173 BCE:

> Larisa sold to Apollo Pythios a male body called Mithradates, Cappadocian in origin, for a price of four mnas . . . and if anything were to happen to Larisa, Mithradates should do all the customary things from the property of Larisa, which he should use best in the first year, and when the time allows him, and if there is anything left from Larisa's property, he should have it, if her son does not come back.[36]

A Cappadocian slave, originating outside the city of Delphi, enters the community through the slave trade and ends up with the right to inherit his mistress's property, provided that her son does not return from abroad. Equally significant is the fact that this woman has the ability to, and opts to, leave her property to her manumitted slave in the absence of her child; in Athens one would have expected that the relatives would have claimed any remaining property instead of the freedman.

The next inscription, again from Delphi, and dating between 170 and 157/6 BCE, concerns a manumission by a citizen of the nearby community of Lilaia:

> Epicharidas, son of Eudamos, a citizen of Lilaia, sold . . . a female body called Asia, Syrian in origin . . . on condition that she will be free, living in Lilaia, and untouchable by all for all time, doing what she wants . . . Asia should not reside (*oikein*) away from Lilaia, nor enjoy civic rights (*politeuein*) without the approval of Epicharidas; and if she resides [*sc.* away from Lilaia] or enjoys civic rights (*politeuein*), her sale will be null and void.[37]

A number of inscriptions from central Greece mention regulations concerning the civic rights of freed persons, usually employing the verb *politeuein*, which normally

---

[32] *I.Bouthrôtos* 17.31–2.
[33] *I.Bouthrôtos* 25.29–31.
[34] See also the parallel case in *I.Bouthrôtos* 25.10–12 and 31.89–93.
[35] Cabanes 1974: 206–7.
[36] *SGDI* 1799.
[37] *SGDI* 1718.

refs to the possession and exercise of citizenship. This inscription is significant because the juxtaposition of the verb *oikein* (to reside) with the verb *politeuein* makes it clear that the latter verb refers to the exercise of some kinds of civic rights. From an Athenian point of view, it appears remarkable that manumitted slaves might exercise civic rights in the community of their former masters; equally remarkable is what appears to be the creation of civic rights for freed persons through the private act of the manumittor, as well as the manumittor's prerogative to prohibit his slave from exercising those rights. We should probably assume that Lilaia, and other central Greek communities where similar provisions appear, had laws that regulated what rights freed persons could exercise and where, and it is these unknown laws that form the background for the provisions that we see in these manumission inscriptions.[38] The same issue is again illustrated by an inscription from Thessalian Pythion, dating to the latter half of the second century BCE:

> Amyntas manumitted for free according to the law Philoumene, his own slave, and her child, whose name is [. . .]; . . . and when Amyntas dies, Philoumene and E[. . .] should be free and should have the right to acquire a house and property wherever they wish.[39]

The significance of this inscription lies in its relevance to the issue of *enktesis*: the manumittor assumes that it will be possible for the former slaves to buy a house wherever they wish; clearly, the right to buy real estate was not restricted to citizens in this case, but could also apply to freed persons. My final example comes from Delphi, dating to 124 BCE:

> Aristion, son of Anaxandridas, sold to Apollo Pythios a female body, called Dioklea, Egyptian in origin, under those terms . . . and if something human happened to Aristion before . . . Dioklea should inherit all the property of Aristion, and should do all the customary things regarding [Aristion's] burial, unless a child was born to them and grew up after.[40]

Dioklea is manumitted by her master and will inherit his property after his death, unless a child is born to them, in which case presumably it will be the child who will inherit the father's property. Not only is Aristion able and willing to bequeath his property to his former slave, but the manumitted slave's child has the right to be recognised as legal inheritor; both things would have been legally impossible in classical Athens.

Let us drive home some conclusions. The distinction between insiders and outsiders was crucial for all slaving systems; the right to own real property, to marry and to bequeath property were crucial parameters in shaping the distinction. The Athenian institutional order limited the ownership of real property to citizens, prohibited marriage between

---

[38] Zelnick-Abramovitz 2009.
[39] *SEG* **XXVI**, 689.
[40] *FD* III, 2, 243.

free and slave or citizen and non-citizen and prioritised the inheritance rights of citizen relatives over the right of the owner to bequeath his property to whomever he saw fit. These parameters effectively created a closed city, in which slaves and freed persons could not enter. Scholars have usually assumed on the basis of their static approach that the same strictures would apply to other Greek slaving systems apart from Athens. But as we have seen, this is not the case everywhere; from classical Crete to Hellenistic Epirus, Thessaly and central Greece we have seen that some Greek communities recognised mixed marriages between slave and free, allowed freed persons to own real property or gain civic rights and permitted masters to bequeath property to their former slaves. How to explain these divergences is an important question which cannot be explored here. What suffices for our current purposes is the documentation of the co-existence of different epichoric slaving systems and the need to abandon static and misleading labels like 'Greek slavery'.

This chapter has focused on epichoric slave systems in the ancient Aegean; a similar analysis could be extended to various other areas of the ancient Mediterranean and their epichoric systems, including of course Rome. In the course of its expansion, the Roman Empire incorporated a variety of epichoric slave systems with their own particular features and characteristics. Even in the early imperial period, let alone the republican period, slaving in Roman Italy was different in a number of respects from slaving in Roman Africa or Roman Iberia.[41] Nevertheless, it is important to take account of the significantly different impact on slaving that the Roman Empire had in comparison with other past empires, which usually had limited impact on epichoric slaving systems within their orbit. Roman law, as developed by the jurists and the imperial authorities, gradually came to shape the practices of the inhabitants of the empire, even before Caracalla granted Roman citizenship to the majority of the free inhabitants of the empire in 212 CE; this of course had important applications for various slaving practices.[42] Apart from law, Roman slaving practices, like the significance of the aristocratic domus or the use of slaves for prestige creation, undoubtedly had an effect on epichoric slave systems within the Roman Empire.[43] A history of epichoric slave systems in antiquity will have to take into account not only spatial diversity and divergence, but also the convergence created by factors like the Roman Empire and its legal and social institutions and practices.

But perhaps the most difficult task will be to account for wider factors of convergence. If in the classical period there were major differences between the epichoric systems of Athens, Sparta and Crete, by the late Hellenistic period there was undoubtedly greater convergence, as the epichoric systems of Sparta and Crete had lost many of their peculiar features.[44] Whether we should account for this convergence in terms of factors which are purely local and concern Sparta and Crete specifically, or we should posit wider trends and trajectories, is something that will require further study.

---

[41] For general surveys of regional differences in slaving strategies within the Roman Empire, see Whittaker 1980; MacMullen 1987; Štaerman et al. 1987; Samson 1989; Morley 2011. For Italy, see Garnsey 1981; López Barja de Quiroga 2010; Verboven 2012. For Iberia, see Curchin 2017; for Africa, see Lenski 2017.

[42] Youni 2012; Czajkowski and Eckhardt 2018.

[43] Hasenohr 2003, 2007, 2017; Eck 2013; Tran 2014.

[44] For Sparta, see Ducat 1987; Kennell 2003; for Crete, see Pałuchowski 2010; see also van Wees 2003.

## Societies with Slaves and Slave Societies

Given that the traditional approach to ancient slavery is based on static premises, how do historians of ancient slavery account for change? How do they employ slavery to account for major economic, social, political or cultural differences between different societies? As we have seen in Chapter 2, it is the distinction between slave societies and societies with slaves which plays a key role in this respect. To re-capitulate briefly, this distinction was introduced by Finley during the 1960s. Finley distinguished between two major categories of slaveholding societies: **societies with slaves** had relatively few slaves, who did not play a major economic role, while in **slave societies** slaves comprised a significant percentage of the population and constituted the main source of elite income. Societies with slaves have been extremely common in world history, and therefore their existence requires no historical explanation; but slave societies are very rare in global history.

Accordingly, historians need to explain the reasons behind the emergence of this rare historical phenomenon. Finley's explanation has remained particularly influential.[45] He argued that the societies of the Near East, as well as Greek societies before the late archaic period, were societies with slaves characterised by a spectrum of statuses. Elites derived their income by exploiting various dependent groups, with the slaves forming merely one group among many. In these societies, therefore, there was no clear dividing line between slave and free, since the concept of freedom was unknown. In the course of the archaic period, a momentous change took place in certain Greek societies. A deep social crisis was resolved by guaranteeing civic rights to the lower classes; this was the birth point of the concept of freedom. Because the lower classes acquired freedom and civic rights, they could no longer be enslaved at home or directly exploited by the elite; therefore the elite needed to find a labour substitute, and the consequence was the mass importation of foreign slaves. The creation of a clear dividing line between freedom and slavery, the mass importation of foreign slaves and their role as the main source of elite income constitute the genesis of the first slave society in world history.

The traditional historical narrative of ancient slavery has been formed on the basis of this purported emergence of slave societies in ancient Greece. Then, for almost a thousand years, hardly anything changed in all the important parameters: slaves comprised a significant proportion of the population of the classical, Hellenistic and Roman imperial societies, at least in mainland Greece and Italy. But starting from the third century CE the ancient slave societies were gradually transformed, giving their place to new societies with slaves where a small number of slaves co-existed with various other dependent groups. Gradually, the status of slaves was enhanced by being settled as family groups in agricultural tenancies, while at the same time the status of the lower classes was depressed, since they lost the privileges associated with their civic status. The result was the emergence of serfdom, which dominated Europe for many centuries to come.[46]

I wish to argue that the conceptual distinction between societies with slaves and slave societies is deeply flawed and needs to be abandoned for most purposes in favour

---

[45] Assessed extensively in Lenski and Cameron 2018; Lewis 2018.
[46] Finley 1980; cf. Whittaker 1987.

of other frameworks; furthermore, the historical narrative of ancient slavery which is constructed on the basis of Finley's conceptual distinction is equally problematic and needs to be replaced as well. Finley invented the concept of slave society in order to square the economic significance of slavery in Greece and Rome with the fact that the overwhelming majority of the populations of ancient societies consisted of free independent producers; slaves were important only in terms of how the elite derived its surplus, not in terms of the population as a whole. Consequently, the concept focuses on how elites in slave societies derived their surplus from the exploitation of slave labour. But this definition is too abstract for most purposes. As we have seen in Chapter 6 in relation to Roman slavery, we can break down the holistic concept of slave society into four different kinds of slaveholding households. Roman slavery combined two quite distinct forms of slave use: the large-scale use of slaves by the senatorial, equestrian and civic elites in complex hierarchies of urban households and rural estates, and the small-scale employment of slaves for a variety of purposes by a wide and prosperous middling section of Roman society.[47] By focusing exclusively on elite slaveholding, the concept of slave society leaves outside purview the variety of other slaveholders and their historical significance.

Furthermore, by referring abstractly to how elites derived their income the concept of slave society fails to distinguish between different slaving strategies. There are major differences between the slaves working in the mines of Laureion or in rural estates, where masters controlled and directed the labour process, and slaves who worked independently and merely provided revenue to their masters. These diverse slaving strategies created very different forms of slavery and slaves and very different economic processes. We need concepts that will allow us to approach such differences and distinctions; the concept of slave society cannot allow us to do so, given its blunt focus on general surplus extraction. The framework of slaving strategies and contexts that we explored in Chapter 4 offers a significant advance in this respect.

A different problem emerges from the central assumption behind the distinction between societies with slaves and slave societies: that there is a direct correlation between the economic role of slavery and its impact on society, culture and politics. According to this view, because slavery played a fundamental economic role in slave societies, it also shaped their politics, culture and society. The problem with this assumption is illustrated by Bradley's discussion of slavery in Rome: after positing that a slave society in economic terms only existed in Roman Italy between 200 BCE and 200 CE, he goes on to argue:

> The attitudes and habits of mind evident when the slave economy of Roman Italy was at its height long antedated and long outlasted that economy's chronological and territorial limits . . . To the extent that owning slaves always served to express *potestas* in a society highly sensitive to gradations of status, esteem and authority, Rome was always a slave society.[48]

---

[47] Harper 2011: 100–200.
[48] Bradley 1994: 30.

Bradley argues that Rome was socially a slave society before and after it was so economically: but this social definition of slave society undermines the distinction between societies with slaves and slave societies, which is precisely based on the economic role of slaves. If Bradley's argument is correct, it follows that there was no automatic link between the economic role of slavery and its impact on society, politics and culture; furthermore, a slave society could exist irrespective of the economic significance of slavery, because slavery was dominant in society, politics and culture. This means that we need to either redefine the concept of slave society or abandon it in favour of concepts that can better explain the impact of slavery on different fields.

If the concept of slave society was created in order to emphasise the significance of slavery in certain societies, the opposite assumption about societies with slaves faces equally serious problems. The immense growth of studies on societies with slaves keeps facing the same problem: how should we assess the impact of slavery in societies where it did not have a dominant economic role? A recent study has explored the significance of slavery in early modern England, a society where it had long become extinct. Despite its extinction, slavery played a major role in English life and thinking: Englishmen faced the experience of slavery and enslavement in their movements across the globe, encountered the language of slavery in their religious and political texts and debated whether some form of slavery was essential for maintaining the right form of social order.[49] In this respect, it is quite remarkable to observe that although various studies have explored the deep impact of slavery in how Jewish and Islamicate societies conceptualised marriage, there is nothing equivalent for the impact of slavery on Greek or Roman conceptions of marriage.[50] If slavery did not affect Greek and Roman conceptions of marriage as deeply as it affected Jewish and Islamic conceptions, then it should be obvious that the economic impact of slavery does not automatically translate into cultural and social impact and vice versa.

Another problem emerges from Finley's original delimitation of slave societies. Finley argued that slave societies were a rarity in world history and pinpointed only five 'genuine' cases: Greece and Rome in antiquity and the New World societies of the Caribbean, Brazil and the US South.[51] It is evident that the list was restricted to 'Western' societies, and this was by no means accidental.[52] It was linked to Finley's observation that the concept of freedom was also restricted to Western societies; in the rest of the world before the Western colonial impact there was not even a word for it. While the Western origins of freedom had a long historiographical pedigree, Finley offered a paradoxical twist to this Eurocentric narrative; freedom became conceivable only because the predominance of slavery in slave societies obliterated the spectrum of statuses that existed in societies with slaves in favour of a single dividing line between free and slave. This sounded convincing as long as the study of slavery was largely restricted to Greco-Roman antiquity and the colonial New World; but once slavery studies expanded beyond these limits, it gradually dawned on scholars

---

[49] Guasco 2014.
[50] Flesher 1988; Ali 2010.
[51] Finley 1968: 308.
[52] Vlassopoulos 2016b; Lenski 2018a, 2018b.

that slave societies were not so rare in world history. Already in 1982 Patterson presented a long global list of slave societies, although he did not seem to draw any conclusions from this observation as regards the validity of the concept of the 'slave society'.[53] Subsequent studies have documented the existence of large-scale slave societies in various parts of Africa, America and the Indian Ocean.[54] These discoveries shattered the idea that slave societies were exclusively Western, and all the assumptions that went along with this.

The concept of societies with slaves was merely a negative catch-all that could only work as long as interest focused on the better-known ancient and early modern slave societies; what analytical insight is there in a concept that brought together disparate societies for the sole reason that they did not own slaves in sufficient numbers? The distinction between slave societies and societies with slaves fails to explain the major differences among slave societies, as well as the existence of fault lines that put together certain slave societies and societies with slaves, and oppose them to other slave societies.

We can explore these problems in further detail by re-examining the traditional distinction between ancient Greek slave societies and Near Eastern societies with slaves. As we have seen in Chapter 6, the idea that Greek slave societies exhibited a single dividing line between slavery and freedom, while Near Eastern societies employed a spectrum of statuses, is untenable. The legally sanctioned spectrum of statuses that one encounters in the society of the orders in early modern Europe or Thailand was in fact absent from Near Eastern societies.[55] There existed, of course, various distinctive groups, like soldiers, women who lived in 'convents' or debt-bondsmen, and the law stipulated particular rules that pertained to these particular groups; but these groups were not ranked into a hierarchical spectrum of statuses. Instead, and like Greek societies, Near Eastern societies recognised only a single major division between slave and free.[56]

What was the economic role of slavery in Near Eastern societies? We can start with Carthage, which was in the western Mediterranean but had inherited the social and cultural practices of her Phoenician metropolis. Carthage was undoubtedly a major slave society where slaves were employed in large numbers in all sectors of the economy, which shows remarkable resemblances with slave systems like that of Athens; it is in fact remarkable that such a major slave society has so far been absent from all lists of slave societies employed by ancient historians.[57] Next to Carthage, it is Iron Age Israel that comes closest to the Greek slaving systems. Slaves were a routine element in the property portfolios of Israelite elites, and they appear to be employed in significant numbers in agriculture, pastoralism and household service.[58] The Assyrian and Persian Empires comprised a mosaic of ecologies, economies, societies and cultures; as a result, it is impossible to make generalisations about slavery in those empires as a whole, but

---

[53] Patterson 1982: 353–64.
[54] Reid 1983; Donald 1997; Stilwell 2014; Hopper 2015; Lenski and Cameron 2018.
[55] For medieval Europe, Duby 1982; for early modern Europe, Bush 1992; for medieval Ireland, Kelly 1988; for Thailand, Turton 1980.
[56] Lewis 2018: 86–9; see also Azoulay and Ismard 2018.
[57] Lenski 2018a: 26–9; Lewis 2018: 259–66.
[58] Lewis 2018: 199–222.

only about specific societies within them. Large numbers of slaves were employed by the elites in the Assyrian and Persian Empires; whether one looks at the elites in the imperial heartland of Assyria, the Persian imperial diaspora in areas like Asia Minor or Persian governors like Aršama, the satrap of Egypt, we see portfolios of tens or hundreds of slaves employed in agriculture, pastoralism, the crafts and household service.[59] In these Near Eastern societies slaves constituted a major part of elite portfolios and were employed in a variety of ways. The traditional distinction between the dominant role of slavery in the Greek world and its marginality in the Near East is consequently no longer tenable and needs to be abandoned.

Instead of abstract classification as slave societies or societies with slaves, we need to set out a number of major axes around which to explore both similarities and divergences. A first major axis is the extent of slave ownership within a single society. While elite ownership of slaves was extensive in both the Greek and the Near Eastern worlds, and thus constitutes a major similarity, the extent to which other social groups owned slaves might have diverged significantly. In certain cases the evidence allows us to calculate relative prices for slaves and other commodities and wages.[60] We can therefore see that slaves were relatively cheap in classical Athens, but comparatively expensive in Assyria and Babylonia. Accordingly, while in Athens slave ownership extended far beyond the elite, the same does not appear to be the case in Assyria or Babylonia.[61]

A second major axis concerns the existence of other sources of revenue and labour. In many Near Eastern economies, alongside the portfolios and activities of subaltern, middling and elite households, there also existed a command economy directed by the palaces and the temples, which accounted for a significant part of wealth and of economic activities. Elites in those societies derived a major part of their income from their role in the command sector, alongside the wealth they generated from their own resources and households. Furthermore, tenancy and wage labour constituted important alternative sources of labour that were particularly significant in certain societies and periods. Thus, while slavery was everywhere a significant source of elite income, in certain societies in the Near East it was also supplemented by other sources. But despite the existence of other important sources of labour and income, slavery was by no means marginal in the Near East.[62]

A third major difference concerns the employment of the various modalities of slavery. In the Near East, the language of slavery could be deployed in order to convey hierarchy and subordination between free people: thus an inferior could address a superior as his master, and the king's subjects could be described as his slaves. These uses did not define a legal relationship, nor were they necessarily derogatory: they rather tended to express a measure of politeness and deference, depending on the context. The use of the language of slavery to refer to relationships of power and service

---

[59] For Assyria, see Lewis 2018: 223–34; for the Persian Empire, see Lewis 2018: 247–54.

[60] Scheidel 1996b, 2005a; Ruffing and Drexhage 2008; Harper 2010a; Salway 2010; cf. Crawford 2010.

[61] Lewis 2018: 180–96.

[62] For alternative labour sources in the ancient Near East, see Postgate 1987; Jursa 2010: 660–81; Radner 2015; Lewis 2018: 289–90.

among free people in the Greek world was almost exclusively derogatory, and was not employed to express deference or politeness.[63] The same largely applies to the Roman world, though it is worth pointing out how the word for master/mistress (*dominus/ domina*) gradually came to be used to address lovers and family members and to express politeness.[64]

Let us summarise the above observations. The traditional distinction between Greek and Roman slave societies and Near Eastern societies with slaves is no longer tenable. Slaves constituted a major source of elite income in many Near Eastern societies; furthermore, slavery played a significant role in the politics, culture and society of Near Eastern societies, even if its impact was rather different from that on Greek and Roman societies. This does not mean that we should ignore the differences between Greek and Roman slaving systems, on the one hand, and those encountered in the ancient Near East, on the other; but we need an alternative framework that will allow us to account for both similarities and differences without recourse to essentialist juxtapositions.[65]

My final point concerns the traditional narrative that has been constructed on the basis of the distinction between slave societies and societies with slaves; this is based on the idea that Greek societies were originally societies with slaves, which in the course of the archaic period were transformed into slave societies through political and social revolutions, like Solon's reforms. But is this narrative of change remotely true? In this respect, it is telling to observe the extent to which conceptual schemes predetermine how historians approach the evidence. Greek historians have preferred to start from the image of dependent bondsmen as the main source of labour in archaic Attica before the reforms of Solon; this is an image created by late classical and post-classical sources like Aristotle and Plutarch. Accordingly, historians have imagined Greek societies before the radical changes of the archaic period as quasi-feudal societies, in which the aristocracy exploited the labour of dependent peasants.[66]

If one starts from this image, it is impossible to account for the social world presented in the Homeric epics, where slavery is dominant and other forms of dependent labour are invisible. It is not surprising, therefore, that historians have either not paid attention to slavery in the Homeric world, or have tried to dissociate Homeric slavery from the traditional historical conception of slavery, by inventing neologisms like 'patriarchal slavery' in order to sustain their conceptual acrobatics.[67] Over the last thirty years, a number of scholars have pointed out major problems with the traditional narrative as regards Homeric slavery and the purported emergence of slave societies in the archaic period.[68] The earliest evidence we have for Greek history, the Homeric epics and Hesiod, make it abundantly clear that slaves constituted the main

---

[63] Lewis 2018: 81–92.

[64] Dickey 2002: 77–109.

[65] For another comparison between Greek and Near Eastern slaveries from the point of view of integration, see Hezser 2016.

[66] Finley 1980: 67–92; Garlan 1988: 38–9.

[67] Beringer 1982; Garlan 1988: 29–37.

[68] Fisher 1993: 15–20; Rihll 1996; Ndoye 2010; Harris 2012; Lewis 2018: 107–24.

labour source from which Greek elites derived their wealth. It is impossible to tell how far before the eighth century BCE we should extend this situation. But the idea that slavery became important in the Greek world during the archaic period and that slave societies emerged for the first time in this period is simply untenable.

There were undoubtedly important changes that took place in the course of the archaic period: the slave trade expanded across the Mediterranean and the Black Sea and became substantially more important as a source for slaves; the extent of slave ownership might have expanded significantly beyond the elites; the institutionalisation of citizenship affected slavery in important ways; new forms of economic activity, like the production of agricultural staples and manufactured goods for market exchange, developed substantially and slavery became a major factor in these new forms. We need to construct new narratives of the history of slavery in which these developments can be incorporated and given their due; but we will have to abandon the current narrative that misconstrues Homeric slavery and attempts to interpret changes by means of a radical disjuncture between societies with slaves and slave societies.[69]

The concept of slave societies was invented to explain the particular economic importance of slavery in certain societies. But as we have seen above, the concept is far too abstract for many aspects of economic history and obscures the diverse economic processes in which slavery was inscribed. The concept also made some sense as long as it was restricted to very few Western societies. Once it has become clear that slave societies can be found across the globe, the implicit assumptions about, for example, the link between slavery and freedom that made the concept appealing no longer make sense. Finley's conceptual scheme had another implicit assumption: that if slavery was economically important it would also affect all other aspects of economy, society and politics, while if its economic impact was limited, it would have little effect on the other aspects. But these assumptions are unwarranted, as we have seen. What is now required is an alternative framework for exploring the interaction between slavery as an economic phenomenon and its impact on society, politics and culture. In this respect, it will be essential to remember that slavery is not a single and unitary entity, but is rather the historical outcome of the varying entanglements between its different conceptual systems. It is likely that we will discover that certain conceptual systems or their facets affected one aspect of life more than another or one society more than another.

Noel Lenski has recently presented a valuable alternative to the simplistic distinction between slave societies and societies with slaves. He distinguishes between two aspects of slavery: the property aspect, and thus its benefits to the master, and the aspect of social death, and thus its disadvantages for the slave. Lenski cautions against assuming that these two aspects were identical or would move in the same way. Furthermore, he suggests dividing each aspect into further sub-categories: the category of property into the use value and exchange value of slaves as commodity and the use value and exchange value of the slaves' labour products; and the category of social death into the permanence of the slave condition, the level of violent domination, the

---

[69] See the efforts to create such new narratives in van Wees 2003, 2013; Descat 2006, 2015; Zurbach 2013.

degree of natal alienation and the level of dishonour. Consequently, we should study the extent of intensification that different slaveholding societies followed along these two axes and their various sub-categories.[70]

The conceptual framework presented in the previous chapters is easily compatible with Lenski's scheme. His property and social death aspects refer to the definitional and prototypical conceptual systems of slavery analysed in Chapter 3; but I have argued that we also need to take account of a third conceptual system, that of the radial modalities of slavery. Furthermore, the various sub-categories of property and social death have been analysed in more detailed terms as the various slaving strategies explored in Chapter 4, as well as the dialectical relationships explored in Chapter 6. I would finally argue that we need to expand Lenski's vectors of intensification with two further axes: the various slaving contexts, as analysed in Chapter 4, as well as the various forms of slave identity examined in Chapter 5. Lenski's call to analyse the patterns of intensification alongside various co-existing but distinct axes is undoubtedly a crucial step forward; but I hope that the framework analysed in the previous chapters not only allows us to add further important axes, but also to explore how the various axes were entangled and interrelated.

## Accounting for Change

We have seen that the conceptual scheme of slave societies and societies with slaves can no longer be used to construct a narrative of the historical trajectory of ancient slavery. We have also seen how the traditional narrative built on this conceptual scheme presented a deeply static account in which in the millennium between the emergence of Greek slave societies in the archaic period and the collapse of the Roman slave society in late antiquity nothing important changed. This image of a millennium of static history is inherently unlikely, given what we have seen about the historical development of early medieval slavery or slavery in the early modern Atlantic world. But we have also seen how we can set aside static approaches to slavery in favour of a dynamic processual framework that explores the changing historical entanglement between the conceptual systems, the slaving contexts and strategies and the dialectical relationships of slavery.

Consequently, we have reached the point where we can envisage the constructions of new narratives of ancient slaving. What forms of historical change should we envisage as part of this historical account? I will trace four modes of conceiving change that such an account should contain. The first mode is the familiar one of **rise and fall**. A characteristic example of this mode is Philip Curtin's study of the rise and fall of the plantation complex, which has traced its course from its emergence in the late medieval Mediterranean, through its extension and development in the early modern Atlantic, to its collapse in the course of the nineteenth century.[71] An ancient equivalent would be the Roman aristocratic *domus*: the urban household based on a detailed differentiation of roles among hundreds of slaves and freed persons, the rural estate with its villa and

[70] Lenski 2018a: 47–57.
[71] Curtin 1998.

productive installations, the bureaucracy of managers and agents that linked together the various operations, the communities of kinship, cult and burial formed by the slaves and freed persons of the *domus*.[72] By focusing on contexts, strategies and dialectics we can perceive the concatenation of forces that brought the *domus* complex into life and understand how their changing entanglement modified it and brought it to an end; but we also need to note that once it was shaped into a distinctive cultural, social and economic package (a lifestyle), the *domus* complex had a life of its own, irrespective of the concatenation of forces that brought it to life and maintained it. While the *domus* complex appeared in the late Republic and came to an end at some point in late antiquity, Roman slavery was not tantamount to it and had a wider historical trajectory, only one element of which was the rise and fall of the elite *domus* complex.

The second mode concerns **cyclical processes** of intensification and abatement in the scale, forms and purposes of slaving: whether, for example, masters intervened directly in the labour process in order to exact labour, or allowed slaves to live and work on their own in exchange for revenue.[73] This is straightforward enough, but far too often historians conflate cycles of intensification and abatement with large-scale change and transformation. Ancient and medieval historians tend to accept a narrative in which the abatement of Roman slaving led to the abandonment of intensive estate agriculture, the settlement of slaves on individual plots as dependent tenants and ultimately the transformation of slaves into serfs.[74] Engagement with Africanist scholarship would have long ago revealed that abatement is a widely encountered process and by no means leads to the abolition or transformation of slavery.[75] It was common in African societies for second-generation or 'seasoned' slaves to be settled in slave villages, where they worked their plots without direct supervision, submitting regular tribute to their masters. But as long as there were new recruits to the system through war and trade, the process of abatement that affected a part of the slave population did not lead to the transformation of African slavery into 'serfdom'.[76] Intensification and abatement were constant tendencies in all slaveholding societies, as we saw in Chapter 4; but these cycles could have divergent temporalities for different processes within the same society, and should not a priori be conceived holistically.[77]

A third mode is that of **conjuncture**. By this I mean the effects of concatenations of events and conditions on the practices of slaving and the interlinking between different societies and processes as a result of such conjunctures. Excellent illustrations of this mode have emerged from recent studies of the conjuncture created in North America by competing colonial empires and native communities and the entanglements between colonial and native slaveries that resulted from it; once the US gradually eliminated all other colonial empires from North America, the changing conjuncture had a transformational impact on practices of slaving.[78]

---

[72] Harper 2011; Marzano and Métraux 2018.

[73] For intensification and abatement processes, see Horden and Purcell 2000: 263–70.

[74] But see now Wickham 2005; Harper 2011; Rio 2017.

[75] Roth 2016 offers a proper comparison between early imperial and early medieval agricultural slavery.

[76] Inikori 1999.

[77] Lenski 2018a: 47–57.

[78] Snyder 2010; Rushforth 2012.

Lenski has explored in a series of studies the impact of conjunctures on slaving: how the changing context of the relationship between the Roman Empire and the various barbarian communities in Europe affected slavery, as well as how slavery affected those relationships;[79] the significance for slaving of the emergence of the powerful rival state of the Huns and its relationship with the Roman Empire and the various barbarian communities of central Europe and the Black Sea;[80] how the balance of power between the Roman Empire, the Sassanian Empire and the Saracen communities of the Near East affected slaving in late antiquity;[81] and the changing significance of slave labour in the economy of Roman Africa from the early imperial period to late antiquity.[82] Other studies have focused on earlier periods, exploring the impact of Roman imperial expansion during the last century of the Roman Republic: the link between Mediterranean political anarchy and slaving in Syria,[83] and the consequences of the Roman penetration and conquest of Gaul on slaving.[84] Another important conjuncture concerns the impact of the institutional order, slaving practices and conceptual systems of the Roman Empire on slaving in various provincial societies and cultures, such as the Jews,[85] or the province of Macedonia.[86]

While geopolitical and cross-cultural conjunctures are so far the best explored in the study of ancient slavery, the examination of epochal conjunctures is still limited. Unsurprisingly, it is primarily in the field of Roman slavery that some progress has been made, while Greek slavery is still tabula rasa from this point of view: Bradley has explored the impact of late republican politics on Roman slaving,[87] while Fábio Joly has performed a similar exercise for the time of Nero;[88] Pedro López Barja de Quiroga has shown that the imperial conjuncture of Roman Italy between the second century BCE and the first century CE offered major opportunities for a large section of freed persons;[89] finally, Rose MacLean has examined how the emergence of the imperial order transformed the lives of slaves and freed persons and offered new ways of employing the conceptual systems of slavery.[90]

A fourth mode is constituted by **long-term change**: the emergence of novel, and usually irreversible, phenomena with profound effects. This is the least understood phenomenon, usually obliterated by the sociological tradition of searching for the essence of slavery and the historical habit of focusing on specific periods to the neglect of wider global trends. I want to focus on three examples, each relating to different contexts of slaving. My first example concerns sex and marriage. For many ancient

[79] Lenski 2008.
[80] Lenski 2014.
[81] Lenski 2011.
[82] Lenski 2017.
[83] Mavrojannis 2018, 2019.
[84] Fentress 2019.
[85] Hezser 2005.
[86] Youni 2000, 2012; Harper 2011: 367–90. For the entanglement between Egyptian and Greek slaving traditions in Ptolemaic Egypt, see Heinen 1978.
[87] Bradley 2011; see also Jongman 2003; Shaw 2014.
[88] Joly 2010.
[89] López Barja de Quiroga 2010.
[90] MacLean 2018; see also Joly 2003.

societies, marriage is largely a means of producing progeny and transmitting property; given the purposes, it is unsurprising that marriages among slaves are often unimportant and without legal effect. This does not mean that slave marriages were not greatly important to slaves; it only means that they could find little support beyond the customary and the temporary.

This situation changed radically with the emergence of the monotheistic religions of Christianity and Islam; for them, marriage became ultimately not merely a means of getting heirs and transmitting property, but a form of regulating sexuality and arranging relations between humans and God which was valuable in itself. This meant that marriage gradually became something desirable for all members of the monotheistic community, irrespective of their legal status.[91] Islam placed an obligation on masters to find wives for their slaves; in the eighth century CE the Lombard laws stipulated that a master who copulated with his own married female slave would have to liberate both the female slave and her slave husband as punishment; the recognition of slave marriage and its legal consequences could not be better expressed.[92]

That such processes of long-term change are not only due to religion is best seen in the case of China. Early Chinese laws created a clear distinction between the honourable free female, who was solely eligible for the highly ritualised marriage ceremonies, and the dishonoured slave. A master could copulate with his own slaves freely, while punishment for copulating with the slaves of others was on an insignificant scale, compared with the draconian penalties for adultery with free women. But from the Song dynasty onwards, the state gradually came to eliminate this disjuncture in honour and to assimilate penalties for copulating with slaves and protection to slave marriages to those pertaining to the free.[93] The Chinese case highlights the need to think carefully about why in the course of the second millennium CE different societies, religions and cultures across the globe moved in the same direction as regards slave marriage.

The second example concerns the emergence of the conceptual language of freedom. While all slaveholding societies oppose slavery to mastery and community membership, the conceptualisation of freedom as a state which entails certain entitlements to autonomy, respect and inviolability was a profound change that appeared only in certain societies and ultimately led to the abolition of slavery. It is worth remarking that while long-term change can be irreversible, it can also be relativised. The vocabulary of freedom survived through the Middle Ages; but instead of denoting an absolute status, as in antiquity, it became relativised to describe certain aspects and conditions in relation to others: somebody could be a slave from the point of view of the exclusive rights of an individual master, and free from the point of view of being released from lordly charges at will. But the survival of this conceptual vocabulary through late antiquity and the early Middle Ages made possible its revival as an absolute status from the late Middle Ages onwards.[94]

[91] For slave marriage in Orthodox Byzantium, see Rotman 2009: 141–4; for slave marriage in the Catholic West, see Sahaydachny 1994; for slave marriage in Islam, see Ali 2010.

[92] *Laws of Liutprand* 140.2; see Fisher Drew 1973: 208; Rio 2017: 232.

[93] Sommer 2000: 30–65.

[94] Blickle 2003; Carrier 2012.

The third example concerns the process through which the custom of enslaving defeated opponents and the process of slave raiding gradually came to be abolished in large parts of Eurasia and Africa. As we saw in Chapter 4, empires and monotheistic religions ultimately created huge no-slaving zones in which, for the first time in human history, defeat in battle or a victorious siege did not lead to mass enslavement; the form of the wider world had radically changed.[95] The temptation to present long-term change as part of a Hegelian march of progress gradually leading to the abolition of slavery is understandable. But it needs to be balanced with a realisation of the grave consequences that accompanied such long-term changes: the creation of huge no-slaving zones based on religion led ultimately to the fateful emergence of racial slavery and the traumatic intensification of slave raiding and trading in areas outside those zones, as in Africa.[96]

The above are forms of change which are applicable to the study of ancient slavery. But we now need to specify the forces that caused the various forms of change we noted above. We need to distinguish between three different forces. As we saw when we analysed the contexts of slaving in Chapter 4, the history of slaving was deeply affected by factors which had their own autonomous history and possessed their own independent trajectories. The household was a crucial context of slaving; but households, families, kinship and gender systems possessed their own dynamic and changed often for reasons that had little to do with slavery; the same applies to contexts like the political community, the wider world and large-scale economic operations. The history of slaving is fundamentally inscribed in the history of wider forces and changes, and we need to understand the history of these wider forces in their own terms, as well as the specific ways in which these wider forces shaped the history of slaving.

The second force in the history of slaving is slavery itself. If the first force points towards the historical impact of independent factors and processes on slaving, the second force requires us to ask the opposite question: what difference did slavery make in how these factors and processes were constructed and operated? What we need to explore is how slavery affected the economic, social, political and cultural history of antiquity. What did it enable people to do? How did it inflect the various phenomena and processes? Which developments did it forestall? If the history of households shaped the history of slaving, how did slavery shape households?[97] To give one pertinent example, Scheidel has pointed out the peculiarity of Greek and Roman obligatory monogamy from the point of view of global history, as we have seen above (pp. 75–6).[98] In Greek and Roman societies common people could only marry one wife, even if serial monogamy was a usual pattern. This was a particularly egalitarian model, as every man, however rich, could only have one legal wife; as a result, even the poorest men would have a realistic opportunity to find a wife, a possibility usually foreclosed in plutocratic societies which recognised polygyny.[99] Scheidel has argued

---

[95] Fynn-Paul 2009; see also the studies qualifying the concept in Fynn-Paul and Pargas 2018.
[96] Eltis 2000.
[97] Golden 1988.
[98] Scheidel 2009, 2011.
[99] Testart et al. 2001; Testart, Govoroff and Lécrivain 2002.

that it is the importance of slavery that explains why Greek and Roman societies accepted the egalitarian model of monogamy: the existence of high numbers of slave concubines was the factor that made obligatory monogamy feasible and acceptable to rich people. Irrespective of whether one agrees with Scheidel's answer, it is an excellent example of how to study the impact of slavery on wider processes.[100]

In order to explore such questions, we need to stop thinking of slavery in a unitary way. If the arguments of this book have been convincing, slavery was the historically changing entanglement between the three conceptual systems we examined in Chapter 3: the definitional system of slavery as property, the prototypical system of slavery as a particular slave status and the radial system of the various modalities of slavery. This complex conception of slavery will be particularly useful in terms of avoiding searching for some red herrings that have long dominated the study of the impact of slavery.

One such pernicious red herring is that of looking for a pro-slavery ideology in ancient texts.[101] Ancient texts seldom if ever concerned themselves with the justification of slavery; given the fact that nobody in antiquity called for the abolition of slavery, there was no debate in which people took sides in favour of or against slavery. There was plenty of debate involving slavery, but it was always a debate about other things: luxury, the rights of war, emotional and intellectual autonomy, self-control, the management of wealth and human relations, the power of fate and luck.[102] We need to carefully reconstruct the contexts of these debates and realise that they never relate to slavery as a whole, but only to particular conceptual systems or modalities.[103] Another related red herring is that of anxiety: modern scholars presume that post-abolitionist anxiety is also relevant for the ancient world, and spill a lot of ink in search of explicit or repressed expressions of anxiety by ancient slave-owners.[104] But for the reasons expressed above, this is usually highly misleading.[105]

Once we eschew the search for such red herrings, we can explore the complex work that slavery performed. William Fitzgerald has examined how certain modalities of slavery have been employed in various genres of Latin literature; elite Latin authors enjoyed using slavery as a thought exercise, as it provided an external point of view for approaching issues like love and emotion.[106] MacLean has explored how communicative modes initiated by freed persons in order to express their newfound but qualified liberty could be employed by Roman elites in order to negotiate their new position

---

[100] For recent fruitful explorations of the links between demography, family and socio-economic conditions in antiquity, see Harper 2013; Huebner 2013; Huebner and Laes 2019.

[101] For ideas about slavery, see Garnsey 1996.

[102] Cf. Cambiano 1987; Paradiso 1991; Garlan 2006; Alston 2011; Panzeri 2011; Occhipinti 2015.

[103] For a particularly characteristic example and its problems, see Ramelli 2016 and my review in Vlassopoulos 2018b.

[104] McCarthy 2000.

[105] For a critique of such approaches, see McKeown 2007a: 30–51, 77–123; that does not mean that fear of slaves was not an important factor, for which see the studies in Serghidou 2007.

[106] Fitzgerald 2000.

under the autocratic imperial order.[107] A number of recent studies have examined how slavery provided a trope that Greek and Roman authors could employ in order to conceptualise the modalities of empire.[108] The role of slavery for conceptualising various theological, cosmological and moral problems in ancient philosophy and Christian thought is another well-explored theme.[109]

My final example illustrates what is required to approach this force from the point of view of historical change. As recent studies have shown, images of Cupids and human bodies were long-established themes in Greek functional art; but Roman art stressed the slavish body and preferred to depict captive Cupids in a way that stressed the similarity of their condition to that of slavery.[110] How should we account for this peculiar Roman inflection based on slavery, given the fact that slaving was clearly important in both Greek and Roman societies? Can we write a narrative in which slavery gradually affected art in ever more significant ways in the course of antiquity? If true, does this apply to all fields and genres of artistic production or only to some of them? And what are the reasons for such developments?

## The Agency of Enslaved Persons and Historical Change

It is time to explore the third force of change in ancient slaving: the agency of masters, slaves and the other individuals and collectivities we examined in Chapter 6. The agency of masters was until recently the only factor that ancient historians considered as an important force of historical change. Given how much ink has been spilt on master agency, and how little on that of enslaved persons, I think it is appropriate and necessary to focus exclusively on slave agency in this final section. The incorporation of slave agency in a narrative of the historical trajectory of slaving faces an acute problem. From the inception of the Western tradition of historiography, the narrative was inseparably linked with political and military history. Not only was history largely conceived in terms of politics and warfare, but eventful narratives were particularly well suited to them. When social, economic and cultural history became major fields of modern historiography in the twentieth century, they largely avoided the narrative form. Economic, social and cultural history are not easily presented in diachronic narratives based on events; they are more easily comprehended through synchronic analyses of structures. When economic, social and cultural historians tried to comprehend and depict change, they largely avoided recourse to event-based narratives; instead, they divided time in historical still frames, defined as periods, and accounted for change by describing the transition from one period to the next (from archaic to classical culture, or from classical to Hellenistic society). This allowed historians to explore phenomena and processes that could not be accounted for by the short-term

---

[107] MacLean 2018.

[108] Joly 2003; Tamiolaki 2010; Lavan 2013.

[109] For slavery and ancient philosophy, see Vlastos 1941; Shaw 1985; Manning 1989; Schofield 1999; Panzeri 2011. For slavery and Christian thought, see Klein 1988, 2000; Martin 1990; Glancy 2002a, 2012; de Wet 2015, 2018.

[110] George 2013b; Lenski 2013; cf. Grawehr 2019.

perspective of *histoire événementielle* and to explore the historical role of individuals and groups beyond the protagonists of the great events that formed the staple of traditional political history (for example, women and slaves).[111] But in this division of labour and foci lay a great danger: on the one hand, of a social, economic and cultural history based on synchronic analysis that gives a static account completely dissociated from the history of events; on the other, of a political history as a narrative that is little informed by the great advances in our historical understanding contributed by social, economic and cultural history.[112]

The above observations are highly relevant to the study of ancient slavery. Ancient slavery is almost exclusively studied synchronically and in almost total dissociation from narrative history. Apart from the wider historiographical reasons, an important contributing factor is also the nature of our sources. The ancient narrative sources that form the basis of modern historical narratives largely focus on elites and states; one will find few slave actors in the narratives of Herodotus, Thucydides and Polybius. On the other hand, most of our evidence for the lives of enslaved persons comes from sources which are not easily amenable to diachronic narrative. Our evidence for ancient slaves comes overwhelmingly from inscriptions that record their sale or manumission; funerary epigrams that record their death; the depiction of fictional slaves in comedies or novels; their fleeting appearance in private letters or law-court speeches; depictions in vases or material objects like chains.[113] It is thus understandable that historians find it immensely easier to incorporate all this evidence into a synchronic analysis of 'slavery in classical Athens' or 'slavery in republican Rome', rather than into a narrative of Greek or Roman history.[114]

But there is a third reason for this synchronic tendency that relates to the study of slavery in particular. Ancient historians have operated with a very simplistic conception of collective actors and collective agency. In order to count as collective actors, slaves must be shown to have acted collectively *qua* slaves and in order to defend slave interests. In the course of antiquity, this can perhaps be attested in the three major revolts that erupted in Italy and Sicily in the late republican period, although even this has been disputed in recent studies, as I have noted already in Chapter 2.[115] But for most of ancient history, there appears to be limited evidence for this kind of large-scale collective agency of enslaved persons. As a result, even those scholars like de Ste. Croix, who have stressed the significance of slavery as a causal factor in ancient history, have been forced to present slaves as passive victims of domination and exploitation, rather than as active historical agents (as also already discussed in Chapter 2).[116] Even sophisticated historical accounts of ancient slavery can end up leaving no space for slave agency as a force of historical change. Harper's account of slavery in late antiquity is undoubtedly among the most

---

[111] For fundamental reflections on these issues, see Sewell 2005.

[112] Vlassopoulos 2017: 225–30.

[113] For the evidentiary sources for ancient slavery, see Bagnall 2011; George 2011; Hunt 2011; Joshel 2011; Morris 2011; Bruun 2014; Straus 2016; Osborne 2017; Chaniotis 2018; Morris 2018; Gardner 2019.

[114] Vlassopoulos 2017: 230–1.

[115] Bradley 1989; Shaw 2001; Urbainczyk 2008; but see the challenges offered by Donaldson 2012; Morton 2012, 2013, 2014; with p. 33 above.

[116] Ste. Croix 1981.

innovative works to be published over the last twenty years, as I argued in Chapter 2;[117] and yet, while Harper sees factors like the contraction of economic activity or the collapse of the Roman state as forces of change in the history of slaving, the agency of slaves as a historical force is completely missing.[118] It is in fact telling that slave agency is invisible in Harper's latest book on the collapse of the Roman Empire.[119]

The study of slave agency is among the most contentious issues in the global study of slavery. To give a sense of how acrimonious such debates can be, a recent volume has even asked whether slave revolts played any significant role in the abolition of slavery.[120] In the previous chapters I have explored a radically different conception of slave agency. Instead of the unitary conception of slaves as collective agents, we have explored the distinction between slave categorisation, slave self-understanding and slave groupness, and the significant gaps and disjunctures between these three aspects. I have employed the term enslaved persons in order to capture these disjunctures and gaps and avoid reducing slaves to a single and monolithic slave identity. Slave agency was not exclusively based on being slave, nor was it exclusively geared towards resisting or escaping slavery.[121] As we have seen in Chapter 7, a significant part of slave agency intended to limit the impact of slavery on slaves' lives, by creating a world below and beyond slavery, which was run on principles other than slavery. And as we shall shortly see, a significant part of slave agency was exercised in actions which maintained slaving, instead of undermining it.

We have examined how slaving strategies and dialectical relationships provided the contexts within which slave agency was exercised; enslaved persons rarely, if ever, had the opportunity to choose their courses of action and their timing. The deep asymmetries inherent in slaving processes meant that enslaved persons usually had to exercise their agency in situations that were not created by them and did not serve their interests or concerns. But this does not mean that enslaved persons did not try to exploit those situations to their own advantage and that the agency of enslaved persons was not consequential. I will try to illustrate these observations by means of two sets of examples. The first set of examples focuses on the role of slaves as agents in narratives of political history; the second set focuses on their role as agents in cultural history.

Let us start our exploration of enslaved person as political agents[122] by examining the role of slaving and enslaved persons in the Peloponnesian War. Slavery is omnipresent in the Peloponnesian War.[123] This obviously applies to the tens of thousands of slaves on whose labour rested both everyday life and the operation of the war: the slaves who laboured for wealthy Athenian citizens and metics,[124] built the Erechtheion,[125] worked

---

[117] Vlassopoulos 2015b.
[118] Harper 2011: 497–509.
[119] Harper 2017b.
[120] Drescher and Emmer 2010; cf. Berlin 1998; Helg 2016; Brown 2020.
[121] Johnson 2003 is fundamental reading; see also Glancy 2013.
[122] For slaves as political agents, see Oakes 1986.
[123] There is no overall study of slaves in the Peloponnesian War. For slaves in Thucydides, see Hunt 1998: 53–143.
[124] O-R 172.
[125] O-R 181; see Randal 1953.

on the construction of the Argive long walls[126] and manned the Corcyraean navy.[127] Because the history of slavery is written as a static story, with little change in the course of time, modern accounts have little space for the profound impact of events on the history of slaving and the experiences of slaves. A hero of Aristophanes complained that he was not able to punish his slaves properly because of the Peloponnesian War, since he was afraid that they might run away aided by the wartime circumstances.[128] This is an illuminating example of the significance of events and the conditions they created for the history of slaving.

The Peloponnesian War was a process that led concurrently to mass enslavement and mass liberation. Thousands of people were enslaved in the course of the war and exchanged freedom for a life in bondage; among the many examples were the inhabitants of Skione, Melos and Hykkara.[129] But equally significant is the reverse process, in which thousands of enslaved persons won their freedom in the course of the war.[130] Many thousands were liberated in order to serve in the war by states desperate for manpower: the thousands liberated and enfranchised by the Athenians to man their fleet before the crucial battle of Arginousai;[131] the enslaved persons in the Chian fleet who were liberated and enrolled as rowers by the Athenians;[132] the hundreds of helots who were employed in Brasidas' campaign in Thrace with the promise of freedom, and who were later settled in Lepreon.[133] Many enslaved persons used the opportunity of war in order to flee from their former masters and gain freedom, or at least enhance their servile conditions: the slaves in the Chian countryside who used the opportunity of the Athenian invasion to gain their freedom;[134] the numerous helots who escaped to Athenian fortifications in Spartan territory;[135] the 20,000 Athenian slaves who escaped to the Spartan fortification in Dekeleia.[136] Other slaves gained freedom as a result of the civil conflicts that were an essential part of the entangled history of the Peloponnesian War: the slaves who took the part of the democrats in Corcyra are a characteristic example.[137]

The experience and historical significance of those thousands of enslaved freemen and liberated slaves has never affected our modern accounts of the Peloponnesian War. An illuminating example comes from a funerary inscription from Attica, dated on epigraphic grounds to the last third of the fifth century BCE:

> The best of the Phrygians in the broad lands of Athens was Mannes Orymaios, to whom belongs this fine tomb; 'and by Zeus I never saw a better woodman than myself'. He died in the war.[138]

---

[126]  Thucydides 5.82.6.
[127]  Thucydides 1.55.1; see Welwei 1974–88: 91–5.
[128]  Aristophanes, Clouds 5–7.
[129]  Thucydides 5.32.1, 5.116.4, 6.62.3–4.
[130]  Paradiso 2008.
[131]  Hunt 2001.
[132]  Thucydides 8.15.2.
[133]  Thucydides 5.34.1.
[134]  Thucydides 8.40.2.
[135]  Thucydides 7.26.2.
[136]  Thucydides 7.27.5; Hanson 1992.
[137]  Thucydides 3.73.
[138]  IG I³, 1361; CEG 87.

The inscription presents Mannes as proud of his ethnic origins, as well as of his skill as a manual worker. The dating of the inscription and the reference that Mannes died 'in the war' make it practically certain that he died during the Peloponnesian War. If we assume that he died fighting in the war, it is plausible that he served among the metics in the Athenian army, and it is quite likely that he was a former slave. Perhaps we should connect this inscription with Thucydides' reference to a skirmish in the course of the first invasion of Attica, at a place called Phrygia; was this place named after the large number of Phrygian slave and metic inhabitants, like Mannes?[139] It is telling that I have yet to encounter a single narrative of the Peloponnesian War that makes reference to Mannes and explores the historical significance of his experience; and it is hardly accidental that I first came across this inscription in one of the few synchronic accounts of Athenian society, economy and culture that pays attention to politics and events.[140]

The Peloponnesian War was neither a war about slavery, nor a war between masters and slaves. But it was a war in which slave agency played an important role. To start with, one of the grievances that led to the Megarian decree, which was one of the key bones of contention, was that Megara allegedly harboured Athenian fugitive slaves.[141] The agency of fugitive slaves would not have led to the Peloponnesian War on its own, but it was one of the sparks that lit the fire. More significantly, the protracted course of the Peloponnesian War is to an important extent the result of slave agency. The depredations of the Messenian former helots and the continuous flight of helots after Pylos had a deep impact on the Spartans and how they conducted the war;[142] the memories of the earlier helot revolt of the 460s conditioned Spartan policy in the course of the fifth century.[143] On the other hand, the ability of the Spartan state to avoid a helot revolt and to use hundreds of helots for various important campaigns, including Amphipolis, Mantineia and Syracuse, was crucial for the shape of the war.[144] While not unconstrained, the exercise of helot agency in support of the Spartan cause was undoubtedly historically significant.[145] The same applies to the Athenian side as well: on the one hand, the participation of thousands of slaves at Arginousai in 406 BCE saved Athens from defeat;[146] on the other hand, the mass flight of slaves severely debilitated the Athenian economy and war effort.[147]

If the implications of slave agency for the course of the Peloponnesian War are fairly evident, the same phenomena have important implications for the study of slavery. The fact that slave agency could simultaneously face in opposing directions is an excellent illustration of why essentialist approaches to slavery are deeply misleading. Instead of assuming that the imposed identity of being slave fully determined the slaves' lives, identities and actions, we need to explore the various processes through

139  Thucydides 2.22.2; Bäbler 1998: 156–63; Hornblower 1991: 276–7.
140  Zimmern 1931: 278.
141  Thucydides 1.139.2.
142  Thucydides 5.14.3.
143  Thucydides 1.101–3.
144  Thucydides 4.80, 5.57, 7.19.3.
145  Thucydides 4.26.
146  Hunt 2001; Hamel 2015.
147  Hanson 1992; Rihll 2010.

which slaves created identities, communities and networks.[148] War both brings these processes into light and tests their strength. To give an example I have explored in Chapter 6, historians of ancient slavery have failed to ask themselves through what processes the majority of Corcyraean rural slaves decided to take the side of the democrats within a few hours.[149]

I have used the Peloponnesian War as an illustrative example, but the same approach could be applied to many other cases. The 'Roman Revolution', like the Peloponnesian War, was not a conflict between masters and slaves, or a clash about slavery. But while it was at heart a conflict between rival elite factions, it was also an entanglement between various factors and actors.[150] Enslaved and freed persons played a variety of roles in these conflicts and experienced various fortunes.[151] The so-called 'barbarian invasions' of late antiquity were not caused by enslaved persons and did not represent 'slave interests', but the role of the agency of enslaved persons in this process was significant. Like in the Peloponnesian War or the Roman Revolution, many people became enslaved in the course of those events, but equally many people gained their freedom and new opportunities, and played their role in how these processes turned out.[152]

Enslaved persons played important roles in scripts that were constructed by other people; but it would be misleading to assume that slave agency was only exercised under conditions that were not chosen by enslaved persons. We should therefore also pay attention to various situations in which enslaved persons exercised initiative in generating events and developments, rather than reacting to events and developments set by others. Initiative could take both individual and collective forms.[153] When the emperor Augustus died in 14 CE, his ultimate successor, Tiberius, needed to do away with all potential claimants to the throne and gave the order to secretly execute Agrippa Postumus, Augustus' exiled grandson. Clemens, Agrippa's slave, tried to rescue his master and take him to the Roman troops in Germany, from where he could stage a revolt against Tiberius. But when he found out that Agrippa had been killed, he decided to spread the rumour that Agrippa was still alive and to pretend he was him. Clemens moved around Italy convincing many people to follow his cause, until he was finally arrested by agents of Tiberius and executed secretly.[154] There are numerous other stories of slaves or freedmen who acted as impostors and/or tried to take revenge for the death of their powerful masters.[155] Towards the end of the second century CE, a Christian member of the *familia Caesaris* entrusted his slave Callistus with investing various funds in banking. Callistus allegedly defrauded his master and the other creditors, tried to escape and failed, ended

---

[148]   Taylor and Vlassopoulos 2015a.
[149]   Vlassopoulos 2017: 236–7.
[150]   Osgood 2006; Alston 2015.
[151]   Annequin 1973; Sartori 1973; Létroublon 1974; Flambard 1977; Bradley 1978, 2011; Mavrojannis 2007; Thein 2013.
[152]   Lenski 2008, 2011b, 2014.
[153]   See Hunt 2017b; McKeown 2019.
[154]   Grünewald 2004: 140–4.
[155]   Grünewald 2004: 137–60.

up working in a treadmill and, despairing of his condition, decided to end his life by instigating a religious conflict between Jews and Christians. He was condemned to work in the mines of Sardinia, until he was pardoned alongside other Christian convicts. He then managed to gradually ascend the Church hierarchy, until in 218 CE he was elected bishop of Rome, in which capacity he played a highly controversial role, before dying as a martyr probably around 222–3 CE.[156]

Let us move to cases of collective initiative of enslaved persons. In the early sixth century CE the Ethiopian kingdom of Aksum invaded the Himyarite kingdom of Yemen in order to protect the local Christian communities. The invading army overthrew the Himyarite king and put Esimphaios, another Himyarite, in his place, on condition of paying tribute to the Ethiopians. But, according to the historian Procopius, the slaves and other malcontents in the Ethiopian army refused to return to Ethiopia, decided to stay in Yemen, overthrew Esimphaios and gave the throne to Abramos, a Himyarite Christian who was originally a slave based at the Ethiopian port of Adulis, where he had taken care of the shipping interests of his Roman master.[157] These events illustrate the significance of the agency of enslaved persons; any account about developments in this particularly important area of late antiquity that does not accord importance to slave agency would be misleading.[158]

Slave agency was also important in processes of ethnogenesis in various ancient societies.[159] While the process has been studied in detail as regards the early modern world, a comprehensive study for antiquity is thoroughly missing.[160] In the fourth century BCE a new ethnic community emerged in South Italy, which was until then controlled by the Lucanians and the Greek colonies. As various sources report, this new community emerged out of the mingling of fugitive slaves, slave shepherds (whose mode of life required substantial autonomy and mobility) and the local free communities.[161] This new ethnic community became known as the Brettians, which in the Lucanian language meant fugitives or apostates, and quickly became a powerful force in the complex politics of southern Italy. While Brettian ethnogenesis involved many groups of people, it is obvious that the role of slaves in this process was significant.[162] In the fourth century CE, the Sarmatians dominated central Europe. Faced with a Gothic attack in 334 CE, they decided to liberate their slaves, who, according to our sources, were more numerous than the free Sarmatians. But while this mass manumission enabled the Sarmatians to defeat the Goths, the liberated slaves soon revolted and forced their erstwhile masters to flee into the Roman territory. Not only is this one of the few successful slave revolts in global history, but it also led to a process of ethnogenesis, as the new community of freed slaves became known as the Limigantes.[163]

---

[156]  Hippolytus, *Refutation against all heresies* 9.11–12.
[157]  Procopius, *Wars* 1.20.
[158]  Cf. Bowersock 2013.
[159]  For slavery and ethnogenesis in the case of the Hebrews, see Na'aman 1986.
[160]  For early modern ethnogenesis and slavery, see Sidbury and Cañizares-Esguerra 2011.
[161]  Diodorus 16.15.1–2; Strabo 6.1.4; Justin, *Epitome of Trogus* 23.3–12.
[162]  Lombardo 1987; Mele 1994.
[163]  Eusebius, *Life of Constantine* 4.6.1–2; Ammianus Marcellinus 19.11.1; see Lenski 2018a: 29–30.

Individual slaves like Clemens, Callistus and Abramos and collective initiatives like those of the Brettians and the Limigantes are generally absent from histories of ancient slavery, as they do not fit any of the roles ascribed to slaves in modern accounts and narratives. But it is high time that ancient historians follow the stimulating example of our colleagues in modern history, and strive to better incorporate slaves in historical narratives and events in the histories of slavery.[164]

My second cluster of examples concerns cultural history; we commonly think of enslaved persons in their economic and social roles, but we rarely think of them as cultural agents. And yet, slaves are implicated in many important cultural phenomena of antiquity in ways which have never been studied systematically. The black- and red-figure pottery industry of archaic and early classical Athens is of course justly famous; it is also relatively well known that among those potters and painters whose names we know, some bore ethnic or foreign names that were overwhelmingly borne by slaves in Athens: potters and painters named Lydos, Brygos, Syriskos and Amasis.[165] It is of course not impossible that these potters and painters could have been free Greeks who had adopted foreign and ethnic names;[166] but at least one of them is explicitly attested as slave, and the concentration of many such names among artisans makes it in my view highly implausible that none of them had at least started their careers as foreign slaves.[167] If this is true, we encounter a situation in which enslaved potters and painters of foreign origin were in a position to paint vases with images steeped in Greek religion and culture; most of these vases are impossible to distinguish in any way from vases painted by artisans with proper Greek names.[168] It is remarkable how little classical archaeologists and ancient historians have wondered about what processes of ethnographic knowledge and cross-cultural transfer and learning would account for such a phenomenon; it is equally remarkable that the phenomenon has exercised historians of ancient slavery equally little.[169]

Given that Athenian vases generally exhibit similar features, irrespective of their artisan makers, perhaps one could argue that even if there were foreign slave potters in Athens, it did not make any appreciable difference.[170] The same, though, is not true for the process through which Rome acquired a literary culture in the course of the last three centuries BCE. This process is usually characterised as Hellenisation, because Roman literature, philosophy, science and art employed Greek models to a very significant degree. Hellenisation is in many ways a misleading term for this complex process, as is increasingly realised.[171] But slaves and freed persons were at the forefront of this immense process of cultural and technological transfer from the Greek-speaking eastern Mediterranean to Roman Italy. Livius Andronicus initiated Latin literature by

---

[164] For the history of slavery as narrative, see Berlin 1998; for slaves in historical narratives, see Nash 2005.
[165] Sparkes 1996: 110–11; for Athenian slave names, see Vlassopoulos 2010, 2015a.
[166] Cook 1948.
[167] For the slave potter Lydos, see Canciani and Neumann 1978.
[168] For a possible exception, see Pevnick 2010; see also Lewis 1998.
[169] For such processes, see Vlassopoulos 2013a, 2013b.
[170] But see Grawehr 2019 for slaves and pottery in the Roman world.
[171] Wallace-Hadrill 2008.

translating Homer into Latin; Terence played a major role in the emergence of Latin drama; Staberius Eros was the first Latin grammarian, while Caecilius Epirota wrote the first commentary on Virgil; Verrius Flaccus was one of the earliest antiquarians; Publilius Syrus was the earliest writer of mimes, while his cousin, Manilius, was the first writer of astrology in Latin.[172]

While the antiquarian collection of evidence about such slaves has been accomplished, the study of the wider processes in which they were imbricated is still missing.[173] This is possibly the first time in global history when a massive cultural and technological transfer was accompanied by the mass enslavement and transportation of members of the donor culture. This should raise a series of questions. While slaves and freed persons were undoubtedly important in these processes, there were also free Romans and Italians and free immigrants from the eastern Mediterranean that played a significant part in them. Given this fact, what exact difference did slavery make? Did enslaved grammarians, poets and scholars contribute to cultural and technological transfer in ways which were different from the contributions of free cultural agents?[174] And once we have understood the role of slaving in this process, what earlier examples can we identify?[175] What role did slaves play in cultural and technology transfer in the Greek world?[176] If the role of slaves in cultural and technology transfer in the Greek world appears more circumscribed, what were the reasons for this?[177]

I turn now to a third example of enslaved persons in processes of cultural exchange: that of Christianisation. Once upon a time, it was thought that Christianity was a religion of slaves, and accordingly the study of slavery was strongly linked to Christianity in the 'slavery and humanity' debate we have examined in Chapter 2. This idea has been fully discredited over the last few decades; but because Christianity can no longer be seen as a slave religion, this does not mean that slavery and enslaved persons did not play an important role in its history.[178] According to the *Acts of the Apostles*, the first gentile to be baptised Christian was an Ethiopian eunuch who was in charge of the treasury of Queen Candace.[179] Although his legal status is not explicitly stated, he was probably a royal slave of the Ethiopian queen, a slaving strategy widely attested, as we saw in Chapter 4. The baptism of this Ethiopian slave was a crucial step in the process of the expansion of Christianity beyond its original Jewish nucleus.[180] Slaves and freed persons also played various roles in the internal organisation of Christian churches.[181] Slave agency was also crucial in the process of the Christianisation of various societies

---

[172] Shaw 2014: 193–6; Hunt 2018a: 92–8; Moatti 2015: 47–50.

[173] Christes 1979; Treggiari 1969: 110–42.

[174] For a fascinating argument in regard to the role of slave experience in Roman comedy, see Richlin 2017.

[175] The role of captives in culture and technology transfer is brought out well in Cameron 2016.

[176] For one particular aspect of this, see Harrison 2019.

[177] For the role of Muslim slaves in technological and cultural transfers in late medieval Europe, see van Koningsveld 1995.

[178] Kyrtatas 1987.

[179] *Acts of the Apostles* 8.27–38.

[180] Ismard 2017a: 120–5.

[181] Shaner 2018.

outside the Roman Empire.[182] Ulfila, who created a Gothic alphabet and translated the Bible into Gothic, was the child of Christian Roman parents who were captured and enslaved by the Goths.[183] Saint Patrick was famously captured and enslaved in Ireland, before escaping into freedom and returning to convert his former masters.[184] Female captives were traditionally accorded a major role in the Christianisation of Armenia, Georgia and Yemen.[185] Christianisation in the territory of Sassanian Iran was the consequence of the captivity and mass transfer of Christian populations from Roman Syria.[186] All these examples illustrate well a point raised in Chapter 5: enslaved persons could understand themselves as free people in captivity, and thinking of slaves in essentialist and monolithic terms obscures the historical consequences of the agency of people who had lived part of their life as free.

Studying the agency of enslaved persons requires facing some difficult methodological problems. Perhaps the most intractable concerns the links between individual and collective action and between change at the micro- and the macro-scale. As Kolchin has argued, slave agency tends to take an individual form to a much greater extent than among any other exploited group.[187] But how should we examine whether millions of individual acts of slave agency created large-scale trends? And how did the individual exercise of slave agency connect with the collective exercise of slave agency?[188] If enslaved persons exercised agency *qua* slaves primarily in individual terms, while their collective agency took place as members of familial, kinship, ethnic, religious and professional groups, how should we join the dots between these highly divergent forms of agency? This is particularly tricky because of the fragility of slave groupness and the difficulty of consolidating and institutionalising hard-won gains. Community was not something that slaves were necessarily born into, but often had to be constructed from scratch and was unusually fragile; and the master–slave dialectic often made individual strategies much more effective than collective action in achieving many aims. Furthermore, while medieval peasants and modern workers had institutionalised communes and trade unions that allowed them to solidify gains in laws, contracts and custumals, this was usually unthinkable in the case of slaves; the written list of demands for such solidifications that a group of Brazilian slaves submitted to their master is remarkable precisely because of its rarity.[189]

These are admittedly difficult questions to answer; but we should not attempt to reinvent the wheel. To focus on one of the issues raised above, it is well known that the biological process of evolution is the cumulative outcome of innumerable small changes in the micro-scale of individuals, which gradually become developments in the macro-scale as the evolution of species. It would of course be misleading to assume that the form of micro–macro links in biology, where it refers to non-conscious and

[182]  Lenski 2011b: 195–6.
[183]  Lenski 1995.
[184]  Pelteret 1980; Thompson 1985: 16–34; McLuhan 2001.
[185]  Sterk 2010.
[186]  Mosig-Walburg 2010; Smith 2016.
[187]  Kolchin 1983.
[188]  For individual strategies of ancient slaves, see Hunt 2017b; for collective strategies, see McKeown 2019.
[189]  Schwartz 1977.

non-volitional events, would be directly relevant to historical processes that also include volitional and conscious choices. But historians trying to understand the link between the micro- and the macro-scale can learn a lot by looking at how scholars in historical disciplines like biology approach variation, change and narrative globally.[190]

Whether we look at the Peloponnesian War, the Athenian pottery industry, Roman literature, scholarship and art, or Christianisation, the agency of enslaved persons played an important role in all of them. It was not a role freely chosen by enslaved persons, nor a role that expressed exclusively or primarily their interests *qua* slaves. But it is an urgent task to re-write our political, social and cultural histories of ancient societies in ways which recognise the constitutive role of the agency of enslaved persons. Enslaved persons need to move out of the synchronic analyses they have so far largely inhabited in order to populate as historical agents our narratives of ancient history. This is undoubtedly a Herculean task; but it is also a necessary act of historical balance.

---

[190] See the argument of Gaddis 2002.

# 9

# CONCLUSIONS

I̵T IS TIME TO TAKE STOCK of what this book has tried to achieve and to point out some implications for future directions of study. One of the major aims of this book is methodological: to offer a new, processual and historicist way of approaching a complex phenomenon like slavery, instead of the essentialist and atemporal approaches that have so far dominated the field. Traditional approaches to slavery have sought to identify its trans-historical essence, whether they identify it as property, social death, or a mixture of the two. I have argued that slavery must be rather seen as a historically changing conglomerate of three conceptual systems: the definitional system of slavery as property, the prototypical system of slave status and the radial system of the various modalities of slavery. While the existence of the conceptual system of property was crucial for enabling the interlinking between different slaving practices within one society and between diverse forms of slavery in different societies, the definitional conceptual system never existed on its own: it always required the other two conceptual systems in its realisation in actual historical processes. But while the three conceptual systems are cross-cultural, both their content and the way in which they were entangled could vary significantly across space and time. Accordingly, this approach allows us to incorporate both diversity and historical change in our framework.

I have then challenged the traditional distinction between slave societies and societies with slaves, which has played a fundamental role in how ancient historians approach ancient slavery. My critique has focused on the same essentialist and atemporal approaches and the need to adopt processual and historicist perspectives. Instead of the essentialist and monolithic concept of the slave society, I have suggested that we need to focus on the entanglement between three different factors: the various slaving strategies of the masters, the different contexts in which slaving took place and the dialectical relationships between masters and slaves, between free and slave and within slave communities. It is again a framework that can incorporate both diversity and historical change. Instead of the monolithic concept of slave societies, the concept of slaving strategies enables us to explore the various aims served by the tool of slavery and the contradictions created by the co-existence of different slaving strategies within the same society. By distinguishing between different kinds of masters and between slaving strategies and slaving lifestyles, we now have a rich palette of concepts through which to explore diversity.

But this new framework also makes three other important contributions. The first contribution challenges the idea that there is some inherent and automatic link between the economics of slavery and its social, political and cultural impact. The distinction between slave societies and societies with slaves was based on the assumption that where slavery was economically important, it would also affect significantly society, politics and culture, while where its economic role was limited, it would also have little effect on other facets of human life. But as we have seen, this assumption is unwarranted and untenable in both of its versions. By creating a framework with four independent variables (conceptual systems of slavery, slaving strategies, slaving contexts and dialectical relationships) it is possible to analyse the specific links between economic, social, political and cultural processes in different societies.

The second contribution concerns the need to escape the exclusive focus on the master–slave relationship that has so far dominated the study of ancient slavery. Slavery was not unilaterally defined by the masters, as the traditional top-down approach posits; by incorporating into the framework the political community and its various institutions, as well as the various communities in which slaves took part, it is now possible to explore the entanglement between various historical agents and their diverse interests and ideologies. It is in this context that the various modalities of slavery offer a powerful tool of analysis for exploring how these various historical agents used different modalities to achieve their diverse aims and shape things in particular ways.

The third contribution concerns the concept of the various slaving contexts of the household, the political community, the wider world and large-scale economic operations. Instead of a monolithic category of slave society, we can now explore how slaving took place in different contexts, which stressed different aspects, placed different priorities and moved in different directions. Apart from highlighting diversity, this concept also stresses the potential contradictions between the different contexts. But equally important is the fact that each of these contexts had its own balance of forces and historical trajectory, which were distinct from slaving as such: accordingly, the history of slaving was inscribed within larger processes, and we need to study how these larger processes affected slaving, as well as how slaving shaped these larger processes in particular ways.

This book has called for a historicist approach which recognises that diversity, contradiction and change are defining aspects of historical processes and their entanglements. A single phenomenon could have contradictory implications at the very same time. The slave family was an important factor of stability in slaveholding societies. It facilitated the natural reproduction of the slave force; it made slaves more dependable, as they were less likely to flee and abandon their families; finally, masters could employ the threat of selling family members away as a powerful tool in disciplining their slaves. But at the same time family and kinship were major tools for creating slave communities of emotion, support and solidarity. The slave family was both a tool in the hands of masters and a means through which slaves could organise their resistance. The history of slavery was shaped by the interaction between processes and tendencies that faced in different and even contradictory directions; this is the reason why the concept of slavery as a static and atemporal institution should be replaced by one of slaving as an entanglement of processes that employed slavery and slaves for a variety of purposes.

Slaving was shaped by the interaction between the master–slave and the free–slave dialectical relationship. If the free community decided not to intervene in the master–slave relationship, this allowed masters to treat their slaves as brutally or as leniently as they saw fit. In such circumstances, the fact that slaves of a powerful master could become more important and connected than many free people created tensions and conflicts of its own. The free community could also decide to intervene and superimpose its own concerns and interests on masters and slaves. This could subordinate the highest slave to the lowest freeman, but could also create conflicts and tensions by limiting how masters could profitably employ their slaves. The political community could also decide to intervene in order to limit master cruelty and domination, giving slaves the opportunity to take advantage of community institutions and conflicts in order to enhance their condition or even gain freedom and incorporation into the community.

Instead of a static and ahistorical slave system, we see a number of interlinked processes which partly complemented and partly contradicted each other. The processes and dialectical relationships of slavery involved a variety of tendencies and choices, which could move in tandem or in different directions. The stability of this entanglement could depend on the preponderance of one process or tendency, or the equilibrium between tendencies facing in different directions. But it always involved major contradictions, which could result in crises, explosions or revolutions depending on conjuncture, long-term trends, events, struggles and choices.

Such a framework requires a new approach to slave agency. Slaves are usually considered as passive victims of domination and exploitation, instead of active historical agents; furthermore, because slavery is usually explored within synchronic analyses rather than diachronic narratives, there is no conceptual space for exploring the interaction between the significance of events and the long-term structures and continuities. By distinguishing between processes of rise and fall, intensification and abatement, conjunctures and long-term changes, we now have a conceptual repertoire with which to bridge the gap between events and long-term structures. The role of slave agency in this narrative was shaped by the various identities of enslaved persons; we have seen how categorisation, self-understanding and groupness provide a framework for studying how slaves created their identities and how they acted on the basis of these identities and the hopes and interests that they fostered. Enslaved persons often had to act in conditions not of their own choosing; and it is remarkable how much they achieved under such circumstances. But while rarely having the chance to choose their timing, enslaved persons consistently fought to enhance their material conditions, to defy social death by finding love and esteem and by gaining freedom.

It is important to point out a final desideratum of future work. The study of ancient slavery will need to be freed from the impact of its three major labels, as currently practised: 'ancient', 'Greek' and 'Roman'. As we saw, the 'Greek' label is effectively tantamount to 'slavery in classical Athens'. This use is legitimised by the twin assumptions that systems like helotage are not 'proper' slavery, and that the remaining Greek societies practised forms of slavery which were practically identical to that of classical Athens. But as we have seen, not only are helotage and other related systems forms of slavery, but the systems of other Greek communities exhibited significant differences from that of Athens. The 'Roman' label has largely avoided accounting for the co-existence of quite different slave systems within the Roman Empire. Finally, the label 'ancient' obscures some major differences between the various Greek and Roman slave systems and conjures a static history of ancient slavery in which hardly anything changed in the millennium between the alleged emergence of slave societies in the archaic period and their apparent transformation in late antiquity. I have suggested that these misleading labels can be substituted by the notion of epichoric slaving systems: these slaving systems differed across space and changed across time as a result of the impact of various economic, social, political and cultural processes that shaped them in diverse directions.

This suggestion is important, but ultimately insufficient. It is not enough to explore the diversity and transformation of Greek and Roman epichoric slaving systems; we need to escape from the clutches of a conceptual framework which is exclusively Greco-Roman. We have seen how modern historians have gradually abandoned focusing exclusively on local and national societies and the 'Western World' in favour of new geo-spatial frameworks like that of the Atlantic world, which brings together European metropolitan societies, Native American and colonial societies and African societies. It is telling in this respect to compare the different volumes of the *Cambridge World History of Slavery*: while the third volume, devoted to the early modern period, is a truly global account, the first volume, devoted to antiquity, is exclusively Greco-Roman; apart from a token chapter on slavery in the ancient Near East,[1] covering over three millennia of history, the evidence from Near Eastern slaveries does not appear in any of the remaining chapters.[2]

The study of 'ancient slavery' can no longer be restricted to Greek and Roman societies, along with the occasional stray reference to other societies: it needs to incorporate systematically the slaving systems of the Assyrians;[3] the Babylonians;[4] the Elamites and Iranians;[5] the Hittites and other Anatolian societies;[6] the Egyptians and other Nilotic communities;[7] the Syrians, Phoenicians, Jews, Samaritans and other Levantines;[8] the Saracens and other steppe and desert communities of western Asia;[9] the Carthaginians;[10] the Garamantes and other North African communities;[11] the Etruscans and other Italian societies;[12] the Thracians and other Balkan societies;[13] the Scythians, Sarmatians, Huns and other societies of the Black Sea and central Europe;[14] the Celtic societies of Atlantic Europe;[15] and the various Germanic communities of northern Europe.[16]

Admittedly, such a project would face serious evidentiary problems: while for some of these societies, like the Assyrians, Babylonians and Jews, the available evidence is relatively plentiful, for many others it is strictly limited. But the problem

---

[1] Snell 2011.
[2] Bradley and Cartledge 2011; Eltis and Engerman 2011.
[3] Radner 1997; Galil 2007; Fales 2009–10; Ponchia 2017; Lewis 2018: 223–34.
[4] Dandamaev 1984; Seri 2013; Dromard 2017; Lewis 2018: 235–45.
[5] Jusifov 1978; Faist 2009; Potts 2011.
[6] Bayram and Çeçen 1996; Hoffner 2008; Bryce 2018: 144–58; Lewis 2018: 247–51.
[7] Bakir 1952; Menu 1997; Heinen 1978; Cruz-Uribe 1982; Loprieno 1997, 2012; Hofmann 2005.
[8] Elayi 1981; Flesher 1988; Hezser 2005; Dušek 2007; Lemaire 2015; Lewis 2018: 199–222.
[9] Lenski 2011a.
[10] Lenski 2018a: 26–9; Lewis 2018: 259–66.
[11] Fentress 2011; Wilson 2017: 192–3.
[12] Torelli 1976; Rix 1994; Nash Briggs 2002; Benelli 2013.
[13] Velkov 1964, 1986; Ducat 1993; Testart and Brunaux 2004.
[14] Khazanov 1975; Braund 2008; Lenski 2014, 2018a: 29–30.
[15] Arnold 1988; Martin 2002; Nash Briggs 2003.
[16] Thompson 1957; Lenski 2008, 2011b.

is primarily conceptual rather than evidentiary. The relatively limited evidence that exists for slaving in Carthage should have made it fairly evident that it was a slave society on a par with classical Athens and Rome; the fact that Carthage was until recently not included in lists of 'genuine' slave societies that were constructed even by major ancient historians like Finley and Hopkins says a lot about many entrenched and often implicit assumptions that ancient historians share. Whether looking at slaving strategies, processes of slave-making, slave prices, household forms, forms of marriage or modalities of slavery, the incorporation of evidence from other ancient slaving systems has allowed us to avoid conceptual mistakes, to clarify our assumptions, to ask new questions and to avoid taking various aspects of Greek and Roman slaving as self-evident or unproblematic.

But the call to enlarge the field of ancient slavery is not primarily about inclusivity, although this is obviously important. It is rather about the fact that, as we have seen, these various slaveholding societies did not constitute separate entities, but entangled systems. Sarmatian, Hunnic, Saracen and Jewish slaving were strongly entangled with the slaving systems of empires like Rome, Iran and Assyria; in their turn, the development of those imperial slaving systems was equally entangled with the slaving systems of various communities both within these empires and in their geopolitical orbits. This entanglement does not apply only to empires, but is also relevant for various other systems of interaction: the Thracian and Scythian slaving systems cannot be understood irrespective of the slaving systems of the Greek communities in the Black Sea and the Aegean, which interacted with them in various ways, but without ever conquering them.

Ancient historians need to construct a wider framework akin to that of the Atlantic World, the Indian Ocean world or the Islamic oecumene adopted by historians working on slaving in other areas and periods. Slaving was an inherent part of the geopolitical, economic, cultural and religious processes that linked the communities of the Mediterranean, the Near East, North Africa, the Black Sea and temperate Europe with central Asia and the Indian Ocean in the course of antiquity. Over the last twenty years historians and archaeologists are gradually constructing a wider framework for studying these interactions; the study of ancient slavery needs to follow suit urgently.[17]

This book has presented a framework for re-writing the history of ancient slavery from new perspectives and in new ways. Such a re-orientation is urgently needed, now that the paradigm that was created back in the 1960s is cracking in front of our very eyes. It is in this way that we can hope to resolve the paradox with which this book started: slavery is everywhere in the ancient world, and yet, as currently studied, it explains so little. Enslaved persons are everywhere, and yet they are completely absent from our modern narratives. It is high time to put slavery and enslaved persons back where they belong.

---

[17] Horden and Purcell 2000; Cunliffe 2001, 2008, 2015; van de Mieroop 2007; Heather 2010; Broodbank 2013; Guarinello 2013; Vlassopoulos 2013a; Benjamin 2018; Preiser-Kapeller 2018.

# BIBLIOGRAPHY

Acton, P. (2014) *Poiesis: Manufacturing in Classical Athens*. New York.

Aitchison, J. (2012) *Words in the Mind: An Introduction to the Mental Lexicon*. Oxford and Cambridge, MA.

Akrigg, B. and Tordoff, R. (eds) (2013) *Slaves and Slavery in Ancient Greek Comic Drama*. Cambridge.

Alexianu, M. (2011) 'Lexicographers, paroemiographers and slaves-for-salt barter in ancient Thrace', *Phoenix*, 65, 389–94.

Ali, K. (2010) *Marriage and Slavery in Early Islam*. Cambridge, MA and London.

Allard, P. (1876) *Les esclaves chrétiens: depuis les premiers temps de l'Église jusqu'à la fin de la domination romaine en Occident*. Paris.

Alston, R. (2011) 'The good master: Pliny, Hobbes, and the nature of freedom' in Hall, Alston and McConnell (2011), 41–64.

Alston, R. (2015) *Rome's Revolution: Death of the Republic and Birth of the Empire*. Oxford.

Alston, R., Hall, E. and Proffitt, L. (eds) (2011) *Reading Ancient Slavery*. London.

Ameling, W. (1998) 'Landwirtschaft und Sklaverei im klassischen Attika', *Historische Zeitschrift*, 266, 281–315.

Amirante, L. (1950) *Captivitas e postliminium*. Naples.

Anastasiadis, V. I. and Doukellis, P. N. (eds) (2005) *Esclavage antique et discriminations socioculturelles*. Bern.

Andreau, J. (1999) *Banking and Business in the Roman World*. Cambridge.

Andreau, J. (2004) 'Les esclaves "hommes d'affaires" et la gestion des ateliers et commerces' in J. Andreau, J. France and S. Pittia (eds), *Mentalités et choix économiques des Romains*, Bordeaux, 111–26.

Andreau, J. (2009) 'Freedmen in the Satyrica' in Prag and Repath (2009), 114–24.

Andreau, J. and Descat, R. (2006) *Esclave en Grèce et à Rome*. Paris.

Annequin, J. (1973) 'Esclaves et affranchis dans la conjuration de Catilina' in *Actes 1971*, 193–238.

Annequin, J. (1987) 'Les esclaves rêvent aussi . . . Remarques sur La "clé des songes" d'Artémidore', *Dialogues d'Histoire Ancienne*, 13, 71–113.

Annequin, J. (2005) 'L'autre corps du maître: les représentations oniriques dans l'Onirocriticon d'Artémidore de Daldis' in Anastasiadis and Doukellis (2005), 305–13.

Annequin, J. (2008) 'Les esclaves et les signes oniriques de la liberté: l'Onirocriticon d'Artémidore' in Gonzalès (2008), 89–93.

Annequin, J. and Garrido-Hory, M. (eds) (1994) *Religion et anthropologie de l'esclavage et des formes de dépendance*. Besançon.

Archer, L. J. (ed.) (1988) *Slavery and Other Forms of Unfree Labour*. London.

Arena, V. (2012) *Libertas and the Practice of Politics in the Late Roman Republic.* Cambridge.

Arnaoutoglou, I. N. (2003) *Thusias heneka kai sunousias: Private Religious Associations in Hellenistic Athens.* Athens.

Arnold, B. (1988) 'Slavery in late prehistoric Europe: recovering the evidence for social structure in Iron Age society' in D. B. Gibson and M. N. Geselowitz (eds), *Tribe and Polity in Late Prehistoric Europe,* Boston, 179–92.

Arnoux, M. (2012) *Le temps des laboureurs: Travail, ordre social et croissance en Europe (XIe–XIVe siècle).* Paris.

Aubert, J.-J. (1994) *Business Managers in Ancient Rome: A Social and Economic Study of Institores, 200 BC–AD 250.* Leiden.

Aubert, J.-J. (2002) 'A double standard in Roman criminal law? The death penalty and social structure in late republican and early imperial Rome' in J.-J. Aubert and B. Sirks (eds), *Speculum Iuris: Roman Law as a Reflection of Social and Economic Life in Antiquity,* Ann Arbor, MI, 94–133.

Aubert, J.-J. (2009) 'Productive investments in agriculture: instrumentum fundi and peculium in the later Roman Republic' in J. Carlsen and E. Lo Cascio (eds), *Agricoltura e scambi nell'Italia tardo-repubblicana,* Bari, 167–85.

Aubert, J.-J. (2013) 'Dumtaxat de peculio: what's in a peculium, or establishing the extent of the principal's liability' in Du Plessis (2013b), 192–206.

Ausbüttel, F. M. (1982) *Untersuchungen zu den Vereinen im Westen des römischen Reiches.* Kallmünz.

Avram, A. (2007) 'Some thoughts about the Black Sea and the slave trade before the Roman domination (6th–1st centuries BC)' in V. Gabrielsen and J. Lund (eds), *The Black Sea in Antiquity: Regional and Interregional Economic Exchanges,* Aarhus, 239–51.

Azoulay, V. and Ismard, P. (2018) 'Honneurs et déshonneurs. Autour des statuts juridiques dans l'Athènes classique' in Moatti and Müller (2018), 213–42.

Baba, M. (1990) 'Slave-owning slaves and the structure of slavery in the early Roman Empire', *Kodai,* 1, 24–35.

Bäbler, B. (1998) *Fleißige Thrakerinnen und wehrhafte Skythen. Nichtgriechen im klassischen Athen und ihre archäologische Hinterlassenschaft.* Stuttgart and Leipzig.

Bäbler, B. (2005) 'Bobbies or boobies? The Scythian police force in Classical Athens' in D. Braund (ed.), *Scythians and Greeks: Cultural Interactions in Scythia, Athens and the Early Roman Empire, Sixth Century BC–First Century AD,* Exeter, 114–22.

Bagnall, R. S. (2011) 'Documenting slavery in Hellenistic and Roman Egypt' in R. S. Bagnall, *Everyday Writing in the Graeco-Roman East,* Berkeley, Los Angeles and London, 54–74.

Bak, J. M. (1980) 'Serfs and serfdom: words and things', *Review,* 4, 3–18.

Baker, H. D. (2017) 'Slavery and personhood in the Neo-Assyrian Empire' in Bodel and Scheidel (2017), 15–30.

Bakir, A. E. M. (1952) *Slavery in Pharaonic Egypt.* Cairo.

Balch, D. L. and Osiek, C. (eds) (2003) *Early Christian Families in Context: An Interdisciplinary Dialogue.* Grand Rapids, MI and Cambridge.

Banaji, J. (2016) *Exploring the Economy of Late Antiquity: Selected Essays.* Cambridge.

Bang, P. F. (2008) *The Roman Bazaar: A Comparative Study of Trade and Markets in a Tributary Empire.* Cambridge.

Baralis, A. (2015) 'Le statut de la main-d'œuvre à Héraclée du Pont et en Mer Noire' in Zurbach (2015), 197–234.

Barcia, M. (2008) *Seeds of Insurrection: Domination and Resistance on Western Cuban Plantations, 1808–1848.* Baton Rouge.

Barcia M. (2012) *The Great African Slave Revolt of 1825: Cuba and the Fight for Freedom in Matanzas.* Baton Rouge.

Barickman, B. J. (1994) '"A bit of land, which they call roça": slave provision grounds in the Bahian Recôncavo, 1780–1860', *Hispanic American Historical Review,* 74, 649–87.

Barker, H. (2018) 'Christianities in conflict: the Black Sea as a Genoese slaving zone in the later Middle Ages' in Fynn-Paul and Pargas (2018), 50–69.

Barschdorf, J. (2012) *Freigelassene in der Spätantike*. Munich.

Barthélemy, D. (2009) *The Serf, the Knight and the Historian*. Ithaca.

Bartlett, R. (1993) *The Making of Europe: Conquest, Colonization and Cultural Change 950–1350*. London.

Bastide, R. (1978) *The African Religions of Brazil: Toward A Sociology of the Interpenetration of Civilizations*. Baltimore.

Bathrellou, E. (2014) 'Relationships among slaves in Menander' in A. H. Sommerstein (ed.), *Menander in Contexts*, New York, 56–73.

Bayram, S. and Çeçen, S. (1996) 'The institutions of slavery in ancient Anatolia in the light of new documents', *Belleten*, 229, 605–30.

Beckert, S. (2015) *Empire of Cotton: A Global History*. New York.

Beckert, S. and Rockman, S. (eds) (2016) *Slavery's Capitalism: A New History of American Economic Development*. Philadelphia.

Bell, S. and Ramsby, T. (eds) (2012) *Free at Last! The Impact of Freed Slaves on the Roman Empire*. London and New York.

Bellen, H. (1971) *Studien zur Sklavenflucht im römischen Kaiserreich*. Stuttgart.

Bellen, H. (1982) 'Antike Staatsräson. Die Hinrichtung der 400 Sklaven des römischen Stadtpräfekten L. Pedanius Secundus im Jahre 61 n. Chr.', *Gymnasium*, 89, 449–67.

Bellen, H. (2001) 'Vom halben zum ganzen Menschen. Der Übergang aus der Sklaverei in die Freiheit im Spiegel des antiken und frühchristlichen Freilassungsbrauchtums' in Bellen and Heinen (2001), 13–29.

Bellen, H. and Heinen, H. (eds) (2001) *Fünfzig Jahre Forschungen zur antiken Sklaverei an der Mainzer Akademie 1950–2000: Miscellanea zum Jubiläum*. Stuttgart.

Bellen, H. and Heinen, H. (2003) *Bibliographie zur antiken Sklaverei, I–II*. 2nd edition. Stuttgart.

Ben-Ur, A. (2018) 'Bound together? Reassessing the "slave community" and "resistance" paradigms', *Journal of Global Slavery*, 3, 195–210.

Bendlin, A. (2011) 'Associations, funerals, sociality, and Roman law: the collegium of Diana and Antinous in Lanuvium (CIL 14.2112) reconsidered' in M. Öhler (ed.), *Aposteldekret und antikes Vereinswesen: Gemeinschaft und ihre Ordnung*, Tubingen, 207–96.

Benelli, E. (2013) 'Slavery and manumission' in J. M. Turfa (ed.), *The Etruscan World*, New York, 447–56.

Benjamin, C. (2018) *Empires of Ancient Eurasia: The First Silk Roads Era, 100 BCE–250 CE*. Cambridge.

Benjamin, T. (2009) *The Atlantic World: Europeans, Africans, Indians and their Shared History, 1400–1900*. Cambridge.

Bergad, L. W. (2007) *The Comparative Histories of Slavery in Brazil, Cuba and the United States*. Cambridge.

Beringer, W. (1982) '"Servile status" in the sources for early Greek history', *Historia*, 31, 13–32.

Berlin, I. (1974) *Slaves Without Masters: The Free Negro in the Antebellum South*. Oxford.

Berlin, I. (1980) 'Time, space and the evolution of Afro-American society on British Mainland North America', *American Historical Review*, 85, 44–78.

Berlin, I. (1998) *Many Thousands Gone: The First Two Centuries of Slavery in North America*. Cambridge, MA.

Berlin, I. and Morgan, P. D. (eds) (1991) *The Slaves' Economy: Independent Production by Slaves in the Americas*. London.

Berlin, I. and Morgan, P. D. (eds) (1993) *Cultivation and Culture: Labor and the Shaping of Slave Life in the Americas*. Charlottesville, VA and London.

Bernard, S. (2016) 'Debt, land and labor in the early republican economy', *Phoenix*, 70, 317–38.

Bielman, A. (1994) *Retour à la liberté. Libération et sauvetage de prisonniers en Grèce ancienne: recueil d'inscriptions honorant des sauveteurs et analyse critique*. Athens.

Bielman, A. (1999) 'De la capture a la liberté: remarques sur le sort et le statut des prisonniers de guerre dans le monde grec classique' in Brun (1999), 179–99.

Bieżuńska-Małowist, I. (1965) 'Les esclavages payant l'apophora dans L'Egypte gréco-romaine', *Journal of Juristic Papyrology*, 15, 65–72.

Bieżuńska-Małowist, I. (1974) *L'esclavage dans l'Égypte gréco-romaine. Première partie: période ptolémaïque*. Wroclaw.

Bieżuńska-Małowist, I. (1977) *L'esclavage dans l'Égypte gréco-romaine. Seconde partie: période romaine*. Wroclaw.

Bieżuńska-Małowist, I. (ed.) (1986) *Schiavitù e produzione nella Roma repubblicana*. Rome.

Binsfeld, A. (2010) 'Archäologie und Sklaverei: Möglichkeiten und Perspektiven einer Bilddatenbank zur antiken Sklaverei' in Heinen (2010a), 161–77.

Binsfeld, A. and Ghetta, M. (eds) (2019) *Ubi servi erant? Die Ikonographie von Sklaven und Freigelassenen in der römischen Kunst*. Stuttgart.

Blackburn, R. (1998) *The Making of New World Slavery: From the Baroque to the Modern, 1492–1800*. London.

Blake, S. (2013) 'Now you see them: slaves and other objects as elements of the Roman master', *Helios*, 39, 193–211.

Blassingame, J. W. (1972) *The Slave Community: Plantation Life in the Antebellum South*. New York.

Blavatskaja, T. V., Golubcova, E. S. and Pavlovskaja, A. I. (1972) *Die Sklaverei in hellenistischen Staaten im 3.-1. Jh. v. Chr*. Wiesbaden.

Blickle, P. (2003) *Von der Leibeigenschaft zu den Menschenrechten: eine Geschichte der Freiheit in Deutschland*. Munich.

Bloch, M. (1947) 'Comment et pourquoi finit l'esclavage antique', *Annales*, 2, 30–44, 161–70.

Blumenthal, D. (2009) *Enemies and Familiars: Slavery and Mastery in Fifteenth-Century Valencia*. Ithaca and London.

Boatwright, M. T. (2015) 'Acceptance and approval: Romans' non-Roman population transfers, 180 BCE–ca 70 CE', *Phoenix*, 69, 122–46.

Bodel, J. (2005) 'Caveat emptor: towards a study of Roman slave-traders', *Journal of Roman Archaeology*, 18, 181–95.

Bodel, J. (2008) 'From Columbaria to catacombs: collective burial in pagan and Christian Rome' in L. Brink and D. Green (eds), *Commemorating the Dead: Texts and Artifacts in Context: Studies of Roman, Jewish and Christian Burials*, Berlin, 177–242.

Bodel, J. (2017) 'Death and social death in ancient Rome' in Bodel and Scheidel (2017), 81–108.

Bodel, J. (2019) 'Ancient slavery and modern ideologies: Orlando Patterson and M. I. Finley among the dons', *Theory & Society*, 48, 823–33.

Bodel, J. and Scheidel, W. (eds) (2017) *On Human Bondage: After Slavery and Social Death*. Chichester.

Bois, G. (1992) *The Transformation of the Year One Thousand: The Village of Lournand from Antiquity to Feudalism*. Manchester.

Bömer, F. (1981) *Untersuchungen über die Religion der Sklaven in Griechenland und Rom. 1: Die wichtigsten Kulte und Religionen in Rom und im lateinischen Westen*. 2nd edition. Wiesbaden.

Bömer, F. (1990) *Untersuchungen über die Religion der Sklaven in Griechenland und Rom. 3: Die wichtigsten Kulte der griechischen Welt*. 2nd edition. Wiesbaden.Bonnassie, P. (1991) *From Slavery to Feudalism in South-Western Europe*. Cambridge.

Booth, A. D. (1979) 'The schooling of slaves in first-century Rome', *Transactions of the American Philological Association*, 109, 11–19.

Borbonus, D. (2014) *Columbarium Tombs and Collective Identity in Augustan Rome*. New York.

Boulvert, G. (1974) *Domestique et fonctionnaire sous le Haut-Empire romain: la condition de l'affranchi et de l'esclave du prince*. Paris.

Bowersock, G. W. (2013) *The Throne of Adulis: Red Sea Wars on the Eve of Islam*. Oxford.

Bowman, S. D. (1993) *Masters and Lords: Mid-19th-Century US Planters and Prussian Junkers*. Oxford.

Boyce, B. (1991) *The Language of the Freedmen in Petronius' Cena Trimalchionis*. Leiden and New York.

Bradley, K. R. (1978) 'Slaves and the conspiracy of Catiline', *Classical Philology*, 73, 329–36.

Bradley, K. R. (1979) 'Holidays for slaves', *Symbolae Osloenses*, 54, 111–18.

Bradley, K. R. (1984) *Slaves and Masters in the Roman Empire: A Study in Social Control*. New York.

Bradley, K. R. (1987) 'On the Roman slave supply and slavebreeding' in Finley (1987), 42–64.

Bradley, K. R. (1989) *Slavery and Rebellion in the Roman World, 140 BC–70 BC*. Bloomington, IN.

Bradley, K. R. (1990) 'Servus onerosus: Roman law and the troublesome slave', *Slavery & Abolition*, 11, 135–58.

Bradley, K. R. (1994) *Slavery and Society at Rome*. Cambridge.

Bradley, K. R. (1997) 'The problem of slavery in classical culture', *Classical Philology*, 92, 273–82.

Bradley, K. R. (2000) 'Animalizing the slave: the truth of fiction', *Journal of Roman Studies*, 90, 110–25.

Bradley, K. R. (2004) 'On captives under the Principate', *Phoenix*, 58, 298–318.

Bradley, K. R. (2008) 'Seneca and slavery' in J. G. Fitch (ed.), *Seneca*, Oxford, 335–47.

Bradley, K. R. (2011) 'Slavery in the Roman Republic' in Bradley and Cartledge (2011), 241–64.

Bradley, K. R. (2015) 'The bitter chain of slavery', *Dialogues d'Histoire Ancienne*, 41, 149–76.

Bradley, K. R. and Cartledge, P. (eds) (2011) *The Cambridge World History of Slavery 1: The Ancient Mediterranean World*. Cambridge.

Braund, D. (2008) 'Royal Scythians and the slave trade in Herodotus' Scythia', *Antichthon*, 42, 1–19.

Braund, D. and Tsetskhladze, G. R. (1989) 'The export of slaves from Colchis', *Classical Quarterly*, 39, 114–25.

Bresson, A. (2014) 'Capitalism and the ancient Greek economy' in L. Neal and J. G. Williamson (eds) (2014), *The Cambridge History of Capitalism: Volume 1, The Rise of Capitalism: From Ancient Origins to 1848*, Cambridge, 43–74.

Bresson, A. (2016) *The Making of the Ancient Greek Economy: Institutions, Markets and Growth in the City-States*. Princeton and Oxford.

Briant, P. (1973) 'Remarques sur les "laoi" et esclaves ruraux en Asie Mineure hellénistique' in *Actes 1971*, 93–133.

Brock, R. (1994) 'The labour of women in classical Athens', *Classical Quarterly*, 44, 336–46.

Brock, R. (2007) 'Figurative slavery in Greek thought' in Serghidou (2007), 217–24.

Broodbank, C. (2013) *The Making of the Middle Sea: An Archaeological History of the Mediterranean from its Earliest Peopling until the Iron Age*. London.

Brooks, G. E. (1993) *Landlords and Strangers: Ecology, Society, and Trade in Western Africa, 1000–1630*. Boulder, San Francisco and Oxford.

Brooks, J. F. (2011) *Captives and Cousins: Slavery, Kinship, and Community in the Southwest Borderlands*. Chapel Hill, NC and London.

Brown, C. L. and Morgan, P. D. (eds) (2006) *Arming Slaves: From Classical Times to the Modern Age*. New Haven and London.

Brown, V. (2009) 'Social death and political life in the study of slavery', *American Historical Review*, 114, 1231–49.

Brown, V. (2020) *Tacky's Revolt: The Story of an Atlantic Slave War*. Cambridge, MA and London.

Browne, G. M. (1983–2001) *Sortes Astrampsychi, I–II*. Leipzig and Munich.

Brubaker, R. and Cooper, F. (2000) 'Beyond "identity"', *Theory & Society*, 29, 1–47.

Brulé, P. (1978) *La piraterie crétoise hellénistique*. Besançon.

Brun, J.-P. (2003) *Le vin et l'huile dans la Méditerranée antique: viticulture, oléiculture et procédés de transformation*. Paris.

Brun, P. (ed.) (1999) *Guerres et sociétés dans les mondes grecs*. Paris.

Brunt, P. A. (1975) 'Two great Roman landowners', *Latomus*, 34, 619–35.

Bruun, C. (2008) 'La familia publica di Ostia antica' in M. L. Caldelli, G. L. Gregori and S. Orlandi (eds), *Epigrafia 2006: atti della XIVe Rencontre sur l'epigraphie in onore di Silvio Panciera con altri contributi di colleghi, allievi e collaboratori*, Rome, 537–56.

Bruun, C. (2013) 'Greek or Latin? The owner's choice of names for *vernae* in Rome' in George (2013a), 19–43.

Bruun, C. (2014) 'Slaves and freed slaves' in C. Bruun and J. Edmondson (eds), *The Oxford Handbook of Roman Epigraphy*, Oxford, 605–26.

Bryce, T. (2018) *Warriors of Anatolia: A Concise History of the Hittites*. London and New York.

Buckland, W. W. (1908) *The Roman Law of Slavery: The Condition of the Slave in Private Law from Augustus to Justinian*. Cambridge.

Buonocore, M. (1984) *Schiavi e liberti dei Volusii Saturnini. Le iscrizioni del colombario sulla via Appia Antica*. Rome.

Burnard, T. (2015) *Planters, Merchants, and Slaves: Plantation Societies in British America, 1650–1820*. Chicago and London.

Bush, M. L. (ed.) (1992) *Social Orders and Social Classes in Europe since 1500: Studies in Social Stratification*. London and New York.

Bush, M. L. (ed.) (1996) *Serfdom and Slavery: Studies in Legal Bondage*. London and New York.

Bussi, S. (2001) *Economia e demografia della schiavitù in Asia minore ellenistico-romana*. Milan.

Bußmann, R. (2014) 'Krieg und Zwangsarbeit im pharaonischen Ägypten' in von Lingen and Gestwa (2014), 57–72.

Cabanes, P. (1974) 'Les inscriptions du théâtre de Bouthrôtos' in *Actes 1972*, 105–209.

Cairns, J. (2006) 'Slavery and the Roman law of evidence in eighteenth-century Scotland' in A. Burrows and Lord Rodger of Earlsferry (eds), *Mapping the Law: Essays in Memory of Peter Birks*, Oxford, 599–618.

Cairns, J. (2012) 'The definition of slavery in eighteenth-century thinking: not the true Roman slavery' in J. Allain (ed.), *The Legal Understanding of Slavery: From the Historical to the Contemporary*, Oxford, 61–84.

Caldelli, M. L. and Ricci, C. (1999) *Monumentum familiae Statiliorum: un riesame*. Rome.

Calhoun, C. (1991) 'Imagined communities and indirect relationships: large scale social integration and the transformation of everyday life' in P. Bourdieu and J. Coleman (eds), *Social Theory for a Changing Society*, Boulder, 95–120.

Calhoun, C. (1992) 'The infrastructure of modernity: indirect social relationships, information technology and social integration' in H. Haferkamp and N. Smelser (eds), *Social Change and Modernity*, Berkeley, 205–36.

Calhoun, C. J. (1997) *Nationalism*. Minneapolis.

Cambiano, G. (1984) 'La Grecia antica era molto popolata? Un dibattito nel XVIII secolo', *Quaderni di Storia*, 20, 3–42.

Cambiano, G. (1987) 'Aristotle and the anonymous opponents of slavery' in Finley (1987), 21–41.

Cameron, C. M. (2016) *Captives: How Stolen People Changed the World*. Lincoln, NE and London.

Campa, N. T. (2018) 'Positive freedom and the citizen in classical Athens', *Polis*, 35, 1–32.

Campbell, G. (ed.) (2004) *The Structure of Slavery in Indian Ocean Africa and Asia.* London.

Campbell, G., Miers, S. and Miller, J. (eds) (2009) *Children in Slavery through the Ages.* Athens, OH.

Campbell, G. and Stanziani, A. (eds) (2013) *Debt and Slavery in the Mediterranean and Atlantic Worlds.* London.

Canciani, F. and Neumann, G. (1978) 'Lydos, der Sklave?', *Antike Kunst,* 21, 17–20.

Canevaro, M. (2018) 'The public charge for hubris against slaves: the honour of the victim and the honour of the hubristēs', *Journal of Hellenic Studies,* 138, 100–26.

Capozza, M. (1966) *Movimenti servili nel mondo romano in età repubblicana. 1: Dal 501 al 184 a. Cr.* Rome.

Capozza, M. (ed.) (1979) *Schiavitù, manomissione e classi dipendenti nel mondo antico.* Rome.

Carandini, A. (1988) *Schiavi in Italia: gli strumenti pensanti dei Romani fra tarda Repubblica e medio Impero.* Rome.

Carandini, A. and Ricci, A. (1985) *Settefinestre. Una villa schiavistica nell' Etruria romana, I–III.* Modena.

Carlsen, J. (1995) *Vilici and Roman Estate Managers until AD 284.* Rome.

Carlsen, J. (2013) *Land and Labour: Studies in Roman Social and Economic History.* Rome.

Carrier, N. (2012) *Les usages de la servitude. Seigneurs et paysans dans le royaume de Bourgogne (VIe – XVe siècle).* Paris.

Carsten, J. (ed.) (2000) *Cultures of Relatedness: New Approaches to the Study of Kinship.* Cambridge.

Carsten, J. (2004) *After Kinship.* Cambridge.

Cartledge, P. (1985) 'Rebels and sambos in classical Greece: a comparative view' in P. Cartledge and F. D. Harvey (eds), *Crux: Essays in Greek History Presented to G. E. M. de Ste. Croix on his 75th Birthday,* London, 16–46.

Cartledge, P. (1988) 'Serfdom in classical Greece' in Archer (1988), 33–41.

Cartledge, P. (2011) 'The helots: a contemporary review' in Bradley and Cartledge (2011), 74–90.

Cartledge, P., Cohen, E. E. and Foxhall, L. (eds) (2002) *Money, Labour, and Land: Approaches to the Economies of Ancient Greece.* London.

Cataldi, S. (2000) 'Akolasia e isegoria di meteci e schiavi nell'Atene dello Pseudo-Senofonte: una riflessione socio-economica' in M. Sordi (ed.), *L'opposizione nel mondo antico,* Milan, 75–101.

Chaniotis, A. (2005) *War in the Hellenistic World: A Social and Cultural History.* Malden, MA and Oxford.

Chaniotis, A. (2009) 'Ritual performances of divine justice: the epigraphy of confession, atonement and exaltation in Roman Asia Minor' in Cotton et al. (2009), 115–53.

Chaniotis, A. (2018) 'Epigraphic evidence' in Hodkinson, Kleijwegt and Vlassopoulos (2016–), published online, DOI: 10.1093/oxfordhb/9780199575251.013.3.

Chantraine, H. (1967) *Freigelassene und Sklaven im Dienst der römischen Kaiser: Studien zu ihrer Nomenklatur.* Wiesbaden.

Cheyette, F. L. (2003) 'Some reflections on violence, reconciliation and the "feudal revolution"' in W. C. Brown and P. Gorecki (eds), *Conflict in Medieval Europe: Changing Perspectives on Society and Culture,* Aldershot, 243–64.

Chioffi, L. (2010) 'Congressus in venalicio: spazi urbani e mercato degli schiavi a Capua e a Roma', *Mélanges de l'École française de Rome-Antiquité,* 122, 503–24.

Chirichigno, G. (1993) *Debt-Slavery in Israel and the Ancient Near East.* Sheffield.

Christes, J. (1979) *Sklaven und Freigelassene als Grammatiker und Philologen im antiken Rom.* Stuttgart.

Ciccotti, E. (1899) *Il tramonto della schiavitù nel mondo antico.* Turin.

Clastres, P. (1987) *Society against the State: Essays in Political Anthropology.* New York.

Clegg, J. J. (2015) 'Capitalism and slavery', *Critical Historical Studies*, 2, 281–304.

Coarelli, F. (1982) 'L' "Agora des Italiens" a Delo: il mercato degli schiavi?' in F. Coarelli, D. Musti and H. Solin (eds), *Delo e l'Italia: Raccolta di studi*, Rome, 119–45.

Coarelli, F. (2005) 'L' "Agora des Italiens": lo statarion di Delo?', *Journal of Roman Archaeology*, 18, 196–212.

Cohen, D. (1989) 'Seclusion, separation and the status of women in classical Athens', *Greece & Rome*, 36, 3–15.

Cohen, E. E. (2000) *The Athenian Nation*. Princeton.

Cohen, E. E. (2013) 'Sexual abuse and sexual rights: slaves' erotic experience at Athens and Rome' in T. K. Hubbard (ed.), *A Companion to Greek and Roman Sexualities*, Chichester, 184–98.

Cohen, E. E. (2015) *Athenian Prostitution: The Business of Sex*. New York.

Cohen, E. E. (2018) 'Slaves operating businesses: legal ramifications for ancient Athens – and for modern scholarship' in P. Perlman (ed.), *Ancient Greek Law in the 21ˢᵗ Century*, Austin, TX, 54–69.

Condominas, G. (ed.) (1998) *Formes extrêmes de dépendance: contributions à l'étude de l'esclavage en Asie du Sud-est*. Paris.

Connolly, S. (2004–5) '"Quasi libera, quasi ancilla": Diogenia and the everyday experience of slaves', *American Journal of Ancient History*, n.s., 3, 171–88.

Connolly, S. (2006) 'Roman ransomers', *Ancient History Bulletin*, 20, 115–31.

Connolly, S. (2010) *Lives behind the Laws: The World of the Codex Hermogenianus*. Bloomington, IN.

Cook, R. M. (1948) 'Ἄμασις μεποιεσεν', *Journal of Hellenic Studies*, 68, 148.

Cooley, C. H. (1962) [1909] *Social Organization*. New York.

Corcoran, S. (2011) 'Softly and suddenly vanished away: the Junian Latins from Caracalla to the Carolingians' in K. Muscheler (ed.), *Römische Jurisprudenz – Dogmatik, Überlieferung, Rezeption: Festschrift für Detlef Liebs zum 75. Geburtstag*, Berlin, 129–52.

Cornell, T. (1993) 'The end of Roman imperial expansion' in J. Rich and G. Shipley (eds), *War and Society in the Roman World*, London and New York, 139–70.

Coşkun, A. (2016) 'The Latins and their legal status in the context of the cultural and political integration of pre- and early Roman Italy', *Klio*, 98, 526–69.

Cotton, H. M., Hoyland, R. G., Price, J. J. and Wasserstein, D. J. (eds) (2009) *From Hellenism to Islam: Cultural and Linguistic Change in the Roman Near East*. Cambridge.

Courrier, C. and Magalhães de Oliveira, J. C. (eds) (forthcoming) *Ancient History from Below: Subaltern Studies in Context*. London and New York.

Couvenhes, J. C. (2012) 'L'introduction des archers scythes, esclaves publics, à Athènes: la date et l'agent d'un transfert culturel' in Legras (2012), 99–119.

Crawford, M. H. (2010) 'From Alcibiades to Diocletian: slavery and the economy in the *longue durée*' in Roth (2010a), 61–73.

Crone, P. (1980) *Slaves on Horses: The Evolution of the Islamic Polity*. Cambridge.

Crossley, P. K. (2011) 'Slavery in early modern China' in Eltis and Engerman (2011), 186–213.

Crowther, N. B. (1992) 'Slaves and Greek athletics', *Quaderni Urbinati di Cultura Classica*, 40, 35–42.

Crowther, N. B. and Frass, M. (1998) 'Flogging as a punishment in the ancient games', *Nikephoros*, 11, 51–82.

Cruz-Uribe, E. (1982) 'Slavery in Egypt during the Saite and Persian periods', *Revue Internationale des Droits de l'Antiquité*, 29, 47–71.

Culbertson, L. (ed.) (2011) *Slaves and Households in the Near East*. Chicago and London.

Cunliffe, B. W. (2001) *Facing the Ocean: The Atlantic and its Peoples, 8000 BC–AD 1500*. New York.

Cunliffe, B. W. (2008) *Europe between the Oceans: 9000 BC–AD 1000*. New Haven.

Cunliffe, B. W. (2015) *By Steppe, Desert, and Ocean: The Birth of Eurasia*. New York.

Curchin, L. A. (2017) 'Slaves in Lusitania: identity, demography and social relations', *Conimbriga*, 56, 75–108.

Cursi, M. F. (2001) 'Captivitas e capitis deminutio. La posizione del servus hostium tra ius civile e ius gentium' in *Iuris vincula: Studi in onore di Mario Talamanca*, II, Naples, 295–340.

Curtin, P. D. (1998) *The Rise and Fall of the Plantation Complex: Essays in Atlantic History*. Cambridge.

Curto, J. C. and Lovejoy, P. E. (eds) (2004) *Enslaving Connections: Changing Cultures of Africa and Brazil during the Era of Slavery*. Amherst, NY.

Curto, J. C. and Soulodre-LaFrance, R. (eds) (2005) *Africa and the Americas: Interconnections during the Slave Trade*. Trenton.

Czajkowski, K. and Eckhardt, B. (2018) 'Law, status and agency in the Roman provinces', *Past & Present*, 241, 3–31.

D'Ambra, E. and Métraux, G. P. (eds) (2006) *The Art of Citizens, Soldiers and Freedmen in the Roman World*. Oxford.

D'Arms, J. H. (1991) 'Slaves at Roman convivia' in W. Slater (ed.), *Dining in a Classical Context*, Ann Arbor, 171–83.

Da Costa e Silva, A. (2000) 'Portraits of African royalty in Brazil' in Lovejoy (2000), 129–36.

Dal Lago, E. (2005) *Agrarian Elites: American Slaveholders and Southern Italian Landowners, 1815–1861*. Baton Rouge.

Dal Lago, E. and Katsari, C. (eds) (2008a) *Slave Systems Ancient and Modern*. Cambridge.

Dal Lago, E. and Katsari, C. (2008b) 'The study of ancient and modern slave systems: setting an agenda for comparison' in Dal Lago and Katsari (2008a), 1–31.

Dal Lago, E. and Katsari, C. (2008c) 'Ideal models of slave management in the Roman world and in the ante-bellum American South' in Dal Lago and Katsari (2008a), 187–213.

Dalby, A. (2000) *Empire of Pleasures: Luxury and Indulgence in the Roman World*. London.

Daloz, J.-P. (2009) *The Sociology of Elite Distinction: From Theoretical to Comparative Perspectives*. Basingstoke.

Dandamaev, M. (1984) *Slavery in Babylonia: From Nabopolassar to Alexander the Great (626–331 BC)*. DeKalb, IL.

Dantas, M. (2008) *Black Townsmen: Urban Slavery and Freedom in the Eighteenth-Century Americas*. New York.

Daoust, A. B. (2019) 'Philonicus Demetriusque: craft specialization in the funerary relief of two freedmen', *Mouseion*, 16, 227–48.

Darmezin, L. (1999) *Les affranchissements par consécration en Béotie et dans le monde grec hellénistique*. Paris.

Dasen, V. and Späth, T. (eds) (2010) *Children, Memory and Family Identity in Roman Culture*. Oxford.

Daube, D. (1946) 'Two early patterns of manumission', *Journal of Roman Studies*, 36, 57–75.

Daubner, F. (2006) *Bellum Asiaticum. Der Krieg der Römer gegen Aristonikos von Pergamon und die Einrichtung der Provinz Asia*. 2nd edition. Munich.

Daverio Rocchi, G. (1975) 'Considerazioni a proposito della schiavitù come pena nell'Atene del V e IV secolo', *Acme: Annali della Facoltà di lettere e filosofia dell'Università degli studi di Milano*, 28, 257–79.

Davidson, J. (2001) 'Dover, Foucault and Greek homosexuality: penetration and the truth of sex', *Past & Present*, 170, 3–51.

Davidson, J. (2007) *The Greeks and Greek Love: A Radical Reappraisal of Homosexuality in Ancient Greece*. London.

Davies, P. A. (2017) 'Articulating status in ancient Greece: status (in)consistency as a new approach', *Cambridge Classical Journal*, 63, 29–52.

Davies, W. (1996) 'On servile status in the early Middle Ages' in Bush (1996), 225–46.

de Carvalho Soares, M. (2011) *People of Faith: Slavery and African Catholics in Eighteenth-Century Rio de Janeiro*. Durham, NC and London.

de Churruca, J. (1982) 'L'anathème du Concile de Gangres contre ceux qui sous prétexte de christianisme incitent les esclaves à quitter leurs maîtres', *Revue historique de droit français et étranger*, 60, 261–78.

de la Fuente, A. (2004) 'Slave law and claims-making in Cuba: the Tannenbaum debate revisited', *Law & History Review*, 22:2, 339–69.

de la Fuente, A. (2007) 'Slaves and the creation of legal rights in Cuba: coartación and papel', *Hispanic American Historical Review*, 87, 659–92.

de la Fuente, A. and Gross, A. J. (2020) *Becoming Free, Becoming Black: Race, Freedom, and Law in Cuba, Virginia, and Louisiana*. Cambridge.

de Ligt, L. (2004) 'Poverty and demography: the case of the Gracchan land reforms', *Mnemosyne*, 57, 725–57.

de Mello, M. (2002) *Reis negros no Brasil escravista: história da festa de coroação de Rei Congo*. Belo Horizonte.

de Souza, P. (2011) 'War, slavery and empire in Roman imperial iconography', *Bulletin of the Institute of Classical Studies*, 54, 31–62.

de Ste. Croix, G. E. M. (1981) *The Class Struggle in the Ancient Greek World*. London.

de Ste. Croix, G. E. M. (1988) 'Slavery and other forms of unfree labour' in Archer (1988), 19–32.

De Vito, C. G. and Lichtenstein, A. (eds) (2015) *Global Convict Labour*. Leiden and Boston.

de Wet, C. L. (2015) *Preaching Bondage: John Chrysostom and the Discourse of Slavery in Early Christianity*. Auckland, CA.

de Wet, C. L. (2018) *The Unbound God: Slavery and the Formation of Early Christian Thought*. London and New York.

de Zwart, P. and van Zanden, J. L. (2018) *The Origins of Globalization: World Trade in the Making of the Global Economy, 1500–1800*. Cambridge.

Degler, C. N. (1971) *Neither Black nor White: Slavery and Race Relations in Brazil and the United States*. Madison, WI.

Deissler, J. (2000) *Antike Sklaverei und Deutsche Aufklärung im Spiegel von Johann Friedrich Reitemeiers 'Geschichte und Zustand der Sklaverey und Leibeigenschaft in Griechenland' 1789*. Stuttgart.

Deissler, J. (2001) 'Friedrich Nietzsche und die antike Sklaverei' in Bellen and Heinen (2001), 457–84.

Deissler, J. (2007) 'Sklaven in der römischen Buchproduktion' in S. Günther, K. Ruffing and O. Stoll (eds), *Pragmata: Beiträge zur Wirtschaftsgeschichte der Antike im Gedenken an Harald Winkel*, Wiesbaden, 1–15.

Deissler, J. (2010) 'Cold case? Die Finley-Vogt-Kontroverse aus deutscher Sicht' in Heinen (2010a), 77–93.

Dell, H. J. (1967) 'The origin and nature of Illyrian piracy', *Historia*, 16, 344–58.

Derlien, J. (2003) *Asyl: die religiöse und rechtliche Begründung der Flucht zu sakralen Orten in der griechisch-römischen Antike*. Marburg.

Desbiens, J. (2017) *Les esclaves dans les lamelles de Dodone*. PhD dissertation, University of Montreal.

Descat, R. (2006) 'Argyrōnetos: les transformations de l'échange dans la Grèce archaïque' in P. G. van Alfen (ed.), *Agoranomia: Studies in Money and Exchange Presented to John H. Kroll*, New York, 21–36.

Descat, R. (2015) 'Autour de la naissance de la société esclavagiste en Grèce archaïque' in Zurbach (2015), 235–42.

Di Nardo, A. and Lucchetta, G. A. (eds) (2012) *Nuove e antiche schiavitù*. Naples.

Dickey, E. (2002) *Latin Forms of Address: from Plautus to Apuleius*. Oxford.

Dixon, S. (2004) 'Exemplary housewife or luxurious slut? Cultural representations of women in the Roman economy' in F. McHardy and E. Marshall (eds), *Women's Influence on Classical Civilization*, New York and London, 56–75.

Domingues, J. M. (1995) *Sociological Theory and Collective Subjectivity*. London.

Donald, L. (1997) *Aboriginal Slavery on the Northwest Coast of North America*. Berkeley, Los Angeles and London.

Donaldson, A. E. (2012) *Peasant and Slave Rebellion in the Roman Republic*. PhD dissertation, University of Arizona.

Donderer, M. and Spiliopoulou-Donderer, I. (1993) 'Spätrepublikanische und kaiserzeitliche Grabmonumente von Sklavenhändlern', *Gymnasium*, 100, 254–66.

Dondin-Payre, M. and Tran, N. (eds) (2012) *Collegia: Le phénomène associatif dans l'Occident romain*. Bordeaux.

Dondin-Payre, M. and Tran, N. (eds) (2017) *Esclaves et maîtres dans le monde romain: expressions épigraphiques de leurs relations*. Rome.

Dossey, L. (2010) *Peasant and Empire in Christian North Africa*. Berkeley and Los Angeles.

Dover, K. J. (1988) 'The freedom of the intellectual in Greek society' in K. J. Dover, *The Greeks and their Legacy: Collected Papers*, volume II, Oxford, 135–58.

Drescher, S. and Emmer, P. C. (eds) (2010) *Who Abolished Slavery? Slave Revolts and Abolitionism*. New York.

Dromard, B. (2017) *Esclaves, dépendants, déportés: les frontières de l'esclavage en Babylonie au premier millénaire avant J.-C.* PhD dissertation, Université Paris I, Panthéon-Sorbonne.

Du Plessis, P. J. (2012) *Letting and Hiring in Roman Legal Thought: 27 BCE–284 CE*. Leiden and Boston.

Du Plessis, P. J. (2013a) 'Damaging a slave' in A. Burrows, D. Johnston and R. Zimmermann (eds), *Judge and Jurist: Essays in Memory of Lord Rodger of Earlsferry*, Oxford, 157–65.

Du Plessis, P. J. (ed.) (2013b) *New Frontiers: Law and Society in the Roman World*. Edinburgh.

duBois, P. (2003) *Slaves and Other Objects*. Chicago and London.

Duby, G. (1971) *La société aux XI et XII siècles dans la région mâconnaise*. 2nd edition. Paris.

Duby, G. (1982) *The Three Orders: Feudal Society Imagined*. Chicago and London.

Ducat, J. (1987) 'Cléomène III et les Hilotes', *Ktema*, 12, 43–52.

Ducat, J. (1990) *Les Hilotes*. Paris.

Ducat, J. (1993) 'L'esclavage collectif en Illyrie. À la recherche d'un hilotisme barbare' in P. Cabanes (ed.), *L'Illyrie méridionale et l'Épire dans l'antiquité*, Paris, 211–17.

Ducat, J. (1994) *Les pénestes de Thessalie*. Besançon.

Ducat, J. (2015) 'Les Hilotes à l'époque archaïque' in Zurbach (2015), 165–95.

Duchêne, H. (1986) 'Sur la stèle d'Aulus Caprilius Timotheos, sômatemporos', *Bulletin de Correspondance Hellénique*, 110, 513–30.

Ducrey, P. (1968) *Le traitement des prisonniers de guerre dans la Grèce antique, des origines à la conquête romaine*. Paris.

Ducrey, P. (1999) 'Prisonniers de guerre en Grèce antique 1968–1999' in Brun (1999), 9–23.

Dumont, J. C. (1987) *Servus: Rome et l'esclavage sous la République*. Rome.

Duncan, A. (2006) *Performance and Identity in the Classical World*. Cambridge.

Duncan-Jones, R. (2016) *Power and Privilege in Roman Society*. Cambridge.

Dušek, J. (2007) *Les Manuscrits araméens du Wadi Daliyeh et la Samarie vers 450–332 av. J.-C.* Leiden.

Ebrey, P. B. and Watson, J. L. (eds) (1986) *Kinship Organization in Late Imperial China, 1000–1940*. Berkeley, Los Angeles and London.

Eck, W. (2013) 'Sklaven und Freigelassene von Römern in Iudaea und den angrenzenden Provinzen', *Novum Testamentum*, 55, 1–21.

Eck, W. and Heinrichs, J. (1993) *Sklaven und Freigelassene in der Gesellschaft der römischen Kaiserzeit*. Darmstadt.

Eder, W. (1980) *Servitus publica: Untersuchungen zur Entstehung, Entwicklung und Funktion der öffentlichen Sklaverei in Rom*. Stuttgart.

Edmondson, J. (2011) 'Slavery and the Roman family' in Bradley and Cartledge (2011), 337–61.

Egerton, D. R. (2006) 'Slaves to the marketplace: economic liberty and black rebelliousness in the Atlantic world', *Journal of the Early Republic*, 26, 617–39.

Eidinow, E. (2007) *Oracles, Curses and Risk among the Ancient Greeks*. Oxford.

Eidinow, E. (2012) '"What will happen to me if I leave?" Ancient Greek oracles, slaves and slave owners' in Hodkinson and Geary (2012), 244–78.

Eidinow, E. and Taylor, C. (2010) 'Lead-letter days: writing, communication and crisis in the ancient Greek world', *Classical Quarterly*, 60, 30–62.

Elayi, J. (1981) 'La révolte des esclaves de Tyr relatée par Justin', *Baghdader Mitteilungen*, 12, 139–50.

Elkins, S. M. (1959) *Slavery: A Problem in American Institutional and Intellectual Life*. Chicago.

Eltis, D. (2000) *The Rise of African Slavery in the Americas*. Cambridge.

Eltis, D. and Engerman, S. L. (eds) (2011) *The Cambridge World History of Slavery 3: AD 1420–AD 1804*. Cambridge.

Evans-Grubbs, J. (1993) '"Marriage more shameful than adultery": slave-mistress relationships, "mixed marriages" and late Roman law', *Phoenix*, 47, 125–54.

Evans-Grubbs, J. (1995) *Law and Family in Late Antiquity: The Emperor Constantine's Marriage Legislation*. Oxford.

Evans-Grubbs, J. (2000) 'The slave who avenged her master's death: Codex Justinianus 1.19.1 and 7.13.1', *Ancient History Bulletin*, 14, 81–8.

Evans-Grubbs, J. (2010) 'Hidden in plain sight: *expositi* in the community' in Dasen and Späth (2010), 293–310.

Evans-Grubbs, J. (2013) 'Between slavery and freedom: disputes over status and the Codex Justinianus', *Roman Legal Tradition*, 9, 31–93.

Faist, B. (2009) 'An Elamite deportee' in G. Galil, M. J. Geller and A. Millard (eds), *Homeland and Exile: Biblical and Ancient Near Eastern Studies in Honour of Bustenay Oded*, Leiden, 59–69.

Fales, F. M. (2009–10) 'On Assyrian "lower stratum" families', *State Archives of Assyria Bulletin*, 18, 163–86.

Falola, T. and Childs, M. D. (eds) (2005) *The Yoruba Diaspora in the Atlantic World*. Bloomington and Indianapolis.

Faraguna, M. (2014) 'Citizens, non-citizens, and slaves: identification methods in classical Greece' in M. Depauw and S. Coussement (eds), *Identifiers and Identification Methods in the Ancient World*, Leuven, Paris and Walpole, MA, 165–83.

Fenoaltea, S. (1984) 'Slavery and supervision in comparative perspective: a model', *Journal of Economic History*, 44, 635–68.

Fentress, E. (2005) 'On the block: *catastae, chalcidica* and *cryptae* in early imperial Italy', *Journal of Roman Archaeology*, 18, 220–34.

Fentress, E. (2011) 'Slavers on chariots' in A. Dowler and E. R. Galvin (eds), *Money, Trade and Trade Routes in Pre-Islamic North Africa*, London, 65–71.

Fentress, E. (2019) 'The Domitii Ahenobarbi and tribal slaving in Gaul' in M. Modolo et al. (eds), *Una lezione di archeologia globale: Studi in onore di Daniele Manacorda*, Bari, 149–55.

Fentress, E., Goodson, C. and Maiuro, M. (eds) (2016) *Villa Magna: An Imperial Estate and its Legacies*. London.

Fentress, E. and Maiuro, M. (2011) 'Villa Magna near Anagni: the emperor, his winery and the wine of Signia', *Journal of Roman Archaeology*, 24, 333–69.

Ferreira, R. A. (2012) *Cross-Cultural Exchange in the Atlantic World: Angola and Brazil during the Era of the Slave Trade*. Cambridge.

Fikhman, I. F. (1973) 'Sklaven und Sklavenarbeit im spätrömischen Oxyrhynchos', *Jahrbuch für Wirtschaftsgeschichte*, 2, 149–206.

Finkenauer, T. (ed.) (2006) *Sklaverei und Freilassung im römischen Recht: Symposium für Hans Josef Wieling zum 70. Geburtstag*. Berlin and Heidelberg.

Finley, M. I. (1959) 'Was Greek civilisation based on slave labour?', *Historia*, 8, 145–64.

Finley, M. I. (ed.) (1960a) *Slavery in Classical Antiquity: Views and Controversies*. Cambridge.

Finley, M. I. (1960b) 'The servile statuses of ancient Greece', *Revue Internationale des Droits de l'Antiquité*, 7, 165–89.

Finley, M. I. (1962) 'The slave trade in antiquity: the Black Sea and Danubian regions', *Klio*, 40, 51–9.

Finley, M. I. (1964) 'Between slavery and freedom', *Comparative Studies in Society and History*, 6, 233–49.

Finley, M. I. (1965a) 'La servitude pour dettes', *Revue historique de droit français et étranger*, 43, 159–84.

Finley, M. I. (1965b) 'Technical innovation and economic progress in the ancient world', *Economic History Review*, 18, 29–45.

Finley, M. I. (1968) 'Slavery', *International Encyclopaedia of the Social Sciences*, XIV, 307–13.

Finley, M. I. (1973) *The Ancient Economy*. London.

Finley, M. I. (1979a) 'Slavery and the historians', *Histoire sociale*, 12, 247–61.

Finley, M. I. (ed.) (1979b) *The Bücher-Meyer Controversy*. New York.

Finley, M. I. (1980) *Ancient Slavery and Modern Ideology*. London.

Finley, M. I. (1981) *Economy and Society in Ancient Greece*. London.

Finley, M. I. (1983) *Politics in the Ancient World*. Cambridge.

Finley, M. I. (ed.) (1987) *Classical Slavery*. London.

Finley, M. I. (1998) *Ancient Slavery and Modern Ideology*. Expanded edition. Princeton.

Fischer, J. (2010) 'Unfreiheit und Sexualität im klassischen Athen' in J. Fischer and M. Ulz (eds), *Unfreiheit und Sexualität von der Antike bis zur Gengenwart*, Hildesheim, Zurich and New York, 58–82.

Fischer, J. (2016) 'Der Schwarzmeerraum und der antike Sklavenhandel. Bemerkungen zu einigen ausgewählten Quellen' in M. Frass, H. Graßl and G. Nightingale (eds), *Akten des 15. Österreichischen Althistorikertages*, Salzburg, 53–71.

Fischer, J. (2017) 'Sklaverei und Religion im klassischen Griechenland' in J. Fischer (ed.), *Studien zu antiken Religionsgeschichte*, Cracow, 67–107.

Fisher, N. (1993) *Slavery in Classical Greece*. London.

Fisher, N. (1995) 'Hybris, status and slavery' in Powell (1995), 58–98.

Fisher, N. (2008) 'Independent slaves in Athens and the ideology of slavery' in Katsari and Dal Lago (2008), 121–46.

Fisher Drew, K. (1973) *The Lombard Laws*. Philadelphia.

Fitzgerald, W. (2000) *Slavery and the Roman Literary Imagination*. Cambridge.

Flambard, J. M. (1977) 'Clodius, les collèges, la plèbe et les esclaves. Recherches sur la politique populaire au milieu du Ier siècle', *Mélanges de l'École française de Rome-Antiquité*, 89, 115–56.

Fleming, R. (1999) 'Quae corpore quaestum facit: the sexual economy of female prostitution in the Roman Empire', *Journal of Roman Studies*, 89, 38–61.

Flesher, P. V. M. (1988) *Oxen, Women or Citizens: Slaves in the System of the Mishnah*. Atlanta, GA.

Flory, M. B. (1978) 'Family in "familia": kinship and community in slavery', *American Journal of Ancient History*, 3, 78–95.

Fogel, R. W. and Engerman, S. L. (1974) *Time on the Cross: The Economics of American Negro Slavery, I–II*. New York.

Forbes, C. A. (1955) 'The education and training of slaves in antiquity', *Transactions and Proceedings of the American Philological Association*, 86, 321–60.

Forsdyke, S. (2012) *Slaves Tell Tales and Other Episodes in the Politics of Popular Culture in Ancient Greece*. Princeton.

Forsdyke, S. (2019) 'Slave agency and citizenship in classical Athens' in G. Thür, U. Yiftach and R. Zelnick-Abramovitz (eds), *Symposion 2017: Vorträge zur griechischen und hellenistischen Rechtsgeschichte*, Vienna, 345–66.

Fountoulakis, A. (2007) 'Punishing the lecherous slave: desire and power in Herondas 5' in Serghidou (2007), 251–64.

Foxhall, L. (1998) 'Cargoes of the heart's desire: the character of trade in the archaic Mediterranean world' in N. Fisher and H. van Wees (eds), *Archaic Greece: New Approaches and New Evidence*, Cardiff, 295–309.

Foxhall, L. (2005) 'Village to city: staples and luxuries? Exchange networks and urbanization' in R. Osborne and B. Cunliffe (eds), *Mediterranean Urbanization, 800–600 BCE*, Oxford, 233–48.

Freamon, B. K. (2019) *Possessed by the Right Hand: The Problem of Slavery in Islamic Law and Muslim Cultures*. Leiden and Boston.

Freedman, P. (1999) *Images of the Medieval Peasant*. Stanford.

Freedman, P. and Bourin, M. (eds) (2005) *Forms of Servitude in Northern and Central Europe: Decline, Resistance, and Expansion*. Turnhout.

Freire, G. (1945) *Brazil: An Interpretation*. New York.

Friedl, C. (2000) *Polygynie in Mesopotamien und Israel: sozialgeschichtliche Analyse polygamer Beziehungen anhand rechtlicher Texte aus dem 2. und 1. Jahrtausend v. Chr.* Munster.

Fröhlich, P. and Hamon, P. (eds) (2013) *Groupes et associations dans les cités grecques (IIIe siècle av. JC.–IIe siècle apr. JC.)*. Geneva.

Fromont, C. (2013) 'Dancing for the king of Congo from early modern Central Africa to slavery-era Brazil', *Colonial Latin American Review*, 22, 184–208.

Fuhrmann, C. J. (2012) *Policing the Roman Empire: Soldiers, Administration and Public Order*. New York.

Fynn-Paul, J. (2009) 'Empire, monotheism and slavery in the greater Mediterranean region from antiquity to the early modern era', *Past & Present*, 205, 3–40.

Fynn-Paul, J. and Pargas, D. (eds) (2018) *Slaving Zones: Cultural Identities, Ideologies and Institutions in the Evolution of Global Slavery*. Leiden.

Gabrielsen, V. (2001) 'Economic activity, maritime trade and piracy in the Hellenistic Aegean', *Revue des Études Anciennes*, 103, 219–40.

Gabrielsen, V. (2003) 'Piracy and the slave-trade' in A. Erskine (ed.), *A Companion to the Hellenistic World*, Oxford, 389–404.

Gabrielsen, V. (2007) 'Brotherhoods of faith and provident planning: the non-public associations of the Greek world', *Mediterranean Historical Review*, 22, 183–210.

Gabrielsen, V. (2013) 'Warfare, statehood and piracy in the Greek world' in N. Jaspert and S. Colditz (eds), *Seeraub im Mittelmeerraum*, Paderborn, 131–53.

Gabrielsen, V. and Thomsen, C. A. (eds) (2015) *Private Associations and the Public Sphere*. Copenhagen.

Gaca, K. L. (2010) 'The andrapodizing of war captives in Greek historical memory', *Transactions of the American Philological Association*, 140, 117–61.

Gaddis, J. L. (2002) *The Landscape of History: How Historians Map the Past*. New York.

Gagarin, M. (2010) 'Serfs and slaves at Gortyn', *Zeitschrift der Savigny-Stiftung für Rechtsgeschichte: Romanistische Abteilung*, 127, 14–31.

Gagarin, M. and Perlman, P. (2016) *The Laws of Ancient Crete, c. 650–400 BCE*. Oxford.

Galil, G. (2007) *The Lower Stratum Families in the Neo-Assyrian Period*. Leiden and Boston, MA.

Gallay, A. (ed.) (2009) *Indian Slavery in Colonial America*. Lincoln, NE.

Galvao-Sobrinho, C. R. (2012) 'Feasting the dead together: household burials and the social strategies of slaves and freed persons in the early Principate' in Bell and Ramsby (2012), 130–76.

Gamauf, R. (1999) *Ad statuam licet confugere: Untersuchungen zum Asylrecht im römischen Prinzipat*. Frankfurt.

Gamauf, R. (2001) 'Zur Frage "Sklaverei und Humanität" anhand von Quellen des römischen Rechts' in Bellen and Heinen (2001), 51–72.

Gamauf, R. (2009) 'Slaves doing business: the role of Roman law in the economy of a Roman household', *European Review of History / Revue européenne d'histoire*, 16, 331–46.

Garcia Ventura, A. (2014) 'Ur III biopolitics. Reflections on the relationship between war and work force management' in D. Nadali and J. Vidal (eds), *The Other Face of the Battle: The Impact of War on Civilians in the Ancient Near East*, Munster, 7–23.

Gardner, J. (1986) 'Proofs of status in the Roman world', *Bulletin of the Institute of Classical Studies*, 33, 1–14.

Gardner, J. (1993) *Being a Roman Citizen*. London and New York.

Gardner, J. (2019) 'Legal evidence: Rome' in Hodkinson, Kleijwegt and Vlassopoulos (2016–), published online, DOI: 10.1093/oxfordhb/9780199575251.013.12.

Garlan, Y. (1987) 'War, piracy and slavery in the Greek world' in Finley (1987), 7–21.

Garlan, Y. (1988) *Slavery in Ancient Greece*. Ithaca.

Garlan, Y. (2006) "L'anti-esclavagisme a-t-il existé en Grèce ancienne?" in M. Cottias, A. Stella and B. Vincent (eds), *Esclavage et dépendances serviles*, Paris, 187–94.

Garnsey, P. (1970) *Social Status and Legal Privilege in the Roman Empire*. Oxford.

Garnsey, P. (1981) 'Independent freedmen and the economy of Roman Italy under the Principate', *Klio*, 63, 359–71.

Garnsey, P. (1996) *Ideas of Slavery from Aristotle to Augustine*. Cambridge.

Garrido-Hory, M. (1981) *Martial et l'esclavage*. Paris.

Gavriljuk, N. A. (2003) 'The Graeco-Scythian slave-trade in the 6th and 5th centuries BC' in P. Guldager Bilde, J. Munk Hojte and V. F. Stolba (eds), *The Cauldron of Ariantas: Studies Presented to A. N. Shcheglov on his 70th Birthday*, Aarhus, 75–85.

Geary, D. and Vlassopoulos, K. (eds) (2009) 'Slavery, citizenship and the state in classical antiquity and the modern Americas', *European Review of History / Revue européenne d'histoire*, 16.3, 295–436.

Gelb, I. J. (1973) 'Prisoners of war in early Mesopotamia', *Journal of Near Eastern Studies*, 32, 70–98.

Genovese, E. D. (1961) *The Political Economy of Slavery: Studies in the Economy and Society of the Slave South*. Hanover, CT.

Genovese, E. D. (1967) 'Rebelliousness and docility in the Negro slave: a critique of the Elkins thesis', *Civil War History*, 13, 293–314.

Genovese, E. D. (1969) *The World the Slaveholders Made: Two Essays in Interpretation*. Hanover, CT.

Genovese, E. D. (1974) *Roll, Jordan, Roll: The World the Slaves Made*. New York.

Genovese, E. D. (1979) *From Rebellion to Revolution: Afro-American Slave Revolts in the Making of the Modern World*. Baton Rouge.

George, M. (1997) 'Servus and domus: the slave in the Roman house' in Laurence and Wallace-Hadrill (1997), 15–24.

George, M. (2002) 'Slave disguise in ancient Rome', *Slavery & Abolition*, 23, 41–54.

George, M. (2006) 'Social identity and the dignity of work on freedmen's reliefs' in d'Ambra and Métraux (2006), 19–29.

George, M. (2010) 'Archaeology and Roman slavery: problems and potential' in Heinen (2010a), 141–60.

George, M. (2011) 'Slavery and Roman material culture' in Bradley and Cartledge (2010), 385–413.

George, M. (ed.) (2013a) *Roman Slavery and Roman Material Culture*. Toronto.

George, M. (2013b) 'Cupid punished: reflections on a Roman genre scene' in George (2013a), 158–79.

Gerbner, K. (2018) *Christian Slavery: Conversion and Race in the Protestant Atlantic World*. Philadelphia.

Giannella, N. J. (2014) *The Mind of the Slave: The Limits of Knowledge and Power in Roman Law and Society*. PhD dissertation, University of Southern California.

Giardina, A. and Schiavone, A. (eds) (1981) *Società romana e produzione schiavistica, I–III*. Rome.

Gibson, E. L. (1999) *The Jewish Manumission Inscriptions of the Bosporus Kingdom*. Tubingen.

Giliberti, G. (1981) *Servus quasi colonus. Forme non tradizionali di organizzazione del lavoro nella società romana*, Naples.

Gillingham, J. (2012) 'Surrender in medieval Europe: an indirect approach' in H. Afflerbach and H. Strachan (eds), *How Fighting Ends: A History of Surrender*, Oxford, 55–72.

Gillingham, J. (2015) 'Crusading warfare, chivalry, and the enslavement of women and children' in G. I. Halfond (ed.), *The Medieval Way of War: Studies in Medieval Military History in Honor of Bernhard S. Bachrach*, Farnham, 133–52.

Giuffrida Ientile, M. (1983) *La pirateria tirrenica: momenti e fortuna*. Rome.

Glancy, J. A. (1998) 'Obstacles to slaves' participation in the Corinthian Church', *Journal of Biblical Literature*, 117, 481–501.

Glancy, J. A. (2002a) *Slavery in Early Christianity*. Oxford and New York.

Glancy, J. A. (2002b) 'Family plots: burying slaves deep in historical ground', *Biblical Interpretation*, 10, 57–75.

Glancy, J. A. (2012) 'Slavery in Acts of Thomas', *Journal of Early Christian History*, 2:2, 3–21.

Glancy, J. A. (2013) 'Resistance and humanity in Roman slavery', *Biblical Interpretation*, 21, 497–505.

Glancy, J. A. (2018) '"To serve them all the more": Christian slaveholders and Christian slaves in antiquity' in Fynn-Paul and Pargas (2018), 23–49.

Glassman, J. (1991) 'The bondsman's new clothes: the contradictory consciousness of slave resistance on the Swahili coast', *Journal of African History*, 32, 277–312.

Glazebrook, A. (2014) 'The erotics of manumission: prostitutes and the πρᾶσις ἐπ᾽ἐλευθερίᾳ', *Eugesta: Journal on Gender Studies in Antiquity*, 4, 53–80.

Glazebrook, A. (2017) 'Gender and slavery' in Hodkinson, Kleijwegt and Vlassopoulos (2016–), published online, DOI: 10.1093/oxfordhb/9780199575251.013.13.

Glazebrook, A. and Henry, M. M. (eds) (2011) *Greek Prostitutes in the Ancient Mediterranean, 800 BCE-200 CE*. Madison, WI.

Gnoli, T. (2005–8) 'C. Iulius Mygdonius: un Parto a Ravenna', *Felix Ravenna*, 161/4, 141–56.

Golden, M. (1988) 'The effects of slavery on citizen households and children: Aeschylus, Aristophanes and Athens', *Historical Reflections / Réflexions historiques*, 15, 455–75.

Golden, M. (2008) *Greek Sport and Social Status*. Austin.

Golden, M. (2011) 'Slavery and the Greek family' in Bradley and Cartledge (2011), 134–52.

Goldman, M. L. (2015) 'Associating the *aulêtris*: flute girls and prostitutes in the classical Greek symposium", *Helios*, 42, 29–60.

Gomez, M. A. (1998) *Exchanging our Country Marks: The Transformation of African Identities in the Colonial and Antebellum South.* Chapel Hill, NC.

Gonzalès, A. (2003) *Pline le jeune: esclaves et affranchis à Rome.* Paris.

Gonzalès, A. (ed.) (2008) *La fin du statut servile (affranchissement, libération, abolition)? Hommage à Jacques Annequin, Volume 1.* Besançon.

Goody, J. (1969) 'Inheritance, property, and marriage in Africa and Eurasia', *Sociology*, 3, 55–76.

Gordon, M. S. (2001) *The Breaking of a Thousand Swords: A History of the Turkish Military of Samarra (AH 200–275/815–889 CE).* Albany.

Graeber, D. (2006) 'Turning modes of production inside out: or, why capitalism is a transformation of slavery', *Critique of Anthropology*, 26, 61–85.

Grawehr, M. (2019) 'Of toddlers and donkeys: Roman lamps with slaves and self-representations of slaves' in Binsfeld and Ghetta (2019), 91–119.

Gray, C. (2015) *Jerome, Vita Malchi: Introduction, Text, Translation, and Commentary.* Oxford.

Greene, K. (2000) 'Technological innovation and economic progress in the ancient world: M. I. Finley re-considered', *Economic History Review*, 53, 29–59.

Grenouilleau, O. (2014) *Qu'est-ce que l'esclavage? Une histoire globale.* Paris.

Grey, C. (2011) *Constructing Communities in the Late Roman Countryside.* Cambridge.

Grieser, H. (2001) 'Asketische Bewegungen in Kleinasien im 4. Jahrhundert und ihre Haltung zur Sklaverei' in Bellen and Heinen (2001), 381–400.

Grieshaber, C. (2012) *Frühe Abolitionisten: die Rezeption der antiken Sklaverei zur Zeit der schottischen Aufklärung und deren Einfluss auf die britische Abolitionsbewegung (1750–1833).* Hildesheim, Zurich and New York.

Grig, L. (ed.) (2017) *Popular Culture in the Ancient World.* Cambridge.

Groen-Vallinga, M. J. (2013) 'Desperate housewives? The adaptive family economy and female participation in the Roman urban labour market' in Hemelrijk and Woolf (2013), 295–312.

Groen-Vallinga, M. J. (2017) *The Roman World of Work: Social Structures and the Urban Labour Market of Roman Italy in the First Three Centuries AD.* PhD dissertation, Leiden University.

Groen-Vallinga, M. J. and Tacoma, L. E. (2015) 'Contextualising condemnation to hard labour in the Roman Empire' in De Vito and Lichtenstein (2015), 49–78.

Grünewald, T. (2004) *Bandits in the Roman Empire: Myth and Reality.* London and New York.

Guarinello, N. L. (2013) *História antiga.* Sao Paulo.

Guasco, M. (2014) *Slaves and Englishmen: Human Bondage in the Early Modern Atlantic World.* Philadelphia.

Gudmestad, R. (2018) 'What is a slave society? The American South' in Lenski and Cameron (2018), 272–89.

Guerci, L. (1979) *Liberta degli Antichi e liberta dei moderni. Sparta, Atene e i 'philosophes' nella Francia del 700.* Naples.

Gundlach, R. (1994) *Die Zwangsumsiedlung auswärtiger Bevölkerung als Mittel ägyptischer Politik bis zum Ende des mittleren Reiches.* Stuttgart.

Günther, R. (1987) *Frauenarbeit – Frauenbindung. Untersuchungen zu Unfreien und Freigelassenen Frauen in den Stadtrömischen Inschriften.* Munich.Gustafson, M. (1994) 'Condemnation to the mines in the later Roman Empire', *Harvard Theological Review*, 87, 421–33.

Guyot, P. (1980) *Eunuchen als Sklaven und Freigelassene in der griechisch-römischen Antike.* Stuttgart.

Hackl, J. (2013) 'Frau Weintraube, Frau Heuschrecke und Frau Gut – Untersuchungen zu den babylonischen Namen von Sklavinnen in neubabylonischer und persischer Zeit', *Wiener Zeitschrift für die Kunde des Morgenlandes*, 103, 121–87.

Hahn, I. (1992) *Traumdeutung und gesellschaftliche Wirklichkeit: Artemidorus Daldianus als sozialgeschichtliche Quelle.* Konstanz.

Hall, E., Alston, R. and McConnell, J. (eds) (2011) *Ancient Slavery and Abolition: From Hobbes to Hollywood*. Oxford and New York.

Hall, G. M. (2005) *Slavery and African Ethnicities in the Americas: Restoring the Links*. Chapel Hill, NC.

Hamel, D. (2015) *The Battle of Arginusae: Victory at Sea and its Tragic Aftermath in the Final Years of the Peloponnesian War*. Baltimore.

Hammer, C. I. (2002) *A Large-Scale Slave Society of the Early Middle Ages: Slaves and their Families in Early Medieval Bavaria*. Aldershot and Burlington, VT.

Hanson, V. D. (1992) 'Thucydides and the desertion of Attic slaves during the Decelean War', *Classical Antiquity*, 11, 210–28.

Hansson, A. (1996) *Chinese Outcasts: Discrimination and Emancipation in Late Imperial China*. Leiden, New York and Cologne.

Hanß, S. and Schiel, J. (eds) (2014) *Mediterranean Slavery Revisited (500–1800) / Neue Perspektiven auf mediterrane Sklaverei (500–1800)*. Zurich.

Haour, A. (2007) *Rulers, Warriors, Traders and Clerics: The Central Sahel and the North Sea, 800–1500*. Oxford.

Harland, P. (2003) *Associations, Synagogues and Congregations: Claiming a Place in Ancient Mediterranean Society*. Minneapolis.

Harper, K. (2008) 'The Greek census inscriptions of late antiquity', *Journal of Roman Studies*, 98, 83–119.

Harper, K. (2010a) 'Slave prices in late antiquity (and in the very long term)', *Historia*, 59, 206–38.

Harper, K. (2010b) 'The SC Claudianum in the Codex Theodosianus: social history and legal texts', *Classical Quarterly*, 60, 610–38.

Harper, K. (2011) *Slavery in the Late Roman World, AD 275–425*. Cambridge.

Harper, K. (2013) *From Shame to Sin: The Christian Transformation of Sexual Morality in Late Antiquity*. Cambridge, MA and London.

Harper, K. (2016) 'Christianity and the roots of human dignity in late antiquity' in A. D. Hertzke and T. S. Shah (eds), *Christianity and Freedom: Historical Perspectives*, Cambridge, 123–48.

Harper, K. (2017a) 'Freedom, slavery and female sexual honor in antiquity' in Bodel and Scheidel (2017), 109–21.

Harper, K. (2017b) *The Fate of Rome: Climate, Disease, and the End of an Empire*. Princeton.

Harper, K. and Scheidel, W. (2018) 'Roman slavery and the ideal of "slave society"' in Lenski and Cameron (2018), 86–105.

Harries, J. and Du Plessis, P. J. (2013) 'The senatus consultum Silanianum: court decisions and judicial severity in the early Roman empire' in Du Plessis (2013b), 51–70.

Harrill, J. A. (1995) *The Manumission of Slaves in Early Christianity*. Tubingen.

Harrington, J. D. (1994) '"Res" or "persona": Roman civil law's influence on Southern slave law', *Labeo*, 40, 236–45.

Harris, E. M. (2002a) 'Did Solon abolish debt-bondage?', *Classical Quarterly*, 52, 415–30.

Harris, E. M. (2002b) 'Workshop, marketplace and household: the nature of technical specialisation in classical Athens and its influence on economy and society' in Cartledge, Cohen and Foxhall (2002), 67–99.

Harris, E. M. (2004) 'Notes on a lead letter from the Athenian agora', *Harvard Studies in Classical Philology*, 102, 157–70.

Harris, E. M. (2012) 'Homer, Hesiod and the "origins" of Greek slavery', *Revue des Études Anciennes*, 114, 345–66.

Harris, E. M. (2014) 'Wife, household, and marketplace: the role of women in the economy of classical Athens' in U. Bultrighini and E. Dimauro (eds), *Donne che contano nella storia greca*, Lanciano, 185–207.

Harris, E. M., Lewis, D. M. and Woolmer, M. (eds) (2015) *The Ancient Greek Economy: Markets, Households and City-States*. Cambridge and New York.

Harris, J. W. (ed.) (1992) *Society and Culture in the Slave South*. London.

Harris, W. V. (1979) *War and Imperialism in Republican Rome, 327–70 BC*. Oxford.

Harris, W. V. (1980a) 'Towards a study of the Roman slave trade', *Memoirs of the American Academy in Rome*, 36, 117–40.

Harris, W. V. (1980b) 'Roman terracotta lamps: the organization of an industry', *Journal of Roman Studies*, 70, 126–45.

Harris, W. V. (1994) 'Child-exposure in the Roman Empire', *Journal of Roman Studies*, 84, 1–22.

Harris, W. V. (1999) 'Demography, geography and the sources of Roman slaves', *Journal of Roman Studies*, 89, 62–75.

Harris, W. V. (ed.) (2013a) *Moses Finley and Politics*. Leiden and Boston.

Harris, W. V. (2013b) '*Politics in the Ancient World* and politics' in Harris (2013a), 107–22.

Harrison, A. R. W. (1968) *The Law of Athens I: The Family and Property*. Oxford.

Harrison, T. (2019) 'Classical Greek ethnography and the slave trade', *Classical Antiquity*, 38, 36–57.

Harvey, F. D. (1988) 'Herodotus and the man-footed creature' in Archer (1988), 42–52.

Harvey, D. (2007) '"The severity of the master, and misery of the slave": fears and evils in David Hume's essay *Of the Populousness of Ancient Nations*' in Serghidou (2007), 347–60.

Hasegawa, K. (2005) *The Familia Urbana during the Early Empire: A Study of Columbaria Inscriptions*. Oxford.

Hasenohr, C. (2003) 'Les Compitalia à Délos', *Bulletin de Correspondance Hellénique*, 127, 167–249.

Hasenohr, C. (2007) 'Les Italiens à Délos: entre romanité et hellénisme', *Pallas*, 73, 221–32.

Hasenohr, C. (2017) 'L'emporion délien, creuset de mobilité sociale? Le cas des esclaves affranchis italiens' in A. Rizakis, F. Camia and S. Zoumbaki (eds), *Social Dynamics under Roman Rule: Mobility Status Change in the Provinces of Achaia and Macedonia*, Athens, 119–31.

Hawkins, C. (2016) *Roman Artisans and the Urban Economy*. Cambridge.

Head, R. (2010) *The Business Activities of Neo-Babylonian Private 'Slaves' and the Problem of Peculium*. PhD dissertation, Johns Hopkins University.

Heather, P. (2010) *Empires and Barbarians: Migration, Development and the Birth of Europe*. London.

Heinen, H. (1976) 'Zur Sklaverei in der hellenistischen Welt (I)', *Ancient Society*, 7, 127–49.

Heinen, H. (1977) 'Zur Sklaverei in der hellenistischen Welt (II)', *Ancient Society*, 8, 121–54.

Heinen, H. (1978) 'Ägyptische und griechische Traditionen der Sklaverei im ptolemäischen Ägypten' republished in Heinen (2006), 486–96.

Heinen, H. (2001) 'Sklaverei im nördlichen Schwarzmeerraum: zum Stand der Forschung' in Bellen and Heinen (2001), 487–503.

Heinen, H. (2005) 'Das Mainzer Akademieprojekt "Forschungen zur antiken Sklaverei": Geschichte und Bilanz, Perspektiven und Desiderate' in Herrmann-Otto (2005), 371–94.

Heinen, H. (2006) *Vom hellenistischen Osten zum römischen Westen. Ausgewählte Schriften zur Alten Geschichte*. Stuttgart.

Heinen, H. (ed.) (2008) *Menschenraub, Menschenhandel und Sklaverei in antiker und moderner Perspektive*. Stuttgart.

Heinen, H. (ed.) (2010a) *Antike Sklaverei, Rückblick und Ausblick: Neue Beiträge zur Forschungsgeschichte und zur Erschließung der archäologischen Zeugnisse*. Stuttgart.

Heinen, H. (2010b) 'Aufstieg und Niedergang der sowjetischen Sklavereiforschung. Eine Studie zur Verbindung von Politik und Wissenschaft' in Heinen (2010a), 95–138.

Heinen, H. (ed.) (2012) *Kindersklaven-Sklavenkinder: Schicksale zwischen Zuneigung und Ausbeutung in der Antike und im interkulturellen Vergleich.* Stuttgart.

Heinen, H. and Eppers, M. (1984) 'Zu den "servi venerii" in Ciceros Verrinen' republished in Heinen (2006), 506–19.

Helg, A. (2016) *Plus jamais esclaves! De l'insoumission à la révolte, le grand récit d'une émancipation (1492–1838).* Paris.

Hellie, R. (1982) *Slavery in Russia 1450–1725.* Chicago and London.

Hemelrijk, E. A. and Woolf, G. (eds) (2013) *Women and the Roman City in the Latin West.* Leiden.

Herrmann-Otto, E. (1994) *Ex ancilla natus: Untersuchungen zu den "hausgeborenen" Sklaven und Sklavinnen im Westen des römischen Kaiserreiches.* Stuttgart.

Herrmann-Otto, E. (ed.) (2005) *Unfreie Arbeits- und Lebensverhältnisse von der Antike bis in die Gegenwart. Eine Einführung.* Hildesheim, Zurich and New York.

Herrmann-Otto, E. (2009) *Sklaverei und Freilassung in der griechisch-römischen Welt.* Hildesheim, Zurich and New York.

Herrmann-Otto, E. (2010) 'Das Projekt "Forschungen zur antiken Sklaverei" an der Akademie der Wissenschaften und der Literatur, Mainz' in Heinen (2010a), 61–75.

Herrmann-Otto, E. (ed.) (2011) *Sklaverei und Zwangsarbeit zwischen Akzeptanz und Widerstand.* Hildesheim, Zurich and New York.

Herschbell, J. P. (1995) 'Epictetus: a freedman on slavery', *Ancient Society*, 26, 185–204.

Herz, P. (2001) 'Das Bürgerrechtsdekret von Ephesos. Inschriften von Ephesos 8. Gedanken zur Gesellschaft im spätrepublikanischen Kleinasien' in Bellen and Heinen (2001), 185–207.

Heywood, L. M. and Thornton, J. K. (2007) *Central Africans, Atlantic Creoles and the Foundation of the Americas, 1585–1660.* Cambridge.

Hezser, C. (2005) *Jewish Slavery in Antiquity.* Oxford.

Hezser, C. (2016) 'Greek and Roman slaving in comparative ancient perspective: the level of integration' in Hodkinson, Kleijwegt and Vlassopoulos (2016–), published online, DOI: 10.1093/oxfordhb/9780199575251.013.16.

Hillner, J. (2001) 'Die Berufsangaben und Adressen auf den stadtrömischen Sklavenhalsbändern', *Historia*, 50, 193–216.

Himmelmann, N. (1971) *Archäologisches zum Problem der griechischen Sklaverei.* Wiesbaden.

Hind, J. G. F. (1994) 'The trade in Getic slaves and the silver coins of Istros' in M. Lazarov and C. Angelova (eds), *Thracia Pontica V: Les ports dans la vie de la Thrace ancienne*, Sozopol, 153–8.

Hirt, M. (2018) 'In search of Junian Latins', *Historia*, 67, 288–312.

Hodkinson, S. (2000) *Property and Wealth in Classical Sparta.* London.

Hodkinson, S. (2008) 'Spartiates, helots and the direction of the agrarian economy: toward an understanding of helotage in comparative perspective' in Dal Lago and Katsari (2008a), 285–320.

Hodkinson, S. and Geary, D. (eds) (2012) *Slaves and Religions in Graeco-Roman Antiquity and Modern Brazil.* Newcastle upon Tyne.

Hodkinson, S. and Hall, E. (2011) 'Appropriations of Spartan helotage in British antislavery debates of the 1790s' in Hall, Alston and McConnell (2011), 65–102.

Hodkinson, S., Kleijwegt, M. and Vlassopoulos, K. (eds) (2016–) *The Oxford Handbook of Greek and Roman Slaveries*, published online, DOI: 10.1093/oxfordhb/9780199575251.001.0001.

Hoffner, H. A. (2008) 'Slavery and slave laws in ancient Hatti and Israel' in D. I. Block (ed.), *Israel – Ancient Kingdom or Late Invention?*, Nashville, 131–55.

Hofmann, T. (2005) *Zur sozialen Bedeutung zweier Begriffe für 'Diener': bak und ḥm. Untersucht an Quellen vom Alten Reich bis zur Ramessidenzeit.* Basel.

Holleran, C. (2013) 'Women and retail in Roman Italy' in Hemelrijk and Woolf (2013), 313–30.

Honneth, A. (1996) *The Struggle for Recognition: The Moral Grammar of Social Conflicts.* Cambridge, MA.

Honneth, A. (2012) 'From desire to recognition: Hegel's grounding of self- consciousness' in A. Honneth, *The I in We: Studies in the Theory of Recognition,* Cambridge, 3–18.

Honoré, A. M. (1961) 'Ownership' in A. G. Guest (ed.), *Oxford Essays in Jurisprudence,* Oxford, 107–47.

Hopkins, K. (1978) *Conquerors and Slaves: Sociological Studies in Roman History, Volume I.* Cambridge.

Hopkins, K. (1993) 'Novel evidence for Roman slavery', *Past & Present,* 138, 3–27.

Hopper, M. S. (2015) *Slaves of One Master: Globalization and Slavery in Arabia in the Age of Empire.* New Haven and London.

Horden, P. and Purcell, N. (2000) *The Corrupting Sea: A Study of Mediterranean History.* Malden, MA.

Hornblower, S. (1991) *A Commentary on Thucydides I: Books I–III.* Oxford.

Horsmann, G. (1998) *Die Wagenlenker der römischen Kaiserzeit: Untersuchungen zu ihrer sozialen Stellung.* Stuttgart.

Howard, P. A. (1998) *Changing History: Afro-Cuban Cabildos and Societies of Color in the Nineteenth Century.* Baton Rouge.

Huebner, S. R. (2013) *The Family in Roman Egypt: A Comparative Approach to Intergenerational Solidarity and Conflict.* Cambridge.

Huebner, S. R. and Laes, C. (eds) (2019) *The Single Life in the Roman and Later Roman World.* Cambridge.

Hülsen, K. (2008) *'Tempelsklaverei' in Kleinasien: Ein Beitrag zum Tempeldienst in hellenistischer und römischer Zeit.* PhD dissertation, Universität Trier.

Humbert, M. (1976) 'Libertas id est civitas: autour d'un conflit négatif de citoyennetés au IIe s. avant J.-C.', *Mélanges de l'École française de Rome-Antiquité,* 88, 221–42.

Humphreys, S. C. (2018) *Kinship in Ancient Athens: An Anthropological Analysis, I–II.* Oxford.

Hunt, P. (1998) *Slaves, Warfare and Ideology in the Greek Historians.* Cambridge.

Hunt, P. (2001) 'The slaves and the generals of Arginusae', *American Journal of Philology,* 122, 359–80.

Hunt, P. (2011) 'Slaves in Greek literary culture' in Bradley and Cartledge (2011), 22–47.

Hunt, P. (2015) 'Trojan slaves in classical Athens: ethnic identity among Athenian slaves' in Taylor and Vlassopoulos (2015a), 129–54.

Hunt, P. (2016) 'Violence against slaves in classical Greece' in Riess and Fagan (2016), 136–61.

Hunt, P. (2017a) 'Slaves or serfs? Patterson on the thetes and helots of ancient Greece' in Bodel and Scheidel (2017), 55–80.

Hunt, P. (2017b) 'Slaves as active subjects: individual strategies' in Hodkinson, Kleijwegt and Vlassopoulos (2016–), published online, DOI: 10.1093/oxfordhb/9780199575251.013.19.

Hunt, P. (2018a) *Ancient Greek and Roman Slavery.* Malden, MA.

Hunt, P. (2018b) 'Ancient Greece as a "slave society"' in Lenski and Cameron (2018), 61–85.

Hunter, V. (2000) 'Introduction: status distinctions in Athenian law' in Hunter and Edmondson (2000), 1–30.

Hunter, V. and Edmondson, J. C. (eds) (2000) *Law and Social Status in Classical Athens.* Oxford.

Hunter, V. (2006) 'Pittalacus and Eucles: slaves in the public service of Athens', *Mouseion,* 6, 1–13.

Huntzinger, H. (2009) *La captivité de guerre en Occident dans l'antiquité tardive (378–507)*. PhD dissertation, Université de Strasbourg.

Huntzinger, H. (2014) 'Prix des captifs, prix des esclaves: l'estimation du "prix de l'Homme" dans l'Antiquité tardive', *Les Cahiers de Framespa: Nouveaux champs de l'histoire sociale*, 17, published online, DOI: 10.4000/framespa.3098.

Hunwick, J. and Powell, E. T. (eds) (2002) *The African Diaspora in the Mediterranean Lands of Islam*. Princeton.

Hurst, H. and Owen, S. (eds) (2005) *Ancient Colonizations: Analogy, Similarity and Difference*. London.

Husby, T. (2017) *Recognizing Freedom: Manumission in the Roman Republic*. PhD dissertation, City University of New York.

Inikori, J. E. (1999) 'Slaves or serfs? A comparative study of slavery and serfdom in Europe and Africa' in I. Okpewho, C. Boyce Davies and A. A. Mazrui (eds), *The African Diaspora: African Origins and New World Identities*, Bloomington, 49–75.

Ismard, P. (2010) *La cité des réseaux: Athènes et ses associations, VIe-Ier siècle av. J.-C.* Paris.

Ismard, P. (2017a) *Democracy's Slaves: A Political History of Ancient Greece*. Cambridge, MA and London.

Ismard, P. (2017b) 'Écrire l'histoire de l'esclavage: entre approche globale et perspective comparatiste', *Annales. Histoire, Sciences Sociales*, 72, 9–43.

Ismard, P. (2019) *La cité et ses esclaves. Institution, fictions, expériences*. Paris.

Jacob, O. (1979) *Les esclaves publics à Athènes*. New York.

Jameson, M. H. (1977) 'Agriculture and slavery in classical Athens', *Classical Journal*, 73, 122–45.

Janzen, M. D. (2013) *The Iconography of Humiliation: The Depiction and Treatment of Bound Foreigners in New Kingdom Egypt*. PhD dissertation, University of Memphis.

Jenkins, R. (2002) *Foundations of Sociology: Towards a Better Understanding of the Human World*. London.

Jenkins, R. (2008) *Social Identity*. 3rd edition. London and New York.

Jew, D., Osborne, R. and Scott, M. (eds) (2016) *M. I. Finley: An Ancient Historian and his Impact*. Cambridge.

Johnson, W. (1997) 'Review: inconsistency, contradiction, and complete confusion: the everyday life of the law of slavery', *Law & Social Inquiry*, 22, 405–33.

Johnson, W. (2003) 'On agency', *Journal of Social History*, 37, 113–24.

Johnson, W. (2009) *Soul by Soul: Life inside the Antebellum Slave Market*. Cambridge, MA and London.

Johnson, W. (2013) *River of Dark Dreams: Slavery and Empire in the Cotton Kingdom*. Cambridge, MA and London.

Joly, F. D. (2003) *Tácito e a metáfora da escravidão: um estudo de cultura política romana*. Sao Paulo.

Joly, F. D. (2010) *Libertate opus est: escravidão, manumissão e cidadania à época de Nero (54–68 d.C.)*. Curitiba.

Joly, F. D. (2019) 'William L. Westermann entre o antiquarismo e a história comparada da escravidão', *Mare Nostrum*, 10, 187–208.

Joly, F. D. and de Bivar Marquese, R. (2020) 'Slave trade, manumission, and citizenship in ancient Rome and Brazil: a comparative perspective' in Hodkinson, Kleijwegt and Vlassopoulos (2016–), published online, DOI: 10.1093/oxfordhb/9780199575251.013.20.

Jones, A. H. M. (1956) 'Slavery in the ancient world', *Economic History Review*, 9, 185–99.

Jones, C. P. (1987) 'Stigma: tattooing and branding in Graeco-Roman antiquity', *Journal of Roman Studies*, 77, 139–55.

Jongman, W. (2003) 'Slavery and the growth of Rome. The transformation of Italy in the second and first centuries BCE' in C. Edwards and G. Woolf (eds), *Rome the Cosmopolis*, Cambridge, 100–22.

Jordan, D. (2000) 'A personal letter found in the Athenian agora', *Hesperia*, 69, 91–103.

Joshel, S. R. (1986) 'Nurturing the master's child: slavery and the Roman child-nurse', *Signs: Journal of Women in Culture and Society*, 12, 3–22.

Joshel, S. R. (1992) *Work, Identity and Legal Status at Rome: A Study of the Occupational Inscriptions*. Norman, OK and London.

Joshel, S. R. (2010) *Slavery in the Roman World*. New York.

Joshel, S. R. (2011) 'Slaves in Roman literary culture' in Bradley and Cartledge (2011), 214–40.

Joshel, S. R. and Murnaghan, S. (eds) (1998) *Women and Slaves in Greco-Roman Culture*. London.

Joshel, S. R. and Petersen, L. H. (2014) *The Material Life of Roman Slaves*. New York.

Jursa, M. (2010) *Aspects of the Economic History of Babylonia in the First Millennium BC*. Munster.

Jusifov, J. B. (1978) 'Das Problem der Freien und Sklaven nach den Schriftquellen Elams', *Altorientalische Forschungen*, 5, 45–62.

Kamen, D. (2010) 'A corpus of inscriptions: representing slave marks in antiquity', *Memoirs of the American Academy in Rome*, 55, 95–110.

Kamen, D. (2011) 'Reconsidering the status of khôris oikountes', *Dike*, 14, 43–53.

Kamen, D. (2013) *Status in Classical Athens*. Princeton.

Kamen, D. (2014) 'Sale for the purpose of freedom: slave-prostitutes and manumission in ancient Greece', *Classical Journal*, 109, 281–307.

Kamen, D. (2016) 'Manumission and slave-allowances in classical Athens', *Historia*, 65, 413–26.

Kamen, D. and Levin-Richardson, S. (2015) 'Revisiting Roman sexuality: agency and the conceptualization of penetrated males' in N. S. Rabinovitz, J. Robson and M. Masterson (eds), *Sex in Antiquity*, London and New York, 469–80.

Kampen, N. (1981) *Image and Status: Roman Working Women in Ostia*. Berlin.

Karras, R. M. (1988) *Slavery and Society in Medieval Scandinavia*. New Haven and London.

Kaster, R. A. (1988) *Guardians of Language: The Grammarian and Society in Late Antiquity*. Berkeley, Los Angeles and London.

Katsari, C. and Dal Lago, E. (eds) (2008) *From Captivity to Freedom: Themes in Ancient and Modern Slavery*. Bristol.

Kay, P. (2014) *Rome's Economic Revolution*. Oxford.

Kaye, A. E. (2002) 'Neighbourhoods and solidarity in the Natchez district of Mississippi: rethinking the antebellum slave community', *Slavery & Abolition*, 23, 1–24.

Kaye, A. E. (2007) *Joining Places: Slave Neighborhoods in the Old South*. Chapel Hill, NC.

Kazakévich, E. G. (2008) 'Were the *khoris oikountes* slaves?', *Greek, Roman & Byzantine Studies*, 48, 343–80.

Kelly, F. (1988) *A Guide to Early Irish Law*. Dublin.

Kennell, N. M. (2003) 'Agreste genus: helots in Hellenistic Laconia' in Luraghi and Alcock (2003), 81–105.

Khazanov, A. (1975) 'Caractère de l'esclavage chez les Scythes' in C. Parain (ed.), *Formes d'exploitation du travail et rapports sociaux dans l'Antiquité classique*, Paris, 111–28.

Kiddy, E. W. (2005a) *Blacks of the Rosary: Memory and History in Minas Gerais*. University Park.

Kiddy, E. W. (2005b) 'Kings, queens, and judges: hierarchy in lay religious brotherhoods of Blacks' in Curto and Soulodre-LaFrance (2005), 95–123.

Kiechle, F. (1969) *Sklavenarbeit und technischer Fortschritt im römischen Reich*. Wiesbaden.

Kiesling, E. C. (2006) 'Corporal punishment in the Greek phalanx and the Roman legion: modern images and ancient realities', *Historical Reflections / Réflexions Historiques*, 32, 225–46.

King, R. H. (2001) 'Domination and fabrication: re-thinking Stanley Elkins' *Slavery*', *Slavery & Abolition*, 22, 1–28.

Kirschenbaum, A. (1987) *Sons, Slaves and Freedmen in Roman Commerce*. Washington, DC.

Klees, H. (1975) *Herren und Sklaven: die Sklaverei im oikonomischen und politischen Schrifttum der Griechen in klassischer Zeit.* Frankfurt.

Klees, H. (1990) 'Griechisches und Römisches in den Traumdeutungen Artemidors für Herren und Sklaven' in C. Boerker and M. Donderer (eds), *Das antike Rom und der Osten: Festschrift für K. Parlasca*, Erlangen, 53–76.

Klees, H. (1998) *Sklavenleben im klassischen Griechenland.* Stuttgart.

Kleijwegt, M. (ed.) (2006a) *The Faces of Freedom: The Manumission and Emancipation of Slaves in Old World and New World Slavery.* Leiden and Boston, MA.

Kleijwegt, M. (2006b) 'Freedpeople: a brief cross-cultural history' in Kleijwegt (2006a), 3–68.

Kleijwegt, M. (2006c) 'Freed slaves, self-presentation and corporate identity in the Roman world' in Kleijwegt (2006a), 89–116.

Kleijwegt, M. (2009) 'Creating new citizens: freed slaves, the state and citizenship in early Rome and under Augustus', *European Review of History / Revue européenne d'histoire*, 16, 319–30.

Kleijwegt, M. (2012) 'Deciphering freedwomen in the Roman Empire' in Bell and Ramsby (2012), 110–29.

Kleijwegt, M. (2013) 'Debt bondage and chattel slavery in early Rome' in Campbell and Stanziani (2013), 43–52.

Klein, H. S. (2010) *The Atlantic Slave Trade.* New York.

Klein, R. (1988) *Die Sklaverei in der Sicht der Bischöfe Ambrosius und Augustinus.* Wiesbaden.

Klein, R. (2000) *Die Haltung der kappadokischen Bischöfe Basilius von Caesarea, Gregor von Nazianz und Gregor von Nyssa zur Sklaverei.* Stuttgart.

Klingenberg, G. (2005) *Corpus der Römischen Rechtsquellen zur Antiken Sklaverei. Teil X: Juristisch speziell definierte Sklavengruppen, 6: servus fugitivus.* Stuttgart.

Klingshirn, W. (1985) 'Charity and power: Caesarius of Arles and the ransoming of captives in sub-Roman Gaul', *Journal of Roman Studies*, 75, 183–203.

Knoch, S. (2017) *Sklavenfürsorge im Römischen Reich: Formen und Motive zwischen humanitas und utilitas.* 2nd edition. Hildesheim, Zurich and New York.

Kolchin, P. (1983) 'Re-evaluating the antebellum slave community: a comparative perspective', *Journal of American History*, 70, 579–601.

Kolchin, P. (1987) *Unfree Labor: American Slavery and Russian Serfdom.* Cambridge, MA.

Kolchin, P. (1993) *American Slavery: 1619–1877.* London.

Kolendo, J. (1979) 'Éléments pour une enquête sur l'iconographie des esclaves dans l'art hellénistique et romain' in Capozza (1979), 161–74.

Konadu, K. (2010) *The Akan Diaspora in the Americas.* New York.

Koops, E. (2014) 'Masters and freedmen: Junian Latins and the struggle for citizenship' in G. de Kleijn and S. Benoist (eds), *Integration in Rome and in the Roman World*, Leiden and Boston, 105–26.

Kopytoff, I. (1986) 'The cultural biography of things: commoditization as process' in A. Appadurai (ed.), *The Social Life of Things: Commodities in Cultural Perspective*, Cambridge, 64–91.

Kremer, D. (2006) *Ius latinum: le concept de droit latin sous la République et l'Empire.* Paris.

Kriger, D. (2011) *Sex Rewarded, Sex Punished: A Study of the Status 'Female Slave' in Early Jewish Law.* Boston, MA.

Kudlien, F. (1986) *Die Stellung des Arztes in der römischen Gesellschaft: freigeborene Römer, Eingebürgerte, Peregrine, Sklaven, Freigelassene als Ärzte.* Wiesbaden.

Kudlien, F. (1991) *Sklavenmentalität im Spiegel antiker Wahrsagerei.* Stuttgart.

Kuhn, T. S. (1962) *The Structure of Scientific Revolutions.* Chicago and London.

Kyle, D. G. (1998) *Spectacles of Death in Ancient Rome.* London and New York.

Kyrtatas, D. I. (1987) *The Social Structure of the Early Christian Communities.* London.

Kyrtatas, D. I. (2002) 'Domination and exploitation' in Cartledge, Cohen and Foxhall (2002), 140–55.

Laes, C. (2003) 'Desperately different? Delicia children in the Roman household' in Balch and Osiek (2003), 298–324.

Laes, C. (2011) *Children in the Roman Empire: Outsiders Within*. Cambridge.

Lakoff, G. (1987) *Women, Fire and Dangerous Things: What Categories Reveal about the Mind*. Chicago and London.

Lane, E. (1971) *Corpus monumentorum religionis dei Menis, I: The Monuments and Inscriptions*. Leiden.

Lape, S. (2002) 'Solon and the institution of the "democratic" family form', *Classical Journal*, 98, 117–39.

Larsson Lovén, L. (2016) 'Women, trade and production in urban centres of Roman Italy' in M. Flohr and A. Wilson (eds), *Urban Craftsmen and Traders in the Roman World*, Oxford, 200–21.

Laubenheimer, F. (2013) 'Amphoras and shipwrecks: wine from the Tyrrhenian Coast at the end of the Republic and its distribution in Gaul' in J. DeRose Evans (ed.), *A Companion to the Archaeology of the Roman Republic*, Malden, MA and Oxford, 97–109.

Laubry, N. (2017) 'La désignation de la postérité. Autour de la formule libertis libertabusque posterisque eorum dans les inscriptions funéraires romaines' in Dondin-Payre and Tran (2017), 59–72.

Lauffer, S. (1956) *Die Bergwerkssklaven von Laureion, I–II*. Wiesbaden.

Launaro, A. (2011) *Peasants and Slaves: The Rural Population of Roman Italy (200 BC to AD 100)*. Cambridge.

Laurence, R. and Strömberg, A. (eds) (2012) *Families in the Greco-Roman World*. London.

Laurence, R. and Wallace-Hadrill, A. (eds) (1997) *Domestic Space in the Roman World: Pompeii and Beyond*. Portsmouth, RI.

Lavan, M. (2013) *Slaves to Rome: Paradigms of Empire in Roman Culture*. Cambridge.

Legras, B. (ed.) (2012) *Transferts culturels et droits dans le monde grec et hellénistique*. Paris.

Leigh, M. (2004) *Comedy and the Rise of Rome*. Oxford.

Lemaire, A. (2015) 'Esclavage pour dettes et autres formes de travail dépendant au Levant: tradition biblique et épigraphie (Xe-Ve s.)' in Zurbach (2015), 67–84.

Lendon, J. E. (2001) *Empire of Honour: The Art of Government in the Roman World*. Oxford.

Lendon, J. E. (2011) 'Roman honor' in Peachin (2011), 377–403.

Lenski, N. (1995) 'The Gothic civil war and the date of the Gothic conversion', *Greek, Roman & Byzantine Studies*, 36, 51–87.

Lenski, N. (2006) 'Servi publici in late antiquity' in J.-U. Krause and C. Witschel (eds), *Die Stadt in der Spätantike: Niedergang oder Wandel*, Stuttgart, 335–58.

Lenski, N. (2008) 'Captivity, slavery and cultural exchange between Rome and the Germans from the first to the seventh century CE' in C. M. Cameron (ed.), *Invisible Citizens: Captives and their Consequences*, Salt Lake City, 80–109.

Lenski, N. (2009) 'Schiavi armati e formazione di eserciti privati nel mondo tardoantico' in G. Urso (ed.), *Ordine e sovversione nel mondo greco e romano*, Pisa, 146–75.

Lenski, N. (2011a) 'Captivity and slavery among the Saracens in Late Antiquity (ca. 250–630 CE)', *Antiquité Tardive*, 19, 237–66.

Lenski, N. (2011b) 'Captivity and Romano-Barbarian interchange' in R. W. Mathisen and D. Shanzer (eds), *Romans, Barbarians and the Transformation of the Roman World*, Farnham, 185–98.

Lenski, N. (2011c) 'Constantine and slavery: libertas and the fusion of Roman and Christian values', *Atti dell'Accademia Romanistica Costantiniana*, 19, 235–60.

Lenski, N. (2013) 'Working models: functional art and Roman conceptions of slavery' in George (2013a), 129–57.

Lenski, N. (2014) 'Captivity among the barbarians and its impact on the fate of the Roman Empire' in M. Maas (ed.), *The Cambridge Companion to the Age of Attila*, Cambridge, 230–46.

Lenski, N. (2016) 'Violence and the Roman slave' in Riess and Fagan (2016), 275–98.

Lenski, N. (2017) 'Peasant and slave in late antique North Africa, c. 100–600 CE' in R. Lizzi Testa (ed.), *Late Antiquity in Contemporary Debate*, Cambridge, 113–55.

Lenski, N. (2018a) 'Framing the question: what is a slave society?' in Lenski and Cameron (2018), 15–57.

Lenski, N. (2018b) 'Ancient slaveries and modern ideology' in Lenski and Cameron (2018), 106–47.

Lenski, N. (2019) 'Searching for slave teachers in late antiquity' in C. Sogno (ed.), *Ποιμένι λαῶν: Studies in Honor of Robert J. Penella*, Savona, 127–91.

Lenski, N. and Cameron, C. M. (eds) (2018) *What is a Slave Society? The Practice of Slavery in Global Perspective.* Cambridge.

Lepelley, C. (1981) 'La crise de l'Afrique romaine au début du Ve siècle, d'après les lettres nouvellement découvertes de Saint Augustin', *Comptes rendus de l'Académie des Inscriptions et Belles-Lettres*, 125, 445–63.

Lerouxel, F. (2015) 'Bronze pesé, dette et travail contraint (*nexum*) dans la Rome archaïque (VIe s. – IVe s. avant J.-C.)' in Zurbach (2015), 109–52.

Létroublon, M. (1974) 'Les esclaves dans les bandes armées d'après les discours de Cicéron de 57 à 52' in *Actes 1972*, 235–47.

Levin-Richardson, S. (2019) *The Brothel of Pompeii: Sex, Class, and Gender at the Margins of Roman Society.* Cambridge.

Lévy, E. (1997) 'Libres et non-libres dans le Code de Gortyne' in P. Brulé and J. Oulhen (eds), *Esclavage, guerre, économie en Grèce ancienne: Hommages à Yvon Garlan*, Rennes, 25–41.

Lewis, D. M. (2011) 'Near Eastern slaves in classical Attica and the slave trade with Persian territories', *Classical Quarterly*, 61, 91–113.

Lewis, D. M. (2013) 'Slave marriages in the laws of Gortyn: a matter of rights?', *Historia*, 62, 390–416.

Lewis, D. M. (2015) 'The market for slaves in the fifth-and fourth-century Aegean' in Harris, Lewis and Woolmer (2015), 316–36.

Lewis, D. M. (2017a) 'Notes on slave names, ethnicity, and identity in classical and Hellenistic Greece', *U schyłku starożytności-Studia źródłoznawcze*, 16, 183–213.

Lewis, D. M. (2017b) 'Orlando Patterson, property, and ancient slavery: the definitional problem revisited' in Bodel and Scheidel (2017), 31–54.

Lewis, D. M. (2017c) 'Making law grip: inequality, injustice and legal remedy in Solonian Attica and ancient Israel' in I. K. Xydopoulos, K. Vlassopoulos and E. Tounta (eds), *Violence and Community: Law, Space and Identity in the Ancient Eastern Mediterranean World*, London and New York, 28–49.

Lewis, D. M. (2018) *Greek Slave Systems in their Eastern Mediterranean Context, c. 800–146 BC.* Oxford.

Lewis, D. M. (2019) 'Piracy and slave trading in action in classical and Hellenistic Greece', *Mare Nostrum*, 10.2, 79–108.

Lewis, D. M. (forthcoming) 'Greek slavery and honour: institutional and prototypical approaches' in M. Canevaro and D. M. Lewis (eds), *Honour and Slavery*, Edinburgh.

Lewis, S. (1998) 'Slaves as viewers and users of Athenian pottery', *Hephaistos*, 16, 71–90.

Link, S. (1994) *Das griechische Kreta: Untersuchungen zu seiner staatlichen und gesellschaftlichen Entwicklung vom 6. bis zum 4. Jahrhundert v. Chr.* Stuttgart.

Link, S. (2001) 'Dolos und woikeus im Recht von Gortyn', *Dike*, 4, 87–112.

Liu, J. (2009) *Collegia Centonariorum: The Guilds of Textile Dealers in the Roman West.* Leiden.

Llewelyn, S. R. (1992) *New Documents Illustrating Early Christianity, 6: A Review of the Greek Inscriptions and Papyri Published in 1980–81.* North Rydel, NSW.

Llewelyn, S. R. (1997) *New Documents Illustrating Early Christianity, 8: A Review of the Greek Inscriptions and Papyri Published in 1984–85.* Grand Rapids, MI and Cambridge.

Loiseau, J. (2016) *Les Mamelouks (XIIIe–XVIe siècle). Une expérience du pouvoir dans l'islam médiéval.* Paris.

Lombardo, M. (1987) 'I Peridinoi di Platone (Leg., 6, 777c) e l'etnogenesi brettia', *Annali della Scuola normale superiore di Pisa: Classe di lettere e filosofia,* 17, 611–48.

López Barja de Quiroga, P. (1998) 'Junian Latins: status and number', *Athenaeum,* 86, 133–63.

López Barja de Quiroga, P. (2006) 'How (not) to sell a son – Twelve Tables 4, 2', *Zeitschrift der Savigny-Stiftung für Rechtsgeschichte: Romanistische Abteilung,* 123, 297–308.

López Barja de Quiroga, P. (2007) *Historia de la manumisión en Roma: de los orígenes a los Severos.* Madrid.

López Barja de Quiroga, P. (2010) 'Empire sociology: Italian freedmen, from success to oblivion', *Historia,* 59, 321–41.

López Barja de Quiroga, P. (2020) 'Patronage and slavery in the Roman world: the circle of power' in Hodkinson, Kleijwegt and Vlassopoulos (2016–), published online, DOI: 10.1093/oxfordhb/9780199575251.013.31.

Loprieno, A. (1997) 'Slaves' in S. Donadoni (ed.), *The Egyptians,* Chicago and London, 185–219.

Loprieno, A. (2012) 'Slavery and servitude' in E. Frood and W. Wendrich (eds), *UCLA Encyclopedia of Egyptology,* Los Angeles, published online at http://digital2.library.ucla.edu/viewItem.do?ark=21198/zz002djg3j.

Lotze, D. (1959) *Metaxù eleuthéron kaì doúlon: Studien zur Rechtsstellung unfreier Landbevölkerungen in Griechenland bis zum 4. Jh. v. Chr.* Berlin.

Lovejoy, P. E. (ed.) (2000) *Identity in the Shadow of Slavery.* London and New York.

Lovejoy, P. E. (ed.) (2004) *Slavery on the Frontiers of Islam.* Princeton.

Lovejoy, P. E. (2012) *Transformations in Slavery: A History of Slavery in Africa.* 3rd edition. Cambridge.

Lovejoy, P. E. and Trotman, D. V. (eds) (2003) *Trans-Atlantic Dimensions of Ethnicity in the African Diaspora.* London and New York.

Luciani, F. (2019) 'Notes on the external appearance of Roman public slaves' in Binsfeld and Ghetta (2019), 37–52.

Luciani, F. (2020) 'Public slaves in Rome: privileged or not?', *Classical Quarterly,* 70, 1–17.

Luraghi, N. (2002a) 'Helotic slavery reconsidered' in A. Powell and S. Hodkinson (eds), *Sparta: Beyond the Mirage,* Swansea, 227–48.

Luraghi, N. (2002b) ''Becoming Messenian', *Journal of Hellenic Studies,* 122, 45–69.

Luraghi, N. (2009) 'The helots: comparative approaches, ancient and modern' in S. Hodkinson (ed.), *Sparta: Comparative Approaches,* Swansea, 261–304.

Luraghi, N. and Alcock, S. E. (eds) (2003) *Helots and their Masters in Laconia and Messenia: Histories, Ideologies, Structures.* Cambridge, MA and London.

McCarthy, K. (2000) *Slaves, Masters and the Art of Authority in Plautine Comedy.* Princeton.

McClintock, A. (2010) *Servi della pena. Condannati a morte nella Roma imperial.* Naples.

McCurry, S. (1995) *Masters of Small Worlds: Yeoman Households, Gender Relations and the Political Culture of the Antebellum South Carolina Low Country.* New York and Oxford.

McGinn, T. A. J. (1990) 'Ne serva prostituatur', *Zeitschrift der Savigny-Stiftung für Rechtsgeschichte: Romanistische Abteilung,* 107, 315–53.

McGinn, T. A. J. (1991) 'Concubinage and the lex Iulia on adultery', *Transactions of the American Philological Association,* 121, 335–75.

McGinn, T. A. J. (2010) *The Economy of Prostitution in the Roman World: A Study of Social History and the Brothel*. Ann Arbor.

McKeown, N. (2007a) *The Invention of Ancient Slavery?* London.

McKeown, N. (2007b) 'The sound of John Henderson laughing: Pliny 3.14 and Roman slaveowners' fear of their slaves' in Serghidou (2007), 265–79.

McKeown, N. (2010) 'Inventing slaveries: switching the argument' in Heinen (2010a), 39–59.

McKeown, N. (2012) 'Magic, religion, and the Roman slave: resistance, control and community' in Hodkinson and Geary (2012), 279–308.

McKeown, N. (2019) 'Slaves as active subjects: collective strategies' in Hodkinson, Kleijwegt and Vlassopoulos (2016–), published online, DOI: 10.1093/oxfordhb/9780199575251.013.25.

MacLean, R. (2018) *Freed Slaves and Roman Imperial Culture: Social Integration and the Transformation of Values*. Cambridge.

McLuhan, E. (2001) 'Ministerium seruitutis meae: the metaphor and reality of slavery in Saint Patrick's Epistola and Confessio' in J. Carey, M. Herbert and P. Ó Riain (eds), *Studies in Irish Hagiography: Saints and Scholars*, Dublin, 63–71.

MacMullen, R. (1987) 'Late Roman slavery', *Historia*, 36, 359–82.

MacMullen, R. (1990) *Changes in the Roman Empire: Essays in the Ordinary*. Princeton.

Mactoux, M. M. (1980) *Douleia: esclavage et pratiques discursives dans l'Athènes classique*. Paris.

Mactoux, M. M. (1988) 'Lois de Solon sur les esclaves et formation d'une société esclavagiste' in Yuge and Doi (1988), 331–54.

Mactoux, M. M. (2008) 'Regards sur la proclamation de l'affranchissement au théâtre à Athènes' in Gonzalès (2008), 437–51.

Maffi, A. (1997) *Il diritto di famiglia nel codice di Gortina*. Milan.

Maffi, A. (2007) 'Le butin humain dans le monde ancien', *Hypothèses*, 10, 307–12.

Magalhães de Oliveira, J. C. (2012) *Potestas populi: participation populaire et action collective dans les villes de l'Afrique romaine tardive (vers 300–430 apr. J.-C.)*. Turnhout.

Magalhães de Oliveira, J. C. (2020) 'Late antiquity: the age of crowds?', *Past & Present*, 249, 3–52.

Malaspina, E. (2003) 'La terminologia latina delle professioni femminili nel mondo antico', *Mediterraneo Antico*, 6, 347–91.

Malka, O. and Paz, Y. (2019) 'Ab hostibus captus et a latronibus captus: the impact of the Roman model of citizenship on Rabbinic law', *Jewish Quarterly Review*, 109, 141–72.

Mann, M. (1986) *The Sources of Social Power: Volume 1, A History of Power from the Beginning to AD 1760*. Cambridge.

Mann, M. (2012) *Sahibs, Sklaven und Soldaten. Geschichte des Menschenhandels rund um den Indischen Ozean*. Darmstadt.

Manning, C. E. (1989) 'Stoicism and slavery in the Roman Empire' in H. Temporini (ed.), *Aufstieg und Niedergang der Römischen Welt II*, 36:3, Berlin and New York, 1518–43.

Marinović, L. P., Golubcova, E. S., Šifman, I. Š. and Pavlovskaja, A. I. (1992) *Die Sklaverei in den östlichen Provinzen des Römischen Reiches im 1.-3. Jahrhundert*. Stuttgart.

Marti, L. (ed.) (2014) *La famille dans le Proche-Orient ancien: réalités, symbolismes et images*. Winona Lake, IN.

Martin, D. B. (1990) *Slavery as Salvation: The Metaphor of Slavery in Pauline Christianity*. New Haven, CT and London.

Martin, D. B. (1993) 'Slavery and the ancient Jewish family' in S. J. D. Cohen (ed.), *The Jewish Family in Antiquity*, Atlanta, 113–29.

Martin, D. B. (2003) 'Slave families and slaves in families' in Balch and Osiek (2003), 207–30.

Martin, J. D. (2004) *Divided Mastery: Slave Hiring in the American South*. Cambridge, MA.

Martin, M. (2002) 'Le forme di dipendenza nel mondo celtico da Posidonio a Cesare', *Mediterraneo Antico*, 5, 639–76.

Marx, K. and F. Engels (2002) [1848] *The Communist Manifesto*. London.

Marzano, A. (2007) *Roman Villas in Central Italy: A Social and Economic History*. Leiden and Boston, MA.

Marzano, A. (2013) *Harvesting the Sea: The Exploitation of Marine Resources in the Roman Mediterranean*. Oxford.

Marzano, A. and Métraux, G. P. (eds) (2018) *The Roman Villa in the Mediterranean Basin: Late Republic to Late Antiquity*. Cambridge.

Mayr, E. (2006) 'Typological versus population thinking' in E. Sober (ed.), *Conceptual Issues in Evolutionary Biology*, Cambridge, MA and London, 325–8.

Mavrojannis, T. (2007) 'Rébellions d'esclaves et réactions politiques de 137 à 101 av. J.-C.' in Serghidou (2007), 423–34.

Mavrojannis, T. (2018) 'Le commerce des esclaves syriens (143–88 av. J.-C.)', *Syria: Archéologie, Art, Histoire*, 85, 245–74.

Mavrojannis, T. (2019) *Il commercio degli schiavi in Siria e nel Mediterraneo Orientale. Il quadro politico dall'inizio della pirateria cilicia sino a Pompeo (143/2–67 a.C.)*. Rome.

Maximova, A. (2001) 'Joseph Vogt und die Begründung seines Sklavereiprojekts aus russischer Sicht' in Bellen and Heinen (2001), 3–10.

Meier, C. (2011) *A Culture of Freedom: Ancient Greece and the Origins of Europe*. Oxford.

Meillassoux, C. (1991) *The Anthropology of Slavery: The Womb of Iron and Gold*. London.

Mele, A. (1994) 'Rites d'initiation des jeunes et processus de libération: le cas des Brettii' in Annequin and Garrido-Hory (1994), 37–58.

Mélèze-Modrzejewski, J. (1976) 'Aut nascuntur, aut fiunt: les schémas des sources de l'esclavage dans la théorie grecque et dans le droit romain' in *Actes 1973*, 351–84.

Melluso, M. (2000) *La schiavitù nell'età giustinianea: disciplina giuridica e rilevanza sociale*. Paris.

Menu, B. (1977) 'Les rapports de dépendance en Egypte à l'époque saïte et perse', *Revue historique de droit français et étranger*, 55, 391–401.

Menu, B. (ed.) (2004a) *La dépendance rurale dans l'Antiquité égyptienne et proche-orientale*. Cairo.

Menu, B. (2004b) 'Captifs de guerre et dépendance rurale dans l'Égypte du Nouvel Empire' in Menu (2004a), 187–209.

Meyer, E. (1898) *Die Sklaverei im Altertum*. Dresden.

Miers, S. and Kopytoff, I. (eds) (1977) *Slavery in Africa: Historical and Anthropological Perspectives*. Madison, WI.

Millar, F. (1984) 'Condemnation to hard labour in the Roman Empire, from the Julio-Claudians to Constantine', *Papers of the British School at Rome*, 52, 124–47.

Miller, J. C. (2008) 'Slaving as historical process: examples from the ancient Mediterranean and the modern Atlantic' in Dal Lago and Katsari (2008a), 70–102.

Miller, J. C. (2012) *The Problem of Slavery as History: A Global Approach*. New Haven and London.

Mintz, S. W. (1974) *Caribbean Transformations*. Chicago.

Mintz, S. W. (1986) *Sweetness and Power: The Place of Sugar in Modern History*. New York.

Mintz, S. W. (2010) *Three Ancient Colonies: Caribbean Themes and Variations*. Cambridge, MA and London.

Mintz, S. W. and Price, R. (1992) *The Birth of African-American Culture: An Anthropological Perspective*. Boston.

Miura, T. and Philips, J. E. (eds) (2000) *Slave Elites in the Middle East and Africa: A Comparative Study*. London.

Moatti, C. (2015) *The Birth of Critical Thinking in Republican Rome*. Cambridge.

Moatti, C. and Müller, C. (eds) (2018) *Statuts personnels et espaces sociaux: questions grecques et romaines.* Paris.

Moggi, M. and Cordiano, G. (eds) (1997) *Schiavi e dipendenti nell' ambito dell' 'oikos' e della 'familia'.* Pisa.

Molina Vidal, J., Grau Mira, I. and Llidó López, F. (2017) 'Housing slaves on estates: a proposed ergastulum at the Villa of Rufio (Giano dell'Umbria)', *Journal of Roman Archaeology,* 30, 387–406.

Momigliano, A. (1987) 'Moses Finley and slavery: a personal note' in Finley (1987), 1–6.

Montoya, B. (2015) *L'esclavitud en l'economia antiga: fonaments discursius de la historiografia moderna (segles XV–XVIII).* Besançon.

Morgan, J. L. (2004) *Laboring Women: Reproduction and Gender in New World Slavery.* Philadelphia.

Morgan, P. D. (1998) *Slave Counterpoint: Black Culture in the Eighteenth-Century Chesapeake and Lowcountry.* Chapel Hill, NC and London.

Morley, N. (2011) 'Slavery under the Principate' in Bradley and Cartledge (2011), 265–86.

Morris, C. (1998) 'The articulation of two worlds: the master-slave relationship', *Journal of American History,* 85, 982–1007.

Morris, I. (1998) 'Remaining invisible: the archaeology of the excluded in classical Athens' in Joshel and Murnaghan (1998), 193–220.

Morris, I. (2011) 'Archaeology and Greek slavery' in Bradley and Cartledge (2011), 176–93.

Morris, S. (2018) 'Material evidence: looking for slaves? The archaeological record: Greece' in Hodkinson, Kleijwegt and Vlassopoulos (2016–), published online, DOI: 10.1093/oxfordhb/9780199575251.013.8.

Morris, S. and Papadopoulos, J. K. (2005) 'Greek towers and slaves: an archaeology of exploitation', *American Journal of Archaeology,* 109, 155–225.

Morris, T. D. (1996) *Southern Slavery and the Law, 1619–1860.* Chapel Hill, NC.

Morton, P. (2012) *Refiguring the Sicilian Slave Wars: from Servile Unrest to Civic Disquiet and Social Disorder.* PhD dissertation, University of Edinburgh.

Morton, P. (2013) 'Eunus: the cowardly king', *Classical Quarterly,* 63, 237–52.

Morton, P. (2014) 'The geography of rebellion: strategy and supply in the two "Sicilian slave wars"', *Bulletin of the Institute of Classical Studies,* 57, 20–38.

Mosig-Walburg, K. (2010) 'Deportationen römischer Christen in das Sasanidenreich durch Shapur I. und ihre Folgen–eine Neubewertung', *Klio,* 92, 117–56.

Mossé, C. (1991) 'La place de la pallakè dans la famille athénienne' in M. Gagarin (ed.), *Symposion 1990: Vorträge zur griechischen und hellenistischen Rechtsgeschichte,* Cologne, 273–9.

Mouritsen, H. (2011a) *The Freedman in the Roman World.* Cambridge.

Mouritsen, H. (2011b) 'The families of Roman slaves and freedmen' in Rawson (2011), 129–44.

Mouritsen, H. (2013) 'Slavery and manumission in the Roman elite: a study of the columbaria of the Volusii and the Statilii' in George (2013a), 43–68.

Na'aman, N. (1986) 'Habiru and Hebrews: the transfer of a social term to the literary sphere', *Journal of Near Eastern Studies,* 45, 271–88.

Nadel, B. I. (1976) 'Slavery and related forms of labor on the North shore of the Euxine in antiquity' in *Actes 1973,* 195–233.

Nafissi, M. (2005) *Ancient Athens and Modern Ideology. Value, Theory and Evidence in Historical Sciences: Max Weber, Karl Polanyi and Moses Finley.* London.

Naquin, S. and Rawski, E. S. (1987) *Chinese Society in the Eighteenth Century.* New Haven and London.

Nash, G. B. (2005) *The Unknown American Revolution: The Unruly Birth of Democracy and the Struggle to Create America.* New York.

Nash Briggs, D. (2002) 'Servants at a rich man's feast: early Etruscan household slaves and their procurement', *Etruscan Studies*, 9, 153–76.

Nash Briggs, D. (2003) 'Metals, salt and slaves: economic links between Gaul and Italy from the eighth to the late sixth centuries BC', *Oxford Journal of Archaeology*, 22, 243–59.

Ndoye, M. (2010) *Groupes sociaux et idéologie de travail dans les mondes homérique et hésiodique.* Besançon.

Nehlsen, H. (1972) *Sklavenrecht zwischen Antike und Mittelalter: I. Ostgoten, Westgoten, Franken, Langobarden.* Gottingen.

Nehlsen, H. (2001) 'Die servi, ancillae und mancipia der Lex Baiuvariorum. Ein Beitrag zur Geschichte der Sklaverei in Bayern' in Bellen and Heinen (2001), 505–21.

Newman, S. P. (2013) *A New World of Labor: The Development of Plantation Slavery in the British Atlantic.* Philadelphia.

Nicholson, E. (2018) 'Polybios, the laws of war, and Philip V of Macedon', *Historia*, 67, 434–53.

Nieboer, H. J. (1900) *Slavery as an Industrial System: Ethnological Researches.* Hague.

Nietzsche, F. (1997) [1887] *On the Genealogy of Morality.* Cambridge.

Nippel, W. (2005) 'Marx, Weber and classical slavery', *Classics Ireland*, 12, 31–49.

Nishida, M. (2003) *Slavery and Identity: Ethnicity, Gender and Race in Salvador, Brazil, 1808–88.* Bloomington.

North, J. (2012) 'The ritual activity of Roman slaves' in Hodkinson and Geary (2012), 67–93.

Noy, D. (2000) *Foreigners at Rome: Citizens and Strangers.* London.

Nunbhakdi, S. (1998) 'Étude sur le système de sakdina en Thaïlande' in Condominas (1998), 459–81.

Oakes, J. (1982) *The Ruling Race: A History of American Slaveholders.* New York.

Oakes, J. (1986) 'The political significance of slave resistance', *History Workshop Journal*, 22, 89–107.

Oakes, J. (1990) *Slavery and Freedom: An Interpretation of the Old South.* New York and London.

Ober, J. (2015) *The Rise and Fall of Classical Greece.* Princeton and Oxford.

Occhipinti, E. (2015) 'Athenaeus' Sixth Book on Greek and Roman slavery', *Scripta Classica Israelica*, 34, 115–27.

Oded, B. (1979) *Mass Deportations and Deportees in the Neo-Assyrian Empire.* Wiesbaden.

Oppenheim, A. L. (1955) '"Siege-documents" from Nippur', *Iraq*, 17, 69–89.

Osborne, R. (1995) 'The economics and politics of slavery at Athens' in Powell (1995), 27–43.

Osborne, R. (2000) 'Religion, imperial politics and the offering of freedom to slaves' in Hunter and Edmondson (2000), 75–92.

Osborne, R. (2011) *The History Written on the Classical Greek Body.* Cambridge.

Osborne, R. (2017) 'Visual evidence – of what?' in Hodkinson, Kleijwegt and Vlassopoulos (2016–), published online, DOI: 10.1093/oxfordhb/9780199575251.013.27.

Osgood, J. (2006) *Caesar's Legacy: Civil War and the Emergence of the Roman Empire.* Cambridge.

Osiek, C. (1981) 'The ransom of captives: evolution of a tradition', *Harvard Theological Review*, 74, 365–86.

Owens, W. M. (2019) *The Representation of Slavery in the Greek Novel: Resistance and Appropriation.* London and New York.

Owensby, B. P. (2009) 'Legal personality and the processes of slave liberty in early-modern New Spain', *European Review of History / Revue européenne d'histoire*, 16, 365–82.

Oxé, A. (1904) 'Zur älteren Nomenklatur der römischen Sklaven', *Rheinisches Museum für Philologie*, 59, 108–40.

Padilla Peralta, D.-E. (2017) 'Slave religiosity in the Roman Middle Republic', *Classical Antiquity*, 36, 317–69.

Palmeira, M. S. (2018) *Moses Finley e a economia antiga: a produção social de uma inovação histo-riográfica.* Sao Paulo.

Pałuchowski, A. (2010) 'La propriété foncière privée et la main-d'œuvre servile en Crète aux époques hellénistique et romaine', *Palamedes*, 5, 37–70.

Panzeri, A. (2011) *Dione di Prusa: Su libertà e schiavitù. Sugli schiavi. Discorsi 14 e 15.* Pisa and Rome.

Paradiso, A. (1991) *Forme di dipendenza nel mondo greco. Ricerche sul VI libro di Ateneo.* Bari.

Paradiso, A. (1999) 'Schiavitù femminile e violenza carnale: stupro e coscienza dello stupro sulle schiave in Grecia' in Reduzzi-Merola and Storchi Marino (1999), 145–62.

Paradiso, A. (2007) 'Sur la servitude volontaire des Mariandyniens d'Héraclée du Pont' in Serghidou (2007), 23–33.

Paradiso, A. (2008) 'Politiques de l'affranchissement chez Thucydide' in Gonzales (2008), 65–76.

Pargas, D. A. (2006) '"Various means of providing for their own tables": comparing slave family economies in the antebellum South', *American Nineteenth-Century History*, 7, 361–87.

Parker, H. (1989) 'Crucially funny, or Tranio on the couch: the servus callidus and jokes about torture', *Transactions of the American Philological Association*, 119, 233–46.

Parker, H. (1998) 'Loyal slaves and loyal wives: the crisis of the outsider-within and Roman exemplum literature' in Joshel and Murnaghan (1998), 152–73.

Parker, H. (2007) 'Free women and male slaves, or Mandingo meets the Roman empire' in Serghidou (2007), 281–98.

Parmenter, C. S. (2020) 'Journeys into slavery along the Black Sea coast, c. 550–450 BCE', *Classical Antiquity*, 39, 57–94.

Patterson, O. (1982) *Slavery and Social Death: A Comparative Study.* Cambridge, MA.

Patterson, O. (1991) *Freedom in the Making of Western Culture, Volume I.* London.

Peachin, M. (ed.) (2011) *The Oxford Handbook of Social Relations in the Roman World.* Oxford.

Pelteret, D. (1980) 'Slave raiding and slave trading in early England', *Anglo-Saxon England*, 9, 99–114.

Pelteret, D. (2001) *Slavery in Early Mediaeval England: From the Reign of Alfred until the Twelfth Century.* Woodbridge.

Penner, L. (2012) 'Gender, household structure and slavery: re-interpreting the aristocratic columbaria of early imperial Rome' in Laurence and Strömberg (2012), 143–58.

Penningroth, D. C. (2003) *The Claims of Kinfolk: African American Property and Community in the Nineteenth-Century South.* Chapel Hill, NC.

Pérez, C. (1984) *Index thématique des références à l'esclavage et à la dépendance: Cicéron Lettres à Atticus.* Paris.

Perotti, E. (1974) 'Esclaves choris oikountes' in *Actes 1972*, 47–56.

Perotti, E. (1976) 'Contribution à l'étude d'une autre catégorie d'esclaves attiques: les andra-poda misthophorounta' in *Actes 1973*, 181–94.

Perry, J. S. (2011) 'Organized societies: collegia' in Peachin (2011), 499–515.

Perry, J. S. (2014) 'From Frankfurt to Westermann: forced labor and the early development of Finley's thought', *American Journal of Philology*, 135, 221–41.

Perry, M. J. (2013) *Gender, Manumission and the Roman Freedwoman.* New York.

Persson, K. G. (1988) *Pre-Industrial Economic Growth: Social Organization and Technological Progress in Europe.* Oxford.

Petersen, L. H. (2006) *The Freedman in Roman Art and Art History.* New York.

Pétré-Grenouilleau, O. (2004) *Les traites négrières: essai d'histoire globale.* Paris.

Pevnick, S. D. (2010) 'ΣΥΡΙΣΚΟΣ ΕΓΡΦΣΕΝ: loaded names, artistic identity and reading an Athenian vase', *Classical Antiquity*, 29, 222–53.

Philips, J. E. (2003–4) 'Slavery as a human institution', *Afrika Zamani*, 11/2, 27–48.

Phillips, W. D. Jr (2014) *Slavery in Medieval and Early Modern Iberia*. Philadelphia.

Piersen, W. D. (1988) *Black Yankees: The Development of an Afro-American Subculture in Eighteenth-Century New England*. Amherst, NY.

Pipes, D. (1981) *Slave Soldiers and Islam: The Genesis of a Military System*. New Haven, CT.

Pirie, F. (2013) *The Anthropology of Law*. Oxford.

Pomeroy, A. J. (1991) 'Status and status-concern in the Greco-Roman dream-books', *Ancient Society*, 22, 51–74.

Ponchia, S. (2017) 'Slaves, serfs, and prisoners in imperial Assyria (IX–VII cent. BC): a review of written sources', *State Archives of Assyria Bulletin*, 23, 157–79.

Porter, J. D. (2019a) *The Diversity of Private Slaving Strategies in Classical Athens*. PhD dissertation, University of Nottingham.

Porter, J. D. (2019b) 'Slavery and Athens' economic efflorescence', *Mare Nostrum*, 10.2, 25–50.

Postgate, J. N. (1987) 'Employer, employee and employment in the Neo-Assyrian empire' in M. A. Powell (ed.), *Labor in the Ancient Near East*, New Haven, 257–70.

Pottage, A. (2020) 'Finding Melanesia in ancient Rome: Mauss's Anthropology of nexum' in S. Bell and P. J. Du Plessis (eds), *Roman Law before the Twelve Tables: An Interdisciplinary Approach*, Edinburgh, 171–98.

Potts, D. T. (2011) 'The abbuttu and the alleged Elamite "slave hairstyle"' in L. Vacín (ed.), *U4 du11-ga-ni sá mu-ni-ib-du11: Ancient Near Eastern Studies in Memory of Blahoslav Hruška*, Dresden, 183–94.

Powell, A. (ed.) (1995) *The Greek World*. London.

Prachner, G. (1980) *Die Sklaven und Freigelassenen im arretinischen Sigillatagewerbe: epigraphische, nomenklatorische sowie sozial-und wirtschaftsgeschichtliche Untersuchungen der arretinischen Firmen- und Töpferstempel*. Stuttgart.

Prag, J. R. and Repath, I. D. (eds) (2009) *Petronius: A Handbook*. Chichester and Malden, MA.

Preiser-Kapeller, J. (2018) *Jenseits von Rom und Karl dem Großen: Aspekte der globalen Verflechtung in der langen Spätantike, 300–800 n. Chr*. Vienna.

Price, R. (2011) 'The concept of creolisation' in Eltis and Engerman (2011), 513–37.

Pritchett, W. K. (1991) *The Greek State at War, Part V*. Berkeley, Los Angeles and Oxford.

Purcell, N. (1985) 'Wine and wealth in ancient Italy', *Journal of Roman Studies*, 75, 1–19.

Purcell, N. (2005) 'Colonisation and Mediterranean history' in Hurst and Owen (2005), 115–39.

Raaflaub, K. (2004) *The Discovery of Freedom in Ancient Greece*. Chicago and London.

Rabbås, Ø. (2015) 'Virtue, respect and morality in Aristotle', *Journal of Value Inquiry*, 49, 619–43.

Raboteau, A. J. (1999) *African-American Religions*. New York.

Raboteau, A. J. (2004) *Slave Religion: The 'Invisible Institution' in the Antebellum South*. New York.

Radner, K. (1997) *Die neuassyrischen Privatrechtsurkunden als Quelle für Mensch und Umwelt*. Helsinki.

Radner, K. (2015) 'Hired labour in the Neo-Assyrian Empire' in Steinkeller and Hudson (2015), 329–43.

Rädle, H. (1970) 'Selbsthilfeorganisationen der Sklaven und Freigelassenen in Delphi', *Gymnasium*, 77, 1–5.

Raffeiner, H. (1977) *Sklaven und Freigelassene: eine soziologische Studie auf der Grundlage des griechischen Grabepigramms*. Innsbruck.

Ramelli, I. (2016) *Social Justice and the Legitimacy of Slavery: The Role of Philosophical Asceticism from Ancient Judaism to Late Antiquity*. Oxford.

Ramin, J. and Veyne, P. (1981) 'Droit romain et société: les hommes libres qui passent pour esclaves et l'esclavage volontaire', *Historia*, 30, 472–97.

Randall, R. H. (1953) 'The Erechtheum workmen', *American Journal of Archaeology*, 57, 199–210.

Ransmeier, J. S. (2017) *Sold People: Traffickers and Family Life in North China*. Cambridge, MA.

Raskolnikoff, M. (1990) *Des anciens et des modernes*. Paris.

Rauh, N. K. (1997) 'Who were the Cilician pirates?' in S. Swiny et al. (eds), *Res Maritimae: Cyprus and the Eastern Mediterranean from Prehistory to Late Antiquity*, Atlanta, 263–83.

Rauh, N. K., Dillon, M. J. and McClain, T. D. (2008) 'Ochlos nautikos: leisure culture and underclass discontent in the Roman maritime world', *Memoirs of the American Academy in Rome*, supplementary volume 6, 197–242.

Rawson, B. (ed.) (2011) *A Companion to Families in the Greek and Roman Worlds*. Malden, MA.

Rawson, E. (1985) *Intellectual Life in the Late Roman Republic*. London.

Read, I. (2012) *The Hierarchies of Slavery in Santos, Brazil 1822–1888*. Stanford.

Redford, D. (2004) *From Slave to Pharaoh: The Black Experience of Ancient Egypt*. Baltimore.

Reduzzi-Merola, F. (1990) *'Servo parere'. Studi sulla condizione giuridica degli schiavi vicari e dei sottoposti a schiavi nell'esperienza greca e romana*. Naples.

Reduzzi-Merola, F. and Storchi Marino, A. (eds) (1999) *Femmes - esclaves. Modèles d'interprétation anthropologique, économique, juridique*. Naples.

Reid, A. (ed.) (1983) *Slavery, Bondage and Dependency in Southeast Asia*. New York.

Reid, A. (1998) 'Merdeka: the concept of freedom in Indonesia' in D. Kelly and A. Reid (eds), *Asian Freedoms: The Idea of Freedom in East and Southeast Asia*, Cambridge, 141–60.

Reid, A. (2018) '"Slavery so gentle": a fluid spectrum of Southeast Asian conditions of bondage' in Lenski and Cameron (2018), 410–28.

Reid, J. N. (2015) 'Runaways and fugitive-catchers during the Third Dynasty of Ur', *Journal of the Economic and Social History of the Orient*, 58, 576–605.

Reid, J. N. (2017) 'The children of slaves in early Mesopotamian laws and edicts', *Revue d'Assyriologie*, 111, 9–23.

Reinhold, M. (1971) 'Usurpation of status and status symbols in the Roman Empire', *Historia*, 20, 275–302.

Reis, J. J. (1993) *Slave Rebellion in Brazil: The Muslim Uprising of 1835 in Bahia*. Baltimore.

Reis, J. J. (1997) '"The revolution of the ganhadores": urban labour, ethnicity and the African strike of 1857 in Bahia, Brazil', *Journal of Latin American Studies*, 29, 355–93.

Reis, J. J. (2001) 'Candomblé in nineteenth-century Bahia: priests, followers, clients', *Slavery & Abolition*, 22, 91–115.

Reis, J. J. (2003) *Death is a Festival: Funeral Rites and Rebellion in Nineteenth-Century Brazil*. Chapel Hill, NC.

Reis, J. J. (2005) 'Street labor in Bahia on the eve of abolition' in Curto and Soulodre-LaFrance (2005), 141–72.

Reis, J. J., dos Santos Gomes, F. and Carvalho, M. J. (2020) *The Story of Rufino: Slavery, Freedom, and Islam in the Black Atlantic*. New York.

Riccardi, S. (1997) *Die Erforschung der antiken Sklaverei in Italien vom Risorgimento bis Ettore Ciccotti*. Stuttgart.

Richardson, S. (2019) 'Walking capital: the economic function and social location of Babylonian servitude', *Journal of Global Slavery*, 4, 1–58.

Richlin, A. (2017) *Slave Theater in the Roman Republic: Plautus and Popular Comedy*. Cambridge.

Richter, W. (1958) 'Seneca und die Sklaven', *Gymnasium*, 65, 196–218.

Ricl, M. (2009) 'Legal and social status of threptoi and related categories in narrative and documentary sources' in Cotton et al. (2009), 93–114.

Riess, W. and Fagan, G. G. (eds) (2016) *The Topography of Violence in the Greco-Roman World*. Ann Arbor.

Rigsby, K. J. (1997) *Asylia: Territorial Inviolability in the Hellenistic World*. Berkeley and Los Angeles.

Rihll, T. (1996) 'The origin and establishment of ancient Greek slavery' in Bush (1996), 89–111.

Rihll, T. (2008) 'Slavery and technology in pre-industrial contexts' in Dal Lago and Katsari (2008a), 127–47.

Rihll, T. (2010) 'Skilled slaves and the economy: the silver mines of the Laurion' in Heinen (2010a), 203–20.

Rinehart, N. T. (2016) 'The man that was a thing: reconsidering human commodification in slavery', *Journal of Social History*, 50, 28–50.

Ringrose, K. M. (2003) *The Perfect Servant: Eunuchs and the Social Construction of Gender in Byzantium*. Chicago.

Rio, A. (2006) 'Freedom and unfreedom in early medieval Francia: the evidence of the legal formularies', *Past & Present*, 193, 7–40.

Rio, A. (2008) 'High and low: ties of dependence in the Frankish kingdoms', *Transactions of the Royal Historical Society*, 18, 43–68.

Rio, A. (2011) 'Self-sale and voluntary entry into unfreedom, 300–1100', *Journal of Social History*, 45, 661–85.

Rio, A. (2015a) 'Penal enslavement in the early middle ages' in De Vito and Lichtenstein (2015), 79–107.

Rio, A. (2015b) '"Half-free" categories in the early middle ages: fine status distinctions before professional lawyers' in P. Dresch and J. Scheele (eds), *Legalism: Rules and Categories*, Oxford, 129–52.

Rio, A. (2017) *Slavery after Rome, 500–1100*. Oxford.

Rix, H. (1994) *Die Termini der Unfreiheit in den Sprachen Alt-Italiens*. Stuttgart.

Robert, J. C. (2014) 'Vente et rançonnement du butin humain des armées romaines à l'époque des conquêtes (264 av. J.-C. – 117 ap. J.-C.)', *Les Cahiers de Framespa: Nouveaux champs de l'histoire sociale*, 17, published online, DOI: 10.4000/framespa.3079.

Robertson, B. (2008) 'The slave names of *IG* I³ 1032 and the ideology of slavery at Athens' in C. Cooper (ed.), *Epigraphy and the Greek Historian*, Toronto, 79–116.

Rockman, S. (2009) *Scraping By: Wage Labor, Slavery and Survival in Early Baltimore*. Baltimore.

Roediger, D. R. (1981) 'And die in Dixie: funerals, death, and heaven in the slave community 1700–1865', *Massachusetts Review*, 22, 163–83.

Rosenstein, N. S. (2004) *Rome at War: Farms, Families and Death in the Middle Republic*. Chapel Hill, NC and London.

Rositani, A. (2018) 'From freedom to slavery: work and words at the house of prisoners of war in the Old Babylonian period', *Journal of Global Slavery*, 3, 41–67.

Rosivach, V. J. (1993) 'Agricultural slavery in the Northern colonies and in classical Athens: some comparisons', *Comparative Studies in Society and History*, 35, 551–67.

Rosivach, V. J. (1999) 'Enslaving *barbaroi* and the Athenian ideology of slavery', *Historia*, 48, 129–57.

Roth, U. (2004) 'Inscribed meaning: the *vilica* and the villa economy', *Papers of the British School at Rome*, 72, 101–24.

Roth, U. (2005) 'Food, status, and the *peculium* of agricultural slaves', *Journal of Roman Archaeology*, 18, 278–92.

Roth, U. (2007) *Thinking Tools: Agricultural Slavery between Evidence and Models*. London.

Roth, U. (ed.) (2010a) *By the Sweat of your Brow: Roman Slavery in its Socio-Economic Setting*. London.

Roth, U. (2010b) '*Peculium*, freedom, citizenship: golden triangle or vicious circle? An act in two parts' in Roth (2010a), 91–120.

Roth, U. (2011) 'Men without hope', *Papers of the British School at Rome*, 79, 71–94.

Roth, U. (2016) 'Slavery and the Church in Visigothic Spain: the donation and will of Vincent of Huesca', *Antiquité Tardive*, 24, 433–52.

Rotman, Y. (2009) *Byzantine Slavery and the Mediterranean World*. Cambridge, MA and London.

Roubineau, J. M. (2015) *Les cités grecques (VIe–IIe siècle av. J.-C.): Essai d'histoire sociale*. Paris.

Rouge, J. (1983) 'Escroquerie et brigandage en Afrique romaine au temps de Saint Augustin (Ep. 8★ et 10★)' in *Les lettres de Saint Augustin découvertes par Johannes Divjak*, Paris, 177–88.

Roy, J. (2012) 'Cittadini ridotti in schiavitù: il consolidarsi della schiavitù nella Grecia classica' in Di Nardo and Lucchetta (2012), 53–66.

Rowlandson, J. (forthcoming) 'Creating a slave society? The Greek and Roman impact on Egypt' in Hodkinson, Kleijwegt and Vlassopoulos (2016–).

Ruffing, K. and Drexhage, H.-J. (2008) 'Antike Sklavenpreise' in P. Mauritsch et al. (eds), *Antike Lebenswelten: Konstanz - Wandel - Wirkungsmacht. Festschrift für Ingomar Weiler zum 70. Geburtstag*, Wiesbaden, 321–51.

Rugemer, E. B. (2018) *Slave Law and the Politics of Resistance in the Early Atlantic World*. Cambridge MA and London.

Rushforth, B. (2012) *Bonds of Alliance: Indigenous and Atlantic Slaveries in New France*. Williamsburg, VA.

Russell-Wood, A. J. R. (1974) 'Black and mulatto brotherhoods in colonial Brazil: a study in collective behavior', *Hispanic American Historical Review*, 54, 567–602.

Sabin, P., van Wees, H. and Whitby, M. (eds) (2007) *The Cambridge History of Greek and Roman Warfare, Volume I: Greece, the Hellenistic World and the Rise of Rome*. Cambridge.

Sabnis, S. (2011) 'Lucian's Lychnopolis and the problems of slave surveillance', *American Journal of Philology*, 132, 205–42.

Sahaydachny, A. N. (1994) *De Coniugio Seruorum: A Study of the Legal Debate about Marriage of Unfree Persons among Decretists and Decretalists from AD 1140–1215*. PhD dissertation, Columbia University.

Saller, R. (1994) *Patriarchy, Property and Death in the Roman Family*. Cambridge.

Salway, B. (2010) 'Mancipium rusticum sive urbanum: the slave chapter of Diocletian's edict on maximum prices' in Roth (2010a), 1–20.

Samson, R. (1989) 'Rural slavery, inscriptions, archaeology and Marx: a response to Ramsay MacMullen's "Late Roman slavery"', *Historia*, 38, 99–110.

Sánchez León, M. L. and López Nadal, G. (eds) (1996) *Captius i esclaus a l'antiguitat i al món modern*. Naples.

Sandon, T. and Scalco, L. (2020) 'More than mistresses, less than wives: the role of Roman *concubinae* in light of their funerary monuments', *Papers of the British School at Rome*, DOI: 10.1017/S0068246220000057.

Santos-Granero, F. (2009) *Vital Enemies: Slavery, Predation and the Amerindian Political Economy of Life*. Austin.

Sartori, F. (1973) 'Cinna e gli schiavi' in *Actes 1971*, 151–69.

Saxonhouse, A. (2006) *Free Speech and Democracy in Ancient Athens*. Cambridge.

Schäfer, D. (2001) 'Frauen in der Arena' in Bellen and Heinen (2001), 243–68.

Scheidel, W. (1990) 'Free-born and manumitted bailiffs in the Graeco-Roman world', *Classical Quarterly*, 40, 591–3.

Scheidel, W. (1995) 'The most silent women of Greece and Rome: rural labour and women's life in the ancient world (I)', *Greece & Rome*, 42, 202–17.

Scheidel, W. (1996a) 'The most silent women of Greece and Rome: rural labour and women's life in the ancient world (II)', *Greece & Rome*, 43, 1–10.

Scheidel, W. (1996b) 'Reflections on the differential valuation of slaves in Diocletian's Price Edict and in the United States', *Münstersche Beiträge zur Antiken Handelsgeschichte*, 15, 67–79.

Scheidel, W. (1997) 'Quantifying the sources of slaves in the early Roman Empire', *Journal of Roman Studies*, 87, 156–69.

Scheidel, W. (1999) 'The slave population of Roman Italy: speculation and constraints', *Topoi*, 9, 129–44.

Scheidel, W. (2002) 'The hireling and the slave: a transatlantic perspective' in Cartledge, Cohen and Foxhall (2002), 193–202.

Scheidel, W. (2004) 'Human mobility in Roman Italy, I: the free population', *Journal of Roman Studies*, 94, 1–26.

Scheidel, W. (2005a) 'Real slave prices and the relative cost of slave labor in the Greco-Roman world', *Ancient Society*, 35, 1–17.

Scheidel, W. (2005b) 'Human mobility in Roman Italy, II: the slave population', *Journal of Roman Studies*, 95, 64–79.

Scheidel, W. (2008) 'The comparative economics of slavery in the Greco-Roman world' in Dal Lago and C. Katsari (2008a), 105–26.

Scheidel, W. (2009) 'A peculiar institution? Greco-Roman monogamy in global context', *History of the Family*, 14, 280–91.

Scheidel, W. (2011) 'Monogamy and polygyny' in Rawson (2011), 108–15.

Scheidel, W., Morris, I. and Saller, R. (eds) (2007) *The Cambridge Economic History of the Greco-Roman World*. Cambridge.

Schermerhorn, C. (2015) *The Business of Slavery and the Rise of American Capitalism, 1815–1860*. New Haven and London.

Schlaifer, R. (1936) 'Greek theories of slavery from Homer to Aristotle', *Harvard Studies in Classical Philology*, 47, 165–204.

Schloen, J. D. (2001) *The House of the Father as Fact and Symbol: Patrimonialism in Ugarit and the Ancient Near East*. Winona Lake, IN.

Schmitz, W. (2012) 'Sklavenfamilien im archaischen und klassischen Griechenland' in Heinen (2012), 63–102.

Schneider, H. (1988) 'Schottische Aufklärung und antike Gesellschaft' in P. Kneissl and V. Losemann (eds), *Alte Geschichte und Wissenschaftsgeschichte. Festschrift für Karl Christ zum 65. Geburtstag*, Darmstadt, 431–64.

Schofield, M. (1999) 'Ideology and philosophy in Aristotle's theory of slavery' in M. Schofield, *Saving the City: Philosopher-Kings and Other Classical Paradigms*, London, 101–23.

Scholl, R. (1985) 'ΙΕΡΟΔΟΥΛΟΣ im griechisch-römischen Ägypten', *Historia*, 34, 466–92.

Scholl, R. (1990) *Corpus der ptolemäischen Sklaventexte, I–III*. Stuttgart.

Scholten, J. B. (2000) *The Politics of Plunder: Aitolians and their Koinon in the Early Hellenistic Era, 279–217 BC*. Berkeley and Los Angeles.

Schulze, H. (1998) *Ammen und Pädagogen. Sklavinnen und Sklaven als Erzieher in der Antiken Kunst und Gesellschaft*. Mainz am Rhein.

Schumacher, L. (1982) *Servus Index: Sklavenverhör und Sklavenanzeige im republikanischen und kaiserzeitlichen Rom*. Wiesbaden.

Schumacher, L. (2001a) *Sklaverei in der Antike: Alltag und Schicksal der Unfreien*. Munich.

Schumacher, L. (2001b) 'Hausgesinde – Hofgesinde. Terminologische Überlegungen zur Funktion der familia Caesaris im 1. Jh. n. Chr.' in Bellen and Heinen (2001), 331–52.

Schumacher, L. (2006) *Corpus der Römischen Rechtsquellen zur Antiken Sklaverei. Teil VI: Stellung des Sklaven im Sakralrecht*. Stuttgart.

Schumacher, L. (2010) 'On the status of private actores, dispensatores and vilici' in Roth (2010a), 31–47.

Schwartz, S. B. (1977) 'Resistance and accommodation in eighteenth-century Brazil: the slaves' view of slavery', *Hispanic American Historical Review*, 57, 69–81.

Schwartz, S. B. (1985) *Sugar Plantations in the Formation of Brazilian Society: Bahia, 1550–1835*. Cambridge.

Schwartz, S. B. (ed.) (2004) *Tropical Babylons: Sugar and the Making of the Atlantic World, 1450–1680*. Chapel Hill, NC and London.

Schweninger, L. (2009) 'Slave women, county courts and the law in the United States South: a comparative perspective', *European Review of History / Revue européenne d'histoire*, 16, 383–99.

Scott, J. C. (1985) *Weapons of the Weak: Everyday Forms of Peasant Resistance*. New Haven, CT and London.

Scott, J. C. (1990) *Domination and the Arts of Resistance: Hidden Transcripts*. New Haven and London.

Serfass, A. (2006) 'Slavery and Pope Gregory the Great', *Journal of Early Christian Studies*, 14, 77–103.

Serghidou, A. (ed.) (2007) *Fear of Slaves, Fear of Enslavement in the Ancient Mediterranean / Peur de l'esclave, peur de l'esclavage en Méditerranée ancienne (discours, représentations, pratiques)*. Besançon.

Serghidou, A. (2010) *Servitude tragique: esclaves et héros déchus dans la tragédie grecque*. Besançon.

Seri, A. (2013) *The House of Prisoners: Slavery and State in Uruk during the Revolt against Samsu-iluna*. Boston.

Setälä, P. (2002) 'Women and brick production - some new aspects' in P. Setälä et al. (eds), *Women, Wealth and Power in the Roman Empire*, Rome, 181–201.

Sewell, W. H. Jr (2005) *Logics of History: Social Theory and Social Transformation*. Chicago and London.

Shaner, K. A. (2018) *Enslaved Leadership in Early Christianity*. Oxford.

Shaw, B. D. (1984) 'Anatomy of the vampire bat', *Economy & Society*, 13, 208–49.

Shaw, B. D. (1985) 'The divine economy: Stoicism as ideology', *Latomus*, 44, 16–54.

Shaw, B. D. (1998) '"A wolf by the ears": M. I. Finley's *Ancient Slavery and Modern Ideology* in historical context' in Finley (1998), 3–74.

Shaw, B. D. (2001) *Spartacus and the Slave Wars: A Brief History with Documents*. Boston.

Shaw, B. D. (2014) 'The great transformation: slavery and the free republic' in H. I. Flower (ed.), *The Cambridge Companion to the Roman Republic*, Cambridge, 187–212.

Sidbury, J. and Cañizares-Esguerra, J. (2011) 'Mapping ethnogenesis in the early modern Atlantic', *William & Mary Quarterly*, 68, 181–208.

Silva Dias, M. O. (1995) *Power and Everyday Life: The Lives of Working Women in Nineteenth-Century Brazil*. New Brunswick, NJ.

Silver, M. (2011) 'Contractual slavery in the Roman economy', *Ancient History Bulletin*, 25, 73–132.

Simonis, M. (2017) *Cum servis nullum est conubium: Untersuchungen zu den eheähnlichen Verbind-ungen von Sklaven im westlichen Mittelmeerraum des Römischen Reiches*. Hildesheim, Zurich and New York.

Sirks, A. J. B. (1983) 'The lex Junia and the effects of informal manumission and iteration', *Revue Internationale des Droits de l'Antiquité*, 30, 211–92.

Smith, C. J. (2006) *The Roman Clan: The Gens from Ancient Ideology to Modern Anthropology*. Cambridge.

Smith, K. (2016) *Constantine and the Captive Christians of Persia: Martyrdom and Religious Identity in Late Antiquity*. Berkeley and Los Angeles.

Smith, M. M. (1998) *Debating Slavery: Economy and Society in the Antebellum American South*. Cambridge.

Smith, S. D. (2006) *Slavery, Family and Gentry Capitalism in the British Atlantic: The World of the Lascelles*. Cambridge.

Snell, D. C. (2001) *Flight and Freedom in the Ancient Near East*. Leiden, Boston and Cologne.

Snell, D. C. (2011) 'Slavery in the ancient Near East' in Bradley and Cartledge (2011), 4–21.

Snyder, C. (2010) *Slavery in Indian Country: The Changing Face of Captivity in Early America*. Cambridge, MA and London.

Sober, E. (1980) 'Evolution, population thinking and essentialism', *Philosophy of Science*, 37, 350–83.

Solin, H. (2001) 'Griechische und römische Sklavennamen. Eine vergleichende Untersuchung' in Bellen and Heinen (2001), 307–30.

Söllner, A. (2000) *Corpus der Römischen Rechtsquellen zur Antiken Sklaverei. Teil IX: Irrtümlich als Sklaven gehaltene freie Menschen und Sklaven in unsicheren Eigentumsverhältnissen - homines liberi et servi alieni bona fide servientes*. Stuttgart.

Sommer, M. H. (2000) *Sex, Law and Society in Late Imperial China*. Stanford.

Sommer, M. H. (2015) *Polyandry and Wife-Selling in Qing Dynasty China: Survival Strategies and Judicial Intervention*. Berkeley and Los Angeles.

Sosin, J. D. (2015) 'Manumission with paramone: conditional freedom?', *Transaction of the American Philological Association*, 145, 325–81.

Sosin, J. D. (2017) 'Ransom at Athens ([Dem.] 53.11)', *Historia*, 66, 130–46.

Sparkes, B. (1996) *The Red and the Black: Studies in Greek Pottery*. London.

Štaerman, E. M. (1969) *Die Blütezeit der Sklavenwirtschaft in der römischen Republik*. Wiesbaden.

Štaerman, E. M. and Trofimova, M. K. (1975) *La schiavitù nell'Italia imperiale, I–III secolo*. Rome.

Štaerman, E. M., Smirin, V. M., Belova, N. N. and Kosolovskaja, J. K. (1987) Die *Sklaverei in den westlichen Provinzen des römischen Reiches im 1.-3. Jahrhundert*. Stuttgart.

Stahlmann, I. (1992) 'Qu'on ne me cite pas les exemples des anciennes républiques! Antike Sklaverei und Französische Revolution', *Klio*, 74, 447–55.

Stampp, K. M. (1956) *The Peculiar Institution: Slavery in the Antebellum South*. New York.

Steinkeller, P. (2013) 'An archaic "prisoner plaque" from Kiš', *Revue d'Assyriologie*, 107, 131–57.

Steinkeller, P. and Hudson, M. (eds) (2015) *Labor in the Ancient World*. Dresden.

Sterk, A. (2010) 'Mission from below: captive women and conversion on the East Roman frontiers', *Church History*, 79, 1–39.

Stevenson, W. (1995) 'The rise of eunuchs in Greco-Roman antiquity', *Journal of the History of Sexuality*, 5, 495–511.

Stewart, R. (2012) *Plautus and Roman Slavery*. Malden, MA and Oxford.

Stilwell, S. (2000) 'Power, honour and shame: the ideology of royal slavery in the Sokoto Caliphate', *Africa*, 70, 394–421.

Stilwell, S. (2004) *Paradoxes of Power: The Kano 'Mamluks' and Male Royal Slavery in the Sokoto Caliphate, 1804–1903*. Portsmouth, NH.

Stilwell, S. (2014) *Slavery and Slaving in African History*. Cambridge.

Straus, J. (1988) 'L'esclavage dans l'Égypte romaine' in H. Temporini (ed.), *Aufstieg und Niedergang der Römischen Welt: II*, 10.1, Berlin and New York, 841–911.

Straus, J. (2004) *L'achat et la vente des esclaves dans l'Égypte romaine. Contribution papyrologique à l'étude de l'esclavage dans une province orientale de l'Empire romain*. Munich and Leipzig.

Straus, J. (2016) 'Papyrological evidence' in Hodkinson, Kleijwegt and Vlassopoulos (2016–), published online, DOI: 10.1093/oxfordhb/9780199575251.013.35.

Strauss, C. and Quinn, N. (1997) *A Cognitive Theory of Cultural Meaning*. Cambridge.

Strickland, M. (1992) 'Slaughter, slavery or ransom: the impact of the Conquest on conduct in warfare' in C. Hicks (ed.), *England in the Eleventh Century*, Stamford, 41–59.

Strickrodt, S. (2004) '"Afro-Brazilians" of the western Slave Coast in the nineteenth century' in Curto and Lovejoy (2004), 213–44.

Sutt, C. (2015) *Slavery in Árpád-Era Hungary in a Comparative Context*. Leiden and Boston, MA.

Sweet, J. H. (2003) *Recreating Africa: Culture, Kinship, and Religion in the African-Portuguese World, 1441–1770*. Chapel Hill, NC.

Sweet, J. H. (2013) 'Defying social death: the multiple configurations of African slave family in the Atlantic world', *William & Mary Quarterly*, 70, 251–72.

Synodinou, K. (1977) *On the Concept of Slavery in Eyripides*. Ioannina.

Szidat, J. (1985) 'Zum Sklavenhandel in der Spätantike (Aug. Epist. 10★)', *Historia*, 34, 362–71.

Tacoma, L. E. (2016) *Moving Romans: Migration to Rome in the Principate*. Oxford.

Tamiolaki, M. (2010) *Liberté et esclavage chez les historiens grecs classiques*. Paris.

Tannenbaum, F. (1946) *Slave and Citizen: The Negro in the Americas*. New York.

Taylor, C. (2017) *Poverty, Wealth, and Well-Being: Experiencing Penia in Democratic Athens*. Oxford.

Taylor, C. and Vlassopoulos, K. (eds) (2015a) *Communities and Networks in the Ancient Greek World*. Oxford.

Taylor, C. and Vlassopoulos, K. (2015b) 'Introduction: an agenda for the study of Greek history' in Taylor and Vlassopoulos (2015a), 1–31.

Tchernia, A. (1986) *Le vin de l'Italie romaine. Essai d'histoire économique d'après les amphores*. Rome.

Tchernia, A. (2016) *The Romans and Trade*. Oxford.

Terpstra, T. (2019) *Trade in the Ancient Mediterranean: Private Order and Public Institutions*. Princeton and Oxford.

Testart, A. (1998) 'L'esclavage comme institution', *L'Homme*, 145, 31–69.

Testart, A. (2004) *La servitude volontaire, I–II*. Paris.

Testart, A. and Brunaux, J. L. (2004) 'Esclavage et prix de la fiancée: la société thrace au risque de l'ethnographie comparée', *Annales. Histoire, Sciences Sociales*, 59, 615–40.

Testart, A., Govoroff, N. and Lécrivain, V. (2002) 'Les prestations matrimoniales', *L'Homme*, 161, 165–96.

Testart, A., Lécrivain, V., Karadimas, D. and Govoroff, N. (2001) 'Prix de la fiancée et esclavage pour dettes. Un exemple de loi sociologique', *Études rurales*, 159–60, 9–34.

Texier, J. G. (1979) 'Les esclaves et l'esclavage dans l'œuvre de Polybe' in Capozza (1979), 115–42.

Thalmann, W. G. (1996) 'Versions of slavery in the *Captivi* of Plautus', *Ramus*, 25, 112–45.

Thalmann, W. G. (2011) 'Some ancient Greek images of slavery' in Alston, Hall and Proffitt (2011), 72–96.

Thein, A. (2013) 'Rewards to slaves in the proscriptions of 82 BC', *Tyche: Beiträge zur Alten Geschichte Papyrologie und Epigraphik*, 28, 163–75.

Thomas, Y. (1984) 'Vitae necisque potestas. Le père, la cité, la mort' in Y. Thomas (ed.), *Du châtiment dans la cité. Supplices corporels et peine de mort dans le monde antique*, Rome, 499–548.

Thomas, Y. (1999) 'L' "usage" et les "fruits" de l'esclave. Opérations juridiques romaines sur le travail', *Enquête: Anthropologie, Histoire, Sociologie*, 7, 203–30.

Thomas, Y. (2007) 'L'indisponibilité de la liberté en droit romain', *Hypothèses*, 10, 379–89.

Thompson, D. (2011) 'Slavery in the Hellenistic world' in Bradley and Cartledge (2011), 194–213.

Thompson, E. A. (1957) 'Slavery in early Germany', *Hermathena*, 89, 17–29.

Thompson, E. A. (1985) *Who was Saint Patrick?* Rochester, NY.

Thompson, E. P., Thirsk, J. and Goody, J. (eds) (1976) *Family and Inheritance: Rural Society in Western Europe 1200–1800*. Cambridge.

Thompson, F. H. (2003) *The Archaeology of Greek and Roman Slavery*. London.

Thonemann, P. (2013) 'Phrygia: an anarchist history, 950 BC–AD 100' in P. Thonemann (ed.), *Roman Phrygia: Culture and Society*, Cambridge, 1–40.

Thornton, J. K. (1983) 'Sexual demography: the impacts of the slave trade on family structure' in C. C. Robertson and M. A. Klein (eds), *Women and Slavery in Africa*, Madison, WI, 39–48.

Thornton, J. K. (1998) *Africa and Africans in the Making of the Atlantic World, 1400–1800*. New York.

Thornton, J. K. (2012) *A Cultural History of the Atlantic World, 1250–1820*. Cambridge.

Thornton, J. K. (2018) 'How useful is the concept of slaving zones? Some thoughts from the experience of Dahomey and Kongo' in Fynn-Paul and Pargas (2018), 151–68.

Todd, S. C. (1993) *The Shape of Athenian Law*, Oxford.

Todd, S. C. (2013) 'Male slave sexuality and the absence of moral panic in classical Athens', *Bulletin of the Institute of Classical Studies*, 56.2, 37–53.

Toledano, E. R. (2017) 'Ottoman elite enslavement and "social death"' in Bodel and Scheidel (2017), 136–50.

Tomich, D. W. (2004) *Through the Prism of Slavery: Labor, Capital and World Economy*. Oxford.

Tomlin, R. S. O. (2008) '"Paedagogium and septizonium": two Roman lead tablets from Leicester', *Zeitschrift für Papyrologie und Epigraphik*, 167, 207–18.

Tomlin, R. S. O. (2010) 'Cursing a thief in Iberia and Britain' in F. Marco Simón and R. L. Gordon (eds), *Magical Practice in the Latin West*, Leiden and Boston, 245–74.

Toner, J. (2015) 'Barbers, barbershops and searching for Roman popular culture', *Papers of the British School at Rome*, 83, 91–109.

Torelli, M. (1976) 'Pour une histoire de l'esclavage en Etrurie' in *Actes 1973*, 99–113.

Toynbee, A. J. (1965) *Hannibal's Legacy, II: The Hannibalic War's Effects on Roman Life*. Oxford.

Tran, N. (2006a) 'Les affranchis dans les collèges professionnels de l'Italie du Haut-Empire: L'encadrement civique de la mobilité sociale' in M. Molin (ed.), *Les régulations sociales dans l'Antiquité*, Rennes, 389–402.

Tran, N. (2006b) *Les membres des associations romaines: le rang social des collegiati en Italie et en Gaules, sous le Haut-Empire*. Rome.

Tran, N. (2013a) *Dominus tabernae: le statut de travail des artisans et des commerçants de l'Occident romain (Ier siècle av. J.-C. – IIIe siècle ap. J.-C.)*. Rome.

Tran, N. (2013b) 'The work statuses of slaves and freedmen in the great ports of the Roman world (first century BCE–second century CE)', *Annales. Histoire, Sciences Sociales: English Edition*, 68, 659–84.

Tran, N. (2014) 'Esclaves et ministres des Lares dans la société de l'Arles antique', *Gallia*, 71, 103–20.

Tran, N. (2017) 'Ars and doctrina: the socioeconomic identity of Roman skilled workers (first century BC–third century AD)' in Verboven and Laes (2017), 246–61.

Treggiari, S. (1969) *Roman Freedmen during the Late Republic*. Oxford.

Treggiari, S. (1973) 'Domestic staff at Rome during the Julio-Claudian period', *Histoire Sociale / Social History*, 6, 241–55.

Treggiari, S. (1975a) 'Jobs in the household of Livia', *Papers of the British School at Rome*, 43, 48–77.

Treggiari, S. (1975b) 'Family life among the staff of the Volusii', *Transactions of the American Philological Association*, 105, 393–401.

Treggiari, S. (1976) 'Jobs for women', *American Journal of Ancient History*, 1.2, 76–104.

Treggiari, S. (1979) 'Lower class women in the Roman economy', *Florilegium*, 1, 65–86.

Treggiari, S. (1981) '*Contubernales* in CIL 6', *Phoenix*, 35, 42–69.

Trimble, J. (2016) 'The Zoninus collar and the archaeology of Roman slavery', *American Journal of Archaeology*, 120, 447–72.

Trümper, M. (2009) *Graeco-Roman Slave Markets: Fact or Fiction?* Oxford.

Tsai, D. Y. (2014) *Human Rights in Deuteronomy: With Special Focus on Slave Laws*. Berlin and Boston.

Tsetskhladze, G. R. (2008) 'Pontic slaves in Athens: orthodoxy and reality' in R. Rollinger and C. Ulf (eds), *Lebenswelten: Konstanz-Wandel-Wirkungsmacht*, Wiesbaden, 309–19.

Tuci, P. A. (2004) 'Arcieri sciti, esercito e democrazia nell'Atene del V secolo aC.', *Aevum*, 78, 3–18.

Tucker, C. W. (1982) 'Women in the manumission inscriptions at Delphi', *Transactions of the American Philological Association*, 112, 225–36.

Turley, D. (2000) *Slavery*. Oxford and Malden, MA.

Turton, A. (1980) 'Thai institutions of slavery' in Watson (1980a), 251–92.

Urbainczyk, T. (2008) *Slave Revolts in Antiquity*. Berkeley.

van de Mieroop, M. (2007) *The Eastern Mediterranean in the Age of Ramesses II*. Malden, MA and Oxford.

van Koningsveld, P. S. (1995) 'Muslim slaves and captives in western Europe during the late Middle Ages', *Islam and Christian-Muslim Relations*, 6, 5–23.

van Koppen, F. (2004) 'The geography of the slave trade and northern Babylonia in the Late Old Babylonian period' in H. Hunger and R. Pruzsinszky (eds), *Mesopotamian Dark Age Revisited*, Vienna, 9–33.

van Minnen, P. (2000) 'Prisoners of war and hostages in Graeco-Roman Egypt', *Journal of Juristic Papyrology*, 30, 155–63.

van Nijf, O. M. (1997) *The Civic World of Professional Associations in the Roman East*. Amsterdam.

van Norman, W. C. (2013) *Shade-Grown Slavery: The Lives of Slaves on Coffee Plantations in Cuba*. Nashville.

van Wees, H. (2003) 'Conquerors and serfs: wars of conquest and forced labour in archaic Greece' in Luraghi and Alcock (2003), 33–80.

van Wees, H. (2007) 'War and society' in Sabin, van Wees and Whitby (2007), 273–99.

van Wees, H. (2013) 'Farmers and hoplites: models of historical development' in D. Kagan and G. F. Viggiano (eds), *Men of Bronze: Hoplite Warfare in Ancient Greece*, Princeton and Oxford, 222–55.

Vandenberghe, F. (2007a) 'Avatars of the collective: a realist theory of collective subjectivities', *Sociological Theory*, 25, 295–324.

Vandenberghe, F. (2007b) 'Une ontologie réaliste pour la sociologie: système, morphogenèse et collectifs', *Social Science Information*, 46, 487–542.

Vaucher, D. (2017) *Sklaverei in Norm und Praxis: Die frühchristlichen Kirchenordnungen*. Hildesheim.

Veblen, T. (2007) [1899] *The Theory of the Leisure Class*. Oxford.

Velkov, V. (1964) 'Zur Frage der Sklaverei auf der Balkanhalbinsel während der Antike', *Études balkaniques*, 1, 125–38.

Velkov, V. (1986) 'L'esclavage en Thrace antique' in H.-J. Kalcyk, B. Gullath and A. Graeber (eds), *Studien zur Alten Geschichte: Siegfried Lauffer zum 70. Geburtstag, III*, Rome, 1021–30.

Verboven, K. (2007) 'The associative order: status and ethos among Roman businessmen in late republic and early empire', *Athenaeum*, 95, 861–93.

Verboven, K. (2009) 'A funny thing happened on my way to the market: reading Petronius to write economic history' in Prag and Repath (2009), 125–39.

Verboven, K. (2012) 'The freedman economy of Roman Italy' in Bell and Ramsby (2012), 88–109.

Verboven, K. and Laes, C. (eds) (2017) *Work, Labour, and Professions in the Roman World*. Boston and Leiden.

Verhulst, A. (1991) 'Review article: The decline of slavery and the economic expansion of the early middle ages', *Past & Present*, 133, 195–203

Vérilhac, A.-M. and Vial, C. (1998) *Le mariage grec du VIe siècle av. J.C. à l'époque d'Auguste*. Athens.

Verlinden, C. (1942) 'L'origine de sclavus-esclave', *Bulletin Ducange: Archivum Latinitatis Medii Aevi*, 17, 97–128.

Vermote, K. (2016a) *Identity and Stigmatisation: A Qualitative Analysis of the Socialisation and Stratification of and the Interaction between Freed and Freeborn Romans*. PhD dissertation, Universiteit Gent.

Vermote, K. (2016b) 'The macula servitutis of Roman freedmen. Neque enim aboletur turpitudo, quae postea intermissa est?', *Revue belge de Philologie et d'Histoire*, 94, 131–64.

Vernant, J.-P. (1990) *Myth and Society in Ancient Greece*. New York.

Veyne, P. (1961) 'Vie de Trimalcion', *Annales. Histoire, Sciences Sociales*, 16, 213–47.

Veyne, P. (1981) 'Le dossier des esclaves-colons romains', *Revue historique*, 265, 3–25.

Viau, R. (1997) *Enfants du néant et mangeurs d'âmes: guerre, culture et société en Iroquoisie ancienne*. Quebec.

Vidal-Naquet, P. (1986a) 'Reflections on Greek historical writing about slavery' in Vidal-Naquet (1986c), 168–88.

Vidal-Naquet, P. (1986b) 'Were Greek slaves a class?' in Vidal-Naquet (1986c), 159–67.

Vidal-Naquet, P. (1986c) *The Black Hunter: Forms of Thought and Forms of Society in the Greek World*. Baltimore.

Vlassopoulos, K. (2007a) 'Free spaces: identity, experience and democracy in classical Athens', *Classical Quarterly*, 57, 33–52.

Vlassopoulos, K. (2007b) *Unthinking the Greek Polis: Ancient Greek History beyond Eurocentrism*. Cambridge.

Vlassopoulos, K. (2009) 'Slavery, freedom and citizenship in classical Athens: beyond a legalistic approach', *European Review of History / Revue européenne d'histoire*, 16, 347–63.

Vlassopoulos, K. (2010) 'Athenian slave names and Athenian social history', *Zeitschrift für Papyrologie und Epigraphik*, 175, 113–44.

Vlassopoulos, K. (2011a) 'Greek slavery: from domination to property and back again', *Journal of Hellenic Studies*, 131, 115–30.

Vlassopoulos, K. (2011b) 'Two images of ancient slavery: the "living tool" and the "koinônia"' in Herrmann-Otto (2011), 467–77.

Vlassopoulos, K. (2012) 'Review of Bradley and Cartledge 2011', *Mnemosyne*, 65, 877–81.

Vlassopoulos, K. (2013a) *Greeks and Barbarians*. Cambridge.

Vlassopoulos, K. (2013b) 'The stories of the Others: storytelling and intercultural communication in the Herodotean Mediterranean' in E. Almagor and J. Skinner (eds), *Ancient Ethnography: New Approaches*, London, 49–75.

Vlassopoulos, K. (2014) 'Which comparative histories for ancient historians?', *Synthesis*, 21, 31–47.

Vlassopoulos, K. (2015a) 'Plotting strategies, networks and communities in classical Athens: the evidence of slave names' in Taylor and Vlassopoulos (2015a), 101–27.

Vlassopoulos, K. (2015b) 'Recent studies on ancient slavery', *Polifemo's Recent Studies*, 2, 83–106.

Vlassopoulos, K. (2015c) 'Religion within communities' in E. Eidinow and J. Kindt (eds), *The Oxford Handbook of Ancient Greek Religion*, Oxford, 257–71.

Vlassopoulos, K. (2015d) 'Ethnicity and Greek history: re-examining our assumptions', *Bulletin of the Institute of Classical Studies*, 58, 1–13.

Vlassopoulos, K. (2015–16) 'Recent works on ancient slavery', Αριάδνη, 22, 253–73.

Vlassopoulos, K. (2016a) 'Does slavery have a history? The consequences of a global approach', *Journal of Global Slavery*, 1, 5–27.

Vlassopoulos, K. (2016b) 'Finley's slavery' in Jew, Osborne and Scott (2016), 76–99.

Vlassopoulos, K. (2016c) 'Que savons-nous vraiment de la société athénienne?', *Annales. Histoire, Sciences Sociales*, 71, 659–81.

Vlassopoulos, K. (2016d) 'Review of Ober 2015', *Bryn Mawr Classical Review*, published online at http://bmcr.brynmawr.edu/2016/2016-03-04.html.

Vlassopoulos, K. (2017) 'Οι σύγχρονες θεωρίες της ιστοριογραφίας και η μελέτη της αρχαίας ιστορίας' in M. Tamiolaki (ed.), *Μεθοδολογικά ζητήματα στις κλασικές σπουδές*, Herakleion, 225–42.

Vlassopoulos, K. (2018a) 'Historicising the closed city' in M. Dana and I. Savalli-Lestrade (eds), *La cité interconnectée: transferts et réseaux institutionnels, religieux et culturels aux époques hellénistique et impériale*, Bordeaux, 43–57.

Vlassopoulos, K. (2018b) 'Review of Bodel and Scheidel 2017, Rio 2017 and Ramelli 2016', *Journal of Global Slavery*, 3, 319–25.

Vlassopoulos, K. (2018c) 'Marxism and ancient history' in D. Allen, P. Christesen and P. Millett (eds), *How to Do Things with History: New Approaches to Ancient Greece*, Oxford, 209–35.

Vlassopoulos, K. (2018d) 'Hope and slavery' in D. Spatharas and G. Kazantzidis (eds), *Hope in Ancient Literature, History and Art*, Berlin and Boston, 239–62.

Vlassopoulos, K. (2018–19) 'Review article: recent books on ancient slavery II', *Αριάδνη*, 25, 167–99.

Vlassopoulos, K. (2019) 'The end of enslavement, Greek style' in Hodkinson, Kleijwegt and Vlassopoulos (2016–), published online, DOI: 10.1093/oxfordhb/9780199575251.013.39.

Vlastos, G. (1941) 'Slavery in Plato's thought', *Philosophical Review*, 50, 289–304.

Vogt, J. (1958) *Wege zur Menschlichkeit in der antiken Sklaverei*. Tubingen.

Vogt, J. (1974) *Ancient Slavery and the Ideal of Man*. Oxford.

Volkmann, H. (1961) *Die Massenversklavungen der Einwohner eroberter Städte in der hellenistisch-römischen Zeit*. Mainz.

von Behren, C. (2009) *Sklaven und Freigelassene auf den Grabdenkmälern des nördlichen Schwarzmeerraumes*. PhD dissertation, Universität Trier.

von Dassow, E. (2011) 'Freedom in ancient Near Eastern societies' in K. Radner and E. Robson (eds), *The Oxford Handbook of Cuneiform Culture*, Oxford, 205–24.

von Dassow, E. (2013) 'Piecing together the Song of Release', *Journal of Cuneiform Studies*, 65, 127–62.

von Dassow, E. (2014) 'Awīlum and muškēnum in the age of Hammurabi' in Marti (2014), 291–308.

von Dassow, E. (2018) 'Liberty, bondage and liberation in the Late Bronze Age', *History of European Ideas*, 44, 658–84.

von Lingen, K. and Gestwa, K. (eds) (2014) *Zwangsarbeit als Kriegsressource in Europa und Asien*. Paderborn.

Vuolanto, V. (2003) 'Selling a freeborn child: rhetoric and social realities in the late Roman world', *Ancient Society*, 33, 169–207.

Wacke, A. (2001) 'Manumissio matrimonii causa. Die Freilassung zwecks Heirat nach den Ehegesetzen des Augustus' in Bellen and Heinen (2001), 133–58.

Wacke, A. (2006) 'Die libera administratio peculii. Zur Verfügungsmacht von Hauskindern und Sklaven über ihr Sondergut' in Finkenauer (2006), 251–316.

Wade, R. C. (1964) *Slavery in the Cities: The South, 1820–1860*. London, Oxford and New York.

Waldstein, W. (1990) 'Schiavitù e cristianesimo da Costantino a Teodosio II' in *Atti dell'Accademia Romanistica Costantiniana: Atti del VIII Convegno Internazionale*, Perugia and Naples, 123–45.

Waldstein, W. (2001) 'Zum Menschsein von Sklaven' in Bellen and Heinen (2001), 31–49.

Walker, D. E. (2004) *No More, No More: Slavery and Cultural Resistance in Havana and New Orleans*. Minneapolis.

Wall, R., Hareven, T. K. and Ehmer, J. (eds) (2001) *Family History Revisited: Comparative Perspectives*. Newark.

Wallace-Hadrill, A. (2008) *Rome's Cultural Revolution*. Cambridge.

Wallon, H. (1988) [1848] *Histoire de l'esclavage dans l'antiquité*. Paris.

Waltzing, J. P. (1895) *Étude historique sur les corporations professionnelles chez les Romains depuis les origines jusqu'à la chute de l'Empire de l'Occident, Tome I*. Louvain.

Warren, J. F. (2007) *The Sulu Zone, 1768–1898: The Dynamics of External Trade, Slavery and Ethnicity in the Transformation of Southeast Asian Maritime State*. Singapore.

Watson, A. (1961) 'Captivitas and matrimonium', *Tijdschrift voor Rechtsgeschiedenis*, 29, 243–59.

Watson, A. (1989) *Slave Law in the Americas*. Athens, GA and London.

Watson, A. (1992) 'Seventeenth-century jurists, Roman law and the law of slavery', *Chicago-Kent Law Review*, 68, 1343–54.

Watson, J. L. (ed.) (1980a) *Asian and African Systems of Slavery*. Berkeley and Los Angeles.

Watson, J. L. (1980b) 'Slavery as an institution, open and closed systems' in Watson (1980a), 1–15.

Watson, J. L. (1980c) 'Transactions in people: the Chinese market in slaves, servants and heirs' in Watson (1980a), 223–50.

Weaver, P. R. C. (1972) *Familia Caesaris: A Social Study of the Emperor's Freedmen and Slaves*. London.

Weaver, P. R. C. (1990) 'Where have all the Junian Latins gone? Nomenclature and status in the early Empire', *Chiron*, 20, 275–306.

Weber, M. (1896) 'Die sozialen Gründe des Untergangs der antiken Kultur', *Die Wahrheit*, 6, 57–77.

Webster, J. (2005) 'Archaeologies of slavery and servitude: bringing 'New World' perspectives to Roman Britain', *Journal of Roman Archaeology*, 18, 161–79.

Weiler, I. (2001) 'Eine Sklavin wird frei: zur Rolle des Geschlechts bei der Freilassung' in Bellen and Heinen (2001), 113–32.

Weiler, I. (2003) *Die Beendigung des Sklavenstatus im Altertum: ein Beitrag zur vergleichenden Sozialgeschichte*. Stuttgart.

Weiß, A. (2004) *Sklave der Stadt: Untersuchungen zur öffentlichen Sklaverei in den Städten des römischen Reiches*. Stuttgart.

Welwei, K.-W. (1974–88) *Unfreie im antiken Kriegsdienst, I–III*. Stuttgart.

Welwei, K.-W. (2000) *Sub corona vendere: Quellenkritische Studien zu Kriegsgefangenschaft und Sklaverei in Rom bis zum Ende des Hannibalkrieges*. Stuttgart.

Welwei, K.-W. (2008) 'Menschenraub und Deportationen in frühen Kulturen' in Heinen (2008), 21–43.

Wengrow, D. and Graeber, D. (2018) '"Many seasons ago": slavery and its rejection among foragers on the Pacific coast of North America', *American Anthropologist*, 120, 237–49.

Westbrook, R. (1995) 'Slave and master in ancient Near Eastern law' republished in Westbrook (2009a), 161–216.

Westbrook, R. (1998) 'The female slave' republished in Westbrook (2009b), 149–74.

Westbrook, R. (2009a) *Law from the Tigris to the Tiber: The Writings of Raymond Westbrook, Volume 1: The Shared Tradition*. Winona Lake, IN.

Westbrook, R. (2009b) *Law from the Tigris to the Tiber: The Writings of Raymond Westbrook, Volume 2: Cuneiform and Biblical Sources*. Winona Lake, IN.

Westbrook, R. and Jasnow, R. (eds) (2001) *Security for Debt in Ancient Near Eastern Law*. Leiden, Boston and Cologne.

Westermann, W. L. (1941) 'Athenaeus and the slaves of Athens', *Harvard Studies in Classical Philology Supplement*, 451–70.

Westermann, W. L. (1943) 'Slavery and the elements of freedom in ancient Greece', *Quarterly Bulletin of the Polish Institute of Arts and Sciences in America*, 1–16.

Westermann, W. L. (1955) *The Slave Systems of Greek and Roman Antiquity*. Philadelphia.

Whittaker, C. R. (1980) 'Rural labour in three Roman provinces' in Garnsey (1980), 73–99.

Whittaker, C. R. (1987) 'Circe's pigs: from slavery to serfdom in the later Roman world' in Finley (1987), 88–122.

Wickham, C. (2005) *Framing the Early Middle Ages: Europe and the Mediterranean, 400–800*. Oxford.

Wickham, J. (2014) *The Enslavement of War Captives by the Romans to 146 BC*. PhD. dissertation, University of Liverpool.

Wiedemann, T. (2000) 'Fifty years of research on ancient slavery: The Mainz Academy project', *Slavery & Abolition*, 21:3, 152–8.

Wiedemann, T. (2002) *Emperors and Gladiators*. London and New York.

Wieling, H. (1999) *Corpus der Römischen Rechtsquellen zur Antiken Sklaverei. Teil I: Die Begründung des Sklavenstatus nach ius gentium und ius civile*. Stuttgart.

Willetts, R. F. (1955) *Aristocratic Society in Ancient Crete*. London.

Williams, B. (1993) *Shame and Necessity*. Berkeley and Oxford.

Williams, C. A. (2010) *Roman Homosexuality*. 2nd edition. Oxford.

Williams, K. F. (2006) 'Pliny and the murder of Larcius Macedo', *Classical Journal*, 101, 409–24.

Willvonseder, R. (2010) *Corpus der Römischen Rechtsquellen zur Antiken Sklaverei. Teil IV: Stellung des Sklaven im Privatrecht. 1: Eheähnliche Verbindungen und verwandtschaftliche Beziehungen*. Stuttgart.

Wilson, A. (2002) 'Machines, power and the ancient economy', *Journal of Roman Studies*, 92, 1–32.

Wilson, A. (2017) 'Saharan exports to the Roman world' in D. J. Mattingly et al. (eds), *Trade in the Ancient Sahara and Beyond*, Cambridge, 189–208.

Wirszubski, C. H. (1950) *Libertas as a Political Idea at Rome during the Late Republic and Early Principate*. Cambridge.

Witzenrath, C. (ed.) (2015) *Eurasian Slavery, Ransom and Abolition in World History, 1200–1860*. London and New York.

Wood, E. M. (1988) *Peasant-Citizen and Slave: The Foundations of Athenian Democracy*. London and New York.

Wrenhaven, K. L. (2009) 'The identity of the "wool-workers" in the Attic manumissions', *Hesperia*, 78, 367–86.

Wrenhaven, K. L. (2011) 'Greek representations of the slave body: a conflict of ideas?' in Alston, Hall and Proffitt (2011), 97–120.

Wrenhaven, K. L. (2012) *Reconstructing the Slave: The Image of the Slave in Ancient Greece*. London.

Wunsch, C. (2013) 'Glimpses on the lives of deportees in rural Babylonia' in A. Berlejung and M. P. Streck (eds), *Arameans, Chaldeans, and Arabs in Babylonia and Palestine in the First Millennium BC*, Wiesbaden, 247–60.

Wunsch, C. and Magdalene, F. R. (2012) 'A slave is not supposed to wear such a garment!', *KASKAL: Rivista di storia, ambienti e culture del Vicino Oriente Antico*, 9, 99–120.

Wyatt-Brown, B. (1992) 'The mask of obedience: male slave psychology in the Old South' in Harris (1992), 134–67.

Yakobson, A. (2011) 'Political stability and public order – Athens vs. Rome' in G. Herman (ed.), *Stability and Crisis in the Athenian Democracy*, Stuttgart, 139–56.

Youni, M. (2000) *Provincia Macedonia: Θεσμοί ιδιωτικού δικαίου στη Μακεδονία επί Ρωμαιοκρατίας*. Athens.

Youni, M. (2012) 'Droit grec et influences romaines dans le contrat de vente d'une esclave en Macédoine romaine' in Legras (2012), 443–58.

Yuge, T. and Doi, M. (eds) (1988) *Forms of Control and Subordination in Antiquity*. Leiden.

Zaccagnini, C. (1995) 'War and famine at Emar', *Orientalia*, 64, 92–109.

Zanker, P. (1975) 'Grabreliefs römischer Freigelassener', *Jahrbuch des Deutschen Archäologischen Instituts*, 90, 267–315.

Zanovello, S. L. (2016) *From Slave to Free: A Legal Perspective on Greek Manumission*. PhD dissertation, Università di Padova.

Zanovello, S. L. (2018) 'Some remarks on manumission and consecration in Hellenistic Chaeronea', *Journal of Global Slavery*, 3, 129–51.

Zelnick-Abramovitz, R. (2005) *Not Wholly Free: The Concept of Manumission and the Status of Manumitted Slaves in the Ancient Greek World*. Leiden.

Zelnick-Abramovitz, R. (2009) 'Freed slaves, their status and state control in ancient Greece', *European Review of History / Revue européenne d'histoire*, 16, 303–18.

Zelnick-Abramovitz, R. (2013) *Taxing Freedom in Thessalian Manumission Inscriptions*. Leiden and Boston, MA.

Zelnick-Abramovitz, R. (2017) 'Whose grave is this? The status of grave plots in ancient Greece', *Dike*, 18, 51–95.

Zeuske, M. (2013) *Handbuch Geschichte der Sklaverei: eine Globalgeschichte von den Anfängen bis zur Gegenwart*. Berlin and Boston.

Zimmermann, K. (1980) 'Tätowierte Thrakerinnen auf griechischen Vasenbildern', *Jahrbuch des Deutschen Archäologischen Instituts*, 95, 163–96.

Zimmern, E. A. (1931) *The Greek Commonwealth: Politics and Economics in Fifth-Century Athens*. 5th edition. Oxford.

Zoumbaki, S. (2005) 'The collective definition of slaves and the limits to their activities' in Anastasiadis and Doukellis (2005), 217–31.

Zurbach, J. (2013) 'La formation des cités grecques: statuts, classes et systèmes fonciers', *Annales. Histoire, sciences sociales*, 68, 955–98.

Zurbach, J. (ed.) (2015) *La main-d'œuvre agricole en Méditerranée archaïque: statuts et dynamiques économiques*. Paris.

Zurn, C. (2015) *Axel Honneth*. Cambridge and Malden, MA.

# INDEX LOCORUM

## Literary and legal sources

## Epigraphic and papyrological sources

# General Index

## Concepts and subjects

# Places, ethnic groups and societies

## *Ancient*

## Modern

## Ancient personal names

## Modern scholars

CPSIA information can be obtained
at www.ICGtesting.com
Printed in the USA
JSHW011247230323
39371JS00003B/67